Spoken Dialogue Technology

Springer
London
Berlin
Heidelberg
New York
Hong Kong
Milan
Paris
Tokyo

Michael F. McTear

Spoken Dialogue Technology

Toward the Conversational User Interface

Foreword by T. V. Raman

 Springer

Michael F. McTear
School of Computing and Mathematics
University of Ulster
Newtownabbey BT37 0QB
Northern Ireland

British Library Cataloguing in Publication Data
McTear, Michael F., 1943–
    Spoken dialogue technology : toward the conversational user interface
    1. Natural language processing (Computer science)   2. User interfaces (Computer systems)
    I. Title
    006.3'5

    ISBN 1852336722

Library of Congress Cataloging-in-Publication Data
McTear, Michael.
    Spoken dialogue technology : toward the conversational user interface / Michael F. McTear.
        p.   cm.
    Includes bibliographical references and index.
    ISBN 1-85233-672-2 (softcover: alk. paper)
    1. User interfaces (Computer systems)   2. Automatic speech recognition.   I. Title.

QA76.9.U83M45 2004
005.4'37 – dc22   2004045619

ISBN 1-85233-672-2 Springer-Verlag London Berlin Heidelberg
Springer-Verlag is a part of Springer Science+Business Media
Springeronline.com

Typeset by SNP Best-set Typesetter Ltd., Hong Kong
34/3830-543210 Printed on acid-free paper SPIN 10886181

Foreword

The present coming of age of speech technologies coincides with the advent of mobile computing and the accompanying need for ubiquitous information access. This has generated enormous commercial interest around deploying speech interaction to IT-based services.

In his book, Michael gives an in-depth review of the nuts and bolts of constructing speech applications. Notice that creating good speech applications requires more than robust speech technologies; the creation of usable, efficient spoken interaction requires substantial thought toward crafting the man-machine conversation. This book does an excellent job in this regard by focusing on the creation of dialog-based applications.

As speech interaction enters the mainstream Web, these applications need to be developed, deployed and maintained against an efficient cost model. The speech industry is converging on a set of open XML-based standards developed under the auspices of the W3C in order to achieve this goal. VoiceXML, SSML and SRGF together form the underpinnings of the XML-based W3C Voice Web, and this book gives the reader a good foundation on building speech interaction using these interoperable standards. The closing chapters on multimodal interaction gives the reader the necessary background to start actively following and contributing to this exciting area.

T. V. Raman
Human Language Technologies
IBM Research

Preface

Writing this book has been a long process of discovery and learning that dates back to my first explorations in human–computer dialogue using natural language, documented in my book *The Articulate Computer* (Blackwell). Published in 1987, it described research in dialogue modeling where the primary input mode was the keyboard rather than speech. Since then things have come a long way. The fields of natural language processing and speech technology have come together, and the discipline of spoken dialogue technology has emerged. Moreover, there has been an increasing commercial interest in the technology, with a number of large, influential companies actively involved in spoken language technology and offering advanced toolkits and development platforms to researchers wishing to explore the exciting potential of conversing with a computer using spoken natural language.

Along the way I have met many people who have helped me and shaped my work. My first attempts with spoken dialogue interfaces involved acquiring and learning how to use the CSLU toolkit. This brought me into contact with Ron Cole, a pioneer in the development and promotion of freely available, open source software to support teachers and students wishing to learn about spoken language technologies. Through Ron I met several of his colleagues: Jacques de Villiers, Ed Kaiser and John-Paul Hosom at the Center for Spoken Language Understanding, who provided me with invaluable advice and support, and later, when Ron moved to the Center for Spoken Language Research (CSLR), Bryan Pellom and Wayne Ward, who introduced me to the CU Communicator and other toolkits and platforms being developed at CSLR.

More recently, as I started to learn about VoiceXML, I have found Jim Larson to be a tremendous source of inspiration and encouragement. As I moved on to look at more recent developments, such as XHTML + Voice, I found support and advice from a number of people in IBM's Pervasive Computing Group, most notably, T.V. Raman, David Jaramillo, Nick Metianu and Les Wilson. There are also a number of colleagues, who I meet regularly at conferences and other academic occasions and who have been a constant source of ideas. These include Harald Aust, Norman Fraser, Paul Heisterkamp, Alex Rudnicky, Paul McKevitt, Ian O'Neill, David Toney and Colleen Crangle.

Developing the practical chapters of the book would not have been possible without the help of many colleagues and students. At the University of Ulster Stephen Downey spent many hours helping me to get the early versions of the CSLU toolkit installed and running properly and provided untiring support both to myself and to the students we taught together in lab sessions. Lesley-Ann Black has worked with me more recently on VoiceXML practicals and she also provided useful feedback on earlier drafts of the book. Countless students, too many to name, have been subjected to practicals involving the CSLU toolkit, VoiceXML, X+V, and SALT. I would like to single out Elizabeth Rooney and Angela Murphy, on whose Master's dissertations I have drawn extensively in chapters 6, 7 and 8, and also Conor McCluskey, Garth Kennedy and Aislinn McAleer, whose excellent undergraduate dissertations provided me with many useful ideas throughout. I would also like to acknowledge Gerrit Bloothooft and his students at the Utrecht Institute of Linguistics, who provided useful feedback and corrections on chapters 7 and 8 involving the CSLU toolkit, as well as students at the ELSNET summer school at Lille, 2004, who also worked through these chapters with me.

I was encouraged to write this book by Beverley Ford, Editorial Director of Springer-Verlag London. Jean Lovell-Butt provided me with editorial assistance during the writing of the book, and Louise Farkas, Senior Production Editor, Springer-Verlag New York, oversaw the development of the book from the raw typescript that I submitted to the final version of the book. To Beverley, Jean and Louise, and all of their colleagues who helped along the way, I offer my gratitude.

Finally, I must acknowledge my wife Sandra, who has supported and encouraged me throughout, particularly during the long hours away from family life that I have spent working on the book.

Newtownabbey, Northern Ireland   Michael F. McTear

Contents

Introduction

People use speech to interact with one another in a seemingly effortless way. From an early age we speak in order to convey our wishes, express our opinions and ask questions. The ability to use written language comes later and is something that has to be taught rather than being acquired spontaneously. Conversely, when we interact with computers we use either some advanced form of written communication, as in programming languages, or a complex set of iconic symbols that we activate with a pointing device such as a mouse. Speech would seem to be the most natural way to interact with a computer, yet it is only recently that speech-based communication with computers has become possible.

The topic of this book is spoken dialogue technology. A spoken dialogue system enables people to interact with computers using spoken language, in contrast to most computing technology, which requires people to learn sequences of commands in order to use applications such as word processors, spreadsheets and email. Spoken dialogue technology is about developing applications that people can interact with using something that they have been using all their lives – their ability to speak and to understand speech.

Spoken dialogue technology has been the dream of many computer scientists for a long time, going back to the early days of Artificial Intelligence (AI) that saw the vision of an intelligent computer that could do lots of things, including interacting with people using natural language. Speaking to computers is also well-known to many of us through science fiction, with the computer HAL in Space Odyssey 2001 being one of the best-known examples. Considerable progress has been made in the various component technologies required to endow a computer with conversational abilities, such as speech recognition and natural language processing. However, it is only in the last decade or so that the conversational computer has become a reality, not only in scientific terms but also commercially. Within the past few years new technologies have emerged that have driven these advances forward. VoiceXML and SALT (Speech Application Language Tags) are new languages that are used to script spoken dialogues and to bring together the technologies of the Internet and the telephone. These languages are being proposed as standards to the World Wide Web consortium (W3C) and are supported actively by influential companies such as IBM, Microsoft and Intel.

Who Should Read This Book?

This book is intended for two types of reader:

1. Final year undergraduate and graduate students with some background in Computer Science and/or Linguistics who are taking courses in Artificial Intelligence, Natural Language Processing, Spoken Language Technology, Internet Technology, or Human Computer Interaction.
2. Professionals interested or working in the fields of Speech, Internet Technologies or Web Development.

The book aims to fill a gap between academic books on speech technology and computational linguistics on the one hand, and books for practitioners and professional developers on VoiceXML and similar topics on the other. Most of the academic texts are highly technical and suited only for those with specialist backgrounds in the relevant areas. The more practice-oriented texts, on the other hand, while showing how to develop realistic applications, tend not to provide a comprehensive overview of the background to spoken dialogue technology.

How This Book Is Organised

In keeping with the intended readership, this book is organised into three parts. The chapters in Part I examine research in dialogue and provide an introduction to the technologies involved in the development of a spoken dialogue system. Part II is concerned with how to develop spoken dialogue applications using some readily available development tools. The aim of these chapters is to enable readers to get a good feel for what is involved in developing spoken dialogue systems – to see how easy it is in some ways to develop an application, but also to appreciate some of the pitfalls and difficulties. Finally, the chapters in Part III identify and discuss some current research directions in order to provide the reader with an insight into how the technology is developing and how it might look in the future.

The following is a brief summary of the contents of each chapter.

Part I. Background to Spoken Dialogue Technology

Chapter 1. Talking with Computers: Fact or Fiction?

This chapter introduces spoken dialogue technology and illustrates aspects of the technology that have already been achieved in research laboratories and, in some cases, in commercial products.

Chapter 2. Spoken Dialogue Applications: Research Directions and
Commercial Deployment

This chapter describes a range of application areas that are suitable for spoken
dialogue technology and presents a brief historical review of research in this
area. The commercial potential of the technology is explored.

Chapter 3. Understanding Dialogue

This chapter is concerned with the key characteristics of dialogue. It is important for developers of dialogue systems to appreciate how dialogues are structured and how people engage in dialogue. A number of influential approaches
to dialogue are examined.

Chapter 4. Components of a Spoken Dialogue System – Speech Input
and Output

In this chapter the main contributing technologies for spoken dialogue systems
are discussed – speech recognition, language understanding, language generation, and text-to-speech synthesis.

Chapter 5. Dialogue Management

This chapter introduces dialogue management – the central component of a
spoken dialogue system. Techniques for dialogue management are reviewed and
illustrated.

Part II. Developing Spoken Dialogue Applications

Chapter 6. Dialogue Engineering: The Dialogue Systems
Development Lifecycle

In this chapter the development lifecycle of a spoken dialogue system is examined and issues of best practice are discussed.

Chapter 7. Developing a Spoken Dialogue System Using the CSLU Toolkit

This chapter shows through a series of tutorials how to develop a spoken dialogue system using RAD. RAD is a component of the CSLU toolkit, a freely
available development platform that has been widely used in educational environments to support research and teaching of spoken language technology.

Chapter 8. Developing Multimodal Dialogue Systems Using the CSLU Toolkit

This chapter shows how to develop multimodal dialogue systems in RAD. A
series of educational applications for teaching elementary concepts to young
children are developed. These applications use a talking head along with pictures and sound recordings.

Chapter 9. Developing a Directed Dialogue System Using VoiceXML

This chapter follows the same pattern as Chapters 7 and 8 with a series of tutorials on basic aspects of VoiceXML. The focus in this chapter is on directed dialogues, in which the system controls the dialogue and the user responds to prompts spoken by the system.

Chapter 10. More Advanced VoiceXML

This chapter examines some more advanced aspects of VoiceXML, such as mixed-initiative dialogue and the generation of dynamic VoiceXML in Web server applications. Some important aspects of VoiceXML are explained, such as the Form Interpretation Algorithm, the structure and use of recognition grammars, and the issue of scope in relation to variables and grammars.

Chapter 11. Multimodal Web-based Dialogue: XHTML + Voice and SALT

In this chapter two new languages for multimodal web-based applications – XHTML + Voice and SALT – are introduced. The elements of these languages are explained using simple examples.

Part III. Advanced Applications

Chapter 12. Advanced Dialogue Systems: Some Cases Studies

This chapter examines more advanced dialogue systems that are being developed in a number of research centres. Several well-known examples are presented as case studies.

Chapter 13. Research Topics in Spoken Dialogue Technology

In this chapter a number of current research topics in spoken dialogue technology are examined, including Information State Theory, error handling, adaptive dialogue systems, and systems that learn an optimal dialogue strategy using machine learning techniques.

Chapter 14. Future Directions: The Way Ahead

This chapter examines some issues for the future, including the integration of spoken dialogue technology into advanced multimodal applications. Future directions for academic and industrial research are explored.

Part I
Background to Spoken Dialogue Technology

Talking with Computers: Fact or Fiction?

1

A Little Fantasy

The alarm goes off at 6:30 a.m. Rachel stirs slightly, turns over and mutters "snooze". Ten minutes later the alarm goes off again. Rachel wakes up and says "off". She stretches, yawns and drags herself out of bed. She turns to the small box beside her bed and says "What's the weather like today?" "In Belfast this morning, cloudy at first with some sunshine later, temperature 12 degrees in the morning rising to around 16 in mid-afternoon," comes back the response from the box. "How about tomorrow?" "The outlook for Tuesday is some light showers at first with heavier rain and possibly some thundershowers spreading from the west towards late afternoon." "And in Barcelona?" "The weather forecast for Barcelona is sunny, with temperatures rising from 16 degrees in the early morning to 25 in mid-afternoon." "What about the Costa Brava?" "I'm sorry," replies the box, "I do not know the place you are asking about. Try asking for a city or country. For example, what cities do you know about in Spain?" "Never mind", responds Rachel with a hint of slight irritation on her way to the bathroom.

After her shower Rachel goes into the kitchen, takes a piece of bread from the bread bin and puts it into the toaster. "Not so well done this time." She goes to the fridge, takes out a carton of milk, and notices that it is almost empty. "Don't forget to order another carton of milk", she says to the fridge. "You're having some friends round for hot chocolate later, maybe I should order two cartons", says the fridge. "Okay", says Rachel.

After breakfast Rachel starts to think about the day ahead. She presses a button on the small device on her wrist that displays the time. The device greets her and asks what services she requires. "What meetings do I have today?" asks Rachel. "You have a meeting with Paul at 10, then a meeting with Anna at 11", responds the device. "Call Anna", says Rachel, and the device places a call to Anna. Rachel speaks with Anna to change the time of her meeting. She tells the device to update her calendar and asks to check her email. When she is finished she says "Thanks, bye for now" to the device on her wrist, and gets ready for the day ahead.

How realistic is this scenario? Is it a vision of the future or is it possible today? In this chapter we will see that most of what is described in this short story is not only possible but is in some cases already available commercially. However, before jumping to the conclusion that the Star Trek computer is ready for us to order from the local computing store, we need to ask a few questions about the sorts of technologies that are involved in this scenario and how exactly we can use them.

How Do You Talk to a Computer?

Typically, speech to a desktop computer evokes the image of a person sitting in front of a PC wearing a headset with speakers and speaking into a microphone that is connected to the computer's soundcard. However, this set-up is not required in order to talk to a computer. One of the most common ways to talk to a computer is over the telephone. This mode of conversation with computers is the main topic of this book. As well as this, however, microphones and speakers are increasingly being embedded into appliances or on to surfaces such as walls or automobile dashboards. These can be connected, using wireless technologies such as Bluetooth, to computers and processors that may be embedded in the appliances or worn on the body. In this way it is possible to speak to appliances such as a toaster, VCR or car audio system.

A number of companies specialise in embedded computers. Sensory Inc. has a range of products that allow people to control appliances and machines by speaking to them and by receiving spoken responses from them (www. sensoryinc.com). Sensory's speech technologies include speech recognition, speaker verification, speech and music synthesis, and animated speech. Their Integrated Circuits (ICs) and embedded software are used in consumer electronics, cell phones, Personal Data Assistants (PDAs), internet appliances, interactive toys, automobiles and other appliances. Sensory has also developed technologies for interactive kiosks that assist customers to find the products they are looking for in large stores (Sensory Inc., 2002). In addition to speech recognition and speech synthesis, the kiosk screen displays an animated character that uses facial animation and lip-synching to provide a human-like "persona" for the application.

HAL (Home Automated Living) is a system that allows a person to speak to and control simple devices in the home, such as lights and thermostats, as well as more complex appliances, such as video recorders and digital music players (www.automatedliving.com). The user simply picks up a phone and issues a command. HAL confirms the command and performs the action. HAL can be controlled from outside the home by phone, indeed from anywhere in the world. For example, the user can call HAL to close the garage door or turn on the front door lights when returning home late at night. HAL works on the basis of a series of preprogrammed commands to a device that are associated with and activated by spoken phrases.

Simple applications involving embedded appliances are a matter of the speech technology component capturing the acoustic signal that represents what the user has said, and translating it into a digital code or electronic signal to perform functions such as light control or opening and closing doors. These devices do not normally need to interact with the user, except to confirm that the instruction has been understood.

At a more complex level the appliances may need to engage in dialogue with the user to clarify the instructions or to take the initiative in the dialogue. These points are illustrated in the following scenarios taken from a demonstrator developed in the D'Homme project, an EU sponsored research project that examined language understanding and dialogue management issues for controlling and interacting with networked devices in the home (Milward et al., 2001).

1.1 (Scenario 1)
1 User: Turn the light off. (There is more than one salient light.)
2 System: There is more than one: the living room light, the kitchen light.
(The humidity sensor in the kitchen pot plants reaches its threshold.)
3 User: The kitchen light.
4 System: The kitchen light is now off.
5 User: By the way, the kitchen humidity sensor was triggered.

The instruction in utterance 1 is ambiguous because there is more than one light that could be turned off, so the system initiates a clarification query in utterance 2. At this point the system notices that the humidity sensor in the kitchen pot plants has reached its threshold. As this is not a critical event, the need to inform the user is deferred until the task of switching off the light is completed.

1.2 (Scenario 2)
1 User: Turn off the light. (There is more than one salient light.)
2 System: There is more than one: the living room light, the kitchen light.
(The smoke sensor in the hall reaches its threshold.)
3 System: WARNING! The smoke detector in the hall has been triggered.
(User runs upstairs to find her teenage son smoking an illicit cigarette out of the window.)
4 User: Ok. False alarm.
(The system assumes that utterance 4 closes the subdialogue.)
5 System: Now where were we? There is more than one light.
6 User: The living room light.

This scenario begins in the same way as Scenario 1 but, in this case, the system detects a critical event (the smoke sensor in the hall reaches its threshold) and interrupts the current task to inform the user. After utterance 4 the system assumes that the interruption subdialogue has been completed and resumes the original task, marking the resumption with the discourse marker "Now, where were we?"

Embedded speech technology is an active research area. A number of companies that specialise in speech technology in general, such as IBM (www.ibm.com/speech), Scansoft (www.scansoft.com) and Nuance (www.nuance.com), have moved recently into the embedded speech sector, while companies such as Xybernaut (www.xybernaut.com) have pioneered the development of wearable computer technology that includes voice activation. Embedded speech technology provides an alternative interface to the knobs, switches, buttons and digital displays of consumer appliances. Devices are becoming increasingly complex and, as the range of features increases, it has become more and more difficult for users to produce the appropriate sequences of key presses to set a control. A typical example is the inability of most people to use their remote control to set the timer on their video recorder to record programs broadcast at a later time or date. Moreover, as devices decrease in size, manual manipulation has become more difficult, if not impossible. There are, however, a number of challenges for speech technology, in particular, the issue of robust speech recognition in noisy environments such as a car, requiring techniques such as echo cancellation, noise subtraction and other noise reduction techniques.

What Kinds of Things Can You Ask a Computer to Do?

Speech to computers can be used for a number of different purposes. For example, Rachel used speech to control the alarm clock ("snooze" and "off"), to give instructions to the toaster ("not so well done this time") and to the fridge ("don't forget to order another carton of milk"), to ask for the weather forecast, and to check and amend her appointments. Let us look at some of the more common functions and examine what is involved.

Controlling Devices

Controlling devices are often referred to as a "Command-and-control" function (Markowitz, 1996). Command-and-control involves the use of speech to control equipment, which can include computers, consumer appliances and machinery. There are a number of products that enable users to issue commands to their computer applications, such as word processors, spreadsheets and operating systems, and to control consumer appliances, as described earlier. Some of the earliest applications of command-and-control were battle management applications for military vehicles, and there have been many applications for manufacturing equipment control.

Command-and-control is appropriate for "hands-busy" situations, where the user's hands are not free to control the equipment. For example, car drivers can control the car stereo or dial a number on their car telephone without taking their hands from the steering wheel or their eyes from the road. Users of computer software can also combine speech commands with traditional mouse and keyboard interfaces to accomplish some functions more easily. For example, issuing the speech command "Create a table with five rows and four columns" might be more convenient in Microsoft Word than the mouse sequence `Tools` $\rightarrow$ `Insert Table`, then selecting the required numbers of rows and columns from the Insert Table dialogue box.

Command-and-control is also useful for people with disabilities who would not otherwise be able to manipulate the control functions of the equipment. The Hill-Rom Enhancemate product, for example, described in Markowitz (1996), enables people with severe physical disabilities to control specially equipped hospital beds as well as other objects in their immediate environment.

Many command-and-control applications have a small vocabulary size (between 10 and 50 words), reflecting the operations required to control the equipment. Thus commands to control the lights might include "on", "off", "dim" and a few more words, depending on what additional operations are available. More complex systems such as military aircraft cockpits can require up to 5000 words to control the equipment. As far as embedded consumer products are concerned, a small vocabulary size is essential in order to minimise memory and CPU resources in the target system. Thus Sensory's voice activation software is limited to between 50–100 phrases in speaker-dependent mode and 10–20 phrases in speaker-dependent mode.

Most command-and-control applications involve the use of single words or phrases, such as "yes", "open garage door", or "lights on". Usually there is a straightforward mapping between the word or phrase and its semantics, i.e., the action to be carried out or the meaning to be associated with the words. More complex commands and queries can involve sentence-like structures, such as "open the garage door at 7 a.m." or "Every Saturday and Sunday turn living room lights on at 6 p.m. for three hours." These commands may map directly on to a set of actions such that each phrase is associated with a particular action set. In this case no complex language processing of the phrases is required. However, as the number of phrases and alternative wordings increases, this approach becomes unmanageable. For example, in the last example alternative words could be substituted for the days "Saturday" and "Sunday", for "turn on", "living room lights", "6 p.m." and "for three hours." In some cases the range of alternative words might be restricted, for example, to days of the week or times of the day. Even so, as the number of alternative wordings increases, the task of listing all possible combinations and associating them with a given set of actions becomes unmanageable and so a grammar is required that specifies, in a more abstract way, the words and phrases along with their permissible combinations. A wide coverage system would also need to include different ways of saying the same thing, for example, "turn the lights on at 7" as opposed to "at 7 turn the lights on" or "at 7 turn on the lights".

Data Entry

Data entry involves the use of speech to enter data into a software program. Many early applications were used by the military as well as in factories and warehouses to enable users to perform several tasks at the same time, such as monitoring equipment while entering data. Most data entry applications involve well-defined data items that can be entered into specific software programs. Applications include form completion, package sorting, equipment maintenance and traffic accident reports. Changing an appointment, as in the fantasy scenario, is one example of data entry.

Data entry applications usually involve a small range of words, such as digits, "yes", "no" and a few additional control words. However, there may also be a requirement for a larger number of application-specific words, depending on the application type. For example, a reporting system for an accident reporting system might require vocabulary for the names of all the streets and locations in a city.

Getting Information

There are already a large number of speech-based applications that enable people to obtain information about the weather, travel schedules, share prices and many other information sources and services by calling a number on the telephone and speaking to the system in a fairly natural conversational mode. The example in the fantasy scenario is based on a conversation between Victor Zue, Head of the Spoken Language Systems Group at MIT's Laboratory for Computer Science, and Jupiter, a weather information system (Zue, 1999). Jupiter is one of the applications that have been created on MIT's Galaxy architecture – others include Pegasus, which provides schedules for around 4000 commercial airline flights in the United States, and Voyager, which is a guide to navigation and traffic in the Boston area. These applications provide up-to-date information in near real-time and can be accessed by telephone. In the period from May 1977 to 1999 Jupiter had fielded more than 30,000 calls and had achieved a correct understanding rate of around 80% of queries from first-time users. Calls are recorded and processed so that the system's performance can be evaluated and to provide data for further research.

Data access and information retrieval systems require vocabularies that reflect the names of the database fields and their contents. A weather information system, for example, would require the names of all the cities and regions for which weather reports are generated.

Dictation

Dictation involves the automatic translation of speech into written form, either while the speaker is talking or with the use of a prerecorded speech sample as input to the system. Current dictation systems also allow the user to format the text using voice commands. Dictation is different from the other functions in that the user's input is not interpreted. If the user chooses to speak nonsense, this will be converted blindly by the system into text. There is no dialogue with the system, as in information retrieval applications, and a different type of speech technology is involved, as dictation applications require a large general vocabulary as opposed to the smaller more domain-specific vocabularies of other application types. However, dictation could be embedded within an interactive system. For example, an email reader could allow the user to dictate a response to an email. Currently, however, speech-based email systems record the user's message and send the recording as a voice file.

Dictation systems require large vocabularies and, in some cases, an application will include a specialist vocabulary for the application in question in addition to a more general vocabulary. Vocabulary size is a two-edged sword for speech systems. On the one hand, the smaller the vocabulary the less chance there is that similarly sounding, and thus more easily confusable, words are included. On the other hand, the larger the vocabulary the less likely the system is to encounter an unknown word. Unknown words are a major source of speech recognition errors as they lead to an incorrect guess in which the system assigns the unknown word to a word that is actually within its vocabulary.

A Speech-enabled Virtual Personal Assistant

In the fantasy scenario Rachel was able to call on a virtual assistant to check and rearrange her appointments, place calls and check her email. These tasks involve a combination of functions as well as the integration of speech technology with the telephone. There have been a number of successful speech-based telephone applications since the beginning of the 1990s, such as voice-activated dialling and automated directory enquiry. Call management is a more recent application type, while the most recent innovation involves the integration of speech technology, the telephone and the Internet into what has come to be known as the Voice Web.

One example of such an application is the Voice-Enabled Virtual Assistant, developed by Vialto and running on the VoiceGenie VoiceXML Gateway (Voice-Genie, 2003). The Virtual Assistant handles a number of automated functions, such as looking up and dialling telephone numbers, retrieving email and consulting and updating calendar entries. Users can speak commands such as "Call John Smith at work", "Appointments for January 18 after 11a.m.", and "Read email from John Smith".

Dialogue with a Computer

In some applications the system receives a simple command from the user, such as "off", and the system responds with the required action. In such a case the dialogue between the user and the system is minimal. In other cases there may be a more extended dialogue. For example, in a flight enquiry system the system may have to elicit a number of items of information from the user, such as destination city, departure city, date and time of travel, and so on, before it can retrieve the appropriate information from a database. Extended dialogue introduces a number of additional issues. On the one hand, a dialogue is more than a set of utterances that follow one another in some arbitrary sequence. For this reason it is necessary to keep track of what has been said in a dialogue and to relate new utterances to what has been said previously. A second issue is that in dialogues people sometimes mishear what the other person said or take it up in the wrong way. Thus there needs to be some way of dealing with errors and misunderstandings. The nature and complexity of dialogue will be discussed in Chapter 3, while Chapter 13 will present some ways for keeping track of what has been said in a dialogue and for recovering from errors.

Relations Between Utterances in Dialogue

There are a number of ways in which the utterances in a dialogue can be related to one another. First, the utterances of each speaker should relate to each other in terms of their function and content. So, if the user asks a question, then the system should provide an answer to that question. More specifically, if the question is for information such as a departure time, then the answer should include that information. There are, of course, cases where this basic prescription may be violated, for example, when the system does not have the required information. In such a case the user's question still needs to be addressed, possibly with some account for the inability to answer it.

A second aspect of relations between utterances is that words or phrases may refer back to something previously mentioned. For example, the user might say "Call Anna", followed by "No, change that to Paul". The system needs to know how the second command relates to the first and how to determine what the word "that" refers to. In this case the name of the callee is to be changed. In a different case, the command "No, change that to email" would need to be interpreted as a change in the medium of the communication. More generally, there are many ways in which words and phrases are related within a dialogue and there are a number of theories that address their use and interpretation within a discourse context (see Chapter 3).

A final example of the relations between utterances in a dialogue concerns topical coherence. In the simplest systems only one topic is involved, such as obtaining flight information. More complex systems may include several functions. For example, the scenarios modelled in the DARPA Communicator systems include flight information and reservations, car rental and hotel reservation (http://fofoca.mitre.org). One method of dialogue control would be to require the user to complete each function before moving on to the next. However, a more flexible system might allow the user to move between topics, for example, to decide on whether a car is required based on the location of the hotel that is to be reserved. In such a case, the system needs to keep track of what has been discussed and agreed in order to be able to return to topics that have not been closed.

Dealing with Errors and Misunderstandings

There are many ways in which errors and misunderstandings can arise in a dialogue. One example of these is illustrated in the fantasy scenario when Rachel asks about the weather forecast for the Costa Brava. This mirrors an actual exchange between Victor Zue and Jupiter in the MIT weather information system (Zue, 1999):

> 1.3
> 1 V.Z.: Is it sunny anywhere in the Caribbean?
> 2 Jupiter: Sorry, I am not sure what you said.
> 3 V.Z.: Is it sunny anywhere in the Caribbean?
> 4 Jupiter: I am sorry, I may not know the city you are asking about. Try asking for the state or country. For example, what cities do you know about in Massachusetts?

In the first exchange (1–2) the system responds that it is unsure about the input. One reason could be that one or more key words have not been correctly recognised (a speech recognition issue). As speech recognition cannot be guaranteed to be completely accurate, even in conversations between humans, a spoken dialogue system must include mechanisms for detecting and dealing with misrecognitions. The simplest ploy is to get the user to repeat, as happens in this exchange. However, there are many more sophisticated techniques that can be employed to resolve recognition problems (see Chapter 13).

In the second exchange (3–4) it becomes obvious that misrecognition is not the problem. The user has asked about something that is outside the scope of the system's knowledge, in other words, the item mentioned is not represented in the database. Handling this sort of problem is more complex. The simplest approach is to state that the system does not have any information about the item in question and invite the user to submit a different query. However, this approach is not particularly helpful and could involve the user in submitting several similar queries that the system cannot answer and subsequently giving up in frustration. An alternative strategy is to detect the source of the problem and to propose a solution. In this case, the system makes clear that it can only answer queries about cities, and provides an example of a query that will inform the user about which cities in particular it can handle. While the solution to this particular issue appears simple, it is a major challenge to provide a more general solution that would enable the system to behave in a cooperative way in the face of similar conversational misunderstandings.

Advanced Functions

Some of the features illustrated in the fantasy scenario are beyond the capabilities of current technology and are the subject of ongoing research. For example, when speaking to the toaster, Rachel said "Not so well done this time." There are several ways in which this short phrase would be problematic. The meaning of the expression "well done" is relative to the extent to which the bread had been toasted on the previous occasion, rather than a description of an absolute degree of toasting. If, on the previous occasion, the bread had been toasted to a moderate degree, then the expression would have the meaning "a little less than moderate". If, however, the toast had been burnt, the expression would have the meaning "a little less than burnt". Furthermore, the expressions "moderate" and "burnt" are themselves relative, but at some point there would need to be a correspondence between expressions, degrees of toasting and toaster settings for these expressions to be interpretable.

Another example is the brief conversation with the fridge about ordering milk:

1.4
1 Rachel: Don't forget to order another carton of milk.
2 Fridge: You're having some friends round for hot chocolate later. Maybe you should order two cartons.

In this episode Rachel instructs the fridge to order more milk. However, instead of accepting Rachel's instruction, the fridge makes a counter suggestion along with a justification. To perform this sort of function, the system needs to be able to do more than simply process instructions and translate them into actions or look up items in a database. Complex reasoning is required involving knowledge of Rachel's plans and what is required for these plans to be achievable.

Reasoning such as this has not been implemented in currently deployed systems, although there are a number of research projects that focus on the integration of reasoning and spoken dialogue technology. One of these is the TRIPS project, which is based in the Conversational Interaction and Spoken Dialogue Research Group at the University of Rochester (Allen et al., 2001a, b). The following is an example of an interaction with the TRIPS system (taken from Allen et al., 2001a, p. 40).

1.5
1 User: We need to get the woman in Penfield to Strong.
2 System: OK.
3 User: What vehicles are available?
4 System: There are ambulances in Pittsford and Webster.
5 User: OK. Use one from Pittsford.
6 System: Do you know that Route 96 is blocked due to construction?

The TRIPS system models dialogue as interactive collaborative problem solving. Unlike most other dialogue systems, in which the system responds to the user's questions and commands by looking up a database or executing some action, in TRIPS the system and user engage in dialogue to solve a real-world task. In the example above, which is a rescue task scenario, the objective is to identify a suitable vehicle and route to move an injured woman to hospital. The user makes a proposal in utterance 5 but the system responds with a possible objection to this proposal in utterance 6. To do this the system must be able to reason about the task at hand and evaluate the viability of the proposed solutions. The TRIPS system is described in greater detail in Chapter 12.

Summary

From the examples that have been presented in this chapter it can be seen that the vision of the talking computer, as depicted in science fiction (e.g., Star Trek and Space Odyssey 2001), is already verging on reality. Progress in speech technology is the result of a number of factors:

1. *Technological advances in computer hardware*. Microprocessors have increased dramatically in speed and power over the past few decades so that they are capable of handling the complex mathematical calculations required for advanced speech technology applications in real-time. Miniaturisation of hardware – the ability to put increasingly powerful components on to smaller chips – has facilitated the embedding of speech technology into consumer appliances. Finally, dramatic reductions in the prices of processors, storage and memory have made speech applications more economically feasible.

2. *Developments in software*. More advanced algorithms have been developed to cope more adequately with tasks such as speech recognition, language understanding, dialogue management and sophisticated reasoning. Moreover,

in addition to advancements in each of these component areas, significant advances have been achieved in the integration of the components into working spoken dialogue systems, either as research demonstrators or as commercial products.

3. *Infrastructure for the Voice Web.* With the rapid development of the World Wide Web over the past decade, an infrastructure and universally accepted interface for distributed information and communication systems have been created. The integration of this infrastructure with speech technology, using the telephone rather than the PC, has made possible a new and powerful interface to Internet-based services and information.

4. *Commercial impetus.* A number of commercial benefits have been suggested for speech technology, such as increased productivity, rapid return on investment and access to new markets. This commercial impetus has in turn driven industrially based research in a number of large corporations, such as Microsoft, IBM and Scansoft, and has led to the emergence of several companies specialising in speech technology, such as Nuance, VoiceGenie, BeVocal and Voxpilot.

The next chapter will examine the sorts of application areas that are suitable for spoken dialogue technology and will review the main research thrusts as well as the commercial potential of the technology.

Further Reading

The fantasy scenario presented in this chapter was inspired by a similar scenario "A Day in Jack's Life" presented in a paper by James Larson entitled "Speech-enabled appliances", which appeared in *Speech Technology Magazine* (Larson, 2000).

Speech Technology Magazine is a bimonthly online publication with in-depth papers on the development, application and integration of speech technology for business and consumer applications, covering recent advancements and future trends. Available at: http://www.speechtechmag.com/

Some Other Interesting References

Phillips's "Vision of the Future Project" describes the home of the future, in which wands are personal preference remote controls that are programmed to personalise and preselect media around the house. Simple voice commands offer an intuitive interface to home systems in this vision. Available at: http://www.design.philips.com/vof/toc1/home.htm

Hal's Legacy: 2001's *Computer as Dream and Reality* (Stork, 1998). This is a collection of papers by leading researchers in Artificial Intelligence (AI) describing to what extent the technologies imagined in the 1960s by Arthur Clarke and Stanley Kubrick in Space Odyssey 2001 are possible today.

The Age of Spiritual Machines: How We Will Live, Work and Think in the New Age of Intelligent Machines (Kurzweil, 2001). This book by Ray Kurzweil predicts the future of technology, suggesting that by 2020 computers will outpace the human brain in computational power.

Kurzweilai.net. This web site (http://www.kurzweilai.net/) covers technology of the future and also includes Ramona, a photorealistic, interactive, lifelike chatterbot with which you can converse on the Web. Using natural language processing techniques, Ramona conducts conversations with visitors, responding to typed questions or comments with a life-like face, lip-synched speech and appropriate facial expressions.

ELSNET's Roadmap for Human Language Technologies. ELSNET (European Network of Excellence in Human Language Technologies) is developing views on and visions of the longer-term future of the field of language and speech technologies and neighbouring areas (http://www.elsnet.org/). For the current state of the roadmap, see: http://elsnet.dfki.de

Exercises

The following web sites contain links to spoken dialogue systems, some of which can be tried out by dialling a telephone number. Others can be viewed as demos. Try out some of the systems listed and play some of the demos. Make a note of some systems that you could use for exercises in later chapters.

IBM

http://www-3.ibm.com/software/pervasive/tech/demos/voice_server_demo.shtml (WebSphere Voice Server demo: demonstrates the ease of accessing Internet information over the phone, including movie schedules, nutritional planning tool, and IBM directory dialer).

Nuance Communications

http://www.nuance.com/solutions/bankingcredit/index.html (several demos in the area of financial services: ATM locator, banking transfer funds, and others).

http://www.nuance.com/solutions/utilities/index.html (several demos in the area of utilities: meter reading, start a service, transfer a service).

Scansoft

http://www.scansoft.com/network/solutions/ (demos for financial services, healthcare, telecom, travel and hospitality, utilities).

VoiceGenie

http://www.voicegenie.com/content/10400.html-9d (ATM locator, taxi booking, also includes phone demos).

Spoken Dialogue Applications: Research Directions and Commercial Deployment

2

This chapter consists of three main parts. In the first part different types of spoken dialogue application will be described. The second part of the chapter will provide an overview of past and current research directions in spoken dialogue technology. The final part will discuss the commercial potential of spoken dialogue technology.

Spoken Dialogue Applications

Spoken dialogue systems can be used for many different purposes. Many applications have involved the retrieval of information, in particular, travel information such as flight schedules and train timetables. Other applications have addressed the provision of services, such as call management, and transactions, such as making reservations or managing a bank account. A more advanced type of application is collaborative problem solving, for example, developing a plan to evacuate a disaster area or giving advice on a financial investment. Spoken dialogue systems can also be deployed in educational contexts as an instructional aid. Finally, there are applications within the area of games and entertainment.

Information Retrieval, Services and Transactions

The information age has brought the promise of vast amounts of information that are potentially accessible to anyone at anytime and anywhere. The Internet has made this information available to anyone with a PC and Internet access. However, many people do not have ready access to PCs and it has been estimated that, although there are a quarter of a billion PCs in the world, there are more than 1.3 billion telephones (Larson, 2002). Telephones have the potential to provide a more universal interface to information and, given recent developments in the integration of the telephone and the Internet, a speech interface to this information brings the promise of a natural, efficient and ubiquitous access method. For this reason it is not surprising that most spoken dialogue applications involve some sort of information retrieval. Typical examples include travel schedules, traffic reports, weather forecasts, stock prices, lists of movies at a local cinema, directory enquiries and package tracking.

Information retrieval is a relatively constrained type of application in which the system elicits one or more required parameters from the user and then executes a query to find a response – usually by retrieving information from a database. Such an application is analogous to a form-filling dialogue on a Web page to obtain information or order goods. Implementing a spoken information retrieval application can be achieved using fairly simple methods, in which the system prompts the user with a predefined sequence of queries and accepts narrowly constrained responses. In this way the vocabulary and language structures can be restricted to facilitate speech recognition and language understanding, while dialogue control can be implemented using simple and well-understood techniques.

The following example is taken from a dialogue with the Philips Automatic Train Timetable Information System (available at: +49 241 604020) which provides information over the telephone about train connections between 1200 German cities. The system conducts a natural dialogue in German with the user, who can speak to the system using fluent, unrestricted speech. The text of this dialogue is translated from the original German (Aust et al., 1995).

2.1
1 System: Good morning. This is the automatic timetable information service. How can I help you?
2 User: I need a connection from Hamburg to Munich.
3 System: When would you like to go from Hamburg to Munich?
4 User: Next Friday at eight o'clock.
5 System: So you want to travel on Sunday the 20th of November at eight o'clock a.m.?
6 User: No, on Friday.
7 System: So you want to travel on Friday the 18th of November at eight o'clock a.m.?
8 User: Yes.
9 System: There is the following connection: With IntercityExpress 793, departure from Hamburg at 8:02, arrival in Munich at 14:05. Do you want me to repeat the connection?

The dialogue begins with an open-ended prompt to which the user can respond with some or all of the information that the system requires to consult the database for a suitable train. If more values are required, the system requests these, as in utterance 3, and then confirms the values, as in utterance 5. Note that the user is able to correct the system's attempted confirmation (utterance 6). Details of how this and similar systems are implemented are described in Chapter 5.

Problem-Solving Applications

By their very nature problem-solving applications require more complex dialogue as they require the system and user to act together to solve a problem.

The following example illustrates collaborative problem solving in the Circuit-Fix-It Shop system (Smith and Hipp, 1994, p. 61). This system helps users to fix an electronic circuit. Communication between system and user is motivated by the fact that neither participant is fully equipped to solve the problem alone. The system has all the necessary knowledge about the task but does not have the required sensory abilities to monitor the state of the world nor to perform actions in the world. These are the concern of the human user who also has some knowledge of the task, which can range from that of a novice to that of an expert, depending on the individual user.

2.2

1 System: Is there a wire between connector 84 and connector 99?
2 User: It is not there.
3 System: Add a wire between connector 84 and connector 99.
4 User: I need help.
5 System: Obtain a wire.
6 User: Okay.
7 System: Connect metal of one free end of the wire to connector 84.
8 User: How?
9 System: Bend back connector 84.
10 User: Done.
11 System: Insert free end of wire into connector 84.
12 User: The wire is connecting.

At the beginning of the dialogue, the system does not know whether there is a wire between connector 84 and connector 99. As this is a missing element in the part of the problem to be solved, the system produces utterance 1 to ask the user. The user confirms that the wire is missing. From this the system can infer that the user knows the location of the connectors and these facts are added to the user model – a store of information that the system believes the user knows.

To complete the current subtask, the system instructs the user to add a wire between the connectors. As the user does not know how to do this, the system has to adopt a subgoal to advise the user on how to accomplish this task. This subgoal consists of the following actions:

1. locate connector 84;

2. locate connector 99;

3. obtain a wire;

4. connect one end of the wire to 84; and

5. connect the other end of the wire to 99.

As the user model contains the information that the user can locate connectors 84 and 99, instructions for the first two actions are not required and so the system proceeds with instructions for the third action, which is confirmed in utterance 6, and for the fourth action. Here the user requires further instructions, which are given in utterance 9, with the action confirmed by the user in utterance 10. At this point the user asserts that the wire between 84 and 99 is connecting, so that the fifth instruction to connect the second end to 99 is not required.

In the Circuit-Fix-It Shop system the dialogue evolves dynamically, depending on the current state of the problem being solved, as well as on the system's estimate of what the user needs to be told. As the state of the problem changes constantly, as well as the state of the user's knowledge, the system needs to maintain a record of its current information state about the problem and the user and to update this information dynamically.

Educational Applications

Spoken dialogue interfaces can be used in educational applications to provide a more natural mode of communication between students and computer-based learning materials. One particularly interesting example involves the use of the Center for Spoken Language Understanding (CSLU) toolkit to assist profoundly deaf children to speak. The CSLU toolkit, which was developed by the CSLU at the Oregon Graduate Institute, includes a graphical authoring environment to support the development of interactive speech applications (cslu.cse.ogi.edu/toolkit/). The latest release of the toolkit, version 2.0, also contains an animation engine CUAnimate, donated by the Center for Spoken Language Research (CSLR) of the University of Boulder, Colorado (cslr.colorado.edu/). Previous versions of the toolkit used an animated three-dimension talking head (Baldi), developed at the Perceptual Science Laboratory at the University of California, Santa Cruz (UCSC) (mambo.ucsc.edu/).

The CSLU toolkit's graphical authoring tool enables a wide range of learning and language training applications to be developed. Baldi has been used at the Tucker–Maxon Oral School in Portland, Oregon, to help deaf children to learn how to form their words and practise pronunciation (Cole et al., 1999; Connors et al., 1999). Baldi's lips, tongue and jaw movements are a near-perfect copy of human speech movements. The children mimic Baldi and then find out if their responses are correct through Baldi's feedback. In addition to deaf children, the toolkit is being used to develop applications for children with autism, who have problems with verbal communication. A variety of other instructional aids such as vocabulary tutors and interactive reading tutors have also been developed, and the latest release of the toolkit also includes the CSLU Vocabulary Editor and Tutor. Chapter 8 contains a series of tutorials for the development of educational applications using the CSLU toolkit.

Conversational interfaces are also being used in conjunction with Intelligent Tutoring Systems (ITSs). ITSs are similar to problem-solving applications as they involve a dialogue between the system and the learner, who is trying to solve a problem. However, in an ITS the purpose of the interaction is to enable the learner to learn about the problem, so that important components of the architecture will include a tutoring strategy that determines the system's behaviours and a learner model that represents the learner's current state of knowledge.

Some recent ITSs support mixed-initiative conversational dialogues with the learner, in which the learner types in answers in English and the system conducts a dialogue in which solutions are developed. Graesser et al. (2001) describe a number of such systems that they have been developing, including AutoTutor, a conversational agent with a talking head, that helps college students learn about computer literacy. The talking head uses synthesised speech, intonation, facial expressions, nods and gestures to communicate with the learner, who types in his or her contributions. The learner's answers can be lengthy, exhibiting deep reasoning and thus requiring sophisticated natural language processing in order to interpret them correctly. Usually a lengthy multiturn dialogue evolves during the course of answering a deep reasoning question. The dialogue properties of advanced systems such as this will be discussed in greater detail in Chapter 12.

Most dialogue-based ITSs involve text-based interactions. In a recent paper, Litman (2002) has proposed adding a spoken language interface to an existing text-based ITS. The initial stages will explore the issues involved in replacing the current input and output modalities with speech and, in particular, with investigating the additional problems that arise with speech recognition errors. At this level speech would function as a potentially more convenient mode of input and output compared with text-based interaction. However, in the longer term the pedagogical effectiveness of a speech interface will be explored, by making use of information that is only available in speech, such as prosodic features that can indicate emotional states such as annoyance, confusion, boredom and certainty. The plan is to use this additional information to enable the system to adapt its tutoring strategies to match the learner's perceived emotional and cognitive state.

Games and Entertainment

Spoken dialogue technology has tremendous potential in computer games and entertainment. The simplest applications involve the replacement of the mouse, keyboard and joystick by voice commands. "Hey You, Pikachu!" from Nintendo is a good example (www.pikachu.com). The game consists mainly of the player taking Pikachu to different places and getting him to carry out actions for which the commands that can be recognised are presented on screen. Another example is Game Commander from Sontage Interactive (www.gamecommander.com). Game Commander is a voice control application for games. Game Commander allows players to control many games with verbal commands instead of, or in conjunction with, keyboard, joystick and mouse controls. For example, instead of remembering that Alt+Shift+F8 is the command for lock missiles, you can just say "Lock Missiles". Recently, Scansoft has released a Games Software Development Kit for PlayStation2 that enables integration of speech recognition functions into games and "edutainment" software (www.scansoft.com/games).

Spoken dialogue technology is being combined with computer games technologies in a European research project NICE (Natural Interactive Communication for Edutainment) (www.niceproject.com). NICE is developing a prototype system for children and adolescents that will allow them to have conversations with the fairy-tale author Hans Christian Andersen and to play games with animated characters. Communication will involve spoken conversation combined with two-dimensional input gestures in a three-dimensional dynamic graphics virtual world.

It has been estimated that there is a huge market for advanced edutainment systems that could act as companions to groups such as the elderly, as well as providing useful assistance such as providing help in medical emergencies. There are already some examples of such systems in the form of "chatterbots" – a type of conversing computer. The term "chatterbot" was coined by Michael Maudlin, founder of the Lycos search engine (Maudlin, 1994). A chatterbot is a computer program that accepts verbal input from the user and outputs a verbal response. Generally, the input and output take the form of typed natural language phrases or sentences, although some chatterbots are now also able to handle spoken input and output.

Chatterbots would appear to be most successful when they do not need to simulate an intelligent, cooperative conversational participant. Chatterbots in games do not need to make relevant responses – indeed, their odd behaviour can often be seen as part of the game. Nevertheless, the techniques used to produce chatterbots have also been used successfully in a number of more serious applications, for example, to provide on-line help. Ford Motor Company has an online chatterbot called Ernie who helps technicians at its network of dealerships to diagnose car problems and to order parts. Ernie is an example of a vRep, an automated agent developed by NativeMinds, that uses natural language dialogue to answer customers' questions (www.nativeminds.com). Similarly, IBM's Lotus software division employs a service chatterbot that can diagnose problems in a user's software and upload patches to the user's computer (Nickell, 2002). In these applications the success of the chatterbot depends on an extensive set of patterns that match the user's input within a restricted domain to trigger an appropriate system output. The technology underlying chatterbots and other systems that simulate conversation will be described in more detail below.

Research in Spoken Dialogue Technology

Research in spoken dialogue technology can be traced back to work on natural language processing and artificial intelligence (AI) in the 1960s. The earliest dialogue systems involved typed input of natural language phrases and sentences, and it was not until the late 1980s that the speech and natural language communities started to come together to develop spoken dialogue systems as they are known today.

Two main approaches can be distinguished in dialogue research. One approach has focussed on theoretically motivated models of dialogue based on research in natural language processing and artificial intelligence. The other approach, sometimes known as "simulated conversation" or "human–computer conversation", has used methods ranging from pattern matching to fairly complex data-driven techniques to simulate conversational interaction. The following sections present a brief historical overview of dialogue systems from the 1960s through to the present time.

Natural Language Dialogue Systems in the 1960s

A number of systems developed in the 1960s aimed to provide natural language interfaces to computers. Much of this work disregarded theories of human language processing from theoretical linguistics and cognitive psychology and used a variety of techniques to manipulate language to produce acceptable results.

BASEBALL was an early question–answering system that could answer questions about the dates, locations, teams and scores of baseball games (Green et al., 1963). The system could be queried with questions such as "Who beat the Yankees on July 4?" or "Did any team play at least once in each park in each month?" To illustrate the ad hoc nature of some of the language processing, the meaning of the word "who" in the system's dictionary was given as "Team = ?", a domain specific meaning that could not be generalised to other domains.

STUDENT was a program that was able to solve algebra story problems cast in natural language (Bobrow, 1968). For example,

2.3
Mary is twice as old as Ann was when Mary was as old as Ann is now. If Mary is 24 years old, how old is Ann?

The program converted the natural language input into a set of algebraic equations by breaking it into simple patterns and looking for words and phrases that could be replaced by arithmetic expressions and variables. STUDENT demonstrated some interesting features that foreshadowed later developments. One of these was that the system was able to deal with connected discourse and not simply with isolated sentences. A second feature was that the system used a store of general knowledge to assist with the solution of problems and it could expand its store of knowledge by eliciting further information from the user. Nevertheless, systems such as STUDENT and BASEBALL were generally based on techniques that could be applied successfully within the domain in question but were not easily generalisable to other domains. Moreover, the techniques in question were not based on any more theoretically motivated approaches to dialogue.

Linguistic and Artificial Intelligence Approaches to Dialogue in the 1970s and Early 1980s

The 1970s and early 1980s saw the emergence of more theoretically motivated approaches to dialogue, based on research in natural language processing and artificial intelligence.

SHRDLU

SHRDLU, developed at MIT in the early 1970s, was an attempt to model the processes of natural language understanding on a computer (Winograd, 1972). The system operated within a very limited domain, a tiny world containing a box, a table, blocks and pyramids that could be manipulated according to commands from the user. The system could also answer questions and could "learn" from the interactions. The following is an example of an interaction with SHRDLU:

2.4
1 User: Pick up a red block.
2 SHRDLU: OK.
3 User: Grasp the pyramid.
4 SHRDLU: I don't understand which pyramid you mean.
5 User: Find a block which is taller than the one you are holding and put it into the box.
6 SHRDLU: By "it" I assume you mean the block which is taller than the one I am holding.
7 User: OK. What does the box contain?
8 SHRDLU: The blue pyramid and the blue box.

SHRDLU has to process the user's input, which in some cases is fairly complex. However, the input has to be processed not only linguistically but also in relation to the simulated world in which the positions of objects change continually as a result of the user's commands. Objects can be referred to using pronouns and other referring expressions. In some cases the reference is ambiguous. For example, "grasp the pyramid" is ambiguous, as there are three pyramids in the scene, and "put it into the box" is ambiguous, as "it" could refer either to the block that SHRDLU was holding or to the larger block that SHRDLU was to find.

SHRDLU used a combination of syntactic, semantic and pragmatic analyses to interact within the blocks' world. The syntactic analysis used a comprehensive grammar of English that assigned a syntactic structure to the user's input by determining the parts of speech of each word and the permissible combinations of words as phrases in a sentence. The semantic analysis enabled SHRDLU to reject meaningless sentences based on semantic knowledge about the objects in the domain. For example, the question "Can the table pick up blocks?" was rejected because a table is an inanimate object and the verb "pick up" requires a subject that is animate. The pragmatic component kept track of the objects in the domain, for example, "Block1 supports Block2" and had procedures to represent actions that could be carried out. If there was an instruction to grasp an object, it would be necessary to check if the object was of a type that could be manipulated, if there was another object on top of the object to be grasped, if the robot was currently holding some other object, and so on. These procedures enabled SHRDLU to carry out actions involving several subactions and, more interestingly, to answer questions about its actions. For example, if asked "Why did you put object2 on the table?" SHRDLU could answer "To get rid of object2". If asked "Why did you get rid of object2", SHRDLU would reply "To grasp object1".

SHRDLU was able to combine its processing modules in an interesting way to resolve sentences that might otherwise be ambiguous. The following example illustrates:

2.5 Put the blue pyramid on the block on the box.

Using syntactic analysis alone, these words could be grouped in two different ways:

1 Put (the blue pyramid on the block) in the box.
2 Put the blue pyramid on (the block in the box).

In other words, either there is a blue pyramid on a block or there is a block in the box. SHRDLU would begin to analyse the sentence using its syntactic knowledge. To decide on the meaning of the sentence it would consult its semantic knowledge, for example, whether the sentence is meaningful in terms of objects that can be manipulated. At this stage there would still be two interpretations. However, the pragmatic component would then check the current state of the world to see if one interpretation made more sense in context. If there was a blue pyramid on a block, then the first interpretation would be accepted, otherwise the second interpretation would be investigated. This interaction between different sources of knowledge to interpret natural language sentences in context remains an important area for research in natural language processing.

Artificial Intelligence Approaches: Knowledge Structures and Inference

In addition to knowledge about objects and their attributes, as utilised in SHRDLU, natural language understanding systems require other knowledge structures in order to make sense of natural language text, such as knowledge about event sequences and knowledge about people, their beliefs, desires, motivations and plans. Schank (1975) developed a theory of language in the 1970s called Conceptual Dependency Theory, in which the emphasis was on the content of information rather than on its syntactic form. As the focus moved from the analysis of single sentences to larger structures such as stories, Schank and his colleagues at Yale developed knowledge structures to represent events, goals and plans that would support the interpretation of stories and similar discourse units.

Scripts were used to represent stereotypical sequences of events, such as going to a restaurant or travelling by bus. Schank argued that to understand a story, people (and computers) required knowledge beyond the information contained explicitly in the text. The following example, taken from an interaction with the program SAM (Script Applier Mechanism), illustrates a script for VIP visits (Cullingford, 1981):

2.6
Sunday morning Enver Hoxha, the Premier of Albania, and Mrs Hoxha arrived in Peking at the invitation of Communist China. The Albanian party was welcomed at Peking Airport by Foreign Minister Huang. Chairman Hua and Mr Hoxha discussed economic relations between China and Albania for three hours.

There are several points in this apparently simple story where script knowledge is required to make sense of the story. Words like "invitation" cause SAM to look in its database of scripts and, when it finds VIPVISIT, a number of relevant concepts are activated, such as arrival and mode of travel. Using this information SAM examines the second sentence and can conclude that, as the group has been welcomed at Peking Airport, they are likely to have arrived there and to have travelled by plane. The third sentence makes sense in the context of a VIP visit, as one of the expected events is an "official talks" episode, in this case a discussion about economic relations. Various inferences are made during the processing of the story. There is no mention of where the talks are held, so SAM assumes it was in the city where the Hoxha party arrived. Similarly, SAM can answer questions such as "Who went to China?" although the story does not say explicitly that anyone went to China, only that the Hoxhas arrived in Peking.

Research in scripts showed that understanding connected discourse involves more than analysing the syntactic structure of sentences and examining their literal meanings. Understanding involves finding causal links between events and making assumptions about events and other items that have not been explicitly mentioned. SAM used the notion of scripts, or stereotypical sequences of events, to perform this reasoning. Another program from the same group, PAM (Plan Applier Mechanism), used the notion of plans to make sense of events that, unlike scripts, had not previously been encountered (Wilensky, 1981). PAM encoded general information about how people achieve goals and about what sorts of goals they try to achieve. Another program QUALM was used in conjunction with SAM and PAM to answer questions (Lehnert, 1980). Finally, within this tradition of research, a program called POLITICS modelled political beliefs and the way in which different people can have different interpretations of the same event, illustrated with a conservative and a liberal view of particular events (Carbonell, 1981).

Natural Language Database Queries

Systems that could process natural language queries and translate them into a formal database query language were one of the earliest major successes in natural language processing. LUNAR, which could answer natural language queries to a database containing information about moon rocks, was one of the first such interfaces that appeared in the late 1960s (Woods et al., 1972). Following active research throughout the 1970s and 1980s, a number of systems have become available commercially, such as English Wizard and Access ELF (Androutsopoulos and Ritchie, 2000).

Strictly speaking a natural language database system does not engage in a dialogue with the user. Rather the user submits a query, usually in typed natural language, that is translated by the system into a query in a formal database language such as SQL. Most systems will simply generate an error message if they are unable to process the user's input and invite the user to submit another query. Some systems are able to process a series of queries that are related to one another and that use discourse phenomena such as anaphora and ellipsis, as in the following examples, quoted in (Androutsopoulos and Ritchie, 2000):

2.7
1 User: Who leads TPI?
2 System: E. Feron
3 User: Who reports to him? (example of anaphoric reference: "him" refers back to "E. Feron" in the previous utterance).

2.8
1 User: Does the highest paid female manager have any degrees from Harvard?
2 System: Yes, 1.
3 User: How about MIT? (elliptical question that is understood by replacing "Harvard" in the first question with "MIT").

Systems that employ discourse devices such as these support a user-driven dialogue in which the user can ask a series of questions and the system has to keep track of the people and objects mentioned in the dialogue in order to be able to process subsequent queries. Considerable research has been directed towards the issue of cooperative systems that provide some form of feedback if the user's query cannot be sufficiently processed. For example, problems may arise if the vocabulary of the dialogue does not map directly on to the vocabulary of the application, or if the query makes false assumptions concerning the actual contents of the database so that no straightforward response is possible. Kaplan (1983) addressed the issue of false assumptions, as illustrated in the following example:

2.9
1 User: How many students got As in Linguistics in 1981?
2 System: None.

The system's response is correct if the set of students that got "A" in linguistics is empty, but it would also be correct if there were no students taking linguistics in 1981. However, in the latter case, the system's response is misleading, as it does not correct the user's false assumptions.

Problems may also arise if the user has misconceptions about the world model represented in the database. Carberry (1986) discusses the query "Which apartments are for sale?" which (in an American real-estate context) is inappropriate, as apartments are rented, not sold, although apartment blocks may be sold, for example, to property developers. Resolving this problem involved discerning the user's goal that gave rise to the ill-formed query.

Dialogue systems that enable users to access the contents of a database over the telephone are usually designed in such a way as to assist the user in the construction of the query by eliciting the required parameters. In most commercially deployed systems each parameter is elicited separately and inserted subsequently into a query template. In this way, the issue of ill-formed queries is avoided.

Dialogue as Planning

Another approach involved the application of formalisms and inference mechanisms from research in planning (a subdiscipline of artificial intelligence) to the modelling of the plans and intentions of participants in dialogue. Consider the following simple example, taken from a system that plays the role of a railway employee answering the queries of a client who has one of two possible goals – to board a train or to meet a train (Allen, 1983; Allen and Perrault, 1980):

> 2.10
> 1 User: When does the train to Windsor leave?
> 2 System: 3.15 at Gate 7.

In this example the user asks for the departure time of the train. However, the system reasons that in order to board a train a person will also need to know the departure location, hence the mention of Gate 7. To provide helpful answers in this way the system has to interpret the user's question and then progress through a series of inferences to determine the user's goal and to identify any potential obstacles to the achievement of this goal. Various inference rules are involved, such as the Action–Effect rule, which can be stated informally as follows:

> 2.11
> If an agent wants to achieve a goal, and some action has that goal as its effect, then the agent will probably want to carry out that action.

A chain of inferences leads from the literal interpretation of the user's question to the system's production of a helpful response. This work has continued throughout the 1980s and 1990s and has formed the basis for current research on conversational agency known as the Belief, Desire and Intention (BDI) approach (see Chapter 12).

Using Frames to Guide the Dialogue – The Travel Agent GUS

The Genial Understander System (GUS) combined sophisticated natural language understanding in terms of morphological and syntactic analysis with a frame-based approach to dialogue control. GUS acted as a travel agent that conducted a dialogue in written natural language with a client who wanted to make a simple return trip from Palo Alto to a single city in California. The following is an excerpt from a dialogue with GUS (Bobrow et al., 1977):

> 2.12
> 1 GUS: Where do you want to go to?
> 2 User: I want to go to San Diego on May 28.
> 3 GUS: What time do you want to leave?
> 4 User: I must be in San Diego before 10 a.m.
> 5 GUS: Would you like PSA flight 102 that arrives at 9.15?
> 6 User: What is the next flight?
> 7 GUS: Air California flight 310 that leaves at 8.30 a.m. and arrives at 10 a.m.
> 8 User: I'll take the first one.

GUS used a set of frames to guide the dialogue. For example, the following is part of a simplified version of a frame, consisting of a series of slots and fillers, for one leg of a trip:

Slots	Fillers
Fromplace	City
Toplace	City
Traveldate	Date
Departure	Time range
Arrival	Time range

During the course of the dialogue, slots are filled with values of the appropriate type. Each slot has procedures to generate questions to acquire information from the client. For example, the "Toplace" slot has the question "Where do you want to go to?" If the user supplies more information than is asked for by a question, as in 2 ("I want to go to San Diego on May 28"), then other slots such as the Traveldate will also be filled and it will not be necessary to ask a Traveldate question later in the dialogue. This is similar to the mechanisms used in many current spoken dialogue systems, as described in Chapters 5 and 10.

GUS also uses sophisticated techniques for resolving expressions that are incomplete and are thus potentially difficult to interpret. For example, the phase "the next one" in 6 is interpreted as referring to the flight following the one mentioned in 5. Another example (not cited in this extract) was a relative date expression "Friday in the evening" in response to the question "What date do you want to return?" This expression has to be interpreted as the Friday following the date of arrival and not the Friday following the date of the conversation. Many current systems involving date and time expressions use similar procedures for resolving relative expressions such as these.

Simulated Conversation

Simulated conversation is concerned with the development of systems that simulate conversational interaction. This approach uses methods such as pattern matching rather than models and theories derived from natural language processing and artificial intelligence. Nevertheless many of the systems developed within this approach are able to perform impressively as conversationalists.

Simulated conversational systems can be traced back to the "imitation game" proposed in 1950 by the British mathematician and code-breaker Alan Turing in his seminal paper, "Computing Machinery and Intelligence", in which he considered the question "Can machines think?" (Turing, 1950). In the imitation game a person interacts in natural language via a terminal and has to decide whether they are interacting with a person or a computer. If they are unable to tell, then the computer should be regarded as having intelligence. Although the validity of Turing's test of machine intelligence has come in for considerable criticism on methodological grounds, there has been a long tradition of efforts to develop computer programs that would pass the test. In 1991, Hugh Loebner initiated the annual Loebner Prize competition, offering a prize of $100,000 for the first program to pass an unrestricted Turing test. The prize was won in 2000 and 2001 by a program called A.L.I.C.E. written by Richard Wallace (www.alicebot.org).

ELIZA

The first, and probably the best known, system to simulate conversation was Weizenbaum's ELIZA program, published in 1966. ELIZA simulates a psychotherapist. The following is an example of a typical conversation with ELIZA (Weizenbaum, 1966):

2.13
1 Patient: Men are all alike.
2 ELIZA: In what way?
3 Patient: They're always bugging us about something or other.
4 ELIZA: Can you think of a specific example?
5 Patient: Well, my boyfriend made me come here.
6 ELIZA: Your boyfriend made you come here?
7 Patient: He says I'm depressed much of the time.
8 ELIZA: I am sorry to hear you are depressed.
9 Patient: It's true. I am unhappy.
10 ELIZA: Do you think coming here will help you not to be unhappy?
11 Patient: I need some help, that much seems certain.
12 ELIZA: What would it mean to you if you got some help?
13 Patient: Perhaps I could learn to get along with my mother.
14 ELIZA: Tell me more about your family.
15 Patient: My mother takes care of me.
16 ELIZA: Who else in your family takes care of you?
17 Patient: My father.
18 ELIZA: Your father.
19 Patient: You are like my father in some ways.
20 ELIZA: What resemblance do you see?
21 Patient: You are not very aggressive but I think you don't want me to notice that.
22 ELIZA: What makes you think I am not very aggressive?
23 Patient: You don't argue with me.
24 ELIZA: Why do you think I don't argue with you?
25 Patient: You are afraid of me.
26 ELIZA: Does it please you to believe I am afraid of you?
27 Patient: My father is afraid of everybody.
28 ELIZA: What else comes to your mind when you think of your father?
29 Patient: Bullies.
30 ELIZA: Does that have anything to do with the fact that your boyfriend made you come here?

While this conversation appears impressive and human-like, in reality ELIZA's conversational abilities were limited and were based on the use of a number of keywords and associated responses. For example, a sentence containing "always" could produce the response "Can you think of a specific example?", while a family word such as "mother" would trigger the response "tell me more about your family". A pronoun transformation routine, used in many similar programs, would transform an input pattern such as "You are not very aggressive" into "What makes you think I am not very aggressive?" The patient's input sentences were stored and cycled back at a later point when no specific keyword could be found to trigger a response, giving the illusion of an intelligent conversational partner. Thus ELIZA's final question in this extract, "Does that have anything to do with the fact that your boyfriend made you come here?", goes back to something said earlier by the patient at a time when the patient's input "bullies" does not match any keyword pattern.

PARRY

PARRY, a system developed by Colby (1975), was a contemporary of ELIZA. PARRY simulated a patient with paranoia and was demonstrated in a version of the Turing test in which psychiatrists were unable to distinguish utterances by PARRY from utterances spoken by real paranoids. PARRY had a large set of about 6000 patterns against which any input was matched. While ELIZA did not take the initiative in a conversation but reflected back what the user said, in the manner of a Rogerian psychotherapist, PARRY was able to keep a conversation going because it always had something to say, based on a number of stored resentments that modelled paranoid behaviour. Indeed, when PARRY did not understand the user's input, it would redirect it according to its own interpretation. In this way PARRY simulated the sorts of unpredictable associations that a paranoid person might make. The following is an example of part of a conversation with PARRY:

2.14
   1 Interviewer: Why are you in the hospital?
   2 PARRY: I shouldn't be here.
   3 Interviewer: Who brought you here?
   4 PARRY: The police.
   5 Interviewer: What trouble did you have with the police?
   6 PARRY: Cops don't do their jobs.
   7 Interviewer: What do they do instead?
   8 PARRY: Cops arrest the wrong people.
   9 Interviewer: They arrest the right ones sometimes.
   10 PARRY: The law should get those Italian crooks.
   11 Interviewer: Are you Italian?
   12 PARRY: My background is British, but I was born in this country.
   13 Interviewer: Do you know any Italian crooks?
   14 PARRY: I try to avoid the underworld.
   15 Interviewer: Are you afraid of the underworld?
   16 PARRY: The mafia are the worst gangsters.
   17 Interviewer: Are you connected with the mafia?
   18 PARRY: You know, they know me.
   19 Interviewer: How do they know you?
   20 PARRY: They spy on me.
   21 Interviewer: Why do they?
   22 PARRY: They want to get false evidence to frame me.
   23 Interviewer: What do they have against you?
   24 PARRY: They are out to get me.

25 Interviewer: What for?
26 PARRY: I have incriminating evidence against the mafia.
27 Interviewer: Are you sure of all this?
28 PARRY: You don't believe me?

CONVERSE

CONVERSE (Batacharia et al., 1997) was the 1997 winner of the Loebner prize. The character of CONVERSE is Catherine, a 26-year-old female whose character details – her physical appearance, likes and dislikes, where she works, and so on – are stored in a database. CONVERSE is driven by scripts covering a range of 80 topics, including crime, racism, religion, mobile phones, "The Simpsons" and abortion. The system tries to maintain control of the conversation by asking a question at the end of a system utterance, but is also responsive to a question from the user. A weighting system determines whether the system-driven or system-responsive mode gains control. The following is an extract from the system's output from the Loebner competition, in which the system displayed strong views on the lesbian couple Bill Clinton had welcomed to the White House the night before the competition, and also on Clinton himself:

2.15
1 PROGRAM: Did you see that story on CNN last night about the lesbian couple who came out at a White House party on Sunday?
2 JUDGE: Yes, I did. I think it may all be a publicity stunt for Ellen.
3 PROGRAM: Ellen Degeneres was one of them – she was kissing her lover in front of Bill Clinton. Do you think he was very embarrassed?
4 JUDGE: I think he wants the gay vote. He will do anything to get it and keep it. He does not have a conservative base.
5 PROGRAM: Are you still a friend of Bill Clinton?
6 JUDGE: I am not sure if he has any real friends. He has achieved a lot and has left a lot of people behind.
7 PROGRAM: You really don't like the guy – well, at least that's definite – I thought most people were just indifferent or numb by now.

Comparing Spoken Dialogue Technology and Simulated Conversational Systems

Spoken dialogue systems differ from simulated conversational systems in the following ways:

1. They make use of more theoretically motivated techniques derived from speech technology, natural language processing, and artificial intelligence, as opposed to the pattern-matching techniques used in simulated conversational systems.

2. They are generally domain specific, focussing on transactional dialogues within a specific domain, such as flight enquiries, rather than modelling conversational interactions in general.

3. Simulated conversational systems use techniques and resources derived from empirical natural language processing, such as large databases of dialogue

patterns and thesaurus networks, as well as weighting systems that can bias the control of the dialogue and provide a range of flexible and unpredictable behaviours.

However, these distinctions are becoming increasingly blurred in large simulated conversational systems, such as CONVERSE, which already include knowledge sources such as scripts that represent conversational topics and a database that contains details on the system's personal characteristics. Proposed extensions to CONVERSE include the incorporation of a model of individual agent beliefs and intentions using techniques from artificial intelligence. Another feature to be developed is the use of statistical dialogue modelling and the machine learning of dialogue behaviours. These are features that are also being adopted in more advanced spoken dialogue systems (see Chapter 13).

Speech Technology

The natural language systems that have been described in the preceding sections have all involved typed input and output. This was due partly to the fact that speech technology had not developed sufficiently in the 1960s and 1970s to handle the complex natural language used in these systems. Another reason was that, while there was some interaction between the natural language and the artificial intelligence communities, there was almost no interaction between these communities and the speech technology community until the mid-1980s.

Research in speech recognition in the 1960s focussed on systems that were characterised by the following features:

1. Speaker-dependent recognition – the system had to be trained to recognise the speech of an individual user.
2. Discrete word recognition – the speaker had to pause between each word to enable the system to identify word boundaries.
3. Small vocabularies of less than 50 words.

A major research programme (Speech Understanding Research (SUR)), sponsored by the Advanced Research Projects Agency (ARPA) of the United States Department of Defense, ran from 1971 to 1976 with the aim of overcoming the limitations of the systems of the 1960s. The systems were required to recognise connected speech from several cooperative speakers using a vocabulary of 1000 or more words. One system, HARPY, from Carnegie Mellon University (CMU) met the programme's requirements, being able to recognise more than 1000 words with an error rate of 5%. More important, the HARPY system was one of the first to use the statistically based form of modelling that is used in almost all current commercial and research speech recognition systems.

Subsequent work in speech recognition has focussed on the development of robust statistical models and of systems capable of handling large vocabulary continuous speech, leading to current voice dictation products. Handling difficult speech data, such as speech over the telephone, speech in noisy environments, and the speech typical of naturally occurring conversation, has directed the interest of speech technologists towards spoken dialogue as a prime example of difficult data. As a result, recent research in spoken dialogue technology has brought together the earlier traditions in speech technology, natural language processing and artificial intelligence that developed largely independently of one another throughout the previous decades.

Recent Developments in Spoken Dialogue Technology

Research in spoken dialogue technology emerged around the late-1980s as a result of two major government funded projects: the DARPA Spoken Language Systems programme in the United States and the Esprit SUNDIAL programme in Europe. The DARPA programme was concerned with the domain of Air Travel Information Services (ATIS). A number of research laboratories throughout the United States were involved, with the main focus on the input technologies of speech recognition and spoken language understanding that were required to make a flight reservation using spoken communication with a computer over the telephone (DARPA, 1992; ARPA, 1994). There was no explicit focus on dialogue issues in the ATIS projects. As all of the project participants were required to use the same database, it was possible to compare the performance of different implementations, and regular evaluations were a major focus of the ATIS programme. The ATIS corpora, a collection of task-oriented dialogues in the ATIS domain which is available from the Linguistic Data Consortium (LDC), provide a resource for developers and evaluators of spoken dialogue systems (www.ldc.upenn.edu).

The Esprit SUNDIAL project, funded by the European Community, was concerned with flight and train schedules in English, French, German and Italian (Peckham, 1993). The goal of the project was to build real-time integrated dialogue systems capable of maintaining cooperative dialogues with users. In addition to research on continuous speech recognition and understanding, a major technological focus was spoken dialogue modelling, resulting in significant insights into dialogue management. The SUNDIAL research led to a number of subsequent European-funded projects in spoken dialogue modelling, such as RAILTEL (Lamel et al., 1995), VerbMobil (Wahlster, 1993), ARISE (den Os et al., 1999) and DISC (Bernsen and Dybkjær, 1997). One well-known commercial development arising out of the SUNDIAL research is the Philips Automatic Train Timetable Information System (Aust et al., 1995).

The DARPA Communicator programme is the most recent large-scale government-funded effort in spoken dialogue technology, involving a number of research laboratories and companies across the United States, and including several affiliated partner sites in Europe (http://fofoca.mitre.org). The aim of the programme is to develop the next generation of intelligent conversational interfaces to distributed information, using speech-only as well as multimodal modalities. The Communicator dialogue systems support complex conversational interaction, in which both user and system can initiate the interaction, change topic, and interrupt the other participant. The application domains include meeting coordination and travel planning, requiring access to multiple data sources. In these respects the Communicator projects represent an advance on earlier programmes such as ATIS and SUNDIAL, which focussed on single domain enquiries and permitted less flexible dialogue strategies (see also Chapter 12).

Alongside these major research programmes there are many individual projects involving spoken dialogue technology. In the United States these include: the Spoken Language Systems Group at MIT, the CSLU at Oregon Graduate Institute of Science and Technology, the Sphinx Group at CMU, the CSLR at the University of Colorado at Boulder, and the Conversational Interaction and Spoken Dialogue Research Group at the University of Rochester. Companies involved actively in spoken dialogue research in the United States include AT&T, Bell Laboratories, Microsoft, IBM and SRI. Within Europe there is a large number of research centres, including the Natural Interactive Systems Laboratory in Odense, Denmark, the LIMSI Spoken Language Processing Group at the Laboratory of Computer Science for Mechanical and Engineering Sciences, Paris, the Centre for Speech Technology at the University of Edinburgh, the Speech Communication and Technology group at KTH, Stockholm, the Language Technology group at DFKI, Germany, CSELT in Italy, and the Department of Language and Speech at the University of Nijmegen, the Netherlands. There are also major research programmes in other parts of the world, particularly in Japan. A more extensive list of projects and links is provided in Appendix 5.

The Commercial Deployment of Spoken Dialogue Technology

Speech is a rapidly emerging technology that provides an alternative and complementary interface to the widely accepted graphical user interface. Many large companies, such as IBM, Philips, Microsoft, AT&T, Intel, Apple, Motorola and Unisys, have active research and development programmes in speech technology. IBM has recently initiated an 8 year project entitled the "Super Human Speech Recognition Initiative" involving about 100 speech researchers in the development of new technology to support "conversational computing". Similarly, the Speech Technology Group at Microsoft is involved in a number of projects aimed at their vision of a fully speech-enabled computer. A number of companies, such as Nuance Communications and Scansoft, specialise in speech technology while some, such as VoiceGenie, BeVocal, Tellme, Voxeo, Hey Anita and Voxpilot, focus exclusively on VoiceXML applications. The Web pages of these companies provide a wide range of information about the nature of speech technology products, applications and commercial benefits.

The Market for Speech Applications

A number of market research firms have predicted a rapid growth in the speech technology market. In a recent report the Kelsey Group, a leading authority on the potential of speech technologies, estimated world-wide revenues from speech technologies and the accompanying infrastructure hardware and software to grow from $505 million in 2001 to more than $2 billion in 2006 (Kelsey Group, 2002). This growth in the core technologies is predicted to trigger a multiplier effect that will drive speech and enhanced telephony services revenues to $27 billion by 2006. Similarly Allied Business Intelligence has predicted that the number of fixed voice portal users in North America will grow from 4 million in 2001 to 17 million by 2005, and mobile voice portal users will grow in the same period from 1 million to over 56 million (www.abiresearch.com). Detailed market analysis of the voice portal and speech technology sectors is available from the market research firm DataMonitor (www.datamonitor.com) as well as from TMA Associates (www.tmaa.com).

The Voice Web: An Infrastructure for Interactive Speech Applications

The Voice Web has come about as a result of a convergence of the computing and communications industries that will allow people to access information and services on the Internet with pervasive access devices such as the telephone and Personal Digital Assistants (PDAs). Interactive speech technologies provide the key to the Voice Web as they allow users to interact with the Internet using natural spoken language. The Voice Browser subsection of the World Wide Web Consortium (W3C) is focussed on expanding access to the Web in this way (www.w3.org/Voice/).

One critical factor in the development of the Voice Web is the emergence of an infrastructure for voice-based interfaces. Until recently the development of interactive speech applications with computer–telephone integration required special Application Programming Interfaces (APIs) and proprietary hardware and software. New languages such as VoiceXML (Voice Extensible Markup Language) and SALT (Speech Application Language Tags) allow developers to build on the existing Web infrastructure using standard Internet protocols.

VoiceXML is promoted by the VoiceXML forum (www.voicexmlforum.org), which was founded by AT&T, IBM, Lucent and Motorola. Its aim is to promote VoiceXML, a new language that has been developed to make Internet content and services accessible over the phone using natural speech. By March 2001 the Forum had grown to over 420 members. A series of tutorials on VoiceXML is presented in Chapters 9 and 10.

SALT is promoted by the SALT Forum, which was founded in 2001 by Cisco, Comverse, Intel, Microsoft, Philips and SpeechWorks (www.saltforum.org). The aim of the SALT Forum is to develop and promote speech technologies for multimodal and telephony applications. A series of tutorials on SALT is presented in Chapter 11.

Benefits of Speech Technology

While recent developments in speech technology are interesting from a technological viewpoint, for speech technology to be successful commercially it should have clear benefits within the commercial domain. Two potential beneficiaries of speech technology can be identified:

1. Technology and services providers.
2. End users.

Benefits for Technology and Service Providers

Technology and service providers include companies who develop speech products and applications and those that make use of these products in the delivery of their services, for example, call centres and internet service providers. The main benefit for providers is that speech will enable them to provide a wider range of services at reduced costs. Speech may also enable providers to promote services that will differentiate them from their competitors and that will provide enhanced customer satisfaction.

A number of studies have quantified the return on investment (ROI) for companies adopting speech technology. In a recent report by Nuance Communications on the business case for speech in the call centre, it was estimated that speech could create savings of more than 90% of the cost of a call by off-loading calls from call centre agents (www.nuance.com/learn/buscasespeech.html). The cost of a call handled by an agent was estimated at $1.28, while the cost of a call handled by a speech-enabled automated system was $0.10. These estimates were based on comparisons between the annual costs of an agent – salary, benefits, equipment, recruitment, training, calls handled per hour – and the costs of an automated system, including hardware, software, application development, installation and maintenance. It was shown that the time required to recoup the cost of a complete speech system could be as little as 3 months and that a large-scale system, handling over 100,000 calls per day, could provide savings of around $2 million over the course of a year. Other estimates make similar predictions (see, e.g., Winther, 2001).

Benefits for End Users

End users of speech technology are people who make use of speech-enabled services to perform tasks such as retrieving information, conducting transactions or controlling devices. For these end users the main benefit of speech is convenience, as they are able to access information and services at any time, from any place and using speech, which is a natural mode of communication. This convenience has been referred to as "pervasive computing", described by

IBM as "... personalised computing power" freed from the desktop, enabling information access anywhere, anytime, on demand (www-3.ibm.com/pvc/index.shtml). With the growth of smaller communications devices, such as Internet-enabled mobile phones and PDAs, as well as embedded devices without keyboards, speech provides an interface as an alternative to more cumbersome methods using pens and text entry. For people with physical disabilities speech may be the only useful interface.

Speech is also convenient in other ways. With current IVR (Interactive Voice Response) systems that use touch-tones and menus to obtain services and information, users often have to navigate a series of menus in order to conduct a transaction. For example, to transfer funds between accounts using a traditional phone-based banking system, a customer may have to press keys to select the transfer option, to indicate the source and destination accounts, and to input the required amount – three key presses for the options and several more for the amount. With a speech-based interface an experienced caller can say something like "Transfer three hundred pounds from my current account to my savings account", reducing the transaction time and the cost of the call considerably. Finally, because human agents in call centres can be released from routine information-gathering tasks that can be taken over by automated systems, calls involving simple enquiries can be answered more quickly and the caller is less likely to be put on hold.

Nuance Communications conducted a quantitative survey of customer satisfaction, attitudes and usage of speech based self-service applications (www.nuance.com/assets/pdf/speech_study.pdf). It was found that overall customer satisfaction was high (87%) and that the rate was even higher with wireless users (96%). The main reasons cited for preferring speech over alternative interfaces were speed, efficiency and ease of use. Similar results were reported in a market research survey by Northwest Airlines, who deployed a reservations service system based on Nuance technology and reported that over 66% of respondents rated the speech-based system as better than the Web-based alternative.

Challenges for Speech Technology

There are some contexts in which speech technology is not appropriate. Traditional web interfaces based on a graphical user interface can display information in graphical and tabular form. This form of presentation cannot easily be translated into speech. Long lists, which can be easily scanned on a visual interface, are difficult to process in an auditory mode. Listening to a long list takes much more time than skimming it visually. As speech is transient, long periods of listening tax human short-term memory. Furthermore, speech is not appropriate in environments requiring privacy nor in noisy environments that cause problems for speech recognition.

Even in contexts where speech is an appropriate medium, there are a number of technological challenges, including imperfections in speech technology and unrealistic user expectations. One of the main tasks for providers is to convince potential users and deployers that the technology will work properly in all situations and for all users.

Speech technologies are imperfect in a number of ways. The speech recognition component may misrecognise words, and attempts to correct errors can lead to error amplification. Major advances in speech recognition algorithms along with careful design can reduce error rates and minimise their consequences, but misrecognition errors will always be a challenge for designers of spoken dialogue systems. On the output side there may be problems with speech synthesis errors, when the system pronounces an unfamiliar name incorrectly or mispronounces words that are homophones, that is, words with the same spelling but different pronunciations, such as "tear", which can be pronounced to rhyme with "bear" or with "beer".

While the main focus to date has been on errors of speech recognition, there may also be errors involving other components of the system. The language understanding component may produce an incorrect parse of the user's input, and errors can also be produced by the dialogue manager, for example, in misinterpreting the user's intentions.

Unrealistic user expectations are also a major challenge for speech technology. Users may expect a speech system to perform to the level of systems depicted in science fiction, such as the computer in the television series Star Trek. These expectations may lead users to speak in complex sentences or to ask for services and information that are outside the domain of the system. Problems may also occur if speakers have strong regional or nonnative accents, have speech impediments, or use speech that is too casual or disfluent. Current systems work best with users who behave cooperatively and who adjust their speech to match the capabilities of the system. It is a major challenge for designers to produce systems that enable users to interact appropriately and efficiently with the system in a natural way, without lengthy instructions and training.

Summary

This chapter has examined the sorts of applications that are amenable to spoken dialogue technology. The majority of current systems involve the retrieval of information and the automation of routine transactions. More complex applications, such as problem solving, are still being developed in the research laboratories. Spoken dialogue is also being used in educational contexts and in games and entertainment. An interesting development is the conversational companion whose function is mainly to maintain a conversation with the user rather than conduct a transaction.

The history of spoken dialogue systems can be traced back to early work in artificial intelligence in the 1960s. However, it was only towards the end of the 1980s that speech was used for user input and system output. A number of different approaches have been used, including theory-driven methods such as linguistic processing, planning and representations from artificial intelligence research, as well as data-driven approaches involving various forms of pattern matching. Some of these methods are converging in current conversational systems.

As well as being a fascinating topic for researchers in universities and research laboratories, spoken dialogue technology has become commercially important over the past few years, due in large part to the emergence of the Voice Web – the convergence of the infrastructure of the World Wide Web and the use of speech technology as a mode of communication with automated systems over the telephone.

This chapter has explored the nature of spoken dialogue technology and plotted its historical development. However, so far, the nature of dialogue – how dialogue is structured, and how people engage in dialogue – has not been examined. This is the topic of Chapter 3, in which the key characteristics of dialogue are discussed and a number of theoretical approaches to dialogue are critically evaluated.

Further Reading

McTear (1987) provides an overview of research in dialogue modelling in the 1970s and 1980s and examines what is required for a computer to be able to converse with humans using natural language. Markowitz (1996) is a good account of the applications of speech technology. Raman (1997) is a detailed account of how to develop auditory user interfaces that are particularly useful for users with visual impairment.

Dialogue and Intelligent Tutoring Systems

Publications from the University of Edinburgh tutorial dialogue group: http://www.cogsci.ed.ac.uk/~jmoore/tutoring/papers.html
Publications from the University of Pittsburgh project Spoken Dialogue for Intelligent Tutoring systems: http://www.cs.pitt.edu/~litman/why2-pubs.html

Exercises

1. Examine one of the spoken dialogue systems that you encountered in the exercise at the end of Chapter 1. Determine the extent to which the system focusses on a particular domain, for example, does it involve a restricted vocabulary and a set of grammatical structures? What would be involved in porting the system to another domain?
2. The following web sites contain links to chatterbots. Try out some of the chatterbots. Analyse your interactions in terms of how realistic the dialogues were.

Simon Laven page: http://www.simonlaven.com/
BotSpot Chatbots: http://www.botspot.com/search/s-chat.htm
Google Directory Chatterbots: http://directory.google.com/Top/Computers/
Artificial_Intelligence/Natural_Language/Chatterbots/

Understanding Dialogue

3

It is important for developers of dialogue systems to have a sound understanding of the nature of dialogue, how it is structured and how people engage in dialogue. This is particularly the case where the aim is to model naturally occurring conversation. Even where conversational modelling is not the main aim, as is usually the case with systems intended for commercial deployment, it is also important to understand the complexities of human dialogue, if only to know how to constrain systems in the interests of performance and the avoidance of error.

This chapter begins with a definition of dialogue followed by a discussion of its key characteristics. Dialogue is then examined from two perspectives – its structural properties and the processes involved when people (and computers) engage in dialogue.

Dialogue: A Definition

The term "dialogue" is used in everyday language to describe a process of exchanging views, sometimes with the purpose of finding a solution to a problem or to resolve differences. Often when there is conflict between individuals, communities or nations, there is a proposal that the parties concerned should "engage in dialogue".

Dialogue may be contrasted with "conversation", a term that is generally used to describe more informal spoken interaction in which the main purpose is the development and maintenance of social relationships. Conversation is often used, however, particularly in research in the United States, to refer to more advanced dialogue systems that display human-like conversational competencies. Dialogue, on the other hand, tends to be used to signify more restricted systems that engage in specific types of interaction with a more transactional purpose, such as getting information, issuing instructions or providing a service. Often the phrase "task-oriented dialogue" is used to emphasise this function. Notwithstanding these distinctions, the terms "dialogue" and "conversation" are frequently used almost interchangeably in the literature to refer to computer systems that use spoken language to interact with people. In this book the term "dialogue" will be used generically to cover all types of spoken interaction with computers.

Key Characteristics of Dialogue

Dialogue has been studied within a wide range of academic disciplines, including linguistics, psychology, sociology, anthropology, philosophy, communication sciences and artificial intelligence. The study of dialogue has also been applied in a range of areas, such as management studies, conflict resolution and intercultural relations as a method for promoting negotiation and discussion of differing viewpoints. Much of this work is not directly relevant to current directions in spoken dialogue technology and will not be discussed further here. In the following sections some of the key characteristics of dialogue that are important in the context of spoken dialogue systems will be discussed:

- *Dialogue as discourse.* The analysis of the use of words, phrases and utterances in the context of extended discourse.
- *Dialogue as purposeful activity.* An examination of the purposes for which people engage in dialogue, the actions that they perform and the meanings that they convey.
- *Dialogue as collaborative activity.* How dialogue is best understood as a joint activity in which people work together to engage in conversational turn-taking and to achieve mutual understanding.
- *Utterances in dialogue.* The nature and form of utterances produced in naturally occurring dialogues.

Dialogue as Discourse

A dialogue consists of at least two turns, one by each speaker. A dialogue that is coherent will exhibit discourse phenomena which, broadly speaking, can be viewed as elements whose interpretation depends on the dialogue context. To participate in a dialogue it is necessary to be able to keep track of these elements. In some cases this involves maintaining a record (or history list) of entities that have been introduced into the dialogue model and that can be referred to subsequently using pronouns and other anaphoric devices, that is, linguistic expressions that are used to refer back to something previously mentioned. In other cases it is necessary to draw on a wider notion of context involving general and background knowledge.

The following examples illustrate some of the issues involved in resolving anaphoric reference using pronouns:

3.1
1 A: John won some money.
2 B: What is he going to do with it?

In this example it can be assumed that "it" refers to "some money". The pronoun matches syntactically (whereas "them" or "him" would not), and it refers back to the most recently mentioned entity. Many dialogue systems have been constructed using these two simple strategies to resolve reference. However, it is not difficult to find examples where these strategies do not return the correct result:

3.2
1 A: John won some money in the lottery.
2 B: What is he going to do with it?

The two simple strategies would propose "the lottery" as the referent for "it", yet clearly this is an unlikely interpretation. An additional strategy that would select the item "some money" as the correct referent would be to locate the focus of attention in A's utterance (i.e., "the money") and to propose this as the most likely referent. Similarly, with this example:

3.3
1 A: Jim caught up with Bill outside the pub.
2 B: Did he give him the tickets?

Using the strategy of recency, "he" would be matched with "Bill", i.e., B is asking whether Bill gave Jim the tickets. (Note also that once "he" is assigned to Bill, then "him" cannot also refer to Bill but has to refer to "Jim".) However, using a different strategy, in which the subject of a sentence is preferred over the object of the sentence as being more likely to be the centre of focus, Jim would be the preferred referent of the pronoun "he". Of course, this interpretation could turn out to be wrong if other knowledge could be brought to bear, for example, if A and B both knew that it was Bill who had the tickets.

In some cases, background (or general) knowledge is required to resolve reference. Consider the following example:

3.4
1 A: Did you see Bill in the pub last night?
2 B: No, the barman said he left early.

Definite descriptions, such as "the barman" are often used to refer to some entity that has been previously mentioned in the dialogue. For example, "There's a new barman in the pub" followed later by "What do you think of the barman?" However, in the dialogue presented here, no barman has been mentioned, yet A would be unlikely to have any problem understanding B's utterance in terms of finding a referent for the expression "the barman". The explanation in this case is that A can draw on background knowledge that a barman works in a pub, so that once a scenario involving a pub is introduced, persons and objects relevant to that scenario can be mentioned using definite reference.

Keeping track of elements within a dialogue also applies at a higher level to the different topics that are introduced during the dialogue, as participants need to be able to keep track of shifts in topic in order to resolve reference to previously mentioned items. The following piece of dialogue, in which A is helping B to install some software, illustrates this point:

3.5
1 A: Click on the "install" icon to install the program.
2 B: OK.
3 B: By the way, did you hear about Bill?
4 A: No, what's up?
5 B: He took his car to be fixed and they've found all sorts of problems.
6 A: Poor Bill. He's always in trouble.
7 A: OK. Is it ready yet?

The referent of "it" in A's last utterance (7) is not Bill's car, which is the most recently mentioned element that matches syntactically, but the program that B is installing. In this case the pronoun and its referent are separated by several turns. (Indeed, in one example cited by Grosz (1978, p. 246), the pronoun and its referent were separated by 60 utterances.)

How do participants keep track in cases such as this, as clearly, keeping history lists is not the solution? It has been suggested that participants keep track of the topics introduced in the dialogue, noting shifts to new topics, subtopics, and back to previous topics. In the example presented here, the main topic is the installation of a program. The intervening turns are part of an unrelated topic (or digression) about Bill and his car. However, the main topic remains open and it is possible to refer to elements that belong to the main topic later in the dialogue using anaphoric devices such as pronouns and definite descriptions. In this example the beginning of the digression is signalled by the phrase "by the way" and its end is signalled by the word "OK". Thus to process a dialogue containing a number of topics and to keep track of the entities mentioned and the ways in which they can be referred to subsequently, it is necessary to maintain a representation of the structure of the dialogue in terms of topics and subtopics.

Spoken dialogue systems often involve tasks such as flight reservations that can be broken down into subtasks, such as getting the flight details and making a reservation. Voice portals are similar, as users can make enquiries about a number of topics and services. In the simpler systems the system uses a menu and maintains strict control of the topics. The system offers a choice of topic to the user and the dialogue follows the topic selected, then another choice of topic is offered. The following is an example:

3.6
1 System: You can ask about restaurants, traffic, news, sport or weather.
2 User: Traffic.
⟨traffic dialogue⟩
3 System: What next? You can ask about restaurants, traffic, news, sport or weather.
4 User: Sport.
⟨sport dialogue⟩

A more advanced system would enable the user to take the initiative and switch topics, as in this example:

3.7
⟨Event dialogue in progress⟩
1 System: What sort of event are you interested in?

2 User: A concert.
3 System: There is a concert in the university grounds at 9 this evening.
4 User: What's the weather forecast?

Here the system is engaged in a dialogue about events and the user shifts to a different topic – the weather. Being able to switch topics in this way provides a more flexible system that can address the user's concerns as they arise. However, the disadvantage is that the system has to have a more advanced speech and language processing capability in order to be able to process "out-of-topic" utterances. When topic shifts occur, there may also be a need to keep track of previous topics that may not have been closed in order to be able to return to those topics.

Dialogue as Purposeful Activity

People engage in dialogue for a wide range of purposes, including transactional functions such as requesting, promising, persuading and informing, and inter-personal functions such as maintaining and regulating social relationships. One way to approach dialogue is in terms of the linguistic actions that people perform in order to carry out these functions. Utterances are produced with the aim of achieving certain effects within particular contexts. The following aspects of this use of language will be considered here:

- How the meanings of utterances depend on the context in which they are used.
- How the selection of an appropriate form of language depends on aspects of the context.
- How participants in dialogue often convey meanings in their utterances that go beyond the meanings of the actual words used.

Meaning and Context

To illustrate how meanings depend on context, consider the utterance "It's hot in here." In different contexts this utterance can have many different functions, some of which are as follows:

1. A neutral statement about the temperature.
2. A statement about the temperature with the purpose of persuading the other person to come in from the cold.
3. A statement about the temperature with the purpose of persuading the other person to go out into a cooler place.
4. A statement about the temperature with the purpose of requesting the other person to do something to change the situation, for example, by opening a window or turning on the air conditioning.

As can be seen from the different contexts described in 2–4, the meaning of the utterance depends on factors such as the physical situation and the relative roles of the speaker and hearer. In 2, the speaker is inside some location and the hearer is outside, while in 3 both are inside. In 4, the speaker assumes that the hearer is able to carry out some action that will change the current state of affairs and also that the speaker is entitled to make such a request. Thus the assignment of an interpretation to an utterance depends on various aspects of the context, and slight differences in context can result in quite different meanings for the same set of words.

Speech Acts: Function and Context

The choice of a particular linguistic form to express some purpose or function also depends on considerations of context. Consider, for example, a speaker wishing to get someone to close the door. There are many ways in which this can be accomplished, including the following examples:

3.8
1 Close the door.
2 Would you mind closing the door?
3 I'd appreciate it if you'd close the door.
4 Is that door open?
5 There's a draught in here.

Some of these utterances take the linguistic form of questions, others are statements, and the final one does not even mention a door, yet in the appropriate contexts each utterance may be interpreted as a request to close the door. Some of the utterances differ in terms of politeness, for example, 2 is more polite than 1, and 3 might be interpreted as being rather rude. However, the relative status of speaker and hearer determines which form may be used, so that in the case of a superior speaking to a subordinate, 1 is appropriate, whereas 2 is more appropriate when speaker and hearer are of similar status. Some forms are also more indirect – 3 does not ask the hearer to close the door but states what the speaker would like to happen, while 4 has the form of a question that asks about a particular state of affairs. To be interpreted as a request, it has to be the case that the hearer believes that the speaker does not want this state of affairs – i.e., the open door – to be true. Finally, 5 is even more indirect in that it is a statement of an undesirable condition but with no indication of what would count as a way of changing it. The hearer has to infer that closing the door might be the desired action.

Much of our understanding of the role of context in determining the functions of utterances comes from the theory of speech acts developed originally by philosophers of language such as Austin and Searle. Austin (1962) proposed that utterances should be described in terms of the actions performed by speakers as opposed to traditional descriptions in terms of truth conditions, i.e., what is required for a statement to be considered true or false. Examples of speech acts are informing, requesting, promising, suggesting and threatening. Searle (1969) extended this work by defining the conditions necessary for the performance of a speech act. For example, the conditions that are necessary for an utterance to be intended and understood as a command are (based on Searle (1969, p. 66)):

1. The utterance is concerned with some future act that the hearer should perform.
2. The hearer is able to do the act, and the speaker believes that the hearer can do the act.
3. It is not obvious to the speaker and hearer that the hearer will do the act in the normal course of events.
4. The speaker wants the hearer to do the act.

These conditions incorporate the intuitions that people normally only ask others to do actions that they want to have done, and that they believe the other person is able to carry out the act and would not otherwise have done so without being asked. The conditions underlying the performance of speech acts have also been used to explain the use of indirect speech acts, in which the function of an utterance is not obvious from its form, as in some of the examples discussed above.

Performing a speech act such as a request involves a dialogue agent in reasoning about beliefs, desires and intentions. In making a request an agent must want the action to be done and must bring about a situation in which the other agent wants to do the action. The requesting agent must believe that the other agent is able to do the action and, as a result of the request, the other agent will believe that the requesting agent wants the action to be performed. When planning a speech act, a dialogue agent will reason about mental states such as these in order to generate the plan. Similarly, the addressee of a speech act will engage in a process of plan recognition to determine the meaning of the act in terms of the speaker's beliefs, desires and intentions. The view that dialogue can be explained in this way has been developed within a theory of dialogue known as the BDI (belief, desire, intention) approach (Allen, 1995). This approach will be examined further in Chapter 12 in order to explain more complex processes of dialogue, such as the interpretation of indirect speech acts.

Conversational Implicature: Meaning and Inference

Participants in dialogues often express meanings in their utterances that go beyond the literal meanings of the words used. The recipients of these utterances are expected to make appropriate inferences in order to determine the intended meaning. Indirect speech acts are an example of these indirectly conveyed meanings. To explain these nonliteral meanings, the philosopher Grice proposed a set of conversational maxims that enable hearers to make the appropriate inferences (Grice, 1975). Grice proposed that participants in conversation are guided by a principle of cooperation that states that they should produce utterances that contribute to the purposes and direction of the conversation. This does not mean that they should always agree or comply with each other's demands, but that they should be guided by a set of maxims in order that what they say is relevant, true, informative and clear. The most interesting part of Grice's theory involved conversational implicatures, where speakers blatantly flout one of the maxims for a specific conversational purpose. For example,

> 3.9
> 1 A: Would you lend me some money to buy a coffee?
> 2 B: It's not Christmas.

To make sense of B's response, A needs to read some additional meaning into it beyond what is contained in the actual words uttered. In the example presented above, it appears that B is not following the maxim of relevance because the utterance "It's not Christmas" does not seem to be relevant to A's request for money to buy a coffee. However, if it is assumed by both participants that B is observing the general cooperative principle of conversation (without being cooperative in the conventional sense of the term), then A can conclude that B's utterance must mean more than what it appears to mean and can begin a process of inferencing to work out what B might have meant. In this case some general knowledge would also be required along the lines that Christmas is a time of giving and, since it is not Christmas, giving (or lending) is not appropriate.

Conversational implicature is a very important aspect of conversational competence because people often use indirect language for a variety of purposes – in this example, to be sarcastic, in other cases to be polite, for example, to soften a request. It is also important that the hearer should be able to make the appropriate inferences in order to derive the implicated meaning, otherwise the implicature will fail. In other words, the speaker and hearer need to share assumptions about the cooperative principle and the conversational maxims, and the speaker needs to design the utterance in such a way that the hearer can infer the intended meaning. As spoken dialogue systems become more complex, they will be required to deal with more indirectly conveyed meanings. Consider the following example of a travel system:

> 3.10
> 1 System: What time do you want to depart for London?
> 2 User: I have to be there for a meeting at 10 a.m.

The user does not answer the system's question directly by giving a departure time. In order to make sense of the user's reply, the system has to assume that mention of the time of the meeting is relevant at this point in the dialogue and then work out a departure time that fits in with the user's requirements.

Dialogue as Collaborative Activity

Dialogue is a joint activity between two or more participants. For dialogue to proceed in an orderly fashion there has to be collaborative activity between the participants in the dialogue. Collaboration does not necessarily imply that the participants have to agree with each other, as even in dialogues where there is strong disagreement there are certain processes that participants employ to enable the dialogue to function. Conversational turn-taking and conversational grounding are important aspects of collaborative activity in dialogue.

Turn-taking in Conversation

Participants in dialogues take turns. The length of the turns and the allocation of turns are not specified in advance, except in extremely formal interactions. In naturally occurring conversations turns are negotiated on a turn-by-turn basis according to an intricate set of rules (Sacks et al., 1974). Generally in a conversation one participant speaks at a time and transitions between speakers are accomplished with a minimum of gap between turns and minimal overlap between the speakers. Conversational participants who wish to take the next turn do not appear to wait until the current speaker stops talking, as otherwise there would be regular and noticeable gaps between the turns. Similarly, they do not seem to depend solely on nonverbal or prosodic cues, such as the speaker's gaze or a falling intonation contour, but rather they anticipate the potential completion of the turn and begin at that point. The evidence for this claim is that overlaps tend to occur at transition-relevant positions, for example, at the point where the current speaker's utterance is potentially complete. The following example illustrates this (underlining indicates overlapped speech):

3.11
1 A: That's an interesting house, *isn't it*?
2 B: *Do you* like it?

The overlap occurs because the current speaker continues beyond the transition-relevant point at the end of a potentially complete sentence. The second speaker has already anticipated the potential completion and begins speaking at precisely this point.

Both participants in a conversation are involved in ensuring smooth turn-taking in conversation. As has already been shown, the potential next speaker has to listen to and analyse the current turn to be able to produce a turn that is relevant and that begins at a transition-relevant place. Likewise, speakers need to construct their turn in such a way that the hearer can project its possible completion. When overlaps occur, one of the speakers must decide to relinquish the floor as conversation normally requires that only one speaker talks at a time. Naturally, there are many cases where current speakers refuse to relinquish a turn or when a next speaker cuts in before the current speaker has completed. However, these cases can be seen as violations of the normal turn-taking rules and they are often explicitly marked by phrases such as "If you'd let me finish".

Turn-taking in dialogues between humans and computers differs from conversational turn-taking between humans in two ways. In the first place, turn-taking with computers is generally more carefully regulated. In some cases the computer indicates with a signal, such as a beep, when it is ready to accept input from the human speaker. The benefit of this turn-taking cue is that the speech recognition process only needs to start after the beep, thus saving on computational resources. A major disadvantage occurs if the speaker begins before the beep. In this case the speech preceding the beep is not captured. Furthermore, when this problem is encountered, human speakers tend to break off and repeat the part of their turn that they think has been missed, resulting in many cases in ungrammatical utterances that the system is unable to process. Problems can also occur if the speaker delays speaking after the prompt as the system may detect the leading silence and react accordingly (e.g., by outputting something like "Sorry I didn't hear anything") just as the speaker begins to speak. In this case the computer output may be captured along with the speaker's input, leading to problems for the speech recognition component.

A more advanced facility provided in many spoken dialogue systems allows the human speaker to cut in on the computer's turn, causing the computer to stop speaking and to switch to listening mode. This is known as "barge-in". Barge-in requires a speech recognition platform with full-duplex capability and echo cancellation. It is particularly useful for experienced users who are familiar with a particular dialogue style and can avoid listening to lengthy prompts by anticipating what is being said and providing a response. However, barge-in can also cause problems for the speech recognition process. If the computer's output does not terminate quickly enough, the user may increase the volume of their speech in order to speak over what the computer is saying. This is known as the Lombard effect. The problem here is that the speech signal becomes distorted as a result of loud speech, making speech recognition less reliable. The other possible effect is stuttering, where the user repeats elements of the utterance that were overlapped.

Barge-in is an example of a process that is acceptable in human–computer dialogue but would be considered inappropriate, and even rude, in dialogues between humans. As systems become more "conversational", they will need to incorporate the more sophisticated rules of collaborative turn-taking that have been found in naturally occurring conversations between humans.

Grounding

Participants in conversation cannot be sure that their utterances have been understood. There are several ways in which miscommunication can arise and participants have to actively collaborate to repair misunderstandings. The most obvious case is where something is noticeably wrong and a conversational repair is initiated. However, more generally participants in dialogue seek for and provide evidence that what has been said in the dialogue has been understood (Brennan and Hulteen, 1995). This evidence can include simple indications of attention (utterances such as "uh huh", "hm" or continued eye contact), explicit acknowledgements such as "ok" and "right" and relevant next turns or actions. Feedback is particularly important in spoken dialogue systems due to errors in speech recognition. The process of achieving mutual understanding is often referred to as "grounding".

Clark and Schaefer (1989) proposed a model of grounding based on the notion of "contribution". According to this model a contribution in a dialogue consists of two parts involving two dialogue participants A and B:

- A "presentation" phase, in which A presents an utterance to B with the expectation that B will provide some evidence to A that the utterance has been understood.
- An "acceptance" phase in which B provides evidence of understanding, on the assumption that this evidence will enable A to believe that B understood A's utterance.

The acceptance phase may take several turns including sequences of clarification requests and repairs. Once both phases are complete, it is argued that it will be common ground between A and B, that B has understood what A meant. Thus this model proposes a collaborative view of dialogue in which the participants coordinate their models of what has been understood in the dialogue on a turn-by-turn basis.

The type of feedback provided in the acceptance phase is determined by factors such as the task at hand and the dialogue model. Tasks that can be undone can use lower levels of feedback as opposed to tasks that have a high probability of error or that have destructive or embarrassing consequences, where the feedback needs to be more explicit. Similarly, if the dialogue model indicates that there have been several problems, such as misrecognitions or misunderstandings, then more explicit grounding is required.

The original model of grounding, as proposed by Clark and others, has been developed in a number of ways to address some deficiencies and to make the model more useful computationally. The basic model focuses on dialogue as a product rather than on dialogue as a process. Contributions represent the models of both participants as seen by an analyst using a transcript of a completed dialogue. However, neither partner in a dialogue is omniscient, so that the models should represent the perspective of only one of the participants (Cahn and Brennan, 1999). Furthermore, as the models develop dynamically, they need to include interim representations of the dialogue participant's current dialogue state as a basis for that agent's decisions as to what to do or say next (Traum, 1999). This more dynamic view of grounding has been developed within the "information state" approach to dialogue modelling, which will be presented later in this chapter.

Utterances in Dialogue

In much of the discussion so far, the term "utterance" has been used to refer to what a speaker says in a dialogue without any clear definition of what an utterance actually is. There is considerable debate within linguistics about the relationship between utterances and sentences, with sentences being considered roughly as abstract idealised forms that can be analysed according to well-defined rules of syntax and semantics, while utterances are considered as realisations of sentences in context. However, there are several ways in which utterances in a dialogue cannot be described in terms of grammars for well-formed sentences:

1. They have the form of partial sentences, such as elliptical answers to questions as in 2 (below) and elliptical questions as in 3:

   3.12
   1. Is the milk in the fridge?
   2. Yes.
   3. The ice cream in the freezer?

2. They contain false starts, as in:

   3.13 Did – did you see – have you ever seen a lion in the wild?

In the remainder of this section several issues relating to the forms of utterances in dialogue will be considered.

The Range of Linguistic Structures Used in Spoken Dialogue

Comparisons of spoken and written language have shown that the utterances of spoken language have a simpler form than the sentences of written texts (Brown and Yule, 1983). For example, simple active declarative forms are more common in speech, while written language contains a wider variety of forms with greater use of subordinate clauses, passive constructions, and phrases such as "however", "moreover" and "nevertheless" that indicate the structure of the written text. Moreover, studies comparing speech to a human with speech to a computer have also found that human–computer dialogues are characterised by a more restricted vocabulary, a smaller set of grammatical constructions and slower speech (Hauptmann and Rudnicky, 1988; Richards and Underwood, 1984). These findings are encouraging for developers of spoken dialogue systems as it would appear that human users talk in a simpler way to computer systems so that the grammars required to recognise and understand the user's input would not need to be as comprehensive as grammars required to process written texts.

The Form of Spoken Utterances in Dialogue

On the down side, as mentioned earlier, naturally occurring spoken language is characterised by various types of disfluency, such as hesitations and ungrammatical constructions that make analysis using traditional grammatical approaches difficult. Consider the following examples from a corpus collected from subjects using either a simulated or an actual spoken language system in the ATIS (Air Traffic Information System) project (cited in Moore, 1994):

   3.14 What kind of airplane goes from Philadelphia to San Francisco Monday stopping in Dallas in the afternoon (first class flight)?

   3.15 (Do) (Do any of these flights) Are there any flights that arrive after five p.m.?

Dialogue 3.14 is a well-formed sentence followed by an additional fragment or after-thought, enclosed in brackets. Dialogue 3.15 is a self-correction in which the words intended for deletion are enclosed in parentheses. Neither of these sentences could be parsed by a conventional grammar containing rules for well-formed sentences.

More generally, spoken language is characterised by a number of features of disfluency, including:

1. False starts – as in Dialogue 3.15, where the speaker begins with "Do", stops and replaces this with "Do any of these flights", then stops again and restarts with a syntactically complete question.
2. Hesitation markers, such as "uh", "err", as well as unfilled pauses (periods of silence).
3. The use of fillers, such as "and so on", "you know", and "if you see what I mean".
4. Incomplete sentences and fragments, for example, as elliptical elements in a dialogue (see 3.12.2 and 3.12.3 above).

Some of these features are sufficiently predictable that they can be described using special rules or strategies to filter out the disfluencies and produce sentences that can be parsed using a conventional grammar. For example, utterances including false starts, normally referred to as "self-repairs", have a typical structure of the form: reparandum–editing term–alteration, as illustrated in the following example:

3.16

The meeting will be	on Mon-	uh	on Tuesday
	reparandum	editing term	alteration

The reparandum is the item that is to be corrected or replaced. The editing term, often indicated by a disruption in the prosodic contour, by a word that has been cut off or by a hesitation marker such as "uh", signals that a self-repair is occurring. Finally, the alteration is the corrected version of the reparandum. Frequently there is some similarity between the reparandum and the alteration in terms of the words used as well as their syntactic structures. For example, a word in the alteration that replaces a word in the reparandum will often be of a similar word class and have a similar meaning. Given these features, it is possible to devise methods for detecting and correcting self-repairs and other types of disfluency in naturally occurring speech (Heeman and Allen, 1994).

Prosodic Characteristics of Utterances

The information that is conveyed in utterances in a dialogue does not reside solely in the words themselves, but derives also from the prosodic features of the utterance. Prosody refers to features such as the following:

- *Overall pitch contour.* This can determine the dialogue act that is being performed, for example, "OK" with a rising tone indicates a checking act, whereas a falling tone indicates acceptance or confirmation.
- *Accentuation.* The item that receives prominence is generally being marked by the speaker as being "new" to the discourse as opposed to the other items that are treated as being "given".
- *Phrasing.* The grouping of an utterance into meaningful chunks. For example, "call the ticket office in Belfast" is taken to refer to a ticket office

that is in Belfast, whereas "call the ticket office | in Belfast", with a pause between "office" and "Belfast", would convey the meaning of calling the ticket office while the hearer is in Belfast.

Prosodic information can support the text-to-speech (TTS) synthesis component of a spoken dialogue system by using the correct prosodic forms to distinguish between otherwise ambiguous dialogue acts, to indicate what information is new, and to group the utterance into meaningful chunks that will assist the hearer to more easily understand the utterance (Hirschberg, 2002). Similarly, dialogue understanding can be improved by the use of prosodic information that enables the system to track the dialogue structure, to segment utterances correctly and to predict and interpret dialogue acts (Nöth et al., 2002; Wright et al., 2002).

Nonverbal Behaviour

Nonverbal behaviour, also known as "kinesics", includes gesture, gaze and body orientation. When examining nonverbal behaviour, it is important to distinguish between those behaviours that convey information unintentionally and those that have a communicative function. Clear cases of the former would include dress and gait, which often indicate a person's affiliations and attitudes, though not necessarily intentionally. Pointing as a means of indicating something or nodding to convey assent are clear cases of intentional nonverbal behaviours that function as surrogates or accompaniments of speech. Often it is difficult to distinguish intentional and nonintentional nonverbal behaviours, as the fine-grained analyses of Argyle (1975) and others have shown. Telephone-based dialogue systems do not require the analysis of nonverbal signals. However, with the movement towards multimodal systems, including those that simulate face-to-face interaction, it is becoming increasingly necessary to consider the functions of these signals in conversational interactions.

The Role of Silence in Dialogue

Silences and pauses are closely monitored by participants in dialogues between humans. A pause may indicate that the current speaker has completed their turn, or is unable to do so, thus giving the next speaker an opportunity to take the floor. Research in conversation analysis has indicated that a silence of approximately one second is an acceptable length of silence in conversation and that after such a period of silence speakers will begin talking to end the silence (Jefferson, 1989).

Silence can also cause the participants to make inferences about why the silence has occurred. Consider the following example, taken from Levinson (1983, p. 350):

3.17
1 A: So I was wondering would you be in your office on Monday by any chance?
(2 second pause)
2 A: Probably not.
3 B: Hmm, yes.

In this example A asks B a question. There is a two second pause, following which A continues "probably not". The brief delay in B's response is sufficient to trigger the inference that B is responding negatively. As it turns out in this example, A has made the wrong inference, as B goes on to reply in the affirmative. Nevertheless, the example demonstrates a powerful structural property of silence in conversation in that it is often used in conjunction with responses that in some way do not fill the expectations of the preceding turn, such as disagreements, refusals or rejections. These response types, known as "dispreferred" responses, are discussed further below.

There has been little analysis of silence in spoken dialogue systems (see, however, Wooffitt (1991)). Silence that occurs following an utterance by the user may be due to the time required by the system to process and interpret the user's utterance. If access to information is required before the system can respond, this can also result in a lengthy silence. However, as Wooffitt points out, users may make inferences as to why the silence has occurred, for example, that there was something wrong in their input. This can lead the user to attempt to correct their previous utterance or to provide additional information. However, it is precisely this sort of utterance that could cause trouble for a dialogue system, as the utterance is likely to contain items that are beyond the vocabulary and grammar of the system. Moreover, such corrections are often uttered using more exaggerated articulation – a slower rate, an increase in loudness and a rise in overall pitch – that will be difficult for the speech recognition component to process (Hirschberg et al., 1999).

Summary

This section has introduced some of the key characteristics of dialogue that are relevant to developers of spoken dialogue systems. The words, phrases and utterances of a dialogue have to be interpreted in context – both in terms of discourse phenomena, such as reference using pronouns, and in terms of how meanings are conveyed and understood. Furthermore, dialogue is a joint activity and many of the processes observable in dialogue, such as turn-taking and conversational grounding, make sense only in terms of a collaborative model. Finally, the content of dialogue – the utterances spoken by the participants – displays a number of properties that are important to consider. On the one hand, utterances are different in many ways from the well-formed sentences of written texts. On the other hand, there is additional information, conveyed in the prosodic features accompanying the utterances, in nonverbal behaviours and even in silences, that is a crucial part of the data of dialogue.

Modelling Dialogue: Structure and Process

Dialogue can be examined from two different perspectives. The first involves an analysis of transcripts of dialogues, usually with a dialogue-coding scheme, to discover regularly occurring patterns and structures. This approach is useful in order to gain an understanding of the basic elements of dialogue and to support the labelling of dialogues for corpus annotation. The second approach examines dialogue processes from the perspective of those participating in the dialogue, looking at issues such as how utterances are interpreted in context and what factors are involved in deciding what to say at a particular point in the dialogue. This approach is useful to support the computational modelling of dialogue agents. The following sections examine these two perspectives in greater detail.

Dialogue Structure

Since the 1960s, linguists working in the areas of discourse analysis, sociolinguistics and language acquisition have been developing models of dialogue structure that show how dialogues can be segmented into smaller functional units. Most research has focussed on the smallest unit, the dialogue act, in which a speaker performs a particular speech action, such as making a request. At the next level of analysis there has also been considerable research into sequences of dialogue acts, for example, a question followed by an answer, or more elaborate structures involving embedded sequences such as clarification requests and responses. There has been less research into larger units of analysis, although some attention has been devoted to ways in which topics are introduced, changed and reintroduced, and there has also been extensive research in sociolinguistic and ethnographic studies on speech events such as story-telling, interviews and conversations.

The general assumption behind much of this structural analysis of dialogue is that the units are hierarchically organised. Sinclair and Coulthard (1975), who developed a framework for the analysis of classroom talk between teachers and pupils, proposed a five-level hierarchy. Carletta et al. (1997), who developed a coding scheme for dialogues in the Map Task (see below), proposed a similar set of categories. Similar hierarchies have been described by Grosz and Sidner (1986) and Dahlbäck and Jönsson (1998). These units of dialogue will be discussed in the following sections, beginning with dialogue acts.

Dialogue Acts

The dialogue act can be considered to be the smallest unit of analysis in dialogue. A dialogue act describes the action performed by a speaker in an utterance. The term "dialogue act" was first introduced by Bunt (1979) and has since been used widely in dialogue analysis. Various other terms have been used, such as speech act (Searle, 1975), communicative act (Allwood, 1976), conversational move (Sinclair and Coulthard, 1975; Carletta et al., 1997) and dialogue move (Cooper et al., 1999). One of the first schemes for coding utterance functions was devised by Bales (1950) for the analysis of small group discussions. Several schemes were devised in the 1970s and 1980s to code utterance functions in various types of interaction, such as parent–child discourse, classroom interaction, therapeutic talk and job interviews. More recently, in the 1990s, new schemes were developed that have been used to tag utterances in large collections of dialogues to support automated analysis.

Dialogue act taxonomies differ in the types of dialogue activity they have been designed to describe, including casual conversation (Jurafsky et al., 1997), classroom discourse (Sinclair and Coulthard, 1975), collaborative scheduling (Alexandersson et al., 1998) and direction following (Carletta et al., 1997). Traum (2000) compares eight different schemes, showing how there are major differences in the distribution of act types across the various domains, schemes and corpora. There are also differences in level of detail, as some schemes have a small number of high-level categories while others try to capture finer distinctions, for example, with several subcategories of higher level acts such as "statement". In some cases the categories are grouped into hierarchies and levels so that the appropriate level of detail can be used as required. Two schemes will be briefly described – DAMSL and the coding scheme for the HCRC Map Task corpus.

DAMSL

DAMSL (Dialogue Act Markup in Several Layers) is a system for annotating dialogues (Allen and Core, 1997). The scheme was developed under the Discourse Resource Initiative, a group of researchers from several dialogue projects worldwide, primarily to provide a standard for the coding of task-oriented dialogues involving two agents collaborating to solve a problem. Utterances are tagged according to four main categories:

1. *Communicative Status.* Whether the utterance is intelligible and whether it was successfully completed.
2. *Information Level.* A characterisation of the semantic content of the utterance, in terms of whether it advances the task, discusses the problem-solving process, addresses the communication process or does not fall neatly into any category.
3. *Forward Looking Function.* How the current utterance affects the subsequent dialogue. For example, as the result of an utterance, is the speaker now committed to certain beliefs or to performing certain future actions?
4. *Backward Looking Function.* How the current utterance relates to the previous discourse.

Table 3.1 shows a list of forward-looking acts from the DAMSL scheme. These categories describe the functions of utterances mainly in terms of the speaker's intentions and the speaker's and hearer's obligations. Where there are a number of distinctions within an act, a decision tree is provided to assist the annotation process.

Requests for action (Influencing-addressee-future-action) obligate the hearer to either perform the action or at least acknowledge the request. However, the subcategory "Open-Options" does not oblige the hearer to respond. In the following example, the first utterance is an Open-Option (OO). B does not need to address it and can respond coherently with utterance 2.

Table 3.1. DAMSL: Forward-looking dialogue acts

Statement	A claim made by the speaker or an answer to a question.
Assert	The speaker is trying to change the beliefs of the addressee.
Reassert	The speaker thinks the claim has already been made.
Other-statement	Other categories of statement.
Influencing-addressee-future-action	Request other than to perform an action.
Open-option	Suggests an action without obligating the hearer.
Action-directive	Obligates hearer to perform the action, or to communicate a refusal or an inability to perform the action.
Info-request	Questions and requests for information.
Committing-speaker-future-action	Commits the speaker to some future action.
Offer	Conditional on the hearer's agreement.
Commit	Not conditional on the hearer's agreement, e.g., promise.
Conventional	Conventional conversational acts.
Opening	Greetings, phrases used to start an interaction.
Closing	Saying goodbye, phrases used to close a dialogue.
Explicit-performative	Performing an action by virtue of saying the utterance, e.g., "I apologise" as way of doing an apology.
Exclamation	An exclamation, e.g., "Ouch".
Other-forward-function	Any other forward-looking function.

3.18
1 Open-Option A: There is an engine in Elmira.
2 Action-dir   B: Let's take the engine from Bath.

However, in the following example, utterance 1 is an Action-directive and B has to address this request, by adopting it, explicitly rejecting it or offering an alternative:

3.19
1 Action-dir   A: Let's use the engine in Elmira.
2 Reject(utt1)   B: No.
3 Action-dir   B: Let's take the engine from Bath.

Backward Looking Functions (shown in Table 3.2) indicate how the current utterance relates to the previous discourse. An utterance can answer, accept, reject or try to correct some previous utterance or utterances. Four dimensions are involved: agreement, signalling understanding, answering and relations to preceding discourse in terms of informational content. Backward-looking acts are coded in terms of the type of act as well as the previous elements of discourse that the acts relate to.

There are several subcategories within many of the backward-looking acts, and decision trees are provided to assist annotation. The following example lists a number of responses to an offer within the "agreement" category:

Table 3.2. DAMSL: Backward-looking acts

Agreement	The second participant's response to a previous proposal, request or claim.
Accept	Accepts all of the proposal, request or claim.
Accept-part	Accepts the proposal, request or claim in part.
Maybe	Defers a definite answer.
Reject-part	Rejects part of the proposal, request or claim.
Reject	Reject all of the proposal, request or claim.
Hold	Leaves the proposal, request or claim open, e.g., counterproposal, request for further information.
Understanding	Actions taken by the speakers to ensure they understand. each other as the dialogue proceeds.
Signal-non-understanding	Explicitly indicate a problem in understanding the utterance.
Signal-understanding	Explicitly signal understanding.
Acknowledge	Indicate that the previous utterance was understood without necessarily signalling acceptance.
Repeat-rephrase	Repeat or rephrase the previous utterance to signal understanding.
Completion	Signal understanding by completing the speaker's utterance.
Correct-misspeaking	Correction of the previous speaker's utterance.
Answer	Compliance with an Info-Request.
Information-relations	How the content of the current utterance relates to the content of the previous utterance.

3.20
1   A: Would you like the book and its review?
2a B: Yes please.   Accept(1)
2b B: I'd like the book.   Accept-part(1)
2c B: I'll have to think about it. Maybe(1)
(intended literally rather than a polite reject)
2d B: I don't need the review.   Reject-part(1)
2e B: No thanks.   Reject(1)

The coding scheme permits multiple tags for utterances that achieve several effects simultaneously. Recently a dialogue annotation tool, called "dat", has been made available to support the annotation task (DAMSL Dialog Annotation, 2001).

A more elaborate version of the DAMSL coding scheme, Switchboard Shallow-Discourse Function Annotation (SWBD-DAMSL), has been used to code the Switchboard corpus (Jurafsky et al., 1997). Switchboard is a collection of about 2430 spontaneous conversations between 543 speakers in which the subjects were allowed to converse freely about a given topic for 5 to 10 minutes. Shallow discourse function refers to a level of coding that captures basic information about how one type of utterance is responded to by another type, in contrast to deep discourse function that encodes conversations in terms of the goals and plans of the participants. A set of about 60 tags was used to code 1155 of the Switchboard conversations. Many of the tags provided more subtle distinctions of the original DAMSL categories. For example, there were a number of subcategories of the DAMSL tag "answer", such as "yes answer", "no answer", "affirmative non-yes answer" and several others.

The HCRC Map Task Coding Scheme

This coding scheme was developed in the Human Communicator Research Centre (HCRC) Map Task project at the University of Edinburgh. The HCRC Map Task was a project conducted at the University of Edinburgh designed to provide a corpus of dialogues that could serve as the basis for a variety of empirical studies of dialogue. In the Map Task two speakers sat opposite one another and each had a map which the other could not see. One speaker had a route marked on her map, while the other speaker had no route on her map. The task for the speaker without a map was to mark out a route on her map based on instructions from the speaker whose map had a route. The two maps were not identical, and the speakers had to discover how the maps differed. Dialogues were coded using a scheme that included three levels of dialogue unit – conversational moves, corresponding to dialogue acts, and conversational game and transaction, to be described below (Carletta et al., 1997).

Conversational moves, described here as Initiations and Responses, are similar to the forward- and backward-looking functions in the DAMSL scheme (see Table 3.3). The moves are described in terms of their communicative functions.

The labels for conversational moves are fairly self-explanatory and there is a decision tree to determine move categories. The following example illustrates the "check" move (Carletta et al., 1997, p. 17):

Table 3.3. Coding of conversational moves in the HCRC Map Task project

Initiations	
Instruct	Speaker tells hearer to carry out an action.
Explain	Speaker states information that has not been elicited by hearer.
Check	Speaker requests hearer to confirm some information that speaker is not sure about.
Align	Speaker checks hearer's attention or agreement.
Query-yn	A question that requires a "yes" or "no" answer.
Query-w	Any query not covered by the other categories, e.g., a "who" or "what" question.
Responses	
Acknowledge	Indicates that the previous utterance was heard and understood.
Reply-y	Reply to a Query-yn query indicating "yes".
Reply-n	Reply to a Query-yn query indicating "no".
Reply-w	Reply to a Query-w query.
Clarify	Reply with information over and above what was asked.

3.21
1 G: Ehm, curve round slightly to your right.
2 F: To my right? (check)
3 G: Yes.
4 F: As I look at it? (check)

Comparing the two schemes, the HCRC scheme uses more surface-level definitions while in DAMSL the definitions are more intention-based. Surface-level definitions are easier to operate. However, interpreting dialogue moves involves recognising intentions, which may not be directly expressed in the surface form. In the DAMSL coding manual it is noted that it is often difficult to determine the actions that the speaker intended to perform with an utterance as well as the effect that the utterance might have on the subsequent dialogue. For example, the effect might differ from what the speaker initially intended. To deal with these problems annotators are allowed to look ahead in the dialogue to help determine the effect that an utterance has on the dialogue. However, while this strategy is useful to support annotation of utterances in a dialogue, it is not a resource that is available to the participants. For this reason, representations describing the processes involved in dialogue, such as the participants' information states, need to be constructed dynamically with provision for change as the dialogue proceeds.

Exchanges and Games

A dialogue is not just a sequence of dialogue acts by different speakers. Rather the dialogue acts relate to each other in a number of ways, as suggested already in the notion of forward- and backward-looking functions (or initiations and responses). A number of schemes encoding these relations has been proposed, including adjacency pairs, exchanges, discourse segments and conversational games.

Adjacency Pairs

The term "adjacency pair" was coined by conversation analysts to describe pairs of utterances that belong together, such as greeting–greeting, question–answer and invitation–acceptance/refusal (Schegloff and Sacks, 1973). Instead of initiations and responses, the utterances were called first- and second-pair parts. Other related units are "presequences" and "inserted sequences". A presequence is an utterance that prepares the way for a subsequent utterance. For example, "Are you doing anything tonight?" could be interpreted not only as a question but as a preliminary to an invitation. Inserted sequences interrupt the normal flow of the dialogue, usually to clarify something that is unclear.

Many responses in adjacency pairs have alternatives, as in the pair invitation–acceptance/refusal. However, these alternatives are not equivalent, as the following examples from Atkinson and Drew (1979, p. 58) illustrate:

3.22
1 A: Why don't you come up and see me sometimes?
2 B: I would like to.

3.23
1 A: uh, If you'd care to come and visit a little while this morning I'll give you a cup of coffee.
2 B: heh, Well that's awfully sweet of you.
3 B: I don't think I can make it this morning.
4 B: Uhm, I'm running an ad in the paper and – and, uh, I have to stay near the phone.

The response to the invitation in Example 3.22 is an acceptance. It occurs promptly and is simple in form. In contrast, the response in 3.23 is marked in several ways – it is delayed, an appreciation is proffered and the refusal is explained. The difference between these responses has been described in terms of the notion of "preference". An acceptance to an invitation is preferred, in the sense that it is the default or unmarked response. A refusal is dispreferred, in that it is usually marked in some way, as shown in the example.

More generally, there seem to be three classes of response to an utterance: the preferred response, a set of dispreferred responses and a response (such as a silence) in which no mention is made of either alternative (see below for further discussion of preferred and dispreferred responses). Thus it is possible to explain inferences that arise when a person apparently fails to respond to a prior utterance, whether deliberately or not (Bilmes, 1988). For example, a person can either accept or reject an invitation. However, if the response seems to be neither an acceptance nor a rejection, then that response, which may be a silence, gives rise to the inference that a rejection is intended. The following schema illustrates this process, where X represents a preferred response, Y a dispreferred response and N represents no mention of either X or Y:

3.24
Invitation
X   Accept.
Y   Refuse.
N   No mention of X or Y.
Inference   If N, then assume refusal.

This structure applies to other sequences such as requests and accusations. The following schema illustrates an accusation sequence:

3.25
Accusation
X   Denial.
Y   Acceptance.
N   No mention of X or Y.
Inference   If N, assume acceptance of accusation.

This sequence applies in everyday conversation but has also been adopted in some legal systems where a failure to respond in court is taken as admission of guilt.

A number of similar dispreferred responses has been documented in studies by conversation analysts. As far as spoken dialogue systems are concerned, this difference in the form and organisation of responses to initiations is important for more advanced systems, either to support their interpretation of a user's response or to enable them to generate an appropriately polite response that is a dispreferred category.

Exchanges

Exchanges were proposed as a minimal unit of interaction in classroom discourse and similarly structured dialogues such as doctor–patient interviews. In the original formulation, exchanges were seen to consist regularly of three moves: an initiation, a response and a feedback (or follow-up) move, as in the following example (Sinclair and Coulthard 1975, p. 68):

3.26
1 Teacher:	What makes a road slippery?	Initiation
2 Pupil:	You might have snow or ice on it.	Response
3 Teacher:	Yes, snow, ice.	Follow-up
4 Teacher:	Anything else make a road slippery?	Initiation
5 Pupil:	Erm oil.	Response
6 Teacher:	Oil makes a road slippery when it's mixed with water, doesn't it?	Follow-up

In this example there are six moves which can be grouped into two exchanges comprising utterances 1–3 and 4–6. Furthermore, the teacher's turn at lines 3 and 4 consists of two moves, one of which is a follow-up within the first exchange, while the other initiates the second exchange. Thus the basic unit is not the turn but the move, as speakers can accomplish more than one move within a turn and turns may be divided across exchanges.

Exchange structure has been studied widely and a number of additions to the original scheme were proposed, including a move Response/Initiation that functions simultaneously as a response and an initiation, as in the following example:

3.27
1 A:	Where's the typewriter?	Initiation
2 B:	Is it in the cupboard?	Response/Initiation
3 A:	No.	Response

Various other combinations of moves were proposed within the same general framework (see, e.g., Stubbs (1983)). However, a major problem with the framework was that it could not be easily applied to the analysis of more open-ended dialogue, such as casual conversation. One difficulty is that many utterances appear to be multifunctional and cannot be assigned to a single category. For example, in a casual conversation most utterances might take the form Response/Initiation, as the participants not only respond to what the other has said but also say something that sets up expectations for a further response. Nevertheless, the framework has been influential in studies of dialogue and its spirit has been reflected in similar schemes such as discourse segments and conversational games.

Discourse Segments

In an influential paper on the structure of discourse, Grosz and Sidner (1986) proposed a model in which discourse is represented in terms of three components: linguistic structure, intentional structure and attentional state. The attentional state is a model of the discourse entities – people, objects, events, and so on – that are salient at each point in the discourse. This model changes dynamically as the discourse proceeds. The intentional structure describes the underlying purpose of a discourse (or dialogue) in terms of the intentions of the person who initiates the discourse. A discourse consists of a number of discourse segments, each of which also has a purpose, representing the intentions of the participants at the level of the segment. For example, a dialogue agent might intend that another agent believe some fact. Two relations are specified for discourse purposes. The first, called "dominance" in the theory, represents a hierarchical relationship between discourse purposes. Taking the example of a flight reservation, the purpose "flight reservation" dominates the purposes "ask for destination", "ask for departure date", and so on, because these smaller subtasks have to be completed before the overall task is accomplished. The second relation, called "satisfaction–precedence", represents the ordering of the discourse purposes. For example, in the flight reservation scenario, finding the destination and departure information would, in most circumstances, precede determining the price.

Discourse segments are similar to exchanges and adjacency pairs, but here the analysis focuses on the intentions (or purposes) behind the moves and a discourse segment is defined as a sequence of moves that share a common purpose.

Conversational Games

Conversational game theory was used initially in the HCRC Map Task project to describe sequences of the moves listed in Table 3.3 (Kowtko et al., 1993). Examples of games are instructing, obtaining information and getting the other dialogue participant to carry out an action. As with discourse segments, games are defined on the basis of the intention behind the game. A game begins with an initiating move and continues until the goal of the initiation has been fulfilled. There may also be nesting of games, when a subgame is initiated whose purpose contributes to the overall goal of the current game, for example, to request clarification about some crucial missing information. Games can also be broken off, for example, following a misunderstanding that is not cleared up. Games are similar in structure to exchanges. For example, a Query game might consist of the moves Query-W, Reply-W and Acknowledge.

Transactions

Transactions are considered to be the highest level unit in a dialogue. A dialogue may consist of one transaction but, more typically, dialogues consist of a number of transactions that generally correspond to subtasks or subtopics. In the Map Task dialogues the participants tended to break the task of describing the route into manageable segments that could be dealt with sequentially (Carletta et al., 1997).

Because participants did not always proceed along the route in an orderly fashion, categories were required to describe different transaction types:

- *Normal* – describes a subtask.
- *Review* – reviews parts of the task that have been completed.
- *Overview* – provides a context for an upcoming subtask.
- *Irrelevant* – discussion not relevant to the task.

Coding transactions involves marking the start of a transaction in the dialogue transcripts, assigning the transaction to one of the four types and, except for IRRELEVANT transactions, indicating the start and end point of the relevant route section using numbered crosses on a copy of the route giver's map.

Using Dialogue Coding Schemes

Dialogue coding schemes can be used for a variety of purposes:

1. For annotation and analysis of units of dialogue, occurrences and structures.

Dialogue act taxonomies can be used to provide labels for the annotation of utterances in dialogue corpora. Previously, work on dialogue tended to use isolated examples, which were either constructed or real. Given the capability of storing large corpora of dialogues on computers, it has been possible to develop more realistic analyses of dialogue structures using coded dialogue samples.

2. To support the design of dialogue systems.

Dialogue acts can be used to specify the moves in a spoken dialogue system. The sequencing of these acts can be specified in advance using a dialogue grammar or flow chart so that there is a finite set of ways in which a dialogue can proceed. Dialogue acts and sequences can also be used to encode part of the information state of a dialogue agent thus enabling the agent to interpret the meaning and intent of the other agent's utterances as well as assisting the agent in deciding what to say or do next.

3. To support machine learning of dialogue acts and sequences.

The main purpose of the label set in the Switchboard coding scheme SWBD-DAMSL was to support the labelling of Switchboard conversations for training stochastic dialogue grammars that would enable the construction of better Language Models for Automatic Speech Recognition of the Switchboard conversations. These dialogue grammars could also be used to train dialogue managers (see also Chapter 13).

4. Theoretical analysis.

Finally, dialogue act taxonomies have been used as a basis for the analysis of the pragmatic meanings of utterances in more theoretically oriented studies of dialogue (e.g., Bunt (1979); Allwood (1976)).

Dialogue Processes

The structures that have been described in the previous section are evidence of regularly occurring patterns within dialogues. Given such structures it should be possible to construct dialogue grammars that would specify well-formed sequences of utterances in the same way that grammars for sentences specify well-formed sequences of words and phrases. Such grammars could be used to develop spoken dialogue systems in which the system performs a particular dialogue act and then uses the grammar to predict the set of possible next acts that the user might perform according to the grammar. Given a particular dialogue act from the user, the system could use the grammar to determine which act it should perform next.

However, although dialogue grammars can be used in this way to model simple dialogues between the system and user, it is clear that such grammars are inadequate in several respects:

1. *Descriptive adequacy.* It is difficult to apply existing schemes to the analysis of transcripts of naturally occurring dialogue.

2. *Combinatorial explosion.* Even if more elaborate schemes are devised, given the range of alternative responses to a given dialogue act, and then the number of possible responses to these responses, and so on, the combinations to be described by the grammar quickly grow to unmanageable proportions.

3. *Implication of ill-formed dialogue sequences.* The specification of well-formed sequences implies that sequences that do not conform to these structures are ill-formed. However, it is difficult to find actual examples of ill-formed dialogues. Instead, when an expected response does not occur, participants tend to try to make sense of this nonoccurrence. For example, in Dialogue 3.17, the occurrence of a silence did not lead to a judgement of an ill-formed sequence but rather gave rise to inferences concerning the reasons for the silence.

More generally, dialogue grammars fail to model the processes involved when participants engage in dialogue. The fact that one dialogue act follows another does not explain why such a sequence occurs. The following sections outline some approaches to the analysis of dialogue processes that seek to explain the nature of dialogue behaviour from the perspective of the dialogue participants.

Dialogue as Social Behaviour

The approach to dialogue adopted by the Conversation Analysts was to identify regularly occurring patterns in conversation and to model the procedures used by participants when engaging in conversation. The methodology and theoretical orientation of Conversation Analysis (CA) derives from a branch of sociology known as Ethnomethodology, which sought to study the techniques used by members of society to interpret and act within their social worlds. As far as conversation was concerned, the aim was to identify the orderliness that is displayed in everyday conversation and the methods employed by participants to maintain this orderliness. The essential findings were that conversations are organised locally and that participants engage in ongoing interactional work to create and maintain orderly conversations.

These points can be illustrated with reference to the structural unit of the adjacency pair. Adjacency pairs could be used as a basis for dialogue grammars.

However, in the CA approach, adjacency pairs were viewed as providing a normative framework within which participants could interpret and make sense of the ongoing dialogue. After producing a first-pair part the speaker will examine the next utterance for the anticipated response. On producing this next utterance, the recipient of the first-pair part displays his (or her) understanding of that first-pair part. Thus each turn provides an ongoing opportunity for participants to monitor the conversation and display their understanding. In this sense the structures are locally managed and emergent rather than predetermined, as in a dialogue grammar. Moreover, adjacency pairs are characterised in terms of "conditional relevance" rather than in terms of well-formed and ill-formed sequences. What this means is that if a second-pair part within an adjacency pair fails to occur, then it is seen to be noticeably absent. On the recognition of this absence the speaker of the first-pair part will make inferences to explain the absence. For example, if there is a failure to respond to a question, it might be inferred that the addressee wishes to avoid answering the question. Observations of large samples of conversational data by conversation analysts demonstrated this process across a range of different adjacency pair types. Similarly, in the case of conversational breakdowns, it was shown that participants worked together to locate the problem and to apply an appropriate repair. More generally, the CA approach was able to explain how the patterns that could be identified in transcripts of conversations reflected an orderliness that was oriented to by the participants and that was achieved collaboratively on a turn-by-turn basis.

Dialogue as the Achievement of Mutual Understanding

Clark (1996) views dialogue as a joint action in which the participants work to achieve mutual understanding. The structures that are observable in conversation emerge from this joint activity. As Clark (1996, p. 319) argues:

Conversations look planned and goal-oriented only in retrospect. In reality, they are created opportunistically piece by piece as the participants negotiate joint purposes and then fulfil them. . . . In the opportunistic view, the hierarchical structure of conversation is an emergent property. It appears because of principles that govern any successful joint action.

Achieving mutual understanding involves the process of grounding described earlier. Information contributed by participants has to be mutually acknowledged as having entered the "common ground" (Clark and Schaefer, 1989; Traum, 1994). This can be achieved in a number of ways, including assertions of understanding, producing a relevant next turn and displaying understanding. Grounding is a dynamic process that gives rise to structural units called Common Ground Units (CGUs) (Nakatani and Traum, 1999). CGUs represent all the linguistic material involved in achieving grounding of an initial presentation of information. They can be complex, containing repair and clarification sequences. There can also be overlapping CGUs, in which an utterance may simultaneously ground an open CGU while also initiating a new CGU. Finally, they can also be discontinuous and revisited later in the dialogue, for example, for further confirmation or to initiate a repair.

Table 3.4. Analysis using exchanges and games

3.28	Exchange	Game
1 S: Where are you travelling to?	Initiation	WH-query
2 U: London.	Response	WH-reply
3 S: You want to go to London?	Initiation? Feedback?	Check
4 U: Yes.	?	Clarify

Viewing dialogue structure in terms of CGUs provides some advantages over other structural units such as the exchange or game:

- CGUs provide an explanation of dialogue structure in terms of the motivation of participants to achieve mutual understanding.
- They are a dynamically evolving structure as opposed to the more static structures proposed in exchanges and games.
- As such, they are more descriptively adequate than other structures when describing sequences of dialogue.

For example, the sequence, shown in Table 3.4, would be difficult to analyse in terms of exchange structures or games. Analysing this sequence using exchange structures runs into problems at utterance 3. This utterance could be coded as an initiation, but this would not reflect how utterances 3 and 4 relate to the exchange in 1–2. If coded as feedback, then it would not be clear how to code utterance 4, as feedback utterances do not require a response, yet clearly utterance 4 responds to 3. Coding according to conversational game theory codes 1 and 2 as a WH-question game followed by an embedded Checking game, but fails to capture the intuition that the point of the Checking game is to ground the information requested in utterance 1. Indeed, the WH-question game could be said to be incomplete until the information is grounded – a process that could continue over several further turns.

In this way, CGUs are more adequate from a descriptive viewpoint as well as providing an explanation for the structures that emerge.

Dialogue as Rational Action

Dialogue has also been viewed in terms of a theory of rational action, in which intelligent dialogue behaviour is seen as a special case of general rational behaviour (Cohen, 1994; Sadek and de Mori, 1997). Much of the early work within this tradition in the 1980s focussed on modelling dialogue in terms of planning. Utterances were viewed as actions that are planned in order to achieve a goal. The goal may be some desired physical state, such as having a drink of beer in a bar. In this case, an utterance that functions as a request for a beer is incorporated into a plan that also involves physical actions, such as the customer handing over some money and the barman giving the beer. Interpreting utterances involved recognising the intention behind an utterance and matching this intention with some part of a plan that might achieve a particular goal (Allen,

1983). A cooperative system would adopt the user's goal, anticipate any obstacles to the plan, and produce a response that would promote the completion of the goal.

In more recent work, plans are not predetermined schemas of action but are derived deductively from rationality principles. While agents normally have the goal of behaving cooperatively in dialogue, an agent does not necessarily have to adopt another agent's goals, if there is good reason not to. For example, an agent should not supply information that is confidential or assist in actions that it knows to be illegal or harmful. In other words, an agent has to attempt to achieve a rational balance between its own mental attitudes and those of other agents and between these mental attitudes and desired plans of action. Thus, in this approach, dialogue structure emerges dynamically as a consequence of principles of rational cooperative interaction, and the processes of dialogue can be explained in terms of the plans, goals and intentions of the agents involved in the dialogue.

The view that dialogue is a special case of rational behaviour brings several advantages. Given that dialogue involves a joint commitment to mutual understanding, there is a motivation for agents to make their intentions clear through confirmations, clarifications, repairs and elaborations (Cohen, 1994). Although these behaviours are included in other approaches, there is no theoretical motivation for their inclusion. The theory also accounts for different contexts of interaction and explains why an agent might provide more information than is required by the other agent's query. For example, if a user asks for an address, the system might also provide a telephone number, if one is available. However, this additional information should not be implemented as an automatically generated response schema but rather as something to be determined within a particular context of interaction on the basis of the rationality principles. Finally, the theory provides a basis for more advanced dialogues, for example, those involving negotiation rather than simple information retrieval, where various types of cooperative and corrective responses may be required.

Summary

These three accounts of dialogue processes are similar in many ways. In particular, they emphasise the view that the structures to be found in dialogue evolve as a result of the processes that participants employ when they engage in dialogue. The structures are not used by the participants to determine whether a dialogue is well-formed or not, but are used as a normative framework in which inferences can be made. Furthermore, dialogue structure is viewed not as predetermined but as dynamically evolving and as a process of rational action, in which the participants work together to achieve their goals, including the conversational goal of understanding one another.

Representing Information States in Dialogue

Given the processes described above in which dialogue participants monitor the ongoing dialogue to assist their interpretation of what is being said and to support their decisions as to what to say next, it is clear that one aspect of dialogue processes is the knowledge that participants bring to bear when taking part in a dialogue. There are different types of knowledge that are involved. Some of this knowledge is static, such as knowledge about the domain being discussed in the dialogue and knowledge of general conversational principles. Other knowledge is dynamic, such as knowledge about what has been said so far in the dialogue, what information is part of the common ground, and what actions can be taken next. This dynamic knowledge has been referred to as the "information state". Using this information state a participant can decide what to say next, how to interpret what the other participant has said, and how modify the current information state based on utterances in the dialogue.

In the simplest case the information state may consist of a list of questions to ask and the answers that have been received. Thus an agent providing a travel service might have questions such as:

3.29
1 Where are you travelling from?
2 Where are you travelling to?
3 What date do you wish to travel?
4 What time do you wish to leave?

These might be represented as a set of attributes and values, representing the agent's information at a particular point in the dialogue, for example,

Origin: Belfast.

Destination: London.

Date: Unknown.

Time: Unknown.

There would also be a mechanism for updating the information on the basis of what is said in the dialogue, for example, changing values from "unknown" to one of the values required by the question, or updating the status of a value from known to confirmed. On the basis of such an information state, the agent could determine that it already knew the values for origin and departure, but not for date and time. Using this information, the agent is able to decide that it does not need to ask about origin and destination, but does need to ask the questions to elicit values for date and time. If values have not yet been confirmed, the agent would also have to decide which values to confirm and when. Representations such as this have been used extensively to determine the actions of dialogue agents in simple spoken dialogue systems.

Information state has generally been used to describe more complex representations that capture a wide range of information about the dialogue and its participants. This information may include the following:

- *Mental states.* The beliefs, desires and intentions of the participants.
- *Information status.* Whether the information is private to one participant, shared (part of the common ground) or semi-shared (introduced into the dialogue but not yet grounded).

- *Obligations.* The obligations and commitments of the participants, for example, to respond to a question.
- *Dialogue information.* Who has the current turn? What is the topic? What was the previous utterance? Which dialogue act did the previous utterance perform?
- *Plan.* The overall goals of the participants.
- *Agenda.* The immediate goals and obligations of the participants.

Information states may represent the dialogue information of one or both of the participants, or may even represent an external view of the dialogue. When annotating transcripts of a dialogue it is possible to represent the information states of each participant as well as representing the dialogue from the perspective of an external observer. Modelling each participant's information state is particularly useful when there are misunderstandings between the participants, as these can be identified from the discrepant information states. However, when modelling the processes of a dialogue participant over the course of a dialogue, it is only possible to represent information states from a single perspective, i.e., that of the dialogue agent (or system). Given that the agent is not omniscient, it can have knowledge of its own beliefs, desires and intentions, but it can only infer the beliefs, desires and intentions of the other participant. Thus while agent A might believe on the basis of what B has said that B wishes to travel to X, it could be the case that B had actually expressed a desire to travel to Y, and that A had misrecognised or misunderstood Y as X. For this reason establishing information as common ground is an important part of attempting to ensure that the participants' information states concur.

This brief discussion of dialogue information states has illustrated another aspect of the dynamic processes that are to be modelled in dialogue systems. Much of current research in information state theory is concerned with complex representation formalisms and mechanisms for updating information states. Some of this work will be described in greater detail in Chapter 13.

Summary

This chapter has been concerned with the characteristics of dialogue and with its structures and processes. The following are the main issues covered in this chapter:

- Dialogue is an example of extended discourse. Words, phrases and utterances are produced and interpreted in the context of discourse and not in isolation.
- Dialogue is a purposeful activity. People engage in dialogue for a purpose and their meanings and actions have to be interpreted in the context of these purposes.
- Dialogue is a collaborative activity in which two (or more) people work together to make the dialogue work. Examples of collaborative activity include ensuring smooth turn-taking and achieving mutual understanding.

- The spoken language typical of naturally occurring dialogue can differ considerably in form from the language of written texts. This has implications for the modules involved in processing naturally occurring speech for speech recognition and speech understanding.

- Dialogue is structured hierarchically. These structures can be used to support the design of dialogue systems and to train systems using machine learning techniques.

In addition to these structures, there are processes that participants in dialogue use to engage in dialogue. It is important to consider these processes in order to explain the structures that evolve in a dialogue.

Further Reading

Pragmatics and Discourse Analysis

There are numerous books on pragmatics and discourse analysis. Levinson (1983) is a standard text on pragmatics, covering topics such as speech act theory, conversational implicature and presupposition, with an excellent chapter on Conversation Analysis (CA). Stubbs (1983) and Brown and Yule (1983) provide comprehensive reviews of different aspects of discourse analysis. Schiffrin (1994) discusses a number of different approaches to discourse analysis, accompanied by detailed analysis of examples. See also Schiffrin et al. (2001) for an edited collection of a wide-ranging set of papers on discourse analysis. For an account of dialogue as coordinated action, in which it is argued that language use involves both individual and social processes, see Clark (1996).

Computational Pragmatics and Dialogue

Bunt and Black (2000a) is a recent collection of papers on computational pragmatics, including a useful introductory overview of the field (Bunt and Black, 2000b). Jurafsky (2004) discusses computational pragmatics, looking in particular at different computational models for the interpretation of indirect speech acts. Webber (2001) reviews computational perspectives on dialogue and discourse, while Leech and Weisser (2003) discuss pragmatics in relation to dialogue. The American Association for Artificial Intelligence (AAAI) Fall 1999 Symposium on Psychological Models of Communication in Collaborative Systems provides a useful set of papers on interactive systems from a psychological perspective (http://www.cs.umd.edu/users/traum/PM/papers.html). Button et al. (1995) argue against the possibility of the conversational computer, based on a critique of a wide range of views in modern cognitive science and the philosophy of mind.

Exercises

Transcribe one of the sample dialogues that you encountered in the exercises in Chapters 1 and 2. Annotate the dialogue using the following schemes described in this chapter:

1. DAMSL.
2. The HCRC Map Task coding scheme.

To what extent are these schemes useful for annotating the dialogue? Do they account for all the important aspects of the interaction?

Components of a Spoken Dialogue System – Speech Input and Output

4

A spoken dialogue system consists of a number of components that need to work together for the system to function successfully. Spoken dialogue toolkits provide integrated environments in which some of the components, such as the speech recognition and the text-to-speech (TTS) engines, are built-in. Other components, such as the dialogue manager, will generally require more effort to develop. This chapter presents an overview of the components that are concerned with processing the user's input to the system and the system's output to the user – speech recognition, language understanding, language generation and speech output. The central component of a spoken dialogue system, the dialogue manager, will be described in Chapter 5.

Overview of a Spoken Dialogue System

The following dialogue can be used to introduce the different components of a spoken dialogue system and to explain the roles of each component within the complete system:

> 4.1
> 1 System: Welcome to the Flight Information Service. Where would you like to travel to?
> 2 Caller: I would like to fly to London on Friday arriving around 9 in the morning.
> 3 System: There is a flight that departs at 7.45 a.m. and arrives at 8.50 a.m.

The dialogue begins with the system greeting the user and prompting for some information (utterance 1). The caller responds with utterance 2. In order to process this utterance, the system has to engage in the following processes:

1. Recognise the words that the caller said (Speech Recognition).
2. Assign a meaning to these words (Language Understanding).
3. Determine how the utterance fits into the dialogue so far and decide what to do next, for example, clarify the utterance if it is unclear, confirm it (grounding), ask for further information, or look up an information source (Dialogue Management).

4. Retrieve flights that match the user's requirements (External Communication).

5. Choose the words and phrases to be used in the response (Language Generation).

6. Speak the response (Text-to-speech (TTS) Synthesis).

These processes illustrate the roles played by the different components of a spoken dialogue system. In this example each process was completed smoothly. However, there could be problems at each stage. The speech recognition component might fail to recognise the caller's words correctly, the language understanding component might assign the wrong meaning or be unable to choose the correct meaning if the utterance is ambiguous, and so on. Dialogue management may involve deciding whether the system is in a position to retrieve information from the external information source or whether items in the caller's input need to be clarified. As far as output is concerned, the response generation component needs to formulate the system's utterances in such a way that the information is presented unambiguously and clearly, while the TTS synthesis component has to speak the words with appropriate phrasing so that the message is comprehensible. The basic architecture of a spoken dialogue system that supports these functions is shown in Figure 4.1.

It will be noted that the control flow in this architecture is serial. Speech input by the user is processed by the speech recogniser and passed on to the language understanding component. The representation produced by the language understanding component is then passed to the dialogue manager. At some point the dialogue manager will produce a message to be output to the user. This message will pass through the language generation and TTS synthesis components so that it is in a form to be spoken to the user. The dialogue manager will also interact with an external knowledge source that provides information to be output to the user. Several passes through the system may be

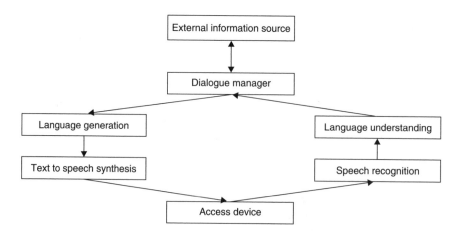

Figure 4.1. Architecture of a spoken dialogue system.

required to complete a dialogue, for example, the dialogue manager may need to clarify some point or may need to ask additional questions before it can retrieve the required information from the external knowledge source.

A large number of spoken dialogue systems, particularly those that are deployed commercially, are designed using a serial control flow. More advanced systems, such as those being developed in research laboratories, may involve different architectures in which the dialogue manager plays a central controlling function and interacts directly with the other components. For example, if there is a problem at the speech recognition stage, the dialogue manager might be able to bring some contextual knowledge to bear that would not otherwise have been available to the speech recognition component. The use of multiple knowledge sources at different stages of the dialogue control process is the subject of current research. These more advanced systems will be examined in Part III of this book. In the remainder of this chapter the components that deal with the input to the system and the output to the user will be discussed.

Speech Recognition

The main task of the speech recognition component is to capture the user's input and convert it into a sequence of words. Considerable progress has been made in speech recognition technologies over the past decades, due to improved algorithms as well as advances in computer hardware that support the complex mathematical calculations required for speech recognition. A detailed technical account of speech recognition is beyond the scope of this book and interested readers are referred to the sources listed at the end of this chapter. Developers should nevertheless have some understanding of speech recognition technology to appreciate why speech recognition is difficult, why recognition errors are inevitable, and how to design systems in such a way as to minimise the occurrence of errors and deal successfully with those that do occur.

Why Is Speech Recognition Difficult?

The main problem with speech recognition is that it cannot guarantee a correct interpretation of the input when compared with keyboard and mouse input. Interpreting speech input can be described in terms of a noisy channel of communication, in which the utterance spoken by the user can be corrupted as it passes through a noisy channel. The task of the recognition system is to decode this noisy utterance by making a best guess at what the original input was. Using advanced statistical methods the speech recognition system considers all the words in its vocabulary and returns the most likely word (or a ranked list of words) given the acoustic input.

There are a number of reasons why the process of speech recognition is uncertain compared with keyboard input, where it can be guaranteed that strik-ing a key such as "k" will result in the character "k" being recognised and displayed on the screen (unless the keyboard is faulty). One of the main problems is that, while there is a finite set of phonemes that represent the sounds of a language – its consonants and vowels – there is no one-to-one relationship between these phonemes and the acoustic patterns that occur in speech. As an example, the phoneme /t/ will have a different acoustic representation depending on its position within a word – in initial position (as in "toy"), between an /s/ and a vowel (as in "stir"), within a consonantal cluster (as in "strong"), and in final position (as in "bit").

These differences are a consequence of coarticulation, in which the pronunciation of a phoneme is affected by the sounds that precede or follow that phoneme. Coarticulation also affects sounds at word boundaries. For example, the word "the" may be pronounced "ni" in a phrase such as "in the event" due to assimilation of the /th/ phoneme to the preceding nasal phoneme /n/ as well as assimilation of the /uh/ vowel to the following vowel in the word "event" (Jurafsky and Martin, 2000). In some cases a phoneme may be omitted altogether. For example, in the phrase "good boy" when spoken quickly, the /d/ at the end of "good" may be omitted entirely, so that the speech recognition system has to return the words "good boy" from an acoustic signal that sounds something more like "gu boy". Most of these processes are predictable from the linguistic context and can be modelled by using triphones (or phonemes in context), in which each phoneme is represented in terms of its preceding and following contexts. For example, the /t/ in "strong" would be represented as s/ t / r. However, some of these processes are probabilistic. The reduction of "the" to "ni" in the context described may occur only some of the time. Probabilities such as these are modelled in the system on the basis of statistics derived from the analysis of large corpora of speech data. Moreover, the particular pronunciation of a word can differ considerably depending on whether the word is stressed or reduced within an utterance, for example, "the" might be pronounced "thee" in the phrase "in the event" if the speaker is articulating very slowly and deliberately, but it is more likely to be pronounced "ni" in more casual speech.

In addition to these linguistic factors that affect the pronunciations of words, there are several other types of variability that make speech recognition problematic:

1. *Inter-speaker variability.* There are differences between speakers in the way they speak and pronounce words. Some of these differences are attributable to physical factors, such as the shape of the vocal tract. Other differences are due to factors such as age, gender and regional origin (accent).

2. *Intra-speaker variability.* The same words spoken on a different occasion by the same speaker can have different acoustic properties. Factors such as tiredness, congested airways due to a cold, and changes of mood have a bearing on how words are pronounced. Even when a person makes a conscious effort to pronounce a word in exactly the same way, there may be subtle differences in the acoustic signal that could cause an error in speech recognition.

3. *Channel variability.* Differences in the transmission channel – microphone or telephone – give rise to differences in the acoustic signal.

4. *Background noise.* The acoustic signal may be distorted due to the effects of background noise, which can be constant, as in the case of the hum of a computer fan, or transient, as in the case of someone sneezing or a door slamming.

Speech Recognition: The Basic Process

Speech recognition involves matching the incoming acoustic signal with a stored set of patterns to return a sequence of words that is estimated to represent the words spoken by the user. Each stored pattern is matched against the input and the one that is the best match is chosen.

The speech recognition process begins when the user speaks into a microphone or telephone handset. The sound that strikes the microphone has the form of an analogue acoustic signal. This signal is captured by the microphone and converted to an electric current, which is then passed to an analogue-to-digital converter within the sound card that translates the current into a stream of bits that represent the sound. This part of the process is known as signal processing and it involves extracting the relevant set of features from the acoustic signal. Following this the extracted features are classified as sequences of phonemes using an acoustic model, and these sequences of phonemes are then combined into words that represent the system's estimate of what the user said. This process is illustrated in Figure 4.2.

Signal Processing

Signal processing faces two major problems:

1. How to deal with the large quantities of data involved.
2. How to extract those features in the acoustic signal that are most relevant for speech recognition.

The acoustic signal is divided into frames, generally with a length of about 10 ms, and each frame is analysed for a number of features, such as the amount of energy at each of several frequency ranges, the overall energy in a frame, and

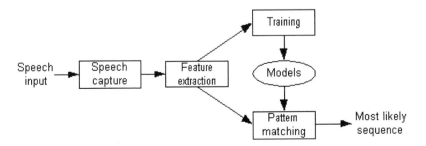

Figure 4.2. The speech recognition process.

differences from the previous frame. Each frame is then represented as a single label rather than as a vector of numbers, resulting in one byte per frame (vector quantisation). In this way the representation of the speech signal is compact as well as encoding those features that will be useful for speech recognition.

Phoneme and Word Identification

The next stage in the process is to take the set of features that were extracted from the acoustic signal and to classify these as phonemes and then combine sequences of phonemes into words. This process involves two models:

1. An acoustic model that shows how each word consists of a sequence of phonemes and how each phoneme relates to the values of the features extracted from the acoustic signal.
2. A language model that specifies permissible sequences of words.

The Acoustic Model

The acoustic model captures variability in pronunciation using probabilities. A word model consists of the phonemes that make up the word. However, a word may be pronounced in different ways. For example, the Camegie Mellon University (CMU) *Pronouncing Dictionary* (available at: http://www.speech.cs.cmu.edu/cgi-bin/cmudict) generates the following two pronunciations for the word "tomato":

1. T AH M EY T OW.
2. T AH M AA T OW.

The first pronunciation represents the way most American speakers pronounce the word, while the second pronunciation represents the pronunciation of British and some eastern American dialects. Given estimates of the probabilities of these alternative pronunciations in American speech data, a word model for "tomato" can be represented as a weighted automaton, as shown in Figure 4.3, in which there are alternative paths through the model with probabilities for each transition (only the alternatives are shown here).

In reality the model would be more complex than this as, in addition to this alternation, the first vowel may be pronounced as "ow" or "ah", while the final

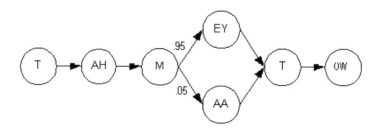

Figure 4.3. Model of the word "tomato".

"t" can be pronounced as "t" or "d" (see Jurafsky and Martin (2000, p. 170), for a more extended model of "tomato", including probabilities).

Hidden Markov Models (HMMs) are used in most current speech recognition systems to represent such variable patterns of speech. Figure 4.4 shows a simple HMM for the word "tomato", based on the model shown in Figure 4.3.

There are three points to note in this model:

1. The HMM consists of a number of states that represent the temporal progression through the word from the start state, through each of the phonemes, to the end state. As the duration of each phoneme can vary due to differences in speaking rate, the arcs have loop back transitions (labelled a_{11}, a_{22}, and so on) that allow the model to remain in the same state to reflect a slower rate of articulation. In this way the HMM deals with temporal variability in the speech signal.

2. Unlike the simpler model shown in Figure 4.3, where each state corresponded to a unique symbol, such as "t" or "ah", in the HMM each state has a probability distribution of possible outputs (labelled $b_1(o_1)$, $b_1(o_2)$, $b_2(o_3)$, and so on). Thus at each state the system matches a portion of the input (a 10 ms frame, as described above, labelled o_1, o_2, o_3, and so on), with all possible outputs, each of which has a different probability. The output that matches is returned along with its probability. In this way acoustic variability in the speech signal is handled.

3. Because there is a distribution probability of outputs at each state and each output can appear in more than one state, it is possible to see that the model outputs a particular symbol but it is not possible to know which state the symbol came from. This is why the model is called a "hidden" model.

Pattern matching using HMMs involves calculating the probability of a state sequence. However, as the number of possible state sequences for a given sequence of frames representing the input acoustic signal is very large, a process called dynamic programming is used to efficiently perform this computation.

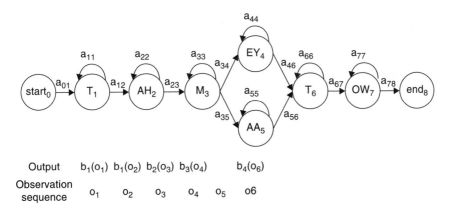

Figure 4.4. Hidden Markov Model of "tomato".

Details of the commonly used algorithms, such as the Viterbi and A* algorithms, are beyond the scope of the current discussion and the interested reader is again referred to the sources listed at the end of this chapter.

The Language Model

The acoustic model is not sufficient on its own as a method for estimating a word or sequence of words given an acoustic signal. For this reason the acoustic model is combined with a language model that contains knowledge about permissible sequences of words and which words are more likely in a given sequence. There are two types of language model in common use:

1. A grammar (or finite state network), in which all the permissible word sequences in the application are specified.
2. An N-gram language model, which provides statistical information on word sequences.

Grammars are often used in spoken dialogue systems to specify the acceptable words and phrases that the user might say at a particular point in the dialogue. (Note that the term "grammar" is confusing, as grammar is also used more traditionally to refer to the analysis of sentences in terms of syntactic categories, such as noun, verb and preposition.)

Figure 4.5 shows a simple grammar network that could be used to parse a user's response to a system prompt in an airline reservations system. This grammar covers several ways in which the user might respond, such as:

4.2
1 I want to book a flight to London on Friday at 11 in the morning.
2 A flight to London?
3 To London in the morning.
4 To London at 11 in the morning.

Given that there is likely to be a finite number of ways in which a user might specify flight requirements, a grammar could be constructed to cover these possibilities. For example, a number of regularly occurring phrases can be identified, such as:

to + Place_Name
on + Day
in the + Period_of_day
at | around | before | after + Time

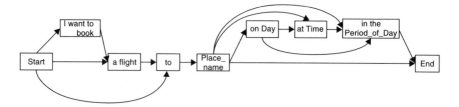

Figure 4.5. A grammar network for flight reservations.

Other phrases may be classified as optional, as they do not contribute to the overall meaning:

(I want a flight)
(I want to book a flight)

Such optional expressions are recognised in the input but discarded as they are not required for further processing. Thus, using such a grammar, the strings returned by the acoustic model can be analysed in terms of whether they conform to the grammar. In this way some of the uncertainties that result from the acoustic analysis can be resolved.

Grammars are useful if all the phrases that are likely to occur in the speech input can be specified in advance. The disadvantage is that perfectly legal strings that were not anticipated are ruled out. Grammars are particularly useful when parsing well-defined sequences, such as dates, expressions of time or terms of address.

N-grams are used in large vocabulary systems where it is not possible to specify all the permissible sentences and word combinations in advance. N-grams provide statistical information on word sequences, indicating how probable a word is in a given context. Jurafsky and Martin (2000, p. 223) present an example in which the acoustic sequence "ni" could represent several different words, such as "need", "knee", "neat" and "new". In their example, based on acoustic scores only, the most likely word was "knee". However, if the preceding word is taken into account and this preceding word is "I", then the most likely word becomes "need". This is because the likelihood of the sequence "I need", as determined by a bigram language model, is greater than "I knee", "I neat" and "I new". Thus combining the acoustic score for a word with N-gram statistics gives a more reliable estimate of the most likely word. N-grams are estimated from large corpora of speech data. In most cases bigrams have proved sufficient to support large vocabulary speech recognition. Problems arise when there is sparse data for particular bigrams or trigrams; however, there are a number of well-understood methods for dealing with this issue. Generally, N-grams have not been used widely in spoken dialogue systems and are more commonly used in large vocabulary applications, such as dictation.

Parameters of Speech Recognition

Speech recognition systems can be defined in terms of a number of parameters:

1. *Enrolment.* A speech recognition system may be speaker-dependent or speaker-independent. A speaker-dependent system has to be trained to the speech patterns of a particular speaker. This process, often known as "enrolment", is required for current dictation systems with large vocabularies. Spoken dialogue systems, which are normally used by a wide variety of casual users, need to be speaker-independent. These systems are trained in advance on samples collected from a variety of speakers whose speech patterns should be

representative of the potential users of the system. Speaker-independent recognition is more error-prone than speaker-dependent recognition, particularly when speakers with nonnative or otherwise unusual accents are involved.

2. *Vocabulary size.* The size of the vocabulary varies with the application and with the particular design of the dialogue system. Thus a carefully controlled dialogue may constrain the user to a vocabulary limited to a few words expressing the options that are available in the system, while in a more flexible system the vocabulary may amount to several thousand words. Dictation systems have very large vocabularies of more than 200,000 words and may also include additional vocabularies for specialist domains, such as legal or medical terminologies.

3. *Speaking mode.* Until recently, many speech recognition systems required the user to pause briefly between each word. These systems used an "isolated" or "discrete" word-speaking mode. Most current systems can process continuous speech, so that the user can talk more naturally. The main difficulty faced by continuous systems is how to segment the speech by correctly detecting the word boundaries. The following often-cited example illustrates this problem:

4.3 It's hard to recognise speech. / It's hard to wreck a nice beach.

Some systems permit connected phrases that have been specified in a form of grammar that allows small variations within the phrases. Connected phrase recognition is used for command-and-control systems, for example, "open X", where X may be any one of a number of application programs on a computer.

4. *Speaking style.* Some speech recognition systems are trained on speech that is read. Others are trained on spontaneous speech. Speech that is read will generally be more fluent and less error-prone. Spontaneous speech is typically more disfluent, with characteristics such as hesitations, false starts and various extralinguistic phenomena, such as coughing (see Chapter 3). A speech recognition system that is trained on and supports spontaneous speech is more appropriate for a spoken dialogue application.

Issues for Developers

It is generally not necessary for developers of spoken dialogue systems to build a speech recognition system from scratch, as speech recognition engines are generally provided as part of a spoken dialogue development environment. These engines normally include acoustic models for a lexicon of the most commonly occurring words in a language. Where such an engine is not included, it is often possible to obtain an appropriate engine for the required language from another vendor. Given this situation, the main tasks for a developer are to fine-tune and extend the acoustic models and to develop or extend the grammars that constitute the language models.

Tuning Recognition

Speech recognition engines usually provide facilities for fine-tuning and extending the acoustic models. Fine-tuning involves adding variant pronunciations to the acoustic models. For example, if the acoustic model for "tomato" was based only on the "tom-eh-to" pronunciation, and it was expected that some users might pronounce the word as "tom-ah-to", then this alternative pronunciation would need to be added. This fine-tuning is usually an iterative process in which an initial system is built and data are collected from a range of users. The data can then be analysed and further changes made to the acoustic model. Often this process is automated, but in some cases the changes have to be made by hand.

Extending the Acoustic Model

Extending the acoustic model involves adding new words to the vocabulary. Generally, the vocabularies of a good speech recognition engine will include the most commonly used words in the language. However, there may be a need to add new words, such as technical terms not included in the general vocabulary and, more especially, names of places and of people. Methods for adding variant pronunciations and new words will be illustrated in Chapters 7 and 9.

Creating Speech Recognition Grammars

Most spoken dialogue toolkits require developers to create speech recognition grammars that specify the permissible input at each point in the dialogue. A number of different notations are used. Speech recognition grammars and some of the notations that are commonly used are discussed in greater detail in Chapters 7–11 in Part II of this book.

Design of Speech Systems

Developers can also take steps to prevent or at least minimise speech recognition errors through careful design. This issue is discussed in detail in a number of texts (e.g., Balentine et al. (2001)). A few examples are presented to illustrate the basic issues.

Design Based on Phonetic Properties of Words

Some sounds cause problems for a speech recognition system so that a sensible strategy could be to design system prompts in such a way that these words will not occur in the user's input. Fricatives (such as /h/, /s/ and /f/) and unvoiced consonants (such as /p/ or /t/) are considered as "noisy" and more difficult to recognise accurately. Thus a word such as "help" would be problematic because the initial /h/ might be lost and the final /p/ might be misrecognised, as final consonants are often voiced or aspirated. Unfortunately, however, the word "help" is likely to be a useful input word in many systems, so that utility might override considerations based on the phonetic properties of the word.

Another example is the word "cancel", in which the /s/ sound in the final syllable might be lost as well as the syllable itself which is unstressed and low energy. For similar reasons words such as "six" are problematic, as here, in addition to the /s/ phoneme, the vowel has a short duration. "Repeat" is another commonly used input word that has a weak initial syllable. Confusion is possible with words that share some of the vowels and also have unstressed initial syllables, for example, "delete". More generally, the recommended strategy is to attempt to require input of several syllables, such as phrases, which is likely to consist of a richer set of phonetic features.

Using Barge-in

Many speech recognition systems allow the developer to select the option of barge-in, which permits the user to interrupt the system's prompt. Barge-in is a useful facility, particularly for experienced users who will not wish to listen to familiar prompts and who can cut in on the prompt with their responses and conclude the dialogue more quickly. However, there are several issues regarding barge-in and its effects on speech recognition that need to be considered carefully at the design stage:

1. Barge-in involves echo cancellation requiring the computationally intensive task of calculating the delay of the echo. Furthermore, barge-in requires the speech recognition engine to be active for most of the call, whereas if barge-in is deactivated, the recognition engine only needs to be active when a response is being processed. Issues such as these place heavy demands on the processor that might detract from the performance of the system.

2. False acceptance, where nonspeech sounds or speech not addressed to the system (e.g., speech spoken to someone else) is treated as intended input, can cause the prompt to be terminated and the user to be left in confusion.

3. At the point where the user cuts in, if the system prompt is not immediately terminated the user may speak louder to be heard over the system prompt. This is known as the "Lombard" effect. The resulting amplified speech may be more difficult to process as it may not match the trained models for speech spoken at a normal volume level.

4. Another problem is that, in the case of overlap between the user and the system, the user may repeat some of the utterance that has been perceived to have been overlapped. This results in what is known as the "stuttering" effect, as the resulting string passed to the recognition component may include hesitations and false starts, in other words, a string that will probably not conform to the grammar specified for that input.

Some systems provide different types of barge-in, each of which has advantages as well as disadvantages:

1. *Barge-in on energy detection.* In this case the system's prompt stops as soon as any sound is detected. One advantage of this method is that it limits distortion caused by barge-in to the first syllables of the user's speech. Furthermore, Lombard speech and the stuttering effect are also minimised. The disadvantage is an increase in the false acceptance of background noise not intended as valid input.

2. *Barge-in on confident word recognition.* In this method audio output only stops after the system determines that the user has spoken a complete valid word or phrase, as defined by the active recognition grammar. The advantage

of this method is that it minimises false acceptance due to accidental interruptions or background noise. However, the disadvantage is that it increases false rejections due to an increased incidence of Lombard speech and the "stuttering" effect.

Language Understanding

The role of the language understanding component is to analyse the output of the speech recognition component and to assign a meaning representation that can be used by the dialogue manager. Traditionally, language understanding has involved two processes: syntactic analysis, to determine the constituent structure of the recognised string (i.e., how the words group together), and semantic analysis, to determine the meanings of the constituents. However, in many current spoken dialogue systems the meaning of the utterance is derived directly from the recognised string using a "semantic grammar".

Language understanding in a spoken dialogue system is problematic for two reasons:

- Ambiguity in natural language.
- Ill-formed input.

There are several ways in which natural language can be ambiguous:

- *Lexical ambiguity.* A word may belong to more than one part of speech, for example, "book" can be a noun or a verb. This sort of ambiguity can usually be resolved within the context of the other words in the sentence, as in the sentence "book a flight to London".
- *Sense ambiguity.* A word can have different meanings, for example, "bank" can be a financial institution or the side of a river.
- *Structural ambiguity.* The relationship between the phrases in the sentence is ambiguous, for example, "a flight to London arriving at 9". On a purely syntactic analysis, there are two possible readings, one in which the flight arrives at 9, and the other in which London arrives at 9 (see further below).

Ill-formed input was discussed in Chapter 3 in which it was shown that the sorts of utterances that occur in spoken dialogues are quite unlike the well-formed sentences that constitute the data for theoretical linguistics. The output from the speech recogniser is likely to contain misrecognised words as well as features of spontaneous speech, such as sentence fragments, after-thoughts, self-corrections, slips of the tongue or ungrammatical combinations.

Wide coverage natural language understanding is uncommon in current spoken dialogue systems, except for the more advanced research prototypes to be discussed in the final part of this book. Most systems use simple techniques involving the extraction of relevant values, such as flight times, from the string returned from the speech recogniser. These methods will be illustrated in greater detail in the chapters in Part II of this book. The remainder of this section will provide a brief introduction to syntactic and semantic approaches to language understanding.

Syntactic Approaches to Language Understanding

Natural language sentences can be described in terms of a set of rules that specify how words and phrases can be grouped together to form legal sentences of the language. For example, the following are some examples of the category Noun Phrase (NP) (see Table 4.1):

These phrases can be captured by a single rule:

NP → (Det) (Modifier) N (Post-Modifier)

which can be interpreted as stating that NP, the category on the left-hand side of the rule, consists of the constituents specified on the right-hand side of the rule. In this rule N is the head word of the phrase and all the other constituents in brackets are optional. Further rules would specify Modifiers and Post-Modifiers. For example, Modifiers can be Adjectives, while Post-Modifiers can be Prepositional Phrases ("to London") and Gerundive Verb Phrases ("arriving at 9"). Rules can be applied recursively. For example, a Noun Phrase can contain a Prepositional Phrase, which contains a Preposition and a further Noun Phrase:

NP → NP PP
PP → Prep NP

Structural ambiguity arises when the phrase structure rules permit more than one legal combination. Consider the following sentence:

4.4 John booked a seat on the train.

This sentence can be interpreted in two ways. In the first, the words "a seat on the train" are grouped together so that the phrase "on the train" modifies (or specifies) the phrase "a seat". In this interpretation, John books "a seat which is on the train", but we are not told where or when the booking takes place. This interpretation is represented by the tree diagram shown in Figure 4.6.

The second grouping separates "on the train" from "a seat", leading to the interpretation that the booking of the seat is done on the train. In this case the phrase "on the train" modifies the verb "booked". This interpretation is represented by the tree diagram shown in Figure 4.7. The main difference between the two trees occurs at the expansion of the VP (Verb Phrase) node:

Table 4.1. Sentences generated by the syntactic grammar rule

NP	Det	Modifier	N	Post-Modifier
1	a		seat	
2	a	cheap	flight	
3	a		flight	to London
4	a		flight	arriving at 9

Figure 4.6. Tree diagram 1 for "John booked a seat on the train."

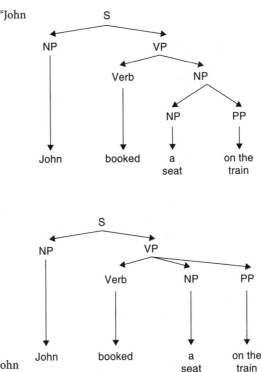

Figure 4.7. Tree diagram 2 for "John booked a seat on the train."

VP → Verb NP (Figure 4.6)
VP → Verb NP PP (Figure 4.7)

Similarly, NP also has two possible expansions:

NP → Det N (Figure 4.7) – "a seat";
NP → NP PP (Figure 4.6) – "a seat on the train";

which gives rise to the different groupings.

On a purely syntactic analysis there are no grounds for choosing between the two readings and disambiguation would have to be carried out at some later stage if the context suggests that one interpretation is more likely.

The type of grammar that has been illustrated here is a context-free grammar (CFG). CFGs can describe most of the structures that occur in natural language and have been widely used in natural language processing as well as in the specification of grammars for speech recognition. Much of theoretical linguistics since the late-1950s has been concerned with alternatives to CFGs, while in computational linguistics the predominant approach involves augmenting phrase structure rules with feature structures that can deal efficiently with complex linguistic phenomena such as agreement.

Syntactic analysis assigns a structure to a sentence that describes its syntactic constituents and the order in which they appear. This structure is not sufficient for meaning extraction, although in the traditional view the syntactic structure is considered necessary for semantic analysis to take place. In this view, often referred to as "compositional semantics", the meaning of a sentence derives from the meaning of its parts. Having determined the parts of the sentence through syntactic analysis, the meanings of those parts are determined through semantic analysis. The meaning of the complete sentence is then simply the combined meanings of its parts. Generally, some form of first-order predicate calculus is used to represent meaning within this view. The semantic analysis can be done after the syntactic analysis, but often syntactic and semantic rules are specified in pairs and the semantic analysis is then built up concurrently with the syntactic analysis.

The syntactic approach provides a detailed analysis of natural language using a small set of categories that can be applied universally. Various fine-grained distinctions can be captured that might be missed in other approaches. Take the following example, in which the distinction between "who" and "which" leads to a different interpretation:

4.5 List all members of the companies who/which are based in the city centre.

In one interpretation involving "who" the request is to list all the members (of some unspecified companies) who are based in the city centre. In the second interpretation involving "which" the request is to take all the companies that are based in the city centre and list all their members. Quite different results are likely to be produced according to which interpretation is selected.

Using logic to represent meaning has the advantage that its properties are well-understood and the logic provides standard mechanisms for reasoning. Logic-based representations are particularly useful for database query systems as the logical representation can act as an intermediate representation between the natural language sentence and a database query in a form such as SQL.

There are, however, some drawbacks to the syntactic approach. Generally a complete utterance has to be analysed before a meaning representation can be obtained. However, it is often the case that the string provided by the speech recognition component does not take the form of a complete sentence or, alternatively, is ill-formed with respect to the rules of the grammar. There are various ways in which the syntactic rules can be relaxed in order to accommodate these cases. An alternative approach, however, is to bypass syntactic analysis altogether and to derive a semantic representation directly from the input string. This approach, which is widely used in current spoken dialogue systems, is known generally as "semantic grammar".

Semantic Grammar: An Alternative Approach

A semantic grammar uses phrase structure rules in the same way as a CFG, but the constituents in a semantic grammar are classified in terms of their function or meaning rather than in terms of syntactic categories. For example, instead of syntactic categories such as NP, VP, PP, and so on, a semantic grammar will have categories such as "flight", "time", "location".

The theoretical basis for semantic grammar has its origins in case theory, a linguistic theory developed by Fillmore (1968). Case theory was concerned with the description of events in terms of a limited set of universal roles. For example, in relation to an action as specified by a verb, there could be a set of case roles such as "agent" (the initiator of the action), "patient" (the undergoer of the action), "location" (the location of the action). Schank's Conceptual Dependency Theory provided a similar set of categories that were used in a number of language understanding applications (Schank, 1975) (see Chapter 2).

Generally, however, semantic grammars for spoken dialogue systems and other natural language understanding systems are domain-specific. So, for example, a system involving flights will have categories relevant to the flight domain, such as "airline", "departure airport" and "flight number", whereas a system involving banking will have categories such as "account", "balance" and "transfer". Some categories are, of course, domain independent, such as dates, times and currencies, and in some development environments, such as VoiceXML, grammars for these categories are provided as built-in, reusable components. Otherwise the grammar for a new domain has to be created from scratch, usually by collecting a representative set of sentences that a user might say to the system and deriving a set of rules that covers this set.

The following example is a set of rules to cover the phrases in Table 4.1. The top level rule describes the domain of flight booking and the relevant concepts within this domain are flight cost, destination and arrival time. Concepts are enclosed in square brackets and can be rewritten as combinations of words and concepts. Optional items are denoted by the symbol*.

```
Semantic grammar: flight booking
flight-booking → [flight] *[destination] *[arrival_time]
[flight] → *a [cost] flight
[destination] → to [place]
[arrival_time] → arriving at [time]
[cost] → cheap | inexpensive | medium priced
[place] → London | Manchester | Glasgow
[time] → 1 | 2 | 3
```

Of course this grammar only covers a small range of phrases and a much larger set of rules would have to be devised to cover all possible ways in which the user might express a flight booking. For example, in specifying departure location and destination, many different phrasings are possible, such as:

```
4.6
1 from Belfast to London
2 to London from Belfast
3 from Belfast to London at 10
4 to London leaving Belfast at 10
5 departing at 10 from Belfast and arriving in London around 12
```

Developing a semantic grammar is often an iterative process of collecting representative data, devising a set of rules to cover the data, testing the system and collecting more data, adding more rules, and so on. The problem is that, compared with the syntactic approach, semantic grammars appear more "ad hoc" with little generalisability. However, their main advantage is that they provide a more robust approach to the analysis of spontaneous speech, which is often ill-formed and therefore less amenable to analysis using the syntactic approach.

Parsing

In the discussion so far, language understanding has been described in terms of the different types of grammar that can be used to represent natural language sentences. However, to produce parse trees such as those illustrated in Figures 4.6 and 4.7, some procedure is required to search through the grammar rules to find various ways of combining the rules to generate the parse trees. Such a procedure is known as "parsing". In many development environments the parsing mechanism is built-in and cannot be altered by the developer. For this reason only a brief description of parsing will be presented here.

One of the main distinctions is between top-down and bottom-up parsing. A top-down parser starts with the goal of proving that the input string matches the start symbol for the structure (e.g., S for a sentence, NP for a noun phrase, and so on). The parser proceeds by expanding the initial symbol using the grammar rules, then expanding this expansion, and so on, until the terminal symbols – the words in the string – are matched. A bottom-up parser works with the words in the input and tries to match them to a symbol in the right-hand side of a rule, then works its way upwards until all the symbols have been combined and a complete structure has been returned that specifies the string.

Top-down parsing has the advantage that it predicts structures from its expansions of rules and so will not consider combinations that cannot result in legal sentences. However, if there are alternative rules to expand, as will be the case for any realistic grammar, the top-down parser will have to systematically explore each of these until it finds the correct rules that specify the input. This process may involve expanding many incorrect rules and having to backtrack to explore alternatives. Bottom-up parsing has the advantage that it only builds structures that are consistent with the input. However, in so doing, it may build many irrelevant phrases that will not ultimately combine to form a complete high-level category, such as NP or S. Alternative rules lead to multiple backtracking, as with top-down parsing.

The solution to the problem of backtracking to explore alternative rules is to use a data structure to keep a record of the constituents parsed so far. This data structure is called a "chart". The chart stores partially parsed results along with a record of rules that have been matched partially but are still incomplete. Using a chart is more efficient as the same constituent never has to be parsed more than once, whereas with the more basic top-down and bottom-up algorithms constituents can be reparsed many times when the parser backtracks to explore alternative solutions. Chart parsing can be either top-down or bottom-up. Generally, in spoken dialogue applications, bottom-up chart parsers have been used as they provide a more robust solution, in that partial results can be returned in the form of phrases from the input without the need to construct a complete sentence. Thus the parser might return well-formed phrases in the input, such as "to London", "arriving at 9" and "a cheap flight" that are sufficient to extract the meaning of the utterance, even though the string is incomplete or ill-formed in terms of the rules of the grammar. The Phoenix parser, one of the most successful semantic grammar systems to be used in spoken dialogue systems, uses bottom-up chart parsing (Ward, 1991). The Phoenix system, which will be described in greater detail in Chapter 12, works by matching semantic fragments in the input with the patterns defined in the grammar. Because the system does not need to handle complete sentences, it is able to deal with many of the phenomena of spontaneous speech, such as restarts, repeats and grammatically ill-formed utterances.

Integration of the Speech Recognition and Natural Language Understanding Components

So far it has been assumed that the speech recogniser and the natural language understanding module are connected serially and that the speech module outputs a single string to be analysed by the language understanding module. Typically, however, the output from the speech recognition component is a set of ranked hypotheses, of which only a few will make sense when subjected to syntactic and semantic analysis. The most likely hypothesis may turn out not to be the string that is ranked as the best set of words identified by the speech recognition component. What this implies is that, as well as interpreting the string (or strings) output by the speech recogniser to provide a semantic interpretation, the language understanding module can provide an additional knowledge source to constrain the output of the speech recogniser. This in turn has implications for the system architecture, in particular for the ways in which the speech recognition and natural language understanding components can be linked or integrated.

The standard approach to integration involves selecting as a preferred hypothesis the string with the highest recognition score and then passing that string on for processing by the natural language component. The disadvantage of this approach is that strings may be rejected as unparsable that nevertheless represent what the speaker had actually said. In this case the recogniser would be over-constrained by the language component. Alternatively, if robust parsing were applied, the recogniser could be under-constrained, as a robust parser will attempt to make sense out of almost any word string.

One alternative approach to integration is word lattice parsing, in which the recogniser produces a set of scored word hypotheses and the natural language module attempts to find a grammatical utterance spanning the input signal that has the highest acoustic score. This approach becomes unacceptable in the case of word lattices containing large numbers of hypotheses, particularly when there is a large degree of word boundary uncertainty.

Another alternative is to use N-best filtering in which the recogniser outputs the n-best hypotheses (where N may range from between 10 to 100 sentence hypotheses), and these are then ranked by the language understanding component to determine the best-scoring hypothesis. This approach has the advantage of simplicity but the disadvantage of a high computational cost given a large value for N. Many practical systems have, however, produced acceptable results with values as low as $N = 5$, using robust processing if strict grammatical parsing was not successful with the top five recognition hypotheses.

Issues for Developers

Developers of spoken dialogue systems will normally be required to create speech recognition grammars that specify the words and phrases that the system can recognise following each prompt. Details of how to create these grammars are covered in Chapter 7 (for the Center for Spoken Language Understanding (CSLU) toolkit) and in Chapters 9 and 10 (for VoiceXML).

Whether a language understanding grammar is also required will depend on the system architecture. In many spoken dialogue systems the words and phrases returned by the speech recognition component are not processed by a natural language understanding component to determine their structure and meaning, but are passed directly to the dialogue management component. This will be the case for the systems to be developed in the CSLU toolkit and in VoiceXML, as shown in the chapters in Part II.

However, most of the more advanced systems, some of which will be described in Chapter 12, include a natural language understanding component that processes the more complex input from the user. Various types of grammar are used in these systems, including syntactic grammars and semantic grammars.

Creating a grammar is usually a matter of handcrafting the rules and testing them against a variety of input, then adjusting and adding to the rules and testing again. This process can continue over several iterations. For a limited application this may not be too difficult, for example, there are not too many ways in which a user can ask for flight information. Furthermore, for many recurring dialogues, reusable grammars are becoming available, for example, to input credit card information or an address. In larger scale applications grammar creation is a complex and costly process. For example, a grammar for an application such as the DARPA Communicator, which permits users to make complex queries for flights, hotels and car rentals, would have to be quite extensive to cover all the ways in which the user's queries might be expressed.

An alternative to handcrafting a grammar is to have the grammar rules acquired automatically from a corpus of dialogues that cover the same domain. Machine learning algorithms can be used to acquire the rules from such a corpus. However, it is often not possible to find a dialogue corpus that has identical coverage to the required domain. Nevertheless, as databanks of dialogues become more common, machine learning of grammars could become a more appropriate way of creating grammars as opposed to handcrafting them from scratch.

Language Generation

Once the requested information has been retrieved from the external source, the language generation component has to construct a natural language message that conveys that information. The retrieved information may take a variety of forms – tables of numeric data, database records, sequences of instructions on how to complete a task. The simplest methods use either canned text or templates, while more sophisticated and more flexible approaches involve the technology of natural language generation.

Canned text is used as output in many software systems. This is the easiest approach to implement and it is useful if the retrieved text represents the information that was requested by the user. A database field that contained textual descriptions of items would be sufficient to provide a response to basic queries. However, this approach is inflexible and wasteful.

Template filling provides a greater degree of flexibility in situations where a message can be produced many times with slight variations. Most current spoken dialogue systems involving information retrieval use template filling to generate the message to be spoken to the user.

In more sophisticated approaches that to date have only been used in research systems, language generation is viewed as a process of planning that begins with a communicative goal and ends with a linguistic message. This process can be divided into three main stages (Reiter and Dale, 2000):

- Document planning.
- Microplanning.
- Surface realisation.

Document Planning

Document planning involves determining what information should be included in the message (content selection) and how the message should be structured (discourse structure). Not all of the information that has been retrieved is appropriate to be spoken to the user. For example, it is not appropriate to convey long lists of information to a user using speech. Similarly, the information to be conveyed might differ according to different users. A user model enables the system to generate output that is appropriate for a particular user. The KNOME system, for example, provided different levels of explanation of Unix commands depending on its categorisation of the user's level of competence and the degree of difficulty of the command in question (Chin, 1989). Similarly, the TAILOR system adapted its output to the user's level of expertise by selecting the type of description and the particular information that would be appropriate for a given user (Paris, 1989). More recently, in the VICO system, which supports car drivers attempting to perform a range of tasks involving several modalities, tasks such as hotel selection are based on knowledge of the user's previous hotel preferences (Bernsen, 2003). Komatani et al. (2003) address the issue of how much information to convey to users of a city bus information system, while Whittaker et al. (2003) discuss the use of multiattribute decision theory to determine an optimal level of conciseness in the generation of information about restaurant and entertainment options in New York City.

The discourse structure of the message is important to support the user's understanding, particularly in a message consisting of several sentences. Some messages have a regular structure. For example, a set of instructions typically describes the required actions in the order of their execution, using connecting words such as "first", "next" and "finally". Well-structured texts can be modelled using schemas (McKeown, 1985). A schema sets out the main components of a text, using elements such as "identification", "analogy", "comparison" and "particular-illustration", which reflect how the text is organised sequentially.

A more elaborate approach, derived from Rhetorical Structure Theory, describes the relations between elements of a text (Mann and Thompson, 1988). The central element of a text ("nucleus") may be related to a more peripheral element ("satellite") by means of rhetorical relations such as "elaboration" and "contrast". Elaboration provides additional information about the content of the nucleus, as in:

4.7 There is a flight to London at 3 p.m. It arrives at 4.05.

Contrast presents items that are similar in some ways but different in others, as in:

4.8 There is an early morning flight to London. However, it has been delayed by 90 minutes.

Schemas can be implemented as grammars for use in text generation. They are computationally efficient and can be acquired fairly easily from a corpus of text. However, they are limited in terms of flexibility as the possible structures have to be determined in advance, and they are not easily ported to different domains. Rhetorical structures are more flexible and they can be implemented using techniques from artificial intelligence (AI) planning.

Microplanning

Microplanning takes the discourse plans output by the document planner and prepares the input that is to be sent to the surface realiser. There are three main tasks in microplanning:

1. Referring expressions.
2. Aggregation.
3. Lexical selection.

Dealing with referring expressions involves determining how to refer to an entity in a text within a particular context. For example, if some entity that has already been mentioned is to be referred to again, it should be possible to refer to that entity using a pronoun, as in Examples 4.7 and 4.8.

Aggregation is the issue of combining content into meaningful portions, for example, by using conjunctions or ellipsis, as in:

4.9
1 The flight departs at 9. It arrives at 10. (No aggregation.)
2 The flight departs at 9 and it arrives at 10. (Aggregation with conjunction.)
3 The flight departs at 9 and [ ] arrives at 10. (Aggregation with conjunction and ellipsis.)

Lexical selection involves choosing the appropriate words to express the content. In most simple systems a single lexical item is associated with each entity in the database. However, using different expressions provides more variation in the text, as in this example.

4.10
1 The first flight departs at 9. The second flight departs at 10. The third flight departs at 11. (No variation.)
2 The first flight departs at 9. The departure times of the next flights are 10 and 11.

Variation in lexical selection may be useful when outputting text to different users with different levels of expertise, for example, more technical terms for experienced users of some technology and more general descriptive terms to novice users.

Surface Realisation

Surface realisation is the process of converting the text specification output by the microplanner into linguistic text. There are two tasks:

1. Structure realisation.
2. Linguistic realisation.

Structure realisation involves the use of markup to convey the document structure. XML is becoming a standard for document markup.

Linguistic realisation involves choosing the words and syntactic structures to express the desired meaning. This includes inserting function words, choosing the correct inflections of content words, ordering the words within the sentence, and applying rules of spelling. A grammar is used that provides a set of choices for linguistic realisation, for example, between active and passive sentences, as in:

4.11
1 Bad weather has delayed the flight.
2 The flight has been delayed by bad weather.

Issues for Developers

As mentioned earlier, few spoken dialogue systems require spoken language generation. This is partly because the focus so far has mainly been on interpreting the spoken input. The results of the query have either been displayed visually, where this is possible, or are preprocessed so that they can be spoken by a TTS component. This preprocessing usually consists of no more than a few adjustments to the content, for example, breaking up long lists to make them more readable and putting the information into predesigned templates. More advanced systems that involve concept-to-speech translation will require much more sophisticated language generation capabilities.

Text-to-Speech Synthesis

Speech output involves the translation of the message constructed by the response generation component into spoken form. In the simplest cases, prerecorded canned speech may be used, sometimes with spaces to be filled by retrieved or previously recorded samples, as in:

4.12 You have a call from <Jason Smith>. Do you wish to take the call?

in which most of the message is prerecorded and the element in angle brackets is either synthesised or played from a recorded sample. This method works well when the messages to be output are constant, but synthetic speech is required when the text is variable and unpredictable, when large amounts of information have to be processed and selections spoken out, and when consistency of voice is required. In these cases TTS synthesis is used.

TTS synthesis can be seen as a two-stage process involving:

1. Text analysis.
2. Speech generation.

Text analysis of the input text produces a linguistic representation that can be used by the speech generation stage to produce synthetic speech by synthesising a speech waveform from the linguistic representation. The text analysis stage is sometimes referred to as "text-to-phoneme conversion", although this description does not cover the analysis of linguistic structure that is involved. The second stage, which is often referred to as "phoneme to speech conversion", involves the generation of a prosodic description (including rhythm and intonation), followed by speech generation which produces the final speech waveform. A considerable amount of research has been carried out in TTS synthesis (see, e.g., Carlson and Granström (1997); Edgington et al. (1996a, b), for recent overviews). This research has resulted in several commercially available TTS systems, such as DECTalk and the BT Laureate system (Page and Breen, 1996). The main aspects of TTS synthesis that are relevant to spoken dialogue systems will be reviewed briefly.

The text analysis stage of TTS synthesis comprises four tasks:

1. Text segmentation and normalisation.
2. Morphological analysis.
3. Syntactic tagging and parsing.
4. The modelling of continuous speech effects.

Text segmentation is concerned with the separation of the text into units such as paragraphs and sentences. In some cases this structure will already exist in the retrieved text, but there are many instances of ambiguous markers. For example, a full stop may be taken as a marker of a sentence boundary, but it is also used for several other functions such as marking an abbreviation "St.", as a component of a date "12.9.97", or as part of an acronym "M.I.5". Normalisation involves the interpretation of abbreviations and other standard forms such as dates, times and currencies, and their conversion into a form that can be spoken. In many cases ambiguity in the expressions has to be resolved, for example, "St." can be "street" or "saint".

Morphological analysis is required, on the one hand, to deal with the problem of storing pronunciations of large numbers of words that are morphological variants of one another and, on the other, to assist with pronunciation. Typically a pronunciation dictionary will store only the root forms of words, such as "write". The pronunciations of related forms, such as "writes" and "writing", can be derived using morphological rules. Similarly, words such as "staring" need to be analysed morphologically to establish their pronunciation. Potential root forms are "star" + "ing" and "stare" + "ing". The former is incorrect on the basis of a morphological rule that requires consonant doubling "starring", while the latter is correct because of the rule that requires "e-deletion" before the – "ing" form.

Tagging is required to determine the parts of speech of the words in the text and to permit a limited syntactic analysis, usually involving stochastic processing. A small number of words – estimated at between 1% and 2% of words in a typical lexicon (Edgington et al., 1996a, p. 69) – have alternative pronunciations depending on their part of speech. For example, "live" as a verb will rhyme with "give", but as an adjective it rhymes with "five". The part of speech also affects stress assignment within a word, for example, "record" as a noun is pronounced 'record (with the stress on the first syllable), and as a verb as re'cord (with the stress on the second syllable).

Modelling continuous speech effects is concerned with achieving naturally sounding speech when the words are spoken in a continuous sequence. Two problems are encountered. First, there are weak forms of words, involving mainly function words such as auxiliary verbs, determiners and prepositions. These words are often unstressed and given reduced or amended articulations in continuous speech. Without these adjustments the output sounds stilted and unnatural. The second problem involves coarticulation effects across word boundaries, which have the effect of deleting or changing sounds. For example, if the words "good" and "boy" are spoken together quickly, the /d/ in "good" is assimilated to the /b/ in "boy". Modelling these coarticulation effects is important for the production of naturally sounding speech.

There has been an increasing concern with the generation of prosody in speech synthesis, as poor prosody is often seen as a major problem for speech systems that tend to sound unnatural despite good modelling of the individual units of sound (Klabbers and van Santen, 2003). Prosody includes phrasing, pitch, loudness, tempo, and rhythm, and is used to convey differences in meaning as well as to convey attitude.

The speech generation process involves mapping from an abstract linguistic representation of the text, as provided by the text analysis stage, to a parametric continuous representation. Traditionally two main methods were used to model speech: "articulatory synthesis", which models characteristics of the vocal tract and speech articulators, and "formant synthesis", which models characteristics of the acoustic signal. Formant synthesis was used in commercial systems such as DECTalk with a high degree of intelligibility.

The most recent approach involves concatenative speech synthesis, in which prerecorded units of speech are stored in a speech database and selected and joined together in speech generation. The relevant units are usually not phonemes, due to the problems that arise with coarticulation, but diphones, which assist in the modelling of the transitions from one unit of sound to the next. Various algorithms have been developed for joining the units together smoothly (Rutten and Fackrell, 2003; Lambert et al., 2003).

Issues for Developers

Generally relatively little emphasis has been put on the speech output process by developers of spoken dialogue systems. This is partly due to the fact that TTS systems are commercially available that can be used to produce reasonably intelligible output. However, there are certain applications where more naturally sounding output is desirable, for example, in applications involving the synthesis of speech for users with disabilities, or in systems for foreign language instruction.

Most TTS systems have facilities for marking up the text that is to be spoken out by the TTS component, for example, to speak a string such as "5767185" as a telephone number, an integer, or as a string of digits. Other regular data structures such as dates, zip codes and currencies can be marked up to ensure that they are spoken correctly. Furthermore, it is also possible in most systems to mark up adjustments such as various prosodic features, volume, rate of speech, and so on. Specific examples of how to mark up text for a TTS will be presented in the chapters in Part II.

Summary

The basic input/output components of spoken dialogue systems that have been described in the preceding sections are technologies, each of which constitutes a major research and development area in its own right. An interesting aspect of spoken dialogue systems is that these separate technologies have to be somehow harnessed and integrated to produce an acceptable, working system. It is essential that the components of the system should work together, indeed, the efficiency of the individual components is less important than the efficiency of the complete system. For example, it can be argued that a system with a high performance speech recogniser would still be ineffective if the dialogue management component functioned poorly. Conversely, a good dialogue management component can often help compensate for the weaknesses of the speech recogniser by producing a reasonable response in the face of unreliable input. One of the major challenges for developers of spoken dialogue systems is to integrate the component technologies to produce a robust and acceptable system, in which the whole is greater than the sum of its parts. These issues are the subject of the next chapter, which examines the role of the dialogue management component.

Further Reading

There are several useful collections of papers on the different components of human language technology, in particular, Cole et al. (1997), Gibbon et al. (1997), Roe and Wilpon (1994) and Mitkov (2003). Allen (1995) is a standard textbook on natural language processing and includes a chapter on speech recognition. Jurafsky and Martin (2000) is a comprehensive textbook on speech and language processing with excellent chapters on speech recognition, language modelling, and syntactic and semantic analysis. See also Huang et al. (2001).

Exercises

Using the dialogue sample you transcribed in the exercise in Chapter 3 as a basis, determine the roles of the following components and assess what sorts of technologies seem to be used:

1. Speech recognition.
2. Language processing.
3. Language generation.
4. TTS synthesis.
5. External communication (e.g., to a database).

Dialogue Management

5

The Dialogue Manager is the central component of a dialogue system. The Dialogue Manager accepts spoken input from the user, produces messages to be communicated to the user, interacts with external knowledge sources, and generally controls the dialogue flow. There are various ways in which these dialogue management functions can be performed, depending to some extent on the type of task that is involved. At one end of the scale the task may involve a fairly simple interaction in which users retrieve information and perform routine transactions. At the other end of the scale are complex tasks involving negotiation and problem solving, which require a more advanced type of interaction.

The complexity of the task will be reflected in the level of spoken language that is to be used. This can range from a minimal subset of natural language, consisting perhaps of only a small set of words such as the digits 0–9 and the words "yes" and "no", through to large vocabulary systems supporting relatively free-form input. The input itself may be spoken or typed and may be combined with other input modes such as Dual Tone Multiple Frequency (DTMF) (touchtone) input, while the output may be spoken or displayed as text on a screen, and may be accompanied by visual output in the form of tables or images. Input and output for multimodal systems will be discussed in Chapter 11.

Dialogue systems can also be differentiated according to the extent to which one of the agents controls the initiative in the dialogue. A dialogue may be system-led, user-led or mixed-initiative. In a system-led dialogue the system asks a sequence of questions to elicit the required parameters of the task from the user. In a user-led dialogue the user controls the dialogue and asks the system questions in order to obtain information. In a mixed initiative dialogue control is shared. The user can ask questions at any time, but the system can also take control to elicit required information or to clarify unclear information.

These distinctions are reflected in the methods that can be used to control the dialogue flow. Controlling the dialogue flow involves, among other things, determining what questions the system should ask, in what order, and when. At one end of the scale the dialogue flow can be scripted as a sequence of choices in a dialogue network (or dialogue grammar). This control strategy is generally used for system-led dialogues. At the other end of the scale are more open-ended systems in which the choice of the next action is determined dynamically, based on the current state of the dialogue. In these systems the dialogue manager acts as an intelligent agent that makes rational decisions about how to manage the dialogue. This approach is often referred to as an "agent-based" approach. An agent-based dialogue manager will allow more flexible dialogues compared with a scripted approach.

Another issue for dialogue management is the way in which grounding is managed. Recall from Chapter 3 that grounding was described as the process whereby participants in dialogue try to ensure that what has been said in the dialogue has been mutually understood. Grounding involves verifying that utterances have been correctly understood and asking for clarification of utterances that are unclear or ambiguous. There are a number of ways to achieve grounding, ranging from simple confirmations to more complex grounding procedures.

This chapter discusses these issues in dialogue management, with a focus mainly on dialogues that are scripted and system-led. Mechanisms for making these dialogues more flexible with a limited degree of mixed-initiative are also discussed. The implementation of these types of dialogue will be presented in the chapters in Part II, while agent-based approaches will be reviewed in the chapters in Part III. The next section presents some examples that illustrate different types of dialogue initiative. Following this, strategies for implementing dialogue control are introduced. The final section examines methods for achieving grounding and, in particular, for dealing with problems of processing the user's input.

Dialogue Initiative

The process of dialogue between two humans can be viewed as an exchange of information in which the initiative may shift between the two participants. For example, at one time A might be asking all the questions, narrating some event, or commenting on some issue, while B might be in the role of listening and responding minimally. At a later point the roles might be reversed. In casual conversation initiative may be fairly evenly distributed and each person may initiate new topics as they see fit.

Generally speaking, in spoken dialogue systems the initiative does not change within a dialogue in the way it does in dialogues between humans. For this reason systems tend to fall into one of the following categories:

1. System-directed (the system has the initiative).
2. User-directed (the user has the initiative).
3. Mixed-initiative (the initiative is shared).

System-directed Dialogue

In a system-directed dialogue the system asks one or more questions to elicit some information from the user so that it can submit an appropriate query to the external knowledge source. Most current spoken dialogue systems are system-directed. The following is a typical example of a travel application in which the system has to find out the user's requirements, that consist of values for parameters such as destination, date and time of travel:

5.1
1 System: Where are you travelling to?
2 User: London.
3 System: What day do you wish to travel?
4 User: Friday.
5 System: At what time?
6 User: 9 a.m.

System-directed dialogues are generally constructed in such a way that the user's input is restricted to single words or phrases that provide responses to carefully designed system prompts. A major advantage of this form of dialogue control is that the required vocabulary and grammar for each response can be specified in advance. In this way speech recognition and language understanding are constrained and are likely to be more accurate. For simple dialogues of this type there are well-understood methods for design and implementation. However, the disadvantage is that these dialogues restrict the user's input to predetermined words and phrases, making correction of misrecognised items (see the section on verification) difficult as well as inhibiting the user's opportunity to take the initiative and ask questions or introduce new topics.

User-directed Dialogues

In a user-directed dialogue the user asks one or more questions that the system interprets and answers. A user-directed dialogue is rather like a natural language interface to a database, in which the user queries the database using natural language input. The dialogue systems developed under the Air Traffic Information System (ATIS) projects and the D'Homme project discussed in Chapter 1 involve user-directed dialogue. The following is an example:

5.2
1 User: How many employees living in the London area earn more than £50,000?
2 System: Fifty four.
3 User: How many are female?
4 System: Eleven.
5 User: And managers?
6 System: Nine.

In a user-directed dialogue the user determines the questions to be asked and the role of the system is to attempt to answer the questions. In some applications the system may ask clarification questions, if some aspect of the user's question is unclear. One disadvantage over system-directed dialogues is that the system needs to have comprehensive speech and language processing capabilities in order to process and interpret a potentially wide range of input. Furthermore, the user needs to be aware of the words and phrases that the system can interpret. As shown in Example 5.2, the system may also need the ability to keep track of the entities discussed in previous queries. For example, the elliptical query in utterance 3 ("how many are female?") has to be expanded into the query:

5.3 How many female employees living in the London area earn more than £50,000?

Similarly, the elliptical query in Example 5.2, utterance 5 ("and managers"), has to be interpreted as further constraining the set of employees to those who are female, living in the London area, earning more than £50,000, and managers.

Mixed-initiative Dialogue

In a mixed-initiative dialogue either participant can take the initiative to ask questions, initiate topics, request clarifications, and so on. The following is an example:

5.4
1 System: Where are you travelling to?
2 User: I want to fly to London on Friday.
3 System: At what time do you want to fly to London?
4 User: Are there any cheap flights?

In utterances 1–3 of this dialogue the system has the initiative and asks questions as in a system-directed dialogue. However, at utterance 4 the user does not respond to the system's question about the departure time, but rather asks a question about cheap flights. This is an example of a shift in initiative and is typical of naturally occurring dialogues between humans. Most current spoken dialogue systems do not attempt to address this type of initiative shifting, although some ways of addressing shifts of initiative have been attempted in more advanced research systems, as will be discussed in Part III.

Recently, the term "mixed-initiative dialogue" has been used in a more restricted sense, particularly within the VoiceXML framework, to describe dialogues in which the system has overall control of the dialogue but the user has some flexibility to volunteer more information than is requested in the system's questions. The following is an example:

5.5
1 System: Where are you travelling to?
2 User: I want to fly to London on Friday.
3 System: At what time do you want to fly to London?
4 User: 9 a.m.

In this example the user's response at utterance 2 is "over-informative" – it provides more information that was requested by the system's question. The analogy of a mixed-initiative system such as this is a form where the user can fill in the answers in any order or can provide answers to more than one question at a time. As long as the system can keep track of which questions in the form have been answered, the dialogue can proceed efficiently and only those questions that still need to be answered will be asked by the system. In this sort of mixed initiative system there is a set number of values to be acquired during the dialogue. The user may provide all of the values in the initial response, in which case the dialogue is complete and the system does not need to ask any further questions (except, perhaps, for verification). If all of the values are not provided initially, the dialogue becomes system-directed and the system asks for each of the remaining values in turn.

Dialogue Control

Alongside these distinctions between different types of dialogue initiative we can distinguish between methods for representing and implementing the flow of the dialogue. Systems in which the dialogue flow can be determined in advance and represented in terms of a dialogue network or grammar are often referred to as "finite state-based" systems. Systems in which the dialogue flow is determined dynamically through a process in which the dialogue manager performs some reasoning in order to determine its next actions are often referred to as "agent-based" systems. In between these two extremes are systems in which the dialogue control is not completely predetermined, as in finite state-based systems, yet not as open-ended, as in agent-based systems. This type of dialogue control, which is a way of implementing the limited mixed-initiative dialogues described earlier, is often referred to as "frame-based".

Finite State-based Dialogue Control

In a finite state-based system the dialogue structure can be represented in the form of a state transition network (or graph) in which the nodes represent the system's questions and the transitions between the nodes represent all the possible paths through the network. The graph specifies all legal dialogues and each state represents a stage in the dialogue in which some information is elicited from or confirmed with the user, or some action is performed by the system. Figure 5.1 is an example of a partial network for a travel system. According to this network the system asks a question about destination and then asks a verification question. If the user answers "yes", the system proceeds to the next question about the day of travel, otherwise the destination question is asked again. This process continues until the network has been traversed.

This is a very simple network that illustrates the basic principles of a finite state-based system. There are many ways in which dialogue networks can be extended to permit more complex dialogue sequencing. For example, subdialogues may be used to represent subasks in the dialogue, or tasks such as eliciting a date that occur frequently. In the Center for Spoken Language Understanding (CSLU) toolkit, for example, there is a default repair subdialogue to handle situations where the system cannot detect any input from the user, or when recognition accuracy is beneath an acceptable threshold (see Chapter 7).

A major advantage of the finite state model is its simplicity. State transition networks are a natural way of modelling dialogues that are system-directed and

Figure 5.1. Dialogue graph for a travel system.

that involve well-structured tasks and information that is to be exchanged in a predetermined sequence. Furthermore, there are some toolkits, such as the CSLU toolkit, that allow the dialogue flow to be represented graphically, thus providing an intuitive interface for the developer.

However, finite state dialogue models are inflexible. Because the dialogue paths are specified in advance, there is no way of managing deviations from these paths. Problems arise if the user needs to correct an item or introduce some information that was not foreseen at the time the dialogue flow was designed. Tasks involving some form of negotiation between system and user cannot be modelled using finite state methods, as the course of the dialogue cannot be determined in advance. For example, planning a journey may require the discussion of constraints that are unknown by either the system or the user at the outset.

Notwithstanding these drawbacks, the finite state-based approach is the most widely used form of dialogue control in commercial systems at the present time. Fewer technological demands are put on the system components, particularly the speech recogniser, as the user's responses can be constrained and therefore predicted. Given this restricted input, there is no requirement for a sophisticated natural language understanding component. Thus the lack of flexibility and naturalness may be justified as a trade-off against these technological demands.

Frame-based Dialogue Control

Frame-based dialogue systems are similar to finite state-based systems in that they are suitable for form-filling tasks in which the system asks the user a series of questions to gather information, and then consults the external knowledge source. However, whereas in a finite state-based system the order of the questions is determined in advance, in a frame-based system the questions do not have to be asked in a predetermined sequence. The frame-based approach is essentially a way of implementing the limited mixed-initiative dialogues discussed earlier. The following is an example:

5.6
1 System: Where are you travelling to?
2 User: I want to fly to London on Friday.

Assuming that there are three items to information to be elicited in this task – destination, date and departure time – two of these have been supplied by the user in one utterance. In a finite state-based system only one item of information can be supplied at a time. Indeed, given that the system would have a recognition grammar to recognise destinations following the system's prompt in 1, the speech recogniser might return "London" and ignore the remainder of the utterance. In this case the system would then proceed to the next question and ask for the travel date – which would obviously be confusing to the user at this point. Alternatively the recogniser might fail to return anything because the user's input did not sufficiently match anything in the recognition grammar. In this case the system would ask the user to repeat, leading potentially to the same problem all over again.

In order to permit this greater degree of flexibility, a frame-based system requires three components:

1. A frame (or template) that keeps track of the items of information that the system has to elicit from the user.
2. A more extensive recognition grammar.
3. A dialogue control algorithm that can determine the system's next actions based on the contents of the frame.

The frame can be a simple data structure consisting of a series of slots to be filled with appropriate values. The following is an example of a frame for Example 5.6 before the system's initial prompt:

Destination: unknown
Date: unknown
Departure time: unknown

The goal of the system is to find values for all the unknown slots. Following the user's utterance (2) in Example 5.6, the Destination and Date slots are filled with the appropriate values. Now the system only has to ask a question about the Departure time.

The frame can be more complex than this, however. For example, instead of having only two possible values – "unknown" and "filled" – a slot might also have a value indicating whether the value has been verified or not. Within this value there could be further distinctions, for example, the level of confidence in the filled value, and the way in which it was verified. These additional elements would have implications for the dialogue control algorithm in terms of the sorts of questions that the system should ask next. For example, a value with low confidence would require a more explicit form of verification, whereas a value with high confidence might not require any further verification and the item could be considered to be implicitly grounded.

A variant on the format of the frame presented here is the E-form, as discussed in Goddeau et al. (1996). E-forms were used in a spoken language interface to a database of classified advertisements for used cars. In E-forms the slots could have different priorities for different users, for example, for some users the colour of a car might be more critical than the model or mileage. Furthermore, information in slots might be related, for example, a more recent model usually costs more. The E-form allowed users to explore multiple combinations to find the car that best suited their preferences.

The second component of a frame-based system is the recognition grammar. This grammar has to be more complex than the grammars used in finite state-based systems, as the user has greater freedom of expression. For example, in response to the system's prompt in Example 5.6, the user's response might include various permutations of the three required elements, such as:

Destination
Destination + Date
Destination + Time
Destination + Date + Time
Destination + Time + Date

The grammar would require rules to match any of these combinations. Similarly, at later points in the dialogue, different combinations would be possible. Indeed, given that there could also be verification questions, the grammars required to handle all the combinations involving verifications and corrections by the users could soon become quite complex.

There are several different approaches to the implementation of mixed-initiative dialogue using frames. In VoiceXML an interaction involves processing a form that consists of one or more fields with values to be filled. In a directed dialogue the fields are filled in sequence (see Chapter 9). In a mixed-initiative form there is an ⟨initial⟩ element that is placed before any other fields in the form. This initial field allows the system to collect several values from the user's response to the initial prompt, given a suitable grammar that recognises these values in the input. The fields for those recognised values are then filled and the Form Interpretation Algorithm (FIA) will not revisit those fields. If any fields have not been filled, the system collects those values using a directed dialogue. This algorithm is an example of a more restricted frame-based approach as the possibility of mixed-initiative input is only available following the system's initial prompt, after which the system reverts to a finite state-based approach using directed dialogue. Implementing a mixed-initiative dialogue in VoiceXML will be illustrated in Chapter 10.

The Philips SpeechMania platform, which was used to develop the Philips Automatic Train Timetable Information System discussed in Chapter 2, permits more flexible mixed-initiative dialogue in which the user can input combinations of values at any point in the dialogue, as long as these combinations are specified in the grammar (Aust et al., 1995). Whereas in VoiceXML the dialogue is designed as a script, in SpeechMania a more declarative approach is taken using rules that take the form of condition-action pairs. The conditions describe the status of the values to be collected by the system and the questions specify how to elicit these values. The following is a simple example:

Condition:	Origin unknown and destination unknown.
Question:	Which route do you want to travel?
Condition:	Origin unknown.
Question:	Where do you want to travel from?
Condition:	Destination unknown.
Question:	Where do you want to travel to?

So, for example, if at a given point in the dialogue the dialogue frame (which is called the "status graph" in SpeechMania) shows that the destination and origin are both unknown, then the system will ask the question "Which route do you want to travel?" If only the origin is unknown, then the question "Where do you want to travel from?" will be asked. Given that all possible states in the dialogue are specified in this way, the dialogue control algorithm loops through these states, selects a state whose conditions are true at that point in the dialogue, and asks the question relevant to that state. If more than one state is returned, there are additional ways of narrowing down the selection until only one state is left. States are also given priorities which, in the default setting, ensure that ambiguities are resolved before values are verified, and values are verified before questions for new values are asked. Thus a dialogue evolves dynamically as a sequence of questions based on the current state of the system – What has been asked so far? What information is ambiguous? What has to be verified? This dynamic type of dialogue control can be contrasted with the finite state approach in which all the paths through the dialogue network are specified in advance.

The E-form discussed earlier uses a similar dynamic approach to determine the system's next response, based on the current status of the E-form, the most recent system prompt, and the number of items returned from the database. The following is a simplified version of the algorithm used in relation to the number of records retrieved by the system:

If no records are found, ask the user to be more general.

If fewer than five records are found, consider the search complete and generate a response that outputs the retrieved records.

Otherwise cycle through an ordered list of prompts choosing the first prompt whose slot in the E-form is empty.

If too many records have been found and all the prompt fields have been filled, ask the user to be more specific.

The frame-based approach has several advantages over the finite-state based approach, for the user as well as the developer. As far as the user is concerned, there is greater flexibility. For example, there is some evidence that it can be difficult to constrain users to the responses required by the system, even when the system prompts have been carefully designed to do just that (Eckert et al., 1995). The ability to use natural language and the use of multiple slot-filling enables the system to process the user's over-informative answers and corrections. In this way the transaction time for the dialogue can be reduced, resulting in a more efficient and more natural dialogue flow.

From a developer's perspective, implementing this degree of flexibility in a finite state-based system becomes cumbersome, if not impossible. A large number of states and transitions are required to deal with all the different paths through the dialogue network. A frame-based system can be specified declaratively and the dialogue control algorithm will find a path dynamically through the implicit dialogue network.

Thus frame-based systems provide a greater degree of flexibility than finite state-based systems. However, the dialogue context that contributes to the determination of the system's next action is fairly limited, being confined essentially to the analysis of the user's previous utterance in conjunction with a frame of slots to be filled and priorities to control the dialogue. Dialogues involving more complex interactions may require more sophisticated dialogue control due to factors such as the following:

- Different users may vary in the level of knowledge they bring to the task, so that a wide range of responses is required by the system.
- The state of the world may change dynamically during the course of the dialogue, with the result that it is not possible to specify all possible dialogue states in advance.
- The aim of the dialogue is not just to obtain sufficient information from the user to execute a database query or carry out some action – instead, the dialogue involves the negotiation of some task to be achieved, involving planning and other types of collaborative interaction.

Agent-based Dialogue Control

Agent-based approaches draw on techniques from Artificial Intelligence (AI) and focus on the modelling of dialogue as collaboration between intelligent agents to solve some problem or task. Compared with the form-filling tasks that can be implemented using finite state-based and frame-based methods, agent-based dialogue control is appropriate for more complex tasks, such as negotiation and problem solving. There are many variants on agent-based systems, depending on what particular aspects of intelligent behaviour are included in the system. The following dialogue illustrates a dialogue agent that displays intelligent, cooperative behaviour when answering the user's question (Sadek and de Mori, 1997):

5.7
1 User: I'm looking for a job in the Calais area. Are there any servers?
2 System: No, there aren't any employment servers for Calais. However, there is an employment server for Pas-de-Calais and an employment server for Lille. Are you interested in one of these?

In this example the system's answer to the user's request is negative. But rather than simply responding "no", the system attempts to provide a more cooperative response that might address the user's needs.

In agent-based systems communication is viewed as interaction between two agents, each of which is capable of reasoning about its own actions and beliefs, and sometimes also about the actions and beliefs of the other agent. The dialogue model takes the preceding context into account with the result that the dialogue evolves dynamically as a sequence of related steps that build on each other. Generally there are mechanisms for error detection and correction, and the system may use expectations to predict and interpret the user's next utterances. These systems tend to be mixed initiative, which means that the user can take control of the dialogue, introduce new topics, or make contributions that are not constrained by the previous system prompts. For this reason the form of the user's input cannot be determined in advance as consisting of a set number of words, phrases or concepts and, in the most complex systems, a sophisticated natural language understanding component is required to process the user's utterances. A number of agent-based systems will be discussed in Chapters 12 and 13 in Part III.

Grounding

The Dialogue Manager of a spoken dialogue system is confronted with a number of problems that do not normally arise in systems using a graphical user interface (GUI):

1. The system cannot guarantee that the representation of the user's input, that it receives from the speech recognition and language understanding components, is accurate.
2. There may be discrepancies between the information that the user requests and what is available in the external knowledge source.

Processing the User's Input

The dialogue manager receives a representation of what the user said from the speech recognition and language understanding components and decides what to do next on the basis of this input. However, the input from the user may be unclear or incomplete for a variety of reasons:

1. The speech recogniser may have detected silence even though the user had spoken. In this case no words will be returned.

2. Only a part of the user's utterance has been recognised and returned. The beginning of the user's input may have been cut off because the user began to speak before the speech recognition engine had started – typically, where the user spoke before a system beep. Alternatively, the end of the user's input could have been lost because the engine stopped listening too early – usually because a pause was detected that was interpreted as the end of the input.

3. All of the input has been captured but some or all of the words were incorrectly recognised.

4. Even though all the words were correctly recognised, the language understanding component was either unable to assign the correct meaning or there were a number of possible meanings due to ambiguity.

Clarification Subdialogues

The simplest approach to handling ill-formed or incomplete input is to simply report the problem back to the user and to request a reformulation of the input. The problem with this method is that it fails to distinguish the different ways in which the input may be ill-formed or incomplete, and it relies on the user knowing how to reformulate the input. A more useful approach is to address the problem explicitly. For example, if silence has been detected, the system can output a message such as:

5.8 Sorry I did not hear anything. Would you please speak a little louder.

If the system is unable to assign a meaning to the words returned by the recogniser, a message could be output such as:

5.9 Sorry I didn't quite understand that. Would you please rephrase?

Facilities exist within most toolkits for handling such commonly occurring problems. In VoiceXML, detection of silence is handled as a ⟨noinput⟩ event for which a default message is output. In the case where the input cannot be interpreted, a ⟨nomatch⟩ event is thrown with an appropriate message. In both cases the developer can change the default message and even devise a sequence of messages that provide increasing help in case the event is repeated without being resolved. These methods will be described in greater detail in Chapter 9. Similarly, in the CSLU toolkit there is a default repair subdialogue that is initiated if the system detects silence or is unable to interpret the input. Default messages are output and these can also be adapted by the developer (See chapter 7).

Verification

Even where no error requiring clarification has been detected, it is important that the system should verify that it has correctly understood the user. This process of "grounding", which was described in Chapter 3, ensures that what is communicated has been mutually understood and that common ground has been established between the system and the user. Verification is common in human–human dialogues where there is a potential for error, for example, human agents in call centres will verify important information such as credit card numbers, addresses and dates before proceeding with a transaction. Establishing common ground is even more necessary in spoken dialogues with computers given the possibility of recognition and understanding errors. There are two commonly used methods for verification: explicit verification and implicit verification.

Explicit Verification

Explicit verification takes the form of a question that asks explicitly for confirmation of the input. This may be accompanied by a request to answer with "yes" or "no":

  5.10 System: So you want to fly to London? (Please answer yes or no.)

Although this is a robust method for confirming values, the disadvantage is that it can become tedious for the user to explicitly verify each value and the number of turns required to complete the dialogue is increased. Verification can be deferred until all the values have been collected. However, this may lead to difficulties when one or more values are incorrect. Consider the following example:

  5.11
  1 System: Where are you travelling to?
  2 User: London.
  3 System: What day?
  4 User: Friday.
  5 System: So you want to travel to London on Sunday?

How is the user to correct "Sunday" to "Friday"? One obvious way would be to say something like "No, not Sunday, I said Friday". However, such a response is likely to be beyond the system's capabilities. (Recall that any user input must conform to the speech recognition grammar.) One way of dealing with the correction of items in the case of deferred verification is to explicitly ask the user which values are incorrect. The following is an example of this strategy:

  5.12
  1 System: Where are you travelling to?
  2 User: London.
  3 System: What day?
  4 User: Friday.
  5 System: So you want to travel to London on Sunday?
  6 User: No.
  7 System: Which value do you wish to correct: the destination or the day?
  8 User: Day.
  9 System: What day?

For this strategy to work, the user must know that only a "yes" or "no" answer is permitted in response to a verification question (as in utterances 5–6).

Following a "no" answer the system can then ask for the value to be corrected. This strategy is fairly robust; however it becomes more complex if more than one value is to be corrected. In this case, can the user say all the values that are to be corrected, which would require the system to have appropriate grammars to represent all possible permutations?

Implicit Verification

With implicit verification the system embeds in its next question a repetition of its understanding of what the user said in the response to the previous question. The user can still correct the repeated value, but if the user answers the next question without correcting the value, then that value has been implicitly confirmed. The following is an example:

> 5.13
> 1 User: I want to fly from Belfast to London.
> 2 System: At what time do you want to fly from Belfast to London?
> 3 User: Seven in the evening.

In utterance 2 the system includes the departure and destination cities that it has recognised in its question about the departure time. In utterance 3 the user gives the departure time but does not mention the departure and destination cities, so that these values are taken to be confirmed implicitly, as otherwise the user should have corrected them.

Using implicit verification can decrease the transaction time for a dialogue, as fewer questions need to be asked. The resulting dialogue also has a more natural flow. Implicit verification can be employed if the system is reasonably confident with the output from the speech recognition and language understanding components. One problem, however, is that implicit requests for verification can give rise to a wider range of possible responses, which may subsequently put greater demands on the recognition and understanding processes. For example, supposing that in utterance 2 in Example 5.13 the user had actually said:

> I want to fly from Belfast to Luton.

but the system had misrecognised "Luton" as "London" and produced the question in Example 5.13, utterance 2 ("At what time do you want to fly from Belfast to London?"). There are a number of ways that the user could correct "London" to "Luton", including the following:

> 5.14
> 1 No, not London, Luton.
> 2 Luton, not London.
> 3 I said Luton.
> 4 Belfast to Luton.
> 5 Belfast Luton.

Indeed there are many ways in which a single value could be corrected and the combinations increase in the case of more than one incorrect value. For the system to be able to interpret these corrections, the grammars supporting the speech recognition and language understanding components would need to cover all the possible ways in which the user might correct an implicit verification.

A further problem is that verification requests involve combining the values elicited from the user (either correctly or incorrectly) with the next value to be queried (e.g., in this case, the departure time). With even a relatively small number of values the combinatorial possibilities expand rapidly, giving rise to a large number of possible verification questions.

Finally, the implicit verification strategy relies on the convention that the user will correct the system if some value in the implicit verification question is incorrect. However, users may not realise that a correction is required, or they may think that they can correct the value later. A further possibility is that the user was more intent on answering the next question and did not attend to the items returned by the system in the implicit verification question, for example, that the system had incorrectly recognised "Luton" as "London".

Verification is one of the most challenging issues in spoken dialogue systems. A failure to verify correctly may lead to miscommunication, while an explicit verification strategy may result in an unreasonably lengthy dialogue, which has an adverse effect on user satisfaction. Considerable research is being directed toward the development of effective and efficient verification strategies that allow the system to degrade gracefully when faced with recognition or inter- pretation problems. For example, when grounding a value the system could first try implicit verification, then move to explicit verification, and finally to a more constrained mode such as an explicit "yes" or "no" or even spelling of the prob- lematic value. The following example illustrates this strategy:

5.15
   1 User: I want to fly from Belfast to Luton.
   2 System: At what time do you want to fly from Belfast to London?
   3 User: No, not London, Luton.
   4 System: Do you want to fly to London? Please answer yes or no.
   5 User: No.
   6 System: Please spell your destination.
   7 User: L-U-T-O-N.
   8 System: So you want to fly to Luton?
   9 User: Yes.
  10 System: At what time do you want to fly from Belfast to Luton?

Accessing Information from an External Knowledge Source

Once the system has elicited sufficient information from the user to determine what the user wants to know or to do, the next task is to consult the external knowledge source. The issue of how to connect a spoken dialogue system to an external knowledge source such as a database using the CSLU toolkit and VoiceXML will be discussed in Chapters 7 and 10. This section will review problems that arise when there are discrepancies between the information that the user requests and what is available in the external knowledge source. The following are common problems that may occur:

- The vocabulary of the dialogue does not map directly on to the vocabulary of the application.
- The data that is retrieved is ambiguous or indeterminate.

Problems with Vocabulary

If the terms extracted from the user's utterances do not correspond to the vocabulary of the knowledge source, then either no information, only partial information, or incorrect information will be returned. Problems can arise due to misspellings, different spellings of items such as names, abbreviations,or different ways of referring to the same item. Some of these problems may be handled in an ad hoc way by providing alternative representations of the items. A more general approach is to enhance the Dialogue Manager with an Information Manager that deals with complex information processing involving the application knowledge source (Whittaker and Attwater, 1996). A key structure in the Information Manager is the data model which contains a number of vocabulary models that are each associated with one vocabulary within the application, so that a distinction can be made between how items are represented in the database and how they may be referenced within a spoken dialogue.

Ambiguous and Indeterminate Data

Various methods have been developed to handle problems of ambiguous or indeterminate data, usually involving some mechanism that has been specifically devised to handle problems that have been predicted in advance. The Philips SpeechMania system had a mechanism for handling under-specified or ambiguous values (Aust et al., 1995). For example, more detailed representations were provided to disambiguate train stations with the same name (such as "Frankfurt am Main" and "Frankfurt an der Oder", which might both be referred to in a dialogue using the shorter name "Frankfurt"). There were also mechanisms for combining values, for example, if a user called in the afternoon with the utterance "today at 8", the two values were combined into the single value 20:00 hours given that the value 08:00 hours was no longer valid. Mechanisms such as these are generally developed on a fairly ad hoc way to handle ambiguity and indeterminacy that may arise in a particular domain.

Database access may be unsuccessful because a value did not find an exact match in the database. For example, a query concerning a flight to London at 8 p.m. might be unsuccessful, although there may be flights to London just before or just after this time. One approach is to relax some of the parameters of the query until a suitable result can be found in the database. A common approach in timetable enquiry systems is to relax the time on the assumption that the user might be satisfied with a departure around the requested time, but not necessarily at exactly the requested time. In other cases, it may not be clear which item should be relaxed. Take, for example, the following query:

5.16 Is there a train from Birmingham to London arriving around 10 in the morning?

Relaxing the time parameter might return trains arriving at 9 a.m. and 11 a.m. However, relaxing the transport parameter might return a flight or a bus that arrives around 10 a.m. In other cases, the user might even be happy with a change in the departure or destination cities, as would be the case with alternative airports in the same city. Making judgements about which parameters to relax requires detailed analysis of the domain, so that there may not be any general solutions to this problem.

Finally, there are problems concerning how the output is to be presented to the user. If a number of database solutions have been found, it is necessary to decide how many to present. While a large number of records can be presented to the user in tabular form in a graphical user interface (GUI), people are generally unwilling to listen to long lists of items and are likely to forget the details by the time the end of the list has been reached. One approach is to divide the records to be listed into small groups of less than five and to read these out in turn. However, this is still unsatisfactory in the case of large numbers of records, for example, 25 flights matching the user's query. An alternative method is to constrain the query so that fewer records are returned. For example, if the user requested flights from London to Boston, the system could ask for more specific parameters to constrain the query, such as flights with particular airlines, specific departure and arrival times, and so on. Again most of these methods are likely to be fairly domain-specific and it is difficult to devise more generally applicable solutions.

Knowledge Sources for Dialogue Management

The dialogue manager may draw on a number of knowledge sources, which are sometimes referred to collectively as the dialogue model. A dialogue model might include the following types of knowledge relevant to dialogue management:

1. *A dialogue history.* A record of the dialogue so far in terms of the propositions that have been discussed and the entities that have been mentioned. This representation provides a basis for conceptual coherence and for the resolution of anaphora and ellipsis.

2. *A task record.* A representation of the information to be gathered in the dialogue. This record, often referred to as a form, template or status graph, is used to determine what information has not yet been acquired. This record can also be used as a task memory (Aretoulaki and Ludwig, 1999) for cases where a user wishes to change the values of some parameters, such as an earlier departure time, but does not need to repeat the whole dialogue to provide the other values that remain unchanged.

3. *A world knowledge model.* This model contains general background information that supports any commonsense reasoning required by the system, for example, that Christmas day is December 25.

4. *A domain model.* A model with specific information about the domain in question, for example, flight information.

5. *A generic model of conversational competence.* This includes knowledge of the principles of conversational turn-taking and discourse obligations, for example, that an appropriate response to a request for information is to supply the information or provide a reason for not supplying it.

6. *A user model.* This model may contain relatively stable information about the user that may be relevant to the dialogue – such as the user's age, gender and preferences – as well as information that changes over the course of the dialogue, such as the user's goals, beliefs and intentions.

These knowledge sources are used in different ways and to different degrees according to the dialogue strategy chosen. In the case of a finite state-based system these models, if they exist at all, are represented implicitly in the system. For example, the items of information and the sequence in which they are acquired are predetermined and thus represented implicitly in the dialogue states. Similarly, if there is a user model, it is likely to be simple and to consist of a small number of elements that determine the dialogue flow. For example, the system could have a mechanism for looking up user information to determine whether the user has previous experience of this system. This information could then be used to allow different paths through the system (e.g., with less verbose instructions), or to address user preferences without having to ask for them.

Frame-based systems require an explicit task model as this information is used to determine what questions still need to be asked. This is the mechanism used by these systems to control the dialogue flow. Generally the user model, if one exists, would not need to be any more sophisticated than that described for state-based systems. Agent-based systems, on the other hand, require complex dialogue and user models as well as mechanisms for using these models as a basis for decisions on how to control the dialogue. Information about the dialogue history and the user can be used to constrain how the system interprets the user's subsequent utterances and to determine what the system should say and how it should be said. These sorts of modelling involve representations of discourse structure, of intentions, goals and beliefs, and of dialogue as a collaborative activity (see also Chapter 12). The different sorts of knowledge sources and how they can be used in conjunction with different dialogue control strategies are summarised in Table 5.1.

Issues for Developers

Dialogue management is the component of a spoken dialogue system where most development work is done. The developer has to make a number of choices regarding dialogue management and has to design and implement the dialogue manager according to these choices. The following are the tasks involved:

Table 5.1. Dialogue control strategies

Feature/Dialogue Control Strategy	State-based	Frame-based	Agent-based
Input	Single words or phrases.	Natural language with concept spotting.	Unrestricted natural language.
Verification	Explicit confirmation – either of each input or at end of transaction.	Explicit and implicit confirmation.	Grounding
Dialogue model	Information state represented implicitly in dialogue states. Dialogue control represented explicitly with control diagram.	Explicit representation of information states. Dialogue control represented with control algorithm.	Dialogue history Context Model of system's intentions, goals, beliefs.
User model	Simple model of user characteristics or preferences.	Simple model of user characteristics or preferences.	Model of user's intentions, goals, beliefs.

- *Choice of dialogue initiative.* Whether the dialogue system will be system-directed, user-directed or mixed-initiative. This choice will be determined partly on the basis of an analysis of the type of interaction that is required to accomplish the selected task, but also in the light of what resources are available. For example, user-directed and mixed-initiative systems will require robust and extensive speech recognition and natural language understanding components.

- *Choice of dialogue control strategy.* Whether the control strategy should be finite state-based, frame-based or agent-based. This choice will be determined partly by the choice of dialogue initiative, but also on the basis of available resources.

- *Design of system prompts.* A carefully designed system prompt can constrain the range of possible user responses and so assist the speech recognition and natural language understanding components, as well as minimising the occurrence of errors.

- *Choice of verification strategy.* Verification is required to ensure grounding of information between the system and the user. Choosing an appropriate verification strategy often involves a compromise between ensuring accuracy at all costs and avoiding very lengthy transactions.

- *Choice of error recovery strategy.* Error recovery involves detecting errors in the first place and methods can range from domain-specific checks to more general methods of error detection.

- *Designing and implementing links to external knowledge sources.* As described earlier, there can be problems in mapping between the vocabularies of a dialogue system and the vocabulary of an external knowledge source. Moreover, the data that is retrieved may often be ambiguous or indeterminate. While it is often maintained that a spoken dialogue system can be easily linked to existing back-end systems, such as application web servers, there are often issues that are unique to the mode of spoken interaction with these back-end systems that require careful consideration.

Many of these issues will be considered in later chapters. Chapter 6 will be concerned with the issues of design mentioned here, while Chapters 7–10 will illustrate various solutions to these issues as well as some of the available design and implementation tools that support the development of dialogue managers.

Summary

This chapter has provided a classification of spoken dialogue systems in terms of dialogue initiative and dialogue control strategy and has examined important issues such as the use of error recovery mechanisms and procedures for grounding. The next chapter considers the development lifecycle of a spoken dialogue system and considers issues of best practice as well as looking at empirical issues, such as the collection and use of corpora of dialogue materials.

Further Reading

There are a number of survey papers on spoken dialogue systems, including Androutsopoulos I and Aretoulaki M (2003), Giachin and McGlashan (1997), McTear (2002) and Sadek and de Mori (1997). Lai (2000) edited a special issue of *Communications of the ACM* on conversational interfaces. Zue (1997) and Glass (1999) review advances and challenges in spoken dialogue dialogue, discussing in particular the research of the Spoken Language Systems Group at MIT.

There are useful chapters on dialogue technology in some of the textbooks on speech processing and computational linguistics. Allen (1995) includes a chapter on conversational agents, Jurafsky and Martin (2000) on dialogue and conversational agents, and Huang et al. (2001) has chapters on spoken language understanding as well as on applications and user interfaces.

Exercise

Select one of the dialogue systems that you have examined in the exercises in earlier chapters that uses system-controlled dialogue. Imagine how the system might work in mixed-initiative mode. Construct some examples of dialogues that illustrate the system working in mixed-initiative mode.

Part II
Developing Spoken Dialogue Applications

Dialogue Engineering: The Dialogue Systems Development Lifecycle

6

The spoken dialogue systems development lifecycle is in many ways similar to the traditional software development lifecycle. There are a number of stages in the lifecycle: requirements analysis, functional specification, design, implementation, testing and evaluation. However, speech interfaces differ in many ways from traditional graphical user interfaces (GUIs). Speech is a very different input mode compared with the keyboard and mouse, particularly with respect to the fact that speech recognition is error-prone. Furthermore, the types of dialogue that can be conducted using speech differ from (GUI)-based interaction in terms of their structure, potential complexity, and the ways in which the dialogue initiative can shift between the system and the user. For these reasons a number of methodologies and guidelines have evolved over the past few years that are specific to speech-based interfaces. This chapter will review some of these methodologies and guidelines. A system for obtaining and updating information about students and courses, the Student Information System[1] will be used to illustrate the different stages in the development process (Rooney, 2002).

Requirements Analysis

The first stage in the development of a spoken dialogue system is to gather and analyse the requirements for the proposed system. The issues to be considered can be grouped into two main categories:

1. *Use case analysis.* The role and function of the system, user profiles, usage patterns.
2. *Spoken language requirements.* Vocabulary, grammars, interaction patterns.

---

[1] This system was developed by Elizabeth Rooney as part of the requirements for the MSc Informatics at the University of Ulster. The speech-based system developed in the dissertation is based on the current GUI-based Student System at Dundalk Institute of Technology (DKIT), Ireland.

Use Case Analysis

A use case analysis will help to determine the type of service to be provided by the system, the types of user who will make use of the system, and the general deployment environment for the system.

One of the first issues to consider is whether the proposed system is to replace or complement an existing system. Analysis of this issue will include analysis of market conditions, pricing, the role of human operators, and the views of unions, suppliers and customers. If the proposed system is to replace or complement an existing system, then it will be important to assess the costs and benefits of the new system. For example, the new system may add benefits such as being available at all times and being accessible to users who do not have access to a PC or the Internet. From the perspective of the service provider it is necessary to investigate whether the proposed system would bring potential savings compared with the current system, for example, in terms of savings on personnel costs. If the system is to replace or complement a system that is human-driven, there are issues to consider such as operator acceptance. Operators may welcome an automated system that relieves them of repetitive aspects of their work, but may feel threatened if the new system might eventually replace them. Customer satisfaction is another factor, as customers must feel that they will receive a service that is at least as good as the currently available service.

Analysis of the purpose of the system includes questions about the type of service to be provided, who will be using it, the tasks they will wish to complete, the sorts of information they will wish to retrieve, and how frequently they will use the system. Before adopting an automated speech system, it is important to consider whether automated speech is an appropriate medium for the proposed system. Some of the factors favouring a speech-based interface include its availability at all times as well as its accessibility, particularly when other modes of access to information and services are not available. A speech-based interface may also be more suitable in hands-free, eyes-busy environments, and for users with visual impairment or with limited use of their hands. Speech will not be suitable if the application involves a lot of graphics and visual material, if the environment in which the application is to be used is very noisy, and if the users have a hearing or speech impairment. The speech mode is suitable for delivering specific items of information, such as a flight time or stock quote, but is limited in comparison to a GUI as information has to be conveyed sequentially, speech is transient, and the user's ability to take in the information is restricted by their short-term memory. Finally, as speech recognition is error-prone and performance may vary across different users and environments, the interface may be less predictable than more traditional technologies such as GUIs.

Analysing the potential users of the system involves questions such as their motivation for using the system, whether many of the intended users will be nonnative speakers of the language in which the application will be written, whether there are major dialect and accent differences in the areas of deployment, and how comfortable the users are with automated applications.

Finally, an analysis of the deployment environment of the system will involve questions concerning the type of environment in which users will use the system (e.g., a quiet office, outdoors, a noisy shopping centre), the type of phone connection to be used (e.g., land-line, cordless, cellular), and how often users will use the system (e.g., regularly, occasionally, or rarely).

Spoken Language Requirements

The spoken language requirements of the system provide a description of the vocabulary, grammar and interaction patterns that are likely to be deployed in the system. Knowing these requirements will assist in determining the technologies that are to be used, for example, isolated versus continuous speech recognition, keyword spotting versus natural language understanding, and directed versus mixed-initiative dialogue. One way to determine these requirements is to study similar systems, using methods such as literature research; interviews with users to elicit the information required to construct the domain and task models; field-study observations or recordings of humans performing the tasks; field experiments, in which some parameters of the task are simulated; full-scale simulations; and rapid prototyping. Two of the most commonly applied methods will be described: the analysis of human–human dialogues and the use of simulations.

Analysis of Human–Human Dialogues

Human–human dialogues provide an insight into how humans engage in different types of dialogue. Considerable effort has gone into collecting corpora of relevant dialogues, many of which are publicly available, such as the Air Traffic Information System (ATIS) collections, the TRAINS corpus, the HCRC Maptask Corpus, and the Monroe corpus. The ATIS, TRAINS, and Maptask corpora involve task-oriented dialogues in fairly simple domains. The Monroe corpus, on the other hand, involves mixed-initiative human–human dialogues in a more complex domain (Stent, 2000). Analysis of a corpus of dialogues can provide information about the structure of the dialogues, the range of vocabulary and language structures used, how topics are introduced and negotiated, and how dialogue initiative is managed.

Analysis of human–human dialogues can also provide useful insights into potential differences between GUIs and speech-based interfaces. In the SpeechActs projects at Sun Microsystems Laboratories, the design of speech-based interfaces was initially influenced by existing graphical interfaces. However, findings from a predesign study of human–human interactions indicated differences in conversational style when users interacted with a human assistant to accomplish certain tasks compared with the interaction patterns that were used with the GUI (Yankelovich et al., 1995). One example involved looking up information in a colleague's calendar. For example, a manager, who was a heavy user of SUN's calendar GUI, asked his assistant "Next Monday – Can you get into John's calendar?" The operations that the assistant had to carry out involved selecting an item from the Browse menu specifying a colleague's ID and a machine name. However, the manager did not use the term "browse" and did not refer to the colleague's ID and machine name. Furthermore, the manager used a relative date ("next Monday") in the instructions spoken to the human operator, whereas absolute dates would be used in the GUI. The lesson learnt from the predesign study was that it was important when designing a speech interface to model the vocabulary and language structures used in human–human conversation rather than the terms used to refer to tasks in the corresponding GUI.

Simulations: The Wizard of Oz Method

One of the main problems with basing the design of a speech-based system on the analysis of human–human dialogues is that it is not always possible to generalise from unrestricted human–human dialogue to the more restricted human–computer dialogues that can be supported by current technology. Speech-based systems are restricted by speech recognition capabilities, limited vocabulary and grammatical coverage, and limited ability to tolerate and recover from error. If there is no existing speech-based system that can be analysed, the best way to collect data on how people might interact with such a system is to simulate the proposed system, collect data from these simulations, and analyse the data as a basis for the design.

The Wizard of Oz (WOZ) method is commonly used to investigate how humans might interact with a computer system (Fraser and Gilbert, 1991). In this method a human (the wizard) simulates the role of the computer, providing answers using a synthesised voice, and the user is made to believe that he or she is interacting with a computer. The two participants should be physically separated, with a partition between them, in separate rooms, or even in different locations, with communication by telephone. The wizard should have a script of the interaction containing the system prompts, and the commands and queries that the user can ask. The interaction usually involves one or more scenarios, in which the user has to find out one or more pieces of information from the system, for example, a flight arrival time and the arrival terminal. The use of a series of carefully designed WOZ simulated systems enables designs to be developed iteratively and evaluation to be carried out before significant resources have been invested in system building (Gibbon et al., 1997). A detailed description of the use of WOZ in the Danish Dialogue Project can be found in Bernsen et al. (1998).

However, one of the greatest difficulties in implementing the WOZ method is that it is difficult for a human experimenter to behave exactly as a computer would, and to anticipate the sorts of recognition and understanding problems that might occur in an actual system. To overcome this disadvantage, the "System in the Loop" method may be used. In this method a system with limited functionality is used to collect data. For example, the system might incorporate on the first cycle speech recognition and speech understanding modules, but the main dialogue management component may still be missing. On successive cycles additional components can be added and the functionality of the system increased, thus permitting more data to be collected. It is also possible to combine this method with the WOZ method, in which the human wizard simulates those parts of the system that have not yet been implemented.

Example: Requirements Analysis for the Student Information System

This example illustrates the process of requirements analysis for a voice-based Student Information System. The system is based on an existing GUI-based system which is used to perform a number of tasks, such as obtaining details about students, creating, editing, deleting and amending course and subject details, recording general statistics on student results, and creating reports for a marks register and for continuous assessment. An important aspect of the requirements analysis is to determine which aspects of the functionality of the current GUI-based system are appropriate for implementation in a speech-based interface and also whether new functionality needs to be introduced in the voice-based system.

A predesign study of human–human dialogue along with observations of how users communicate with the current GUI system were used as a basis for the analysis. User and usage profiles were developed for the proposed system in order to identify the environments in which the system would be used and the user characteristics and requirements that would influence the design of the system. Table 6.1 presents a selection of the questions that were asked in order to determine the user profile. The answers to the questions determine the nature of the application and the level of expertise the users have with spoken language applications. For example, the information obtained has a bearing on the design of prompts, whether barge-in and the Dual Tone Multiple Frequency (DTMF)

Table 6.1. User profile for the student system

Question	Answer
What type of user (admin, academic)?	Both
Demographics (sex, age, education)?	Ranges from 18–60
Experience with spoken language system?	None
How much help will be required?	Basic help until familiar with the application – then option to move quickly to perform tasks.
Motivation for using system?	Simpler way to gain information.
Multilingual dialogue?	Not required.
Most common tasks performed?	Create and query personal details, course details, subject details. Produce student reports.
Familiarity of user with tasks?	Very familiar with GUI-based system.

might be required, and whether the dialogue control should be directed or mixed-initiative.

The usage profile was used to determine system and hardware requirements. Table 6.2 presents some of the questions asked in relation to usage. Once the user and usage profiles had been created, the next stage was to determine the tasks that users were required to carry out in order to achieve their goals when using the existing GUI-based system, and then to identify those tasks that were most suited to a speech-based system. It was decided not to translate all of the elements of the graphical interface to the speech-based interface, partly because of the large number of options in the graphical interface that could be easily manipulated by pointing and clicking but would be more difficult to navigate using speech. The speech-based system was broken down into three main groups – Student Details, Course Details, and Reports. These groups are shown in Table 6.3 along with an indication of the main functionality required.

As a result of the predesign studies of human–human dialogues and of the WOZ studies a corpus of dialogues was collected that could be used in the specification and design of the speech-based system. The following is an example of one of these dialogues:

Table 6.2. Usage profile for the student system

Question	Answer
Number of callers – How often?	One per department – daily during normal term time. 2–3 during exam times.
Frequency of use?	Daily
Availability of application 7 × 24 × 365?	Monday to Friday
Access Hours?	9–5
Concurrency requirements?	None at moment.
Input device type?	Telephone
Output device type?	Telephone
Environment – quiet/noise background, etc.?	Varies

Table 6.3. Task analysis for the speech-based Student Information System

STUDENT INFORMATION SYSTEM		
Component	Functionality	Additional detail
Personal details	View student details Edit student details Add student details	
Course details	Course information	Course code Subject details
Reports	Marks register Exam letters Continuous assessment	
	Results	By subject By course
	Stage stats	Number of students who sat exam.
	Subject stats	Details of who got what results.

6.1
```
 1 System:  Welcome to the Student System Main Menu.
 2         Please say your username.
 3 User:    Liz.
 4 System:  Thank you.
 5         Now please say your four digit pin.
 6 User:    6 5 6 6.
 7 System:  Was that 6 5 6 6?
 8 User:    Yes.
 9 System:  The system provides details on students, courses and reports.
10         For students say students or press 1, for courses say courses or press
           2, for reports say reports or press 3.
11 User:    Students.
12 System:  This is Student Details.
13         Say "View details" to view existing student details.
14         Say "Add details" to add new student details.
15 User:    View details.
16 System:  Viewing student details.
17         What is the student id.
18 User:    96050918.
19 System:  I have the following details: student John Scott, course code DK003, at
           stage 1.
20         Would you like any more information?
21 User:    Courses.
```

This dialogue includes the following elements:

- Prompt and response (e.g., 2–3), also with verification (7–8).
- Digit recognition (6, 18).
- DTMF input (10).
- Retrieval of information from a database (19).
- Global navigation (21).

Analysis of the dialogues revealed that experienced users often preferred to include several parameters within a single utterance. For example, when obtaining details of a particular course, the user might say: "coursecode dk003, stage award, subject code 01".

Once sufficient data has been gathered regarding the requirements of the system, the next stage is to develop a more formal specification of the requirements.

Requirements Specification

Requirements specification (also known as Functional Specification) involves setting out in a formal document the details of what the system should do. The requirements can be listed in natural language under a set of headings or can be specified using a particular notation or tool, such as the Volere template (Robertson and Robertson, 1999). Requirements specification for interactive speech systems has been addressed in a number of projects funded by the

European Union, for example, EAGLES (Gibbon et al., 1997) and DISC (www.disc2.dk), and has also been described in detail in Bernsen et al. (1998).

Volere is an exhaustive requirements specification process in which each requirement is identified and listed. Several different types of requirement are considered, including the following:

Project drivers. These requirements describe the purpose of the project, the project personnel, stakeholders and users.

Project constraints. These requirements identify factors such as how the system might interface with existing systems, including hardware, software or business practice, as well as other constraints, such as budgets and timescales.

Functional requirements. These requirements specify in measurable terms the scope of the system, the services that the system should provide and its data requirements.

Nonfunctional requirements. These are properties of the specified functions, such as "look and feel", performance, usability and operational requirements. Other nonfunctional requirements describe maintainability, portability, security, and cultural, political and legal factors.

Project issues. This is a definition of the conditions under which the project will be done, including factors that contribute to the success or failure of the project.

An alternative approach, based on research in the Danish Dialogue Project and in a number of associated projects funded by the European Union, is described in Bernsen et al. (1998). This method is intended specifically for interactive speech projects and has been recently extended to include multimodal systems. Two sets of documents are used to specify the system requirements:

1. A Design Space Development (DSD).
2. A Design Rationale (DR).

A DSD document (or frame) represents the design space structure and designer commitments at a given point during the system design, so that a series of DSDs provide snapshots of the evolving design process. A DSD contains information about general constraints and criteria as well as the application of these constraints and criteria to the system under development.

A DR frame represents the reasoning about a particular design problem. The DR contains information concerning the justification for the original specification, a list of possible options, the resolution adopted, and comments. In this way the evolving design and its rationale are comprehensively documented.

Example: Requirements Specification for the Student Information System

In this section some examples are presented that illustrate requirements specification using the Volere process. Examples of DSD documents and DR frames can be found in Bernsen et al. (1998, pp. 72–75).

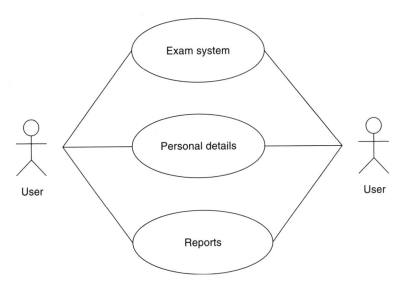

Figure 6.1. Top level Use Case Diagram for the Student Information System.

Use Case Diagrams

Use Case Diagrams are used to describe and model the functionality of the system from the perspective of the user. These diagrams are used to provide a Use Case Specification from which the functional requirements can be derived. Figure 6.1 shows the Top-level Use Case Diagram for the Student Information System, which consists of the following main use cases:

1. Exam system.
2. Personal details.
3. Reports.

   Further Use Case Diagrams would be provided for each additional use case.

Use Case Specifications

The Use Case Specifications detail the elements of each Use Case based on the Use Case Diagrams. An example is shown in Table 6.4.

Functional Requirements

An example of a Functional Requirement for the task of viewing and amending student details is shown in Table 6.5. It is assumed that other Functional Requirements and Use Case Specifications have been listed.

Nonfunctional Requirements

Table 6.6 shows an example of a nonfunctional requirement concerned with the recognition of speech input.

Table 6.4. Use Case Specification for the top-level options

Use Case	3.1.4 Top-level selection
Flow of events	System prompts actor to select from exam system, personal details or reports.
	Actor speaks one of the options: exam system, personal details, reports.
	System recognises the actor's input and enters the selected use case.
Alternative flow	The actor's input is not recognised.
	The system prompts the actor to speak his/her choice again.
Pre-conditions	The actor must be logged into the system.
Post-conditions	If successful, the system enters the selected use case.
	If unsuccessful, the system state is unchanged.

Table 6.5. Functional requirement: Viewing and amending student details

Number	4	Conflicts: N/A
Description	The user must be able to view and amend student details.	
Rationale	Each user should be able to access details on students and update the details with new information.	
Type	Functional User Requirement	
Dependencies	1, 2, 3	Event/Use Case: 3.1.3
Support	Section 7.2.1	
History	N/A	
	Qual. Number	Qualification
	UQ 17.1	The user must be able to view all student details.
	UQ 17.2	The user must be able to amend all student details.

Table 6.6. Nonfunctional requirement: Speech recognition performance

Number	14	Conflicts: Functional Requirements
Description	All valid speech input must be recognised by the system by the third attempt of input.	
Rationale	If the system cannot recognise valid speech input of good audio quality the system will not be used by users.	
Type	Nonfunctional user requirement.	

Hardware/Software Requirements

These requirements will be determined partly by the development platform to be used. Several different development platforms are used in Chapters 7–11 to illustrate the process of implementation of spoken dialogue systems. Details of the hardware and software requirements of these platforms are provided in Appendices 2–4.

Design

Whereas the requirements specification phase is concerned with describing what the system is intended to do, the design phase is concerned with describing how the system will achieve these functional specifications. The end result of the design phase is to provide a basis for the implementation of the system. Design can be broken down into high- and low-level design.

High-level design includes the description of the overall architecture of the system in terms of the different components and how they relate to each other; the flow of data within the system; the tasks to be performed by the user; the dialogue flow; dialogue elements, such as prompts, system help, recognition grammars and navigational commands; and external applications such as databases.

Low-level design is concerned with decisions that involve the usability and performance of the system, such as consistency, sound and feel, word choice and error handling.

Example: Design of the Student Information System

An abstract view of the overall architecture of the Student Information System is shown in Figure 6.2. The system consists of a spoken dialogue system that interacts with the user and an external application (database). The development of the database will not be considered further in this chapter, as the main focus is on issues relating to spoken dialogue technology and there are many excellent texts that cover database development in detail. Of course, in a fully deployed system the database would be an integral part of the system and it could be the case that much of the functionality of the spoken dialogue system would be determined by the nature and structure of the database.

The tasks that the user will perform can be shown in a Task Hierarchical Diagram (THD) that illustrates the user interface from the viewpoint of the user. A THD describes each task, which can be further decomposed into subtasks. Figure 6.3 is a THD for the Student Information System, beginning with login and progressing to the main menu, where a selection is made from one of the

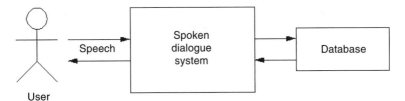

Figure 6.2. Overall architecture of the Student Information System.

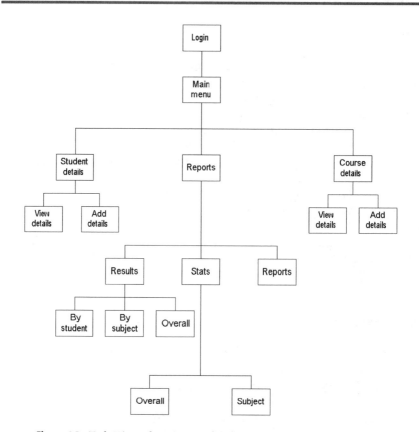

Figure 6.3. Task Hierarchy Diagram for the Student Information System.

three options available. Each of these choices then leads to a further set of selections, as shown in Figure 6.3.

Each task in the THD is likely to involve some sort of interaction between the user and the system which, in the case of the speech-based Student Information System, will take the form of spoken dialogues. The dialogue flow, which can be represented as a flowchart, state transition network, or dialogue grammar, should specify all reachable states in the dialogue. Information should also be included about what actions should be performed in each state, how to decide which state should be the next, and whether there are interactions with other applications such as databases. Figure 6.4 shows the login dialogue, including the prompts, user response types (e.g., username, password) and some indication of how invalid input is handled. Validation of user input at login may consist of two stages:

1. Whether the input is legitimate, e.g., a username may have to be a string of four digits (can be validated locally by the system).
2. Whether the input corresponds to an existing entry in the database (validated by consulting the database).

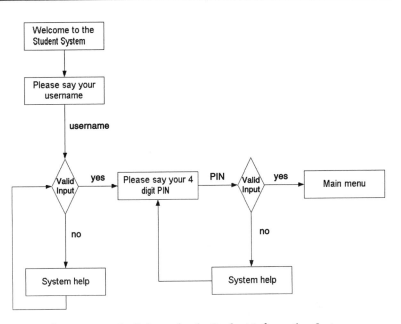

Figure 6.4. Login dialogue for the Student Information System.

For simplicity these interactions are not included in Figure 6.4, but they would need to be included in the specification of a complete system.

Figure 6.5 shows the dialogue flow for the main menu, including prompts, user responses and the handling of invalid input. The user responses are high-level descriptions of what the user can say following each prompt. The actual words that can be recognised by the system would be specified in the recognition grammars associated with each prompt.

Invalid input in this dialogue refers to words that are not specified in the recognition grammar for the prompt. In Figure 6.5 invalid input leads to System Help. A further refinement of this case might involve a reprompt, possibly with some rephrasing. Figure 6.5 also omits further details, such as the dialogues that ensue on transition to the states Student Details, Course Details, Results, Stats and Reports. Normally, further diagrams would be created for these tasks and so on for further subtasks.

The dialogue flow diagrams should also include information about interactions with other applications, such as databases. Figure 6.6 shows the dialogue flow for the "View Student Details" task, which, if successful, results in a database request to retrieve student details.

The design of the system as shown in the diagrams so far is similar to the design of any interactive system. The only difference is that in a GUI-based system the user responses would involve selecting items from drop-down boxes or clicking on choices using the mouse, whereas in a speech-based system these choices are made using speech. Subsequent design issues to be discussed below apply uniquely to speech-based interfaces.

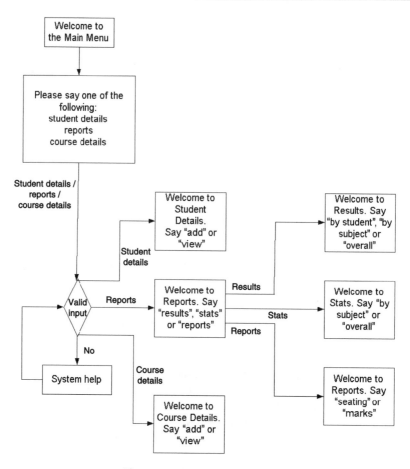

Figure 6.5. Main menu dialogue.

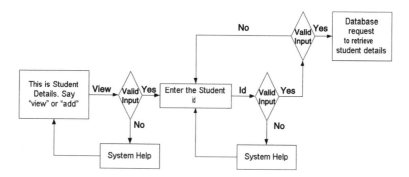

Figure 6.6. Dialogue flow for the "View Student Details" dialogue.

Full-duplex (Barge-in) or Half-duplex Implementation

Barge-in allows experienced users to interrupt system prompts when they know what to say. In this way a dialogue can be completed more quickly and the user does not have to listen to lengthy prompts and instructions. Given the usage patterns identified in the requirements analysis stage, it was decided that barge-in would be appropriate, if available on the selected implementation platform, as users would quickly become familiar with the features of the system and should therefore be able to interrupt the system prompts in order to arrive more quickly at their chosen options.

Prompts

Prompts can be output using either professionally recorded prompts or synthesised speech (text-to-speech (TTS)). Most commercial systems use recorded prompts as these provide a more natural pronunciation. TTS is useful during the development of a system as the TTS prompts can be changed more easily than recorded prompts. TTS is also required when outputting data that cannot be predicted in advance, such as news items or emails. It was decided to use TTS for prompts in the prototype system. Recorded prompts would be recommended for a fully deployed system.

The careful design of system prompts can reduce potential errors by constraining what the user might say in response to the prompt. For this reason prompt design figures extensively in most design guidelines for spoken dialogue systems. The system prompts for the Student Information System were designed with these guidelines in mind. As first-time users would not be likely to have experience of speech-based interfaces, it was important to provide helpful prompts to guide these users. As they became more familiar with the system, there should be prompts that enable them to perform a transaction more quickly and more efficiently.

There are various types of prompts that can be used at different points in a dialogue:

Tapered prompts: These involve shortening the prompt on subsequent attempts to elicit missing information from the user in a reprompt:

    6.2
    1 System: Say the course code, stage, subject code and year.
    2 User: dk003, csm, 2002.
    3 System: What stage?

In this example the system has initially tried to elicit four items of information with a single prompt. The user has responded with three items, so the next prompt asks only for the missing item.

Incremental prompts: These are the opposite of tapered prompts as they provide more detailed instructions on what to do in the case of a problem such as misrecognition:

    6.3
    1 System: Please say view or add.
    2 User: (unrecognized input)

3 System: Sorry I didn't get that. Please say view or add or use the keypad: press 1 for view and 2 for add.

Leading prompts: These prompts guide the user by indicating which words should be provided in the user's response:

6.4
System: This is Student Details. To add Student Details say Add. To view Student Details say View.

Grammars

Grammars specify what a user can say at a given point in the dialogue. Grammars can be simple, including only basic words and phrases, or complex, allowing the user to express a number of concepts in several different ways. Various factors determine the choice of grammar type. A simple grammar is easier to construct and maintain, but restricts what the user can say and may result in lengthier interactions as the user can only say one thing at a time. A complex grammar gives the user more flexibility and provides a more natural interface. However, complex grammars are more difficult to construct and it is not easy to predict all the ways in which a user might say something if they are allowed greater flexibility. This issue can be addressed to some extent by designing prompts in such a way so as to indicate to the user the sorts of things that can be said as a response.

Simple and complex grammars were used in the system, according to the interaction style selected for the dialogues (see Interaction Style, below). The following is an example of a simple grammar for usernames to be used in the Login dialogue:

username → liz | margaret | mike | guest

This grammar requires the user to speak one of the four choices of username.

The following is an extract from a complex grammar to be used when viewing student details:

viewdetails → (give me details on) (student) studentid (on) coursecode (on | at) (stage) coursestage
studentid → 96050918 | 96069783 | 96317159 | 96561921
coursecode → diploma in applications and support | dk003 | diploma in software development | dk004
coursestage → 1 | award

This grammar, in which optional items are in parentheses, would allow a user to speak sentences such as:

6.5
1 Give me details on student 96050918 on dk003 at stage award.
2 96050918 dk003 award.

along with many other variations.

There are also some specific grammar types that are often provided as built-in grammars. These include recognisers for digits, alphanumeric strings, dates, phone numbers and currency. Built-in grammars provide consistency across applications. In the current system special grammars were required for digits (for student IDs) and alphanumeric strings (for course codes).

DTMF grammars may be useful for digit recognition, which is error-prone, and for sensitive transactions that users would not want overheard, such as passwords or credit card numbers. It is important to decide when DTMF is to be used instead of speech to avoid confusing the user as to which mode of input is permitted at a given point in the dialogue. DTMF grammars were used in the current system when initial recognition of digit strings by speech was unsuccessful, or if the system failed to recognize the user's choice of an option, as illustrated in Example 6.3.

Interaction Style: Directed Dialogue or Mixed Initiative

Directed dialogues are easier to design and require simple grammars, but have the disadvantage that they generally require longer transaction times to complete the dialogue. Mixed initiative dialogues are more natural and flexible, but require greater resources in terms of grammars for natural language understanding and structures to keep a record of the dialogue history. It was decided that certain dialogues within the system could be suitable for a mixed-initiative style, for example:

Student details: In this dialogue the user can enter details in any order to retrieve student details, e.g., name, date of birth, address.

Reports: In this dialogue the user can enter details in any order to retrieve student details, e.g., course code, stage, year.

Other dialogues, such as "login" and "main menu" were more suited to a directed dialogue mode.

Navigation Commands

Speech systems should have commands that are always active, such as "help", "go back", "repeat", "exit" and "what-can-i-say". Some implementation platforms provide commands such as these as standard. The Student Information System provides global navigation commands that are available anywhere in the application, including "main menu", "start over", and a series of words for quitting, including "quit", "quit application", "exit". If possible, there should also be commands for switching from one task to another by saying a command such as "Student Details" or "Course Details".

System Help

Help can be implemented either through a separate "help" dialogue or through self-revealing help. Using a separate subdialogue for help means that the system must be able to return to the state that it left when it entered help. Many platforms provide support for this sort of subdialogue. Self-revealing help uses a sequence of prompts that provide progressively greater levels of help at each turn. This type of help is more context-sensitive, but requires multiple prompts to be provided for each turn in the dialogue. It was decided to include both types of help, depending on the facilities provided by the development platform.

Consistency

Consistency in an interface allows the user to become familiar with the application more rapidly. In the current system considerations include:

- Terminology: Using the same words to refer to an object or event rather than synonyms.
- Personality: Using same wording, attitude and style.
- Use of DTMF.
- Timing, e.g., of pauses between menu items.
- Timeout, i.e., how long the system waits for the input before reprompting.
- Consistent and intuitive dialogue structure, enabling the user to know what they should say at any point in the dialogue.

Confirmation

Since speech recognition technology cannot guarantee that the system heard exactly what the user said, the system should confirm what the user wants, especially if the next action could result in unrecoverable consequences. However, confirming user input is time-consuming and interrupts the natural flow of the dialogue. Decisions have to be made as to whether a confirmation needs to be done, and if so, whether it should be done after each item is acquired and whether more than one item can be confirmed at a time. Issues regarding choice of confirmation strategy were discussed in Chapter 5. Generally explicit confirmation following each input of information by the user was recommended for the Student Information System.

Implementation

Implementation involves taking the design documents, selecting a method of implementation, and then translating the design into a working system. The details of how the system is implemented will depend on which development platform has been selected. Chapters 7–11 discuss and illustrate implementation on a number of different platforms. This section describes briefly the toolkits and development platforms that are to be used in Chapters 7–11. An annotated list of toolkits and other resources to support the design and development of spoken dialogue systems can be found in Appendix 6.

CSLU Toolkit

The Center for Spoken Language Understanding (CSLU) toolkit, which was introduced briefly in Chapter 2, was developed at the CSLU at the Oregon Graduate Institute of Science and Technology. The main aim of the toolkit, which is available free-of-charge under a license agreement for educational, research, personal and evaluation purposes, is to support speech-related research and development activities. The toolkit includes core technologies for speech recognition and TTS synthesis, as well as a graphically based authoring environment (Rapid Application Developer (RAD)) for designing and implementing spoken dialogue systems. The RAD component is used in Chapters 7 and 8 to illustrate the process of building directed dialogues that may also make use of a talking head and other multimodal features.

Building a dialogue system with RAD involves selecting and linking graphical dialogue objects into a graph-based dialogue model, which may include branching decisions, loops, jumps and subdialogues. Figure 6.7 shows how a simple dialogue can be constructed by linking together a sequence of dialogue objects on the RAD canvas. The palette of dialogue objects is displayed on the left side of Figure 6.7, while the dialogue flow, displayed as a sequence of linked states, is shown on the main canvas. The functions of the various objects will be explained in greater detail in Chapters 7 and 8.

RAD is a relatively simple tool to use and is thus useful for introducing dialogue systems concepts. Most of the development process involves the

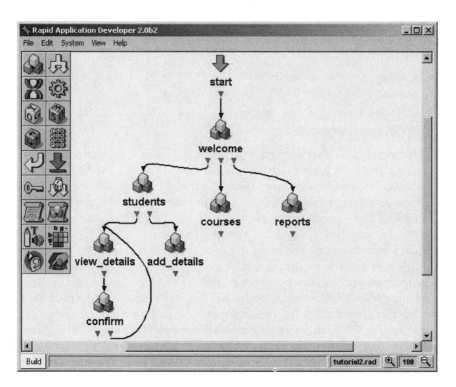

Figure 6.7. A dialogue graph on the RAD canvas (Reprinted with permission from the Center for Spoken Language Understanding. Copyright 2003, OHSU.)

use of intuitive graphical objects and there are comprehensive tutorials and instructional materials provided. It is also possible to develop fairly complex applications with RAD that involve interfaces with external components such as databases (see Chapter 7). RAD can also be used to access information from the World Wide Web, as explained in the RAD tutorial 17. Available at: (http://cslu.cse.ogi.edu/toolkit/docs/2.0/apps/rad/tutorials/tutorial017/index.html). However, this function has to some extent been superseded by platforms developed specifically for speech-based access to the Web, such as VoiceXML and SALT (Speech Application Language Tags).

VoiceXML Platforms

VoiceXML is presented in Chapters 9 and 10 as a language for developing spoken dialogue systems that interface with back-end Web-based applications and services. There are two main options for VoiceXML developers: standalone systems that run on a PC, and web-based environments that are accessed over the Internet.

Standalone Systems

The development platform that is used to illustrate VoiceXML in Chapters 9 and 10 is the IBM WebSphere Voice Server SDK (Software Development Kit). The Voice Server SDK contains all the relevant components for developing and running VoiceXML applications on a standalone PC, including:

- A speech browser to interpret the VoiceXML markup, along with a DTMF Simulator to simulate DTMF input on a desktop PC.
- IBM's speech recognition engine.
- A TTS synthesis engine.

Audio output is played through the PC's speakers or through a headset, and spoken input is through a microphone attached to the PC. The SDK also supports text input and output mode, which is useful in the stages of early development as well as for automated testing. The Voice Server SDK can be used on its own to develop and run applications. In this case a text editor is used to create the applications, which are run in a DOS window (see Appendix 3 for details on downloading and using the Voice Server SDK).

IBM also provide the WebSphere Voice Toolkit, an integrated development environment that contains a number of tools for developing VoiceXML projects, including a VoiceXML editor, tools for creating recognition grammars, tools for building acoustic models for speech recognition, and tools for recording audio prompts. The Voice Toolkit also includes a set of reusable VoiceXML dialog components. The VoiceXML editor, shown in Figure 6.8, contains a "Content Assist" facility that guides developers by displaying valid tags and attributes at relevant points within a VoiceXML file. The Voice Toolkit runs on top of the Voice Server SDK. Applications can be developed using the sophisticated tools provided in

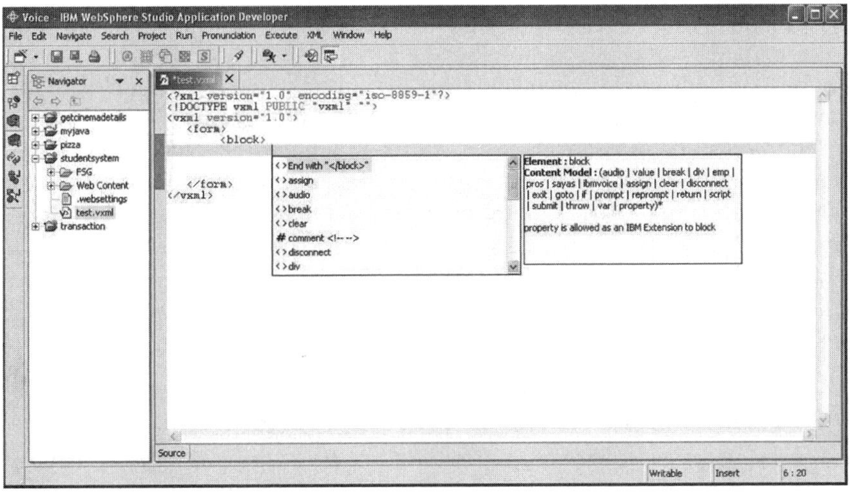

Figure 6.8. The Content Assist tool (IBM WebSphere Voice Toolkit. (Reprinted with permission from IBM Pervasive Computing Division.)

the Toolkit and then the Voice Server SDK is called from within the Toolkit to run and test the applications.

Standalone development environments such as the IBM Voice Toolkit and the VoiceServer SDK provide all the tools required to develop, test and run VoiceXML applications without the need for a telephone connection. On the downside these environments are resource intensive and require large amounts of storage capacity and memory to run efficiently. Although they simulate a telephone conversation, they do not provide direct experience of conversing with an application over the telephone.

Web-based Environments

A web-based VoiceXML development environment provides facilities for developers to create applications without the overhead of installing resource intensive software. A web-based environment normally includes a voice browser, speech recognition and TTS engines, and telephony hardware and software. All that is required to interact with an application is a telephone. Development of an application requires a developer account (which is usually free) and an Internet connection. Applications are developed in a text editor, then they are uploaded, hosted and run on the host Web site. Web-based development environments include a number of additional tools for tasks such as syntax checking, real-time debugging, and logging of interactions. They also provide extensive documentation and tutorials, libraries of audio clips, grammars and code samples. A list of the most common web-based VoiceXML development environments can be found in Appendix 6.

While online environments address the shortcomings of standalone environments, there are certain disadvantages. Most online environments are based in the United States and provide US toll-free numbers. This means that access for developers outside of the United States will be expensive, involving international telephone charges. There may also be difficulty accessing the environments, if servers are down, and some operations may take longer to execute as they depend on Internet access, whereas operations on a standalone PC are limited only by the power of the PC. For this reason tools on the PC are likely to support more powerful applications.

Platforms for Multimodal Web-based Applications

Chapter 11 deals with multimodal web-based applications which are intended to run on devices such as such as advanced mobile (cellular) phones and PDAs (Personal Digital Assistants). Two platforms will be described: the IBM Multimodal Toolkit and the Microsoft .NET Speech SDK.

IBM Multimodal Toolkit

The IBM Multimodal Toolkit is an extension to the WebSphere Voice Toolkit. With the Multimodal Toolkit developers can integrate visual applications written in XHTML and voice applications written in VoiceXML. A number of example applications are developed in Chapter 11. For instructions on installing the IBM Multimodal Toolkit, see Appendix 4.

Microsoft .NET Speech SDK

The Microsoft .NET Speech SDK also enables developers to create and run speech-based multimodal applications, using SALT, a set of XML elements that can be used in conjunction with HTML and XHTML. The SDK provides a set of tools for use within the Visual Studio .NET development environment. A number of example applications are developed in Chapter 11. For instructions on installing the Microsoft .NET Speech SDK, see Appendix 4.

Testing

The purpose of testing is to determine that the system conforms to the specifications set out in the Requirements Specifications document and to identify and correct any defects. There are two commonly used types of testing: white box (or structural) testing and black box (or functional) testing.

White box testing, which includes unit (or module) testing and integration testing, is carried out during the implementation stage with full knowledge of the underlying code, design and file structure. The purpose of unit testing is to ensure that each individual unit (or module) in the system works correctly as specified, independently of other modules in the system. Test cases are designed for each unit, with columns for expected and actual results, and a column for whether the test was passed. In a spoken dialogue system unit testing will include testing of the recognition of the user's spoken input as well as path testing, which involves testing each execution path through the system. Examples are presented below.

Black box testing, which takes place after white box testing, involves validation of the system with reference to its functional specification. The aim of black box testing is to ensure that the system meets its functional and nonfunctional requirements. Black box testing may also include system testing, in which the performance and reliability of the system are tested. System testing may involve the execution of a number of scenarios that include typical as well as exceptional uses of the system. One common technique is Stress testing, in which the system's performance is measured under a given workload.

Example: Testing of the Student Information System

In this section a selection of test procedures are illustrated with reference to the Student Information System.

Unit Testing

Unit testing for spoken dialogue systems involves testing the recognition of the user's input and the execution of paths through the dialogue. These tests are illustrated with reference to the Login dialogue, which was shown in Figure 6.4.

As far as recognition is concerned, the system should correctly recognise the input spoken by the user. Table 6.7 presents an example of recognition test results for the input of the username in the Login dialogue. As shown in Table 6.7, the usernames "Liz" and "Margaret" were recognised correctly, while "Mike" was recognised as "Margaret". In a more realistic test each input item would be tested a number of times and recognition accuracy estimated. Test input should also include words that are not in the recognition grammar for each prompt. In this way items that are problematic over a number of tests can be identified and measures taken to address the errors.

As the system includes mixed-initiative dialogue with grammars that permit multiple input, test input would also include sentences such as the following, spoken within the Student Details component of the system:

Table 6.7. Test case example for the Login dialogue (recognition)

Prompt	*Please enter your username*		
Input	Expected result	Actual result	Pass/fail
Liz	Liz	Liz	Pass
Margaret	Margaret	Margaret	Pass
Mike	Mike	Margaret	Fail

Table 6.8. Test case example for the Login dialogue

Prompt	*Please enter your username*		
Input	Expected result	Actual result	Pass/fail
Liz	Continue to next prompt	Continue to next prompt	Pass
Margaret	Continue to next prompt	Continue to next prompt	Pass
William	System help	System help	Pass
Sarah	System help	Continue to next prompt	Fail

6.6
Add details on student 96050918, coursecode DK003, stage award, year 2000, overall
result pass, overall average 40.

The expected result is that the system is able to extract the appropriate information required to fill the fields "studentid", "coursecode", "stage", "year",
"overall result" and "overall average", while ignoring any other words. Extensive
testing would determine whether complex input of this type was reliable or not.

Table 6.8 shows an example of path testing with reference to the point in the
Login dialogue where the user speaks the username. In this example it is
assumed that "Liz" and "Margaret" are valid usernames (as contained in a database), whereas "William" and "Sarah" are invalid. The aim of path testing is to
determine whether the system makes the correct choice of path following the
user's input. This test should be conducted separately from tests of recognition
accuracy, although misrecognition may cause the system to select an incorrect
path, as shown in the final case in Table 6.8.

In this test case there are two possible paths: continue to the next prompt, or
go to system help. The first two cases involve a valid input and a correct choice
of path. The third case involves invalid input with the correct path selected. The
final case also involves invalid input but incorrect path selection. In this case
the likely explanation is that the item has been misrecognised and has been
treated as a valid username. Failures such as this need to be examined carefully,
as they cause the system to execute an unexpected path. In this case, for
example, the dialogue proceeds to the password stage with an invalid username
and the error may not be detected until much later, if at all. Similar test cases
would be prepared for each unit in the system.

Integration Testing

Integration testing refers to the testing of interfaces between modules. The techniques used to test integration are similar to those used for unit testing, except
that the scope of the test cases covers input for a number of units. The test cases
illustrated in Table 6.8 involved testing of the input of the username (with
limited integration testing, as the system had to look up the database to validate the recognised username). More extensive integration testing can be illustrated using dialogues such as the View Student Details dialogue (Figure 6.6).
In this dialogue the user first has to select whether to view or add student

Table 6.9. Integration testing for the View Student Details dialogue

System prompt	User input	Expected result	Actual result
1			
Say "view" or "add".	View	Continue to next prompt.	Continue to next prompt.
Enter the student ID.	96050918	System retrieves student details: firstname: john, lastname: scott, coursecode: dk003, stage: 1.	System retrieves student details: firstname: john, lastname: scott, coursecode: dk003, stage: 1 (Pass).
2			
Say "view" or "add".	View	Continue to next prompt.	Continue to next prompt.
Enter the student ID.	96069783	System retrieves student details: firstname: david, lastname: wilson, coursecode: dk005, stage: award.	System retrieves student details: firstname: john, lastname: scott, coursecode: dk003, stage: 1 (Fail).

details, and then enter the student ID. For the dialogue to be successfully completed, the system has to retrieve the correct details from the database. Table 6.9 shows how integration testing might be applied to this dialogue.

Test case 1 is successful because the correct student details have been retrieved. Test case 2 fails because the incorrect student details have been retrieved. The most likely cause is that the system misrecognised the student ID, but this would need to be examined, using a log of the interaction, if this is available. However, it would also be important to perform tests of information retrieval from the database to measure whether the database query is correct and whether the results that are returned are accurate in terms of the query. Similar tests would be required to test whether the database was updated when the user added new details.

Integration testing should be carried out for each set of dialogues, and then for interactions with the complete system from Login to Logout, using test case scenarios, such as the following:

Log on to the system with username: liz and PIN: 1234. Ask to view the student details of student: 96050918.

Validation Testing

Validation testing is concerned with checking whether the system meets its functional and nonfunctional requirements. For example, Functional Requirement No. 4, listed in Table 6.5, states that "The user must be able to view and amend student details." The qualification statements associated with this functional requirement were:

UQ 17.1: The user must be able to view all student details.

UQ 17.2: The user must be able to amend all student details.

Each of these qualification statements would be examined to verify that the requirements were satisfied. Similarly, Nonfunctional Requirement No. 14 (listed in Table 6.6) states that "All valid speech input must be recognised by the system by the third attempt of input." Data collected during unit testing would be examined to test whether this requirement was satisfied.

System Testing

System testing could involve a number of tests that were used at the unit and integration testing level, with an emphasis on performance and reliability. For this purpose, a number of performance measures could be deployed, such as transaction time, transaction success and overall reliability. Exceptional scenarios involving the input of unusual user responses could be used to test the robustness of the system. Stress testing could also be used before deployment to assess whether the system will scale up under real conditions, for example, if a large number of callers access the system simultaneously, resulting in potential degradation of performance.

Evaluation

Testing a software system is concerned with identifying differences between expected and actual performance under controlled conditions, with testing conducted by the developers and possibly a team of trained testers. Evaluation, on the other hand, examines how the system performs when used by actual users. Evaluation may involve a number of stages, such as field-testing with a restricted set of users, leading to more extensive evaluation with a large user set. Evaluation can take a variety of forms, for example, analysing user acceptance of the system, and measuring aspects of the performance of the system and its individual components. Evaluation usually involves a series of observational studies in which users interact with the system according to a set of scenarios, such as the scenario presented above to illustrate integration testing. The scenarios can either give precise instructions on each stage of the dialogue or can be more open-ended. In addition, the test suites used in unit testing can also be administered to users to determine word accuracy, sentence accuracy and concept accuracy scores (see below).

Analysis of User Acceptance

Analysis of user acceptance is a qualitative type of evaluation, usually conducted by means of user responses to questions or statements in a Likert-scaled questionnaire. In Table 6.10 a scale of 1 to 5 is used, with 5 being the highest score.

Table 6.10. Qualitative evaluation

	1	2	3	4	5
It was easy to complete a task using the system.					
It was easy to navigate around the system.					
The system understood what you said.					
The system's speech was easy to understand.					
The system responded in a timely manner.					
The system responded in ways that you would expect.					
The system was able to cope with errors.					
You would prefer to use this system rather than a Web-based system.					

Analysis of System Performance

Evaluation of the performance of spoken dialogue systems can involve either the individual components of the system or the complete system. Analysis of system performance is a quantitative type of evaluation using a set of metrics.

Evaluation of Individual Components

Evaluation of individual components is generally based on the concept of a reference answer, which compares the actual output of the component with its desired output. Reference answers are easier to determine for components such as the speech recogniser and the language understanding component, but more difficult with the dialogue manager where the range of acceptable behaviours is greater and sometimes even indeterminate.

The most commonly used measure for speech recognisers is Word Accuracy (WA). WA accounts for errors at the word level. The number of errors is counted in relation to the number of words actually spoken and a WA count (or sometimes a word error rate) is computed. On its own WA is not the most satisfactory metric for a spoken dialogue system, as it is still possible to obtain satisfactory performance in terms of transaction success even if not all of the words spoken have been recognised correctly.

Sentence Accuracy (SA) is a measure of the percentage of utterances that have been completely and correctly recognised. In this case, the recognised string of words is matched exactly with the words in the reference answer. Sentence Understanding Rate (SU), on the other hand, measures the rate of understood sentences in comparison with a reference meaning representation, which consists of the key phrases or semantic structures to be recognised. A similar measure of understanding is Concept Accuracy (CA), which measures the percentage of concepts that have been correctly understood. For example, given the following query:

6.7
Will it rain tomorrow in Boston?

there are three concepts that should be recognised:

weather: *rain*
date: *tomorrow*
city: *boston*

Selection of the appropriate metric is important. For example, in a number of evaluations involving Advanced Research Projects Agency (ARPA) projects, it was found that the error rate for sentence understanding was much lower than that for sentence recognition (10.4% compared with 25.2%), indicating that it is easier to understand sentences than to recognise each word in the sentence and that sentence understanding, by using robust processing techniques, is able to compensate to some extent for errors produced by the speech recognition component (Hirschman, 1995). Similar results were reported by Boros et al. (1996) in a comparison of WA and CA measures. In this study it was found that it is possible to achieve perfect understanding with less than perfect recognition, but only when the misrecognitions affect semantically irrelevant words. When misrecognition affects parts of the utterance that are significant for understanding, CA may be lower than WA. Thus it is important to examine closely the relationships between different measures.

Related to CA are measures of query density and concept density (Glass et al., 2000). Query density measures how effectively the user can provide new information to the system. Consider the following example:

6.8
1 User: I'd like to book a flight from Seattle to Chicago on December twenty-seventh.
2 User: I said December twenty-seventh.

In this example the user has attempted to express three concepts but has taken two utterances to express the concepts (assuming that utterance 2 is spoken in order to correct the system, for example, following a verification attempt). For this example the query density would be $3/2 = 1.5$. Calculating query density over a number of dialogues provides a measure of how effectively the users communicate information, in terms of the number of concepts communicated and the number of turns required.

Concept density is a similar measure that calculates the average number of turns required for all of the required concepts to be understood by the system. Taking Example 6.8, a total of four concepts are communicated (one of which – the date – is repeated), out of three concepts that are required. Thus the concept density for this example is $3/4 = 0.75$. A concept density of 1 would indicate a perfect interaction in which each concept is spoken once only by the user.

Evaluation of Spoken Dialogue Systems

The performance of a spoken dialogue system can be measured in terms of the extent to which it achieves its task, the costs of achieving the task (e.g., the time taken or number of turns required to complete the task), and measures of the quality of the interaction, such as the extent to which the system behaves cooperatively (see the EAGLES handbook (Gibbon et al., 1997) for a detailed account of the measures described below together with annotated examples). Metrics for evaluation of spoken dialogue systems include the following:

Transaction Success (TS). This metric measures how successful the system has been in providing the user with the requested information. TS may be defined as a four-valued measure to account for cases of partial success as well as instances where the user's goal was not clearly identifiable or changed during the course of the interaction: S (succeed), SC (succeed with constraint relaxation), SN (succeed with no answer) and F (fail).

Number of turns/Transaction time. This is a measure of the duration of the dialogue in terms of the number of turns taken to complete the transaction. An alternative measure is the time taken to complete the transaction. These measures can be used in conjunction with different dialogue strategies to give an indication of the costs of the dialogue, which may be compared with other measures such as Transaction Success or User Acceptance.

Correction Rate (CR). This is a measure of the proportion of turns in a dialogue that are concerned with correcting either the system's or the user's utterances, which may have been the result of speech recognition errors, errors in language understanding, or misconceptions. A dialogue that has a high degree of CR might be judged to have high costs in terms of user acceptability, as well as potentially high costs financially.

Contextual Appropriateness (CA). This is a measure of the extent to which the system provides appropriate responses. The metric can be divided into a number of values, such as: TF (total failure), AP (appropriate), IA (inappropriate), AI (appropriate/inappropriate) and IC (incomprehensible). With TF, the system fails to respond to the user. IA is used for responses that are inappropriate. AI is used when the evaluator is in doubt, and IC when the content of an utterance cannot be interpreted.

Dialogue Strategy

Dialogue strategy has been used as an evaluation metric by Danieli and Gerbino (1995), who compared different ways of recovering from errors in the dialogue. "Implicit recovery" (IR), which can be compared with implicit verification as discussed in Chapter 5, was defined as the ability to overcome errors produced by the speech recogniser or parser and to rectify these implicitly. This strategy contrasts with an explicit strategy involving correction that can be measured using the Correction Rate (CR) metric. The following example illustrates implicit recovery (values understood by the system in angle brackets):

6.9
1 User: I want to go from Roma to Milano in the morning.
< arrival-city = MILANO, departure-time = MORNING >
2 System: Sorry, where do you want to leave from?
3 User: From Roma.
< departure-city = ROMA, cost-of-ticket = ? >
4 System: Do you want to go from Roma to Milano leaving in the morning?

Although the user's first utterance contains the concepts that the system requires to retrieve the desired information, the departure city has not been recognised, so the system takes into account the concepts that have been correctly understood and asks for the concept that was not understood. The user's second utterance contains the required information but additional words have been inserted by the recogniser that are interpreted as a request for the cost of the ticket. As this concept is not relevant in the current context, it is disregarded by the system and the user is asked to confirm the correct concepts. In this case the IR score is 100% and the system has succeeded in spite of recognition and parsing errors but without having to engage in explicit correction.

In their study Danieli and Gerbino compared explicit and implicit recovery strategies, also using the other measures described earlier such as Contextual Appropriateness. They found that the system that used an explicit recovery strategy achieved greater robustness in terms of dealing with errors, although at the cost of longer transactions. They also found that, as users became more familiar with the system, the recovery results for the system using implicit recovery improved substantially. Thus several aspects have to be considered and balanced when evaluating a dialogue system, including Transaction Success and Dialogue Duration, which measure the ability of the system to find the required information, and Contextual Appropriateness, which measures the quality of the dialogue. However, it is not possible using these measures to determine whether the higher transaction success of the system using the explicit recovery strategy was more critical to performance than the efficiency of the system using the implicit recovery strategy.

PARADISE Tool for Evaluating Spoken Dialogue Systems

PARADISE (PARAdigm for Dialogue System Evaluation) is a tool for the evaluation of spoken dialogue systems that addresses the limitations of the methods discussed so far by combining various performance measures such as transaction success, user satisfaction, and dialogue cost into a single performance evaluation function, and by enabling performance to be calculated for subdialogues as well as complete dialogues (Walker et al., 1997, 1998). In this framework the overall goal of a dialogue system is viewed in terms of maximising user satisfaction. This goal is subdivided into the subgoals of maximising task success and minimising costs. The latter is in turn subdivided into efficiency measures and qualitative measures.

Transaction Success is calculated by using an attribute value matrix (AVM) that represents the information to be exchanged between the system and the user in terms of a set of ordered pairs of attributes and their possible values. For example, in the Student Information System there might be four users, as shown in the attribute-value table (Table 6.11).

Given a number of interactions with the system, based perhaps on scenarios, data is collected in a confusion matrix according to whether the values have

Table 6.11. Attribute-value table

Attribute	Possible values
Username	Liz, Margaret, Mike, Guest

Table 6.12. Confusion matrix for username values

Data	Username			
	Liz	Margaret	Mike	Guest
Liz	**25**	1	0	5
Margaret	1	**29**	0	1
Mike	1	0	**18**	0
Guest	3	0	2	**14**
Total	30	30	20	20

been recognised correctly by the system or not. The correct values for each attribute, which are referred to as the "keys", are plotted along with any incorrect values that occurred during the actual dialogue. Table 6.12 presents a hypothetical confusion matrix for the recognition of the username values in Table 6.11.

The measure of $P(A)$, as shown in bold on the diagonal, indicates how well the system performed in terms of recognition of each of the usernames. The additional scores within each column indicate misrecognitions. As seen in this example, the username "Guest" was misrecognised five times (25%) as "Liz".

The confusion matrix is used to calculate the Kappa coefficient K that is normally used to measure inter-observer reliability but in the PARADISE tool is used to indicate how well the system has performed a particular task within a given scenario (Sidney and Castellan, 1988). Calculating K involves the following formula:

$$K = P(A) - P(E)/1 - P(E),$$

where $P(A)$ is the proportion of times that the AVMs for the actual dialogues agree with the AVMs for the scenario keys, and $P(E)$ is the proportion of times that the AVMs for the dialogues and the keys are expected to agree by chance. Unlike other measures of Transaction Success and Concept Accuracy, K takes into account the inherent complexity of the task by correcting for expected chance agreement.

Dialogue costs are measured in terms of cost measures that can be applied as a function to any subdialogue. Given a set of cost measures the different measures are combined to determine their relative contribution to performance. Using the formula for measuring performance (see Walker et al. (1997)), it is possible to calculate performance involving multiple dialogue strategies, including performance over subdialogues. User satisfaction is measured using qualitative evaluation measures such as those presented in Table 6.10.

PARADISE is a framework for evaluating dialogue systems that incorporates and enhances previously used measures. It supports comparisons between dialogue strategies and separates the tasks to be achieved from how they are achieved in the dialogue. Performance can be calculated at any level of a dialogue, such as subtasks, and performance can be associated with different dialogue strategies. Furthermore, subjective as well as objective measures can be combined and their cost factors relative to overall performance can be specified. PARADISE has been used as a tool to evaluate a number of applications, including accessing train schedules and email, as well as voice dialling and messaging (Kamm et al., 1999; Walker et al., 1998).

Summary

In this chapter the stages of the software development lifecycle for spoken dialogue systems have been presented. A speech-based Student Information System has been used to illustrate the development process. Chapters 7–11 will provide tutorials on the implementation of many of the features discussed in this chapter, using the different development tools and environments discussed in the implementation section.

Further Reading

Dialogue Systems Development

The most comprehensive account of dialogue systems development is to be found in the book *Designing Interactive Speech Systems: From First Ideas to User Testing* (Bernsen et al., 1998). Following introductory chapters on interactive speech systems and speech interaction theory, the book presents a detailed account with copious examples of the application of the standard software engineering lifecycle model to the development and evaluation of interactive speech systems. Also included are chapters on the WOZ simulation technique and corpus handling.

Design Guidelines

There are a number of books and other resources that discuss design guidelines and human factors issues for interactive speech systems, including Balentine et al. (2001), Gardner-Bonneau (1999), Lai and Yankelovich (2002) and Weinschenk and Barker (2000). The VoiceXML Programmers Guide, provided as documentation for the IBM WebSphere Voice Server Software Developers Kit (SDK), has useful chapters on "Designing a speech user interface" and "Hints, tips and best practices" (see Appendix 3 for download information).

Speech interface development is the topic of a special section on Natural Language Interfaces in the *International Journal of Speech Technology* (Novick, 2002). In this issue Karsenty (2002) discusses the design philosophy of spoken dialogue systems, while Sinha et al. (2002) illustrate the use of the Suede tool for spoken language interface design. See also Glass and Weinstein (2001), Lai and Yankelovich (2002) and Suhm (2003).

Most of the books on VoiceXML listed at the end of Chapter 9 provide chapters on design guidelines. Larson's book *VoiceXML: Introduction to Developing Speech Applications* (Larson, 2002), has a detailed account of testing (Chapter 11), as well as a case study that describes in some detail the process of specifying and developing a speech-based application for a fictional fast foods company (Appendix 1).

Exercises

1. Produce examples of user, usage and task profiles for the dialogue system that you have been examining in earlier exercises.
2. Produce examples of use case specifications and functional and nonfunctional requirement specifications for your system.
3. Produce examples of dialogue flow for your system.
4. List the sorts of considerations required for your system in terms of factors such as: prompt design, barge-in, confirmations, grammars, navigational commands.
5. List some tests that would be useful for the system in terms of unit testing, integration testing, validation testing and system testing.

Developing a Spoken Dialogue System Using the CSLU Toolkit

7

RAD (Rapid Application Developer) is a graphically based authoring environment for designing and implementing spoken dialogue systems. RAD supports directed dialogues using a finite state-based dialogue model. The developer selects various dialogue objects and links them together to make a dialogue graph. These objects perform functions such as speaking a prompt, recognising the user's input, and executing actions related to the dialogue. RAD also includes animated characters and facilities for presenting media objects such as pictures and sounds. Once the dialogue graph has been constructed, it can be tested using speech input and output.

In order to show how to construct spoken dialogue systems in RAD, a series of linked tutorials will be presented that progressively introduce the main features of the toolkit. In this chapter a speech-only system will be developed for accessing student information. Chapter 8 will present a multimodal educational system for young children that makes use of the animated characters as well as media objects such as pictures and sounds.

This chapter consists of the following tutorials:

Tutorial 1: Basic functions in RAD: The Pizza application.
Tutorial 2: Developing basic functions for a Student Information System.
Tutorial 3: The default repair subdialogue.
Tutorial 4: Subdialogues.
Tutorial 5: Digit recognition.
Tutorial 6: DTMF input.
Tutorial 7: Alpha-digit recognition.
Tutorial 8: Recognition grammars.
Tutorial 9: Speech output in RAD.
Tutorial 10: Using Tcl in RAD.
Tutorial 11: Improving recognition and creating a dynamic recogniser.
Tutorial 12: Linking a RAD application to a database using TclODBC.

Tutorial 1: Basic Functions in RAD: The Pizza Application

This tutorial involves running the Pizza example and making some minor changes to the example. The Pizza application, which is provided with the Center for Spoken Language Understanding (CSLU) Toolkit, allows you to order a pizza using spoken input. The application prompts you to select a size and topping and also asks you whether you want salad with your order. The application does not connect to a database and the dialogue terminates once your order has been confirmed.

Starting RAD and Loading the Pizza Application

Download and install the CSLU Toolkit, as described in Appendix 2. To start RAD, go to Start on your PC, then click Start -> CSLU Toolkit -> RAD. This starts the RAD system displaying a palette of dialogue objects and an empty canvas on which the dialogue graph will be developed, as shown in Figure 7.1. (*Note*: For the tutorials in this chapter you should disable the

Figure 7.1. The RAD canvas. (Reprinted with permission from the Center for Spoken Language Understanding. Copyright 2003, OHSU.)

animated face. Click on File -> Preferences, then uncheck the box entitled "Animated Face".)

If this is the first time that RAD has been started on your system a dialogue box will pop-up informing you that a directory called ".rad" is about to be created for you. Note the location in which that directory is being created (because the programs and data you create during these tutorials will be stored in subdirectories of that directory by default), and then click OK.

Also, when starting RAD for the first time, it is possible that you will see another small dialogue box asking you to calibrate your microphone. Click OK and follow the instructions in the ensuing dialogue boxes. You may also choose to do this calibration before running an application. To do this, Click on File -> Preferences -> Audio and then on the Calibrate tab, and then follow the instructions that appear on the screen.

Click on File -> Examples -> pizza to load the Pizza application. This will load the Pizza application, part of which is shown in Figure 7.2. The dialogue is modelled as a graph, beginning at the "start" state and proceeding through states entitled "size", "topping", and so on, until the "Goodbye" state is reached. There is also a loop to repeat the dialogue. In this application all the states are represented using the GENERIC icon, shown in Figure 7.3.

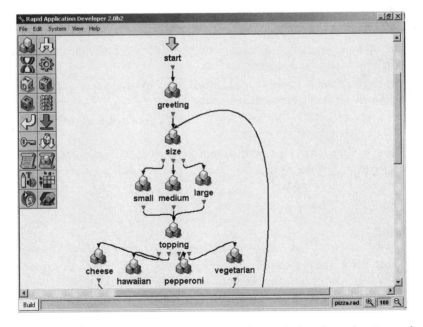

Figure 7.2. The pizza application. (Reprinted with permission from the Center for Spoken Language Understanding. Copyright 2003, OHSU.)

Figure 7.3. The generic icon. (Reprinted with permission from the Center for Spoken Language Understanding. Copyright 2003, OHSU.)

Compiling and Running an Application

An application has to be compiled before it can be run. Click on `build` (either on the tab at the bottom left corner of the canvas, or within the menu item `System -> build`). If there are any errors in the code, these will be reported at this point. Once the application has been compiled, the tab at the bottom left corner displays the word "Run". Click `Run` to run the application. (*Note:* You will need a headset or speakers to hear the system prompts and a microphone to speak your responses. Wait for the beep before speaking.)

Recognition Problems

There are a number of reasons why the system may fail to recognise your responses correctly and each of these should be checked in the case of poor recognition:

1. The microphone is not connected properly. This can be tested using the Windows Sound Recorder application.
2. The microphone is poor quality. You will need to obtain a microphone that is suitable for speech recognition applications.
3. You began to speak before the beep, so that the system did not capture some of your response.
4. There was too great a pause between the beep and the beginning of your response, so that the system may have stopped recording your input before you made your response.

Prompts

The application speaks a series of prompts using the built-in text-to-speech (TTS) system. To see how the prompts are specified, double click on the "size" state. This will open the window shown in Figure 7.4. This window is used for a number of different functions. For the moment we will only examine the TTS function for prompts. By default the window displays this function on opening. The prompt that will be spoken by the TTS component is shown in the Prompt box.

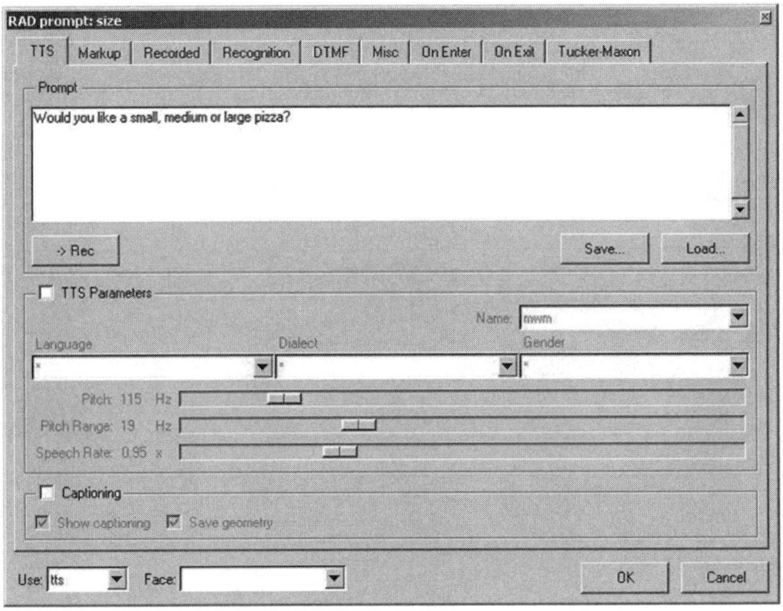

Figure 7.4. The prompt dialogue box. (Reprinted with permission from the Center for Spoken Language Understanding. Copyright 2003, OHSU.)

Exercise 1: Changing the Prompt

1. Edit the prompt so that the system will say "Would you like a small, medium, large or gigantic pizza?"
2. Edit some of the other prompts, including the prompt in the "Goodbye" state.

Recognition Vocabulary

If a response is required from the user, the recognition vocabulary for that response has to be specified. The "greeting" state does not require a response, but responses are required at several other states, including the "size" state. You can see what responses are required by moving the mouse over the icon shaped as a red arrowhead under each state. This icon is known as the "recognition port". You will notice that there is no vocabulary specified for the "greeting" state, but there is a word for each of the recognition ports associated with the "size" state.

To examine the recognition vocabulary in more detail, double click on the leftmost port under the "size" state. This brings up a window showing the recognition vocabulary for this state, as shown in Figure 7.5. The words to be recognised at this state are typed into the box entitled "Words". The box entitled Pronunciation gives the pronunciation of the word in using the Worldbet representation. (To see a list of these symbols, click on Help -> Worldbet symbols.)

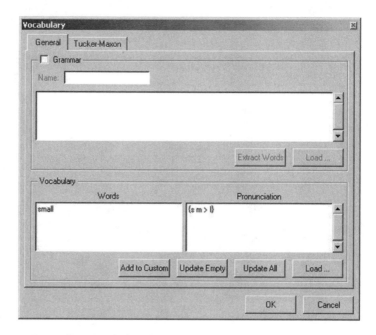

Figure 7.5. Recognition vocabulary box. (Reprinted with permission from the Center for Spoken Language Understanding. Copyright 2003, OHSU.)

Exercise 2: Adding a Pronunciation for a New Word

You can add a new word to the vocabulary by entering it on a new line in the Words box (as will be shown below). For the moment, we will create a new port for the new word.

1. Add a new port by right clicking on the "size" state and selecting Add port.
2. Double left click on the new port and add the word "gigantic" to the vocabulary in the Words window.
3. Click on Update All to generate the pronunciation, then on OK to close the Vocabulary window.

Exercise 3: Adding and Linking a New State

You will need a new state in case the user responds with the word "gigantic". To create a new state:

1. Move the cursor over the GENERIC recognition icon on the icon palette.
2. Left click and drag the icon on to the canvas until it is aligned with the state entitled "large".
3. The new state will have a name with a number, such as "state6". To rename the state to "gigantic" right-click on the new state and select the rename option.

4. Incorporate the state into the dialogue graph: Place the cursor over the recognition port for the state "gigantic", hold down the left button to create an arrowed arc and drag the arc to the state entitled "topping". Release the left button when the arc is within the "topping" state. You will now have an arc linking the "gigantic" and "topping" states.

5. Draw a similar arc to link the port entitled "gigantic" on the "size" state to the state entitled "gigantic".

If you wish to delete a state, right-click on the state and select `delete`.

Build and run your dialogue, asking for a "gigantic" pizza when prompted for size.

If you want to save your amended dialogue, choose `File -> Save`, naming your file something other than "pizza", for example, "mypizza", so as not to overwrite the tutorial application.

Branching

This application illustrates branching within the dialogue graph after the states "size", "topping", "salad" and "confirm". However, branching only has relevance in this example following the "confirm" state. At this point the system can enter the "Goodbye" state and terminate with a prompt. Alternatively, it can enter the "again" state from which it loops back to the "size" state to begin the dialogue again, but this time without the initial greeting.

Branching after the other states is not required in this application, although this might be required if selection of a particular size or topping were to lead the dialogue down a separate dialogue path. In this simple version the recognition vocabulary for states such as "size" and "topping" could have been listed (with each word on a separate line) within the one recognition port, as shown in Figures 7.6 and 7.7.

Verification

In this application the system verifies the order after the values for size, topping and salad have been selected. If the user responds "no", then the dialogue loops back and all the values are collected again. This is not necessarily the most efficient way to handle verification, particularly if only one of the values was incorrect. Some variations on handling verification using RAD will be presented later.

Using Variables to Store Recognised Values

RAD has a built-in mechanism for storing the values recognised by the system at each state in the dialogue. The value for a state can be referenced using the variable "$state(recog)", where "state" is the name of the state in question. An example of this can be seen if you double-click on the "confirm" state and then

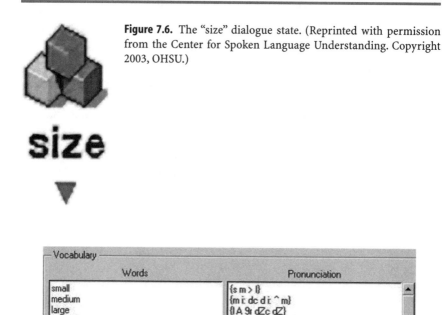

Figure 7.6. The "size" dialogue state. (Reprinted with permission from the Center for Spoken Language Understanding. Copyright 2003, OHSU.)

Figure 7.7. Recognition vocabulary for the "size" dialogue state. (Reprinted with permission from the Center for Spoken Language Understanding. Copyright 2003, OHSU.)

click on the OnEnter tab. You will see that the prompt consists of a conditional statement (in the scripting language Tcl (Tool Command Language)):

```
if [string match yes $salad(recog)] {
    tts "So you want a $size(recog) $topping(recog) pizza with salad, right?"
} else {
    tts "So you want a $size(recog) $topping(recog) pizza, right?"
}
```

The use of Tcl within RAD will be discussed later. For the present the key point to note is that the words recognised by the system at the size and topping states are represented by the variables "$size(recog)", and "$topping(recog)", respectively. Note that what is returned is the word recognised by the system at the state in question. This may not be the same as the word that was actually spoken by the user.

Exercise 4: Adding a Confirmation

A simpler way to provide a confirmation, provided it does not depend on some condition as in this example, would be to use the standard Prompt window, with a text such as:

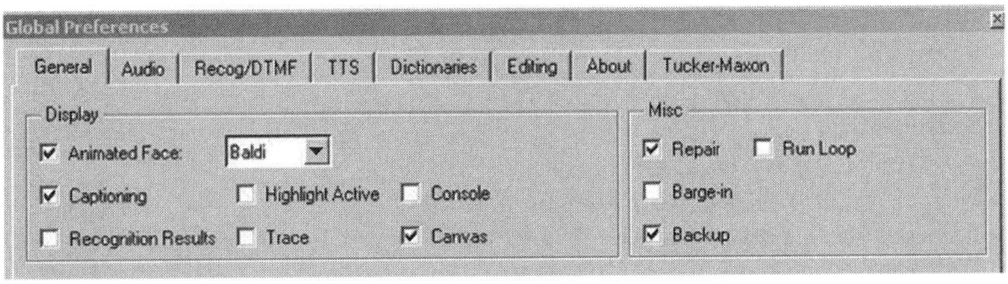

Figure 7.8. The global preference box. (Reprinted with permission from the Center for Spoken Language Understanding. Copyright 2003, OHSU.)

So you want a $size(recog) $topping(recog) pizza?

Insert this prompt into the Prompt window under the TTS tab and delete the text in the OnEnter window. This will allow the system to confirm using the variables specified in your new prompt, although of course whether or not you choose salad will not be confirmed.

Additional Features: Captioning and the Animated Face

You will have noticed that a small caption window displays the systems prompts. You can deselect this feature by clicking on `File -> Preferences` and clicking on the tick against the captioning feature, as shown in Figure 7.8. Other features can also be selected and deselected in this way. For example, while the canvas is important for the developer, you may want to have a different visual display (or even no display at all) for the end-user. This can be achieved by deselecting `Canvas`. Other selections within the Preferences window will be discussed in later tutorials.

Tutorial 2: Developing Basic Functions for a Student Information System

In this tutorial the basic functions illustrated in Tutorial 1 will now be applied in the development of the student information system presented in Chapter 6.

Functional Description of the Application

The Student Information System allows a user to log in using a four-digit PIN, and ask for information about students or courses, or request reports. The system looks up the requested information and speaks it back to the user. The following example, presented originally in Chapter 6, shows the type of dialogue that the system should be able to conduct:

7.1
 1 System: Welcome to the Student System Main Menu.
 2   Please say your username.
 3 User: Liz.
 4 System: Thank you.
 5   Now please say your four-digit pin.
 6 User: 6 5 6 6.
 7 System: Was that 6 5 6 6?
 8 User: Yes.
 9 System: The system provides details on students, courses and reports.
10   For students say students or press 1, for courses say courses or press 2,
           for reports say reports or press 3.
11 User: Students.
12 System: This is Student Details.
13   Say "View details" to view existing student details.
14   Say "Add details" to add new student details.
15 User: View details.
16 System: Viewing student details.
17   What is the student ID?
18 User: 96050918.
19 System: I have the following details: student John Scott, course code DK003, at
           stage 1.
20   Would you like any more information?
21 User: Courses.

This dialogue includes the following elements:

- Prompt and response (e.g., 2–3), also with verification (7).
- Digit recognition (6 and 18).
- DTMF input (10).
- Retrieval of information from a database (19).
- Global navigation (21).

These and some additional functionalities (such as dealing with repair, alpha-digit recognition and customising speech output) will be developed gradually during the course of this chapter.

Exercise 5: Create a Dialogue Graph

1. Open RAD with an empty canvas. If you already have an application on the canvas and wish to develop a new application, then select File -> New.
2. Create a dialogue graph as shown in Figure 7.9. (*Note*: You should regularly save your application. Call it "studentsystem1.rad" and save it in the default location provided by RAD, e.g., c:\.rad\saved\.)
3. Add prompts and recognition vocabulary as follows:

   GENERIC: welcome
   TTS:

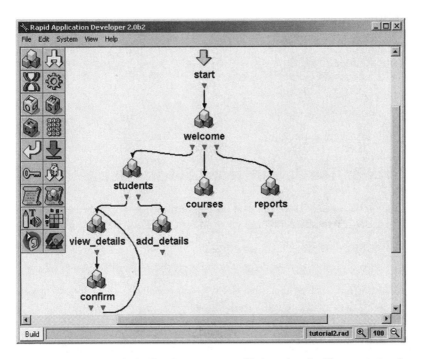

Figure 7.9. Dialogue graph for "studentsystem1.rad". (Reprinted with permission from the Center for Spoken Language Understanding. Copyright 2003, OHSU.)

Welcome to the Student System Main Menu.
The system provides details on students, courses and reports.
To begin say one of the following: students, courses, reports.
Recognition:
Left output port: students
Middle output port: courses
Right output port: reports

GENERIC: students
TTS:
This is Student Details.
Say View details to view existing student details.
Say Add details to add new student details.
Recognition:
Left output port: view details
Right output port: add details

GENERIC: view_details
TTS:
Viewing student details
Please say the student name
Recognition:
John, David, Rosemary, Jennifer

GENERIC: confirm
TTS: was that $view_details(recog)?
Recognition:
Left output port: yes
Right output port: no

GENERIC: add_details
TTS: Adding student details

Save and test your application.

Tutorial 3: The Default Repair Subdialogue

You may have noticed that the system was not always accurate in recognising what you said. Two situations are covered by the default repair subdialogue:

1. The system does not detect any speech.
2. The speech that is detected does not match the recognition vocabulary.

These situations will be tested in the following exercise in order to introduce and explain the default repair subdialogue.

Exercise 6: Examining the Default Repair Subdialogue

To examine the operation of the default repair subdialogue, do the following:

1. Do not speak following a prompt, in this case, the system should say: "Please speak after the tone" and repeat the prompt.
2. Say something that is not in the recognition vocabulary for that state, in this case, if what you say matches closely to a word in the recognition vocabulary, then that matched word will be recognised. Otherwise, the system will say "Sorry" and repeat the prompt.

The default repair subdialogue can be viewed by clicking View -> Repair default (see Figure 7.10). If you open the various states and view the prompts, you will see how the behaviours that you have tested were programmed. You will also note that the system makes two attempts to match the input and closes the dialogue if it has been unsuccessful. Note that the subdialogue terminates either by reaching a state entitled "return: repeat" or by reaching the "Goodbye" state. In the case of Return: repeat the dialogue returns to the state from which the repair subdialogue was launched and repeats the actions specified in that state, such as the prompt. Later we will see some different ways of returning from a subdialogue.

Recognition Results

One of the reasons why the system enters a subdialogue is because the recognition for the user's input was poor. You can view the recognition results for a state by clicking on View -> Recognition results. This is useful if

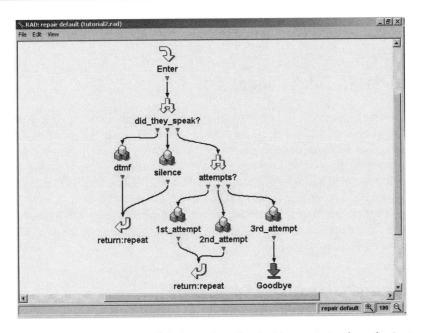

Figure 7.10. The default repair subdialogue. (Reprinted with permission from the Center for Spoken Language Understanding. Copyright 2003, OHSU.)

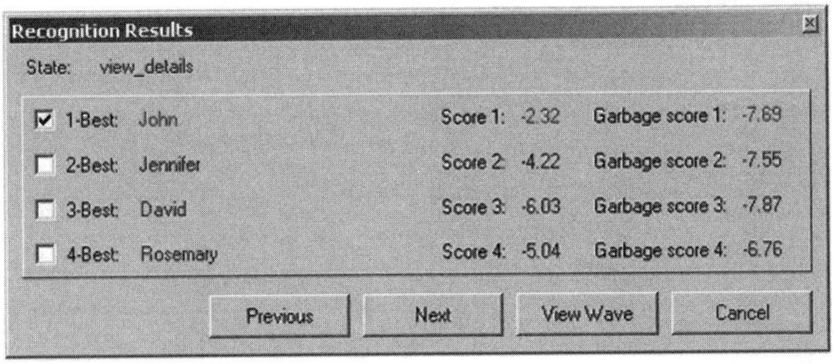

Figure 7.11. Recognition results for student name. (Reprinted with permission from the Center for Spoken Language Understanding. Copyright 2003, OHSU.)

there have been recognition problems. Figure 7.11 shows an example of recognition results in response to the prompt "Please say a student name."

The table displays the four best results along with their scores and garbage scores. The garbage score is the score for silence or the score for extraneous noise, whichever is the greater. The ideal garbage model will have a better score, while noise is occurring, than any of the vocabulary words, and a worse score during speech, provided the speech is in the vocabulary (see Hosom et al. (1997), for a more detailed discussion). In this example, "John" was the best estimate. You can see the results from Previous and Next by clicking on the relevant buttons. Clicking on `View Wave` displays the waveform and spectrogram for the acoustic input.

Tutorial 4: Subdialogues

Subdialogues can be used for commonly occurring interactions, such as validating the user, and collecting standard information, such as times and dates. They are useful when developing in a graphical authoring environment such as RAD as they prevent the top-level canvas from becoming too cluttered. The default repair subdialogue is a built-in subdialogue. This tutorial will show how to develop a subdialogue for user validation.

For the purposes of this tutorial, we will assume that users will log in using names. Validation involving strings of digits and alphanumeric strings will be illustrated in Tutorials 5 and 7.

Exercise 7: Creating a Subdialogue

Construct an application with the top-level dialogue graph as shown in Figure 7.12. The contents of the states will be entered later. Before creating the

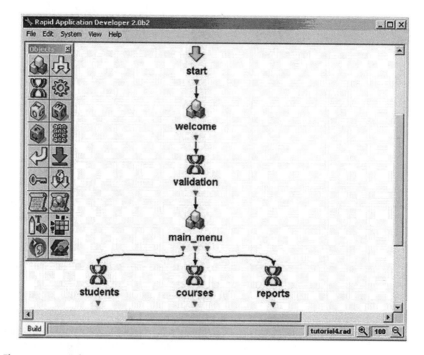

Figure 7.12. Dialogue graph with subdialogues. (Reprinted with permission from the Center for Spoken Language Understanding. Copyright 2003, OHSU.)

subdialogues, you will need to undock the palette of dialogue objects, so that they can be dragged on to the subdialogue screens. To do this:

1. Right click on the palette, select Undock. The subdialogue object can be found on the palette in column 1, row 2.
2. Drag the subdialogue object on to the canvas, release, and select NewMaster Subdialogue from the pop-up window.
3. Right-click on the new subdialogue icon and rename it as "validation".
4. Double click to open. You will see that the subdialogue has an enter icon.
5. Add a generic recognition icon entitled "name".
6. Add a "return:continue icon" – column 1, row 5 (see Figure 7.13).
7. Add further subdialogues entitled "students", "courses" and "reports". These subdialogues will be empty for the moment, but ensure that they each include the return:continue icon.

You can see a list of the subdialogues associated with your application by clicking View. Clicking on Edit provides options for deleting subdialogues.

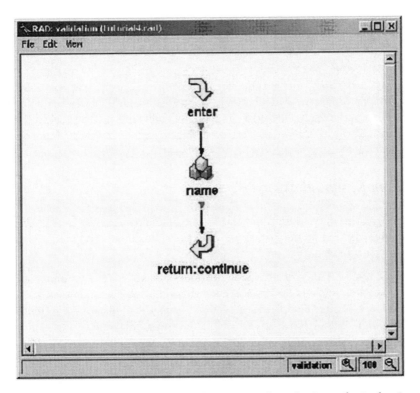

Figure 7.13. A subdialogue. (Reprinted with permission from the Center for Spoken Language Understanding. Copyright 2003, OHSU.)

The following text should be added into the states in the main dialogue and into the subdialogue entitled "validation":

GENERIC: welcome
TTS: Welcome to the Student System Main Menu.
The system provides details on students, courses and reports.

GENERIC: name
TTS: please say your user name.
Recognition:
Liz, Margaret, Mike, Guest

GENERIC: main_menu
TTS: Please say one of the following: students, courses, reports.
Recognition:
students, courses, reports

Save the complete application as "studentsystem2.rad" by clicking on the top level dialogue to highlight it, then File -> Save. Build and run your application, testing it with a range of different inputs.

Saving Subdialogues

It is important to save subdialogues correctly. There are two things to consider:

1. When saving an application that includes subdialogues, you only need to save the main screen. This will automatically include every subdialogue on the main screen.
2. If you explicitly save a subdialogue screen, then only that subdialogue will be saved. You would do this if you wanted to include the saved subdialogue in other applications. To save a subdialogue, right click on it and select Save Subdialogue Object. The saved object can then be inserted into other applications by right clicking on the canvas, and selecting Insert File.

Returning from Subdialogues

There are three options for returning from a subdialogue. These can be viewed by double-clicking on the return icon in the subdialogue, and then selecting the Options tag.

1. Continue. This is the option that should be used for the subdialogues in applications such as the present one, where the subdialogue is similar to a subroutine. After completing the subdialogue, the application continues at the point where it left off in order to enter the subdialogue.
2. Repeat. This is the option used in the default repair subdialogue. In this case the system returns to the state from which the repair subdialogue was launched and repeats the prompt of that state.
3. Goto. With this option you can specify the state that the application should go to following the completion of the subdialogue.

You should consider these options carefully when designing subdialogues for your applications.

Tutorial 5: Digit Recognition

In the application developed in Tutorial 4 students were represented by their names. In a more realistic application students would probably be represented by an ID consisting of a string of digits or an alphanumeric string consisting of digits and letters. Similar strings would also be used for course codes. There are two special dialogue objects provided in RAD for digit and alpha-digit recognition. This tutorial deals with digit recognition.

Exercise 8: Validation Using the Digit Recogniser

This example, which can be called "studentsystemdigit.rad", illustrates the use of the digit recogniser. The digit recogniser in RAD has a special grammar and recogniser which are tailored to recognise digits. It also has only one output port, so any branching on the recognition results must be done with a conditional object (the fork-like object named "check_pin", as shown in Figure 7.14). The example involves the following functions:

1. The user is asked to speak in their four-digit pin.
2. The system checks if it has recognised four digits.
3. If no, the system says that four digits are required and reprompts.
4. If yes, then the user is asked to confirm the four digits
5. If the user confirms the digits, then the system exits.
6. If the user does not confirm the digits, then the user is asked to speak the digits, then to confirm the digits.

The example is built as follows:

1. Create a dialogue graph on the RAD canvas as shown in Figure 7.14.
2. Drag the DIGIT icon from the palette (column 2, row 3) from the palette on to the canvas and attach to the Start icon.
3. Rename the Digit state "pin".
4. Drag a conditional object, rename it "check_pin" and connect it to the "pin" state.
5. Create the other states and links, as shown.
6. Open the recognition port for "pin". The recognition box is shown in Figure 7.15. In the Words box you will see the vocabulary for the digits, including "zero", "oh" and two special words "*sil" and "*any", that will be explained in more detail in Tutorial 8. Above the Words box there is a Grammar box that will also be explained in Tutorial 8.
7. Click on the "pin" state and enter the following prompt: "What is your pin?"

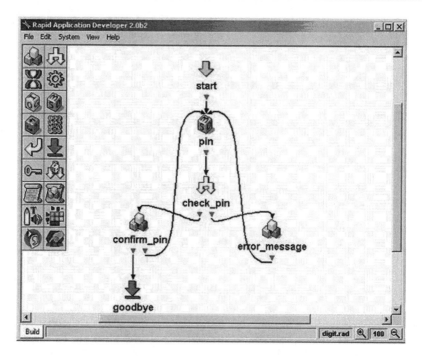

Figure 7.14. Dialogue with digit recognition "studentsystemdigit.rad". (Reprinted with permission from the Center for Spoken Language Understanding. Copyright 2003, OHSU.)

The conditional object is used to check conditions. In this example the pin should consist of four digits. We can state one condition that, if the recognised string consists of four digits, then the dialogue continues to the next state "confirm_pin", otherwise it will go to the state "error_message". To set these conditions:

1. Open the left side port of "check_pin" and insert the text (without the quotation marks) `"[llength $pin(recog)]== 4"`.
2. In the right side port place a "1" (without quotes). This right-hand path evaluates to "true" if, and only if, the left side port, which contains the condition and is checked first, does not evaluate to "true".
3. Add the following prompt to the "error_message" state: `Your pin should consist of 4 digits.`
4. Add the following prompt in the "confirm_pin" state: `Was that $pin(recog)?`

Trailing Silence Duration

You may find that the recogniser cuts off the end of your utterance. To correct this, you need to adjust the Trailing Silence Duration setting. To adjust this

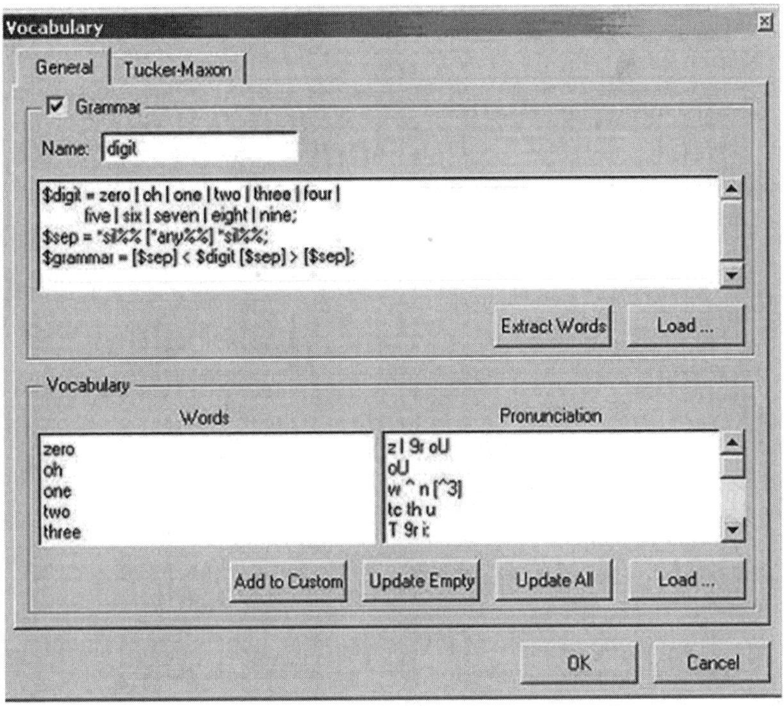

Figure 7.15. Recognition vocabulary box for the digit recogniser. (Reprinted with permission from the Center for Spoken Language Understanding. Copyright 2003, OHSU.)

setting for all the states in the dialogue, click on `File -> Preferences`, click on the `Audio` tab, and adjust `Trailing Silence Duration`.

However, you may only need to make an adjustment for the "pin" state, in which a brief period of silence may be detected between digits. To adjust the "pin" state, double-click on the "pin" state, select the Misc tab, tick Audio Parameters, and adjust the Trailing Silence Duration to a value of around 1000 ms.

Build and run the dialogue. You can give any string of four digits as the correct response. Test the conditional statement with strings consisting of less than and more than four digits. (*Note*: You may find that the system is not as accurate as you may wish when recognising spoken digits. One way of addressing this problem will be presented in Tutorial 6.)

Tutorial 6: DTMF Input

As you may have noticed when running your application in Tutorial 6, accuracy of digit recognition may be unsatisfactory. Bear in mind that the digit recogniser may have been trained on a dialect different from yours in which some of the digits are pronounced differently. For example, there is considerable variation between dialects in the pronunciation of the word "eight". Many digits are short words that provide little acoustic material for the recogniser, as discussed in Chapter 4. This tutorial introduces the use of DTMF (Dual Tone Multiple Frequency) input. In a telephone-based application DTMF input is where the user enters digits on the telephone keypad. Most current automated systems use DTMF (or touch-tone) input. In this tutorial a simulated keypad will be used to illustrate the use of DTMF input in a RAD application. The basic functionality of the application is as follows:

1. The user is asked to speak in their four-digit pin.
2. The system checks if it has recognised four digits.
3. If no, the user is asked to type the digits using the keypad, then to confirm the digits.
4. If yes, then the user is asked to confirm the four digits.
5. If the user confirms the digits, then the system exits.
6. If the user does not confirm the digits, then the user is asked to type the digits using the keypad, then to confirm the digits.

Exercise 9: DTMF Input for Validation

You can use the "studentsystemdigit.rad" application developed in Tutorial 5. If you want to keep that application separate, then save a copy of it as "studentsystemdtmf.rad" for the purposes of this tutorial.

This tutorial involves the use of DTMF input. A DTMF dialogue object is provided in the RAD palette. However, this object will only work in a telephony set-up. In the stand-alone PC environment the following code will simulate the telephony set-up with a DTMF window into which the digits can be entered.[1]

1. Insert a Tcl dialogue object (row 2, column 2) after the "start" icon on the main canvas. Name this state "setup". This state will contain the code to set up the DTMF window. Connect this state to the state named "pin".
2. Delete the "error_message" state and replace it with a DTMF object (row 4, column 2) entitled "dtmf_pin".
3. Add a further Tcl dialogue object called "edit_pin". Draw a connection from the output port of "dtmf_pin" to "edit_pin", and another connection from the output port of "edit_pin" to "confirm_pin".
4. Draw a connection from the output port of "confirm_pin" for the response "no" to "dtmf_pin".

The completed dialogue graph is shown in Figure 7.16. Edit the states as follows:

GENERIC: setup
OnExit:

---

[1] The code for this example was supplied by Jacques de Villiers at CSLU. Permission to use the code is gratefully acknowledged.

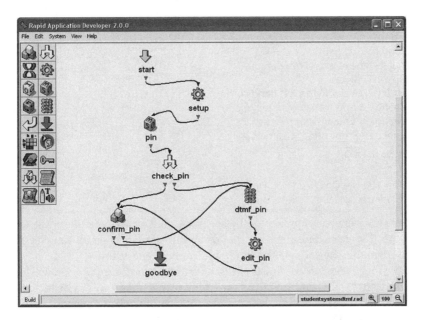

Figure 7.16. Dialogue with DTMF "studentsystemdtmf.rad". (Reprinted with permission from the Center for Spoken Language Understanding. Copyright 2003, OHSU.)

```
set d [toplevel .dtmf]
wm title $d "DTMF"
wm transient $d
wm withdraw $d

proc dtmfKeyRelease w {$w invoke; $w configure -relief raised}
foreach l {0 1 2 3 4 5 6 7 8 9 * # a b c d} {
  button $d.$l -text $l -command [list tcl audio_control Event-> [list dtmf $l]]
  bind $d <KeyPress-$l> [list $d.$l configure -relief sunken]
  bind $d <KeyRelease-$l> [list dtmfKeyRelease $d.$l]
}
grid $d.1 $d.2 $d.3 $d.a -sticky news
grid $d.4 $d.5 $d.6 $d.b -sticky news
grid $d.7 $d.8 $d.9 $d.c -sticky news
grid $d.* $d.0 $d.# $d.d -sticky news
grid columnconfigure $d {0 1 2 3} -weight 1
grid rowconfigure $d {0 1 2 3} -weight 1
update idletasks
wm minsize $d [winfo reqwidth $d] [winfo reqheight $d]

proc showDTMF {} [subst -nocommands -nobackslashes {
  wm deiconify $d
  focus -force $d
}]
proc hideDTMF {} [list wm withdraw $d]
wm protocol $d WM_DELETE_WINDOW hideDTMF
showDTMF
```

```
GENERIC: dtmf
Prompt:
Sorry I didn't get that
Please type in your 4 digit pin.
Open DTMF tab:
Click DTMF box in top left-hand corner.
Change output variable to "pin_recog"
Change Maximum # of tones to 4
Select Interrupt prompt immediately

GENERIC: edit_pin
OnExit
after 100 {set Done 1}; vwait Done
set pin(recog) [split $pin(recog) {}]"
```

Save and test your application by speaking digit strings that have less than or more than four digits, so that the "dtmf_pin" state is entered. You can also disconfirm the pin to cause the "dtmf_pin" to be reentered.

Note that if the user continues to disconfirm the pin, the application will loop between "dtmf_pin" and "confirm_pin". One way to avoid this is to include a count of the number of times the system should try to elicit a response before trying something else. This strategy will be introduced in Chapter 8.

Tutorial 7: Alpha-Digit Recognition

Alpha-digit strings are often used for items such as course codes and product codes. Create a new application, which can be called "course-code". This will be a simple application just to test the alpha-digit recogniser. The dialogue graph for this example is shown in Figure 7.17. This example is similar to the example involving the digit recogniser in that the system checks the alpha-digit string entered by the user, except that in this case a set of alpha-digit strings to be recognised is specified in a vocabulary file. The example involves the following functions:

1. The user is asked to speak in the course code, which is an alphadigit string (e.g., DK003).
2. The system checks if it has recognised something.
3. If no, the system reprompts.
4. If yes, then the user is asked to confirm the course code.
5. If the user confirms the course code, then the system exits.
6. If the user does not confirm the course code, then the user is asked to speak the course code again, then to confirm it.

Exercise 10: Using the Alpha-Digit Recogniser

Create the dialogue graph shown in Figure 7.17, as follows:

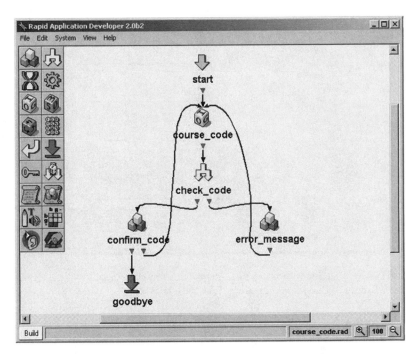

Figure 7.17. Dialogue with alphadigit recogniser "studentsystemalphadigit.rad". (Reprinted with permission from the Center for Spoken Language Understanding. Copyright 2003, OHSU.)

1. Drag the ALPHA-DIGIT icon from the palette (column 1, row 3) from the palette on to the canvas and attach to the Start icon.
2. Rename the state "course_code".
3. Enter the following prompt:

   What is the course code?

Open the recognition port for "course_code". This will bring up an Alphadigit vocabulary box, as shown in Figure 7.18.

   Create a vocabulary file, as follows:

1. Tick Vocabulary.
2. Enter the following words, one on each line: DK003, DK004, DK005 (these are the course codes).
3. Click on the compile tab.
4. Name the file "course_code". It will be given the extension ".dict".
5. Tick Use vocabulary file and browse for your new file "course_code.dict".
6. Click OK to close the window.
7. Adjust the Trailing Silence Duration as described above.

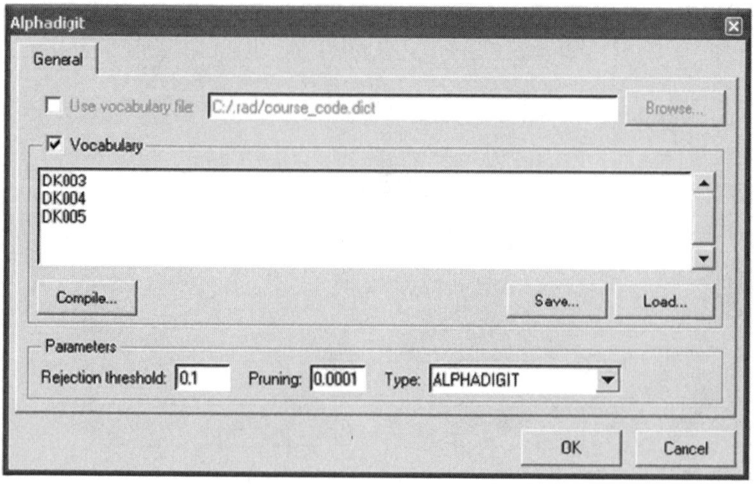

Figure 7.18. Alphadigit vocabulary box. (Reprinted with permission from the Center for Spoken Language Understanding. Copyright 2003, OHSU.)

Note: The file "course_code.dict" will normally reside in c:\.rad\. To create this file, you may also need to create a temporary directory, i.e., c:\.rad\tmp. GENERIC :check_code

1. Open the left side port of "check_code" and insert the expression:
   `$course_code(recog) != ""`
   The dialogue will branch left to the state "confirm_code" if the recognition at "course-code" was not empty. (! = means "not equal to" and " " means "empty string".)

2. In the right side port place a "1" (without quotes). As before, this path evaluates to "true" if the left side port, which contains the condition and is checked first, does not evaluate to "true".

   GENERIC: confirm_code
   Prompt:
   was that $course_code(recog)?
   Recognition:
   Yes, no

   GENERIC: error_message
   Prompt: I didn't get that

Build and run the dialogue. You may find that the TTS has problems speaking the alpha-digit string recognised at the state "course_code". In this case it needs to be translated into a form that can be more easily spoken, i.e., with spaces between the items. This can be done as follows:

1. Click on the "check_code" state and then on the On Exit tab.

2. Enter the following expression in the box, then click
   ```
   OK regsub -all {(.)} $course_code(recog) {/1 }
   speak_code
   ```
   The resulting list of items that can be spoken is now called "speak_code".
3. Adjust the prompt in the state "confirm_code" as follows:
   ```
   was that $speak_code?
   ```

Tutorial 8: Recognition Grammars

Recognition grammars can be used in RAD to allow for input consisting of more than one word or phrase and to enable keyword spotting. In the Pizza example presented in Tutorial 1 there were separate prompts to elicit the size and topping. A recognition grammar could be constructed to allow several values to be submitted within one utterance. Similarly, the confirmation query at the end of the dialogue required the words "yes" or "no" as a response. A recognition grammar could extract keywords from the input that expressed "yes" and "no" in other ways and ignored other irrelevant parts of the input, for example, a response such as "uh right yes that's fine". The rules presented in this tutorial perform both these functions.

Specifying a Recognition Grammar

For the purpose of this tutorial we will define some grammar rules that allow the user to respond to the prompt "What size and type of pizza would you like?" with strings such as:

   (I'd like a) small pepperoni (pizza please)

in which the elements in brackets are optional.

The grammar requires rules for all the words that represent the size choices and the topping choices, such as:

   $size = small | medium | gigantic | large;
   $topping = vegetarian | pepperoni | cheese;

In this notation $size and $topping are variables (indicated by the symbol $). The right-hand side of these rules specifies choices, where the symbol | means "or". According to the $size rule, for example, one of the words "small", "medium", "gigantic" or "large" can be recognised.

The third rule specifies the order in which these variables may occur:

   $pizza = [*sil%% | *any%%] $size $topping [*sil%% | *any%%];

This rule says that a string must include a "size" word followed by a "topping" word. Additionally, there are optional words, which are enclosed in the square brackets. These words are special, built-in features of RAD which are interpreted as follows:

*sil is used to recognise silence;

*any is a garbage word that is used to recognise anything that does not match the specified recognition vocabulary, for example, other words or noises.

Thus the $pizza rule will recognise a string beginning with optional silence or garbage, followed by a $size word and a $topping word, and ending in optional silence or garbage. The %% symbol following a word indicates that the word will not appear in the recognition results, even if it is recognised. A quick check will verify that this rule will match the string "(I'd like a) small pepperoni (pizza please)".

Exercise 11: Creating a Recognition Grammar in RAD

1. Build a small application called "grammar1.rad" consisting of the following states: Start, order, verify.
2. Construct a recognition grammar for the state "order".

Creating a recognition grammar in RAD involves specifying the rules that match all the anticipated input strings and then entering the rules into RAD's recognition vocabulary for the state in question. Let us assume that we have specified the three rules listed above and that these rules constitute the recognition vocabulary for a state in which the user is asked for their order. This grammar is entered as follows:

1. Double click on the recognition port of the state. This will open the vocabulary dialogue, as shown in Figure 7.19.
2. Select Grammar in the box in the upper left corner to indicate that the vocabulary for this state takes the form of a grammar rather than a list of words.
3. Type "pizza" as the name of the grammar.
4. Type in the three grammar rules.
5. Select Extract Words. All of the individual words in your grammar will appear in the vocabulary area.
6. Select Update All to get pronunciation strings for these words.

Notice that RAD uses special, nonphonetic pronunciation strings for *sil and *any. If you were to forget to type the "*" before either of these words in your grammar, then RAD would produce regular pronunciation strings for them and attempt to recognise them literally. The completed grammar is shown in Figure 7.20. You will learn how to extract the elements of the response in Tutorial 10.

GENERIC: order

Note: Increase the trailing silence for this state to enable longer strings to be recorded.

Prompt:
What size and type of pizza would you like?

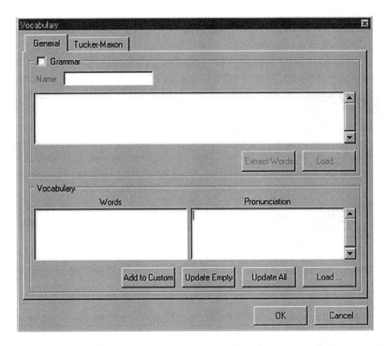

Figure 7.19. Recognition vocabulary box. (Reprinted with permission from the Center for Spoken Language Understanding. Copyright 2003, OHSU.)

> GENERIC: verify
> Prompt:
> You ordered a $order(recog) pizza

Save and test your application using a variety of inputs: Legal inputs that match the grammar, including the two obligatory items (size and topping), and also including some additional words that will be matched by *any. Illegal combinations, for example, including only one of the obligatory items, saying them in the order "topping size", or inserting some other word between the "size" and "topping" words.

Exercise 12: Developing More Complex Grammar Rules

The grammar formalism provided in RAD allows for more complex rules to be developed to represent more varied input. Consider the following grammar rules, slightly adapted from those presented in Chapter 6 to avoid problems with digit recognition:

> viewdetails -> (give me details on) (student) studentname (on) coursecode (on | at) (stage) coursestage
> studentname -> john scott | david wilson | rosemary blackburn | jennifer black

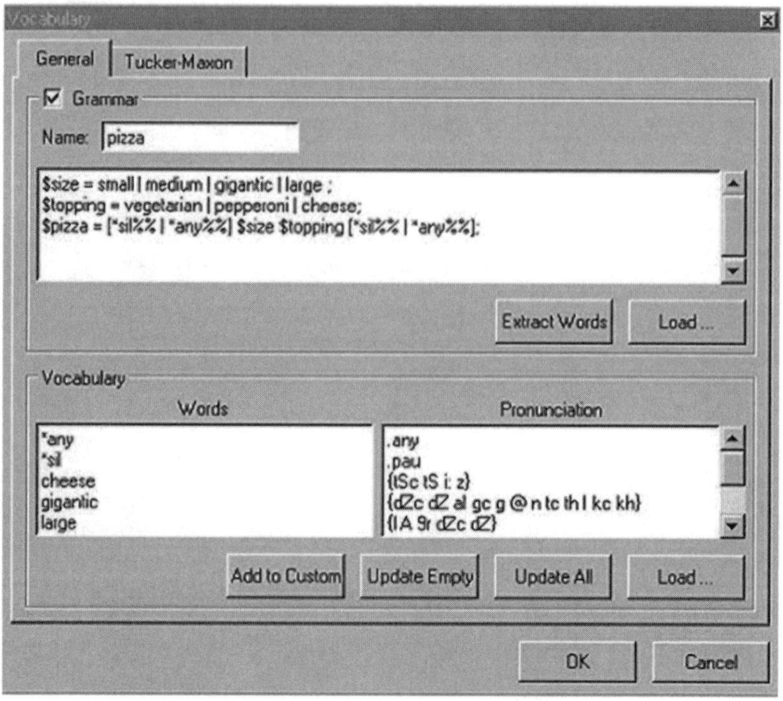

Figure 7.20. Recognition grammar for "grammar1.rad". (Reprinted with permission from the Center for Spoken Language Understanding. Copyright 2003, OHSU.)

```
coursecode -> diploma in applications and support | dk003 | diploma in software
development | dk004
coursestage -> 1 | award
```

These rules allow the user to speak sentences such as:

```
1 Give me details on student john scott on dk003 at stage award.
2 john scott dk003 award.
```

Specify a grammar in RAD that uses these rules and that will accept these sentences. Construct an application called "grammar2.rad" which incorporates this grammar. The application should have a state with a prompt such as "Student details. How may I help you?" A second state should attempt to verify the system's recognition of the user's input according to the grammar. Test your application with a variety of inputs.

The following are some guidelines concerning the notation for the grammar:

```
[ ] indicates words that are optional.
< > indicates items that can be expressed one or more times in a row.
{ } indicates items that can be expressed zero or more times in a row.
| indicates "or".
%% following a word, indicates that word will not appear in the recognition results,
even if it is recognised.
```

% following a word will substitute the next word into the recognition results if the first word is recognised.

The ordering of the rules is also significant. In most grammar formalisms the top-level rules are specified first, followed by rules for smaller constituents, and ending with the lexical rules. In the grammar rules in RAD the lexical rules are specified first, as it is here that the variables are declared that are to be used in the top-level rule. The variable for the top-level rule is declared as the name of the grammar.

Tutorial 9: Speech Output in RAD

It is possible to modify the pronunciation provided by the Festival TTS component in RAD by using SABLE mark-up tags. SABLE is an XML/SGML-based mark-up scheme for TTS synthesis. SABLE tags can be entered into prompts in RAD using a simple graphical tool, as shown in the following exercises.

Exercise 13: Modifying the Rate and Pitch of Speech

1. Open RAD.
2. Drag a generic object on to the canvas and double click on it.
3. Click on the tab Markup (rather than TTS) to enter the following prompt: "Hello this is Baldi. You can make me speak in a lot of different ways."
4. Highlight the prompt.
5. Right click to bring up the dialogue box called TTS Mark-up.
6. Click on the sound icon in the bottom left-hand corner to hear the default output.

Make adjustments to the various parameters such as emphasis, rate, volume, etc., and try them out. If you want to save the modification, click on Apply. (*Note*: You can also highlight a part of the prompt if you only want that part to be modified.)

When you have closed the TTS Mark-up box, you can click on the tab View Source to see how your prompt has been tagged using the SABLE mark-up tags. This is similar to the HTML tags used to mark up a Web page.

Exercise 14: Using SayAs for Special Forms of Output

Edit your prompt as follows:

1. Change the prompt to "banana".
2. Highlight "banana", right click, select SayAs and then select from Speaking Mode: Syllabify. Click on the sound icon to test. Try also using Spell or Digits.

1. Change the prompt to "654137".
2. Highlight and right click, select SayAs and then select from Speaking Mode: Phone Number. Click on the sound icon to test. Try also using Spell or Digits and Ordinal.

Exercise 15: Modifying the Pronunciation

1. Insert a prompt, e.g., "banana".
2. Highlight the prompt and right click, then select Pronounce. You can either enter a word in the Words box, or a phonetic WorldBet representation in the WorldBet box.

Enter the word "apple". Click on the sound icon to test. "Banana" will be pronounced as "apple". (This is probably not what you would want in a real application, but you can use this facility to give words an alternative pronunciation, as required, e.g., words in a foreign language.)

WorldBet entry: right click in the WorldBet box. This will bring up some IPA symbols. Click on a symbol, then click on Audio to hear it. Click on Insert if you want to create a phonetic model for a word. When the word is complete, click on Close, click on the sound icon to test, and on Apply if you want to keep that pronunciation. This feature will be useful for modelling alternative pronunciations or words in a foreign language.

Exercise 16: Inserting a Recording

You can also right click to insert a sound file to accompany other text included as a prompt. For example, insert some text, such as "hello", right click to bring up the Insert option of TTS-Mark-up. Select a sound file from the options provided in the drop-down box for Sound File, e.g., "laugh.wav". Click on Play to test.

Tutorial 10: Using Tcl in RAD

Some examples of Tcl code have been encountered in the tutorials so far. The RAD component of the CSLU Toolkit – the visual elements such as the canvas and dialogue objects – are written in Tcl/TK. (The low-level processing modules such as audio, telephony, and speech recognition and speech synthesis are mostly written in C.) Tcl was created by Ousterhout at the University of California at Berkeley (Ousterhout, 1994). TK, an extension to Tcl, allows the building of graphical user interfaces (GUIs).

In this tutorial some uses of Tcl in RAD will be illustrated. The tutorial is not intended as an introduction to programming in Tcl. Readers who wish to explore Tcl further should consult the Tcl online tutorial provided with RAD and, for more detail, see the on-line Tcl manuals (see references at end of chapter).

Using Tcl/TK Commands

Tcl/TK commands can be typed directly to the Tcl interpreter. This is useful when developing a spoken dialogue system in RAD as the Tcl code can be tested off-line without having to run the spoken application. The Tcl interpreter, which is often referred to as the "command shell", can be accessed by selecting `Start -> CSLU Tookit -> CSLUsh`. Tcl can also be tested in the console window – select `View -> Canvas` from the RAD window. Tcl can also read input from a source file.

Within RAD there are three places where Tcl/TK commands can be inserted:

1. *Start-of-run action*. This code is executed at the start of a RAD application. You enter the start-of-run commands by selecting `System->Start of run action` from the main menu.

2. *State action*. Most RAD objects allow you to enter Tcl/TK code by selecting the `Preferences Menu-> OnEnter-or OnExit` tabs for a state. When the dialogue reaches the state, the Tcl/TK code in these windows is executed. More specifically, the order of execution on entering a state is as follows:

1. Execute code in OnEnter box.
2. Execute prompt.
3. Perform recognition.
4. Default repair.
5. Execute code in OnExit box.

We have already encountered a special Tcl dialogue object for entering Tcl code (see Tutorial 6).

3. *End-of-run action*. The Tcl/TK code is executed at the end of a dialogue (i.e., when a Goodbye Object is reached). You enter the end-of-run commands by selecting the `System->End of run action` from the main menu.

Exercise 17: Using Tcl to Process Recognised Words

In Tutorial 8 the use of a recognition grammar was illustrated, in which the user could specify the size and topping for a pizza order within a single utterance. If recognition was successful then exactly two words would have been recognised, one representing a "size" word and one representing a "topping" word. This phrase can be retrieved using the built-in variable discussed earlier, i.e., "name_of_state(recog)".

However, we may wish to separate the elements of the string and assign each element to its own variable in order to be able to refer to the different elements individually. The following lines of Tcl code will enable this, assuming that the name of the state is "order".

```
set pizzaSize [lindex $order(recog) 0]
set pizzaTopping [lindex $order(recog) 1]
```

The function inside the square brackets uses the function "lindex" to locate an element in the list represented by the variable "$order(recog)". The number 0 indicates that it will be the first element in the list. Similarly, the second line will locate the second element in the list. These elements are assigned to the variables "pizzaSize" and "pizzaTopping" using the assignment function "set".

1. Modify your application "grammar1.rad" to test this code in a Tcl dialogue object, which should be inserted between "order" and "verify".

2. To test that the items have been correctly extracted, change the prompt in "verify" to:

So you want a $pizzaSize pizza. And you want a $pizzaTopping topping.

Some more examples of the use of Tcl in RAD will be presented in Tutorials 11 and 12.

Tutorial 11: Adding New Pronunciations and Creating a Dynamic Recogniser[2]

Adding New Pronunciations

Recognition can be improved by fine-tuning the phonetic representation of the recognition vocabulary. Some tools are provided in RAD to do this fine-tuning, but essentially fine-tuning of the phonetic representation will require some knowledge of phonetics.

It is important to appreciate how the pronunciation models are created in RAD. As you will have seen, phonetic representations are generated automatically when you enter words into the recognition window and click Update All. To create these pronunciations RAD consults the following sources in order until a pronunciation has been found:

1. Custom dictionary. This contains specific pronunciation models produced by the developer (see below).

2. System dictionary. By default, RAD uses the CMU (Carnegie Mellon University) pronunciation dictionary.

3. TTS synthesiser. If the word is not found in any of the above dictionaries, a TTS synthesiser is used to generate a pronunciation via letter-to-sound rules. This pronunciation is then stored in the local dictionary in case it is needed again.

---

[2] This tutorial is based on RAD tutorial 20 "Custom Pronunciations and Word Models", which is available at: http://www.cslu.ogi.edu/toolkit/docs/2.0/apps/rad/tutorials/tutorial020/index.html

RAD uses the Worldbet phonetic symbol set to represent pronunciations of words. (Recall that a table of Worldbet symbols, including examples, is available by clicking on `Help -> Worldbet` symbols.) Hand-crafting a pronunciation is required when the pronunciation generated by the system is inaccurate, because of an incorrect dictionary entry or because of regional pronunciations of the word.

There are two ways to modify a pronunciation that is displayed in the box entitled "Pronunciations":

1. Type in a new pronunciation.
2. Save the hand-built models into the custom dictionary:
   1. Enter the alternate pronunciation.
   2. Click `Add to Custom` from the recognition Vocabulary dialogue box.

This is a more permanent solution.

The entire custom dictionary can be manually edited from the global preferences window under the Dictionaries tab. The dictionary format contains one entry per line. The first element of the line is the word in lowercase letters, followed by white space, then a pronunciation. Words can be composed of any combination of printable characters, except that there can be no white space in the middle of the word.

A pronunciation is a list of phonemes delimited by white space. Extra spaces or tabs are ignored during recognition. Every phoneme must be matched in order for the word to be successfully recognised:

    dZ @ n j u E 9r i:

Optional phonemes are enclosed in square brackets. The following example can be pronounced with or without the E:

    dZ @ n j u [E] 9r i:

Alternate phonemes are enclosed in curly braces. The following pronunciation permits either @ or E for the vowel in the first syllable:

    dZ {@ E} n j u E 9r i:

Phonemes can be forced into alternative groupings using parentheses. The following example allows two alternate pronunciations in the first syllable, either dZ @ n or dZ E m:

    dZ {(@ n) (E m)} j u E 9r i:

Exercise 18: Modifying Pronunciations

Create a hand-crafted pronunciation model for the following words, and then run a test program to see if recognition improves:

portland;

eighty-eight.

Below are some common modifications that often improve the accuracy of words models.

1. Try making the plosive releases optional when followed by consonants or at the end of a word. Example: Change the pronunciation string for "portland" from:

   pc ph > 9r tc th l & n dc d

   to:

   pc ph > 9r tc [th] l & n dc [d]

2. Try changing the alveolar plosives that occur in the middle of a word or phrase to flaps. Example: Change the pronunciation string for eighty-eight from:

   ei tc th i: [.pau] ei tc th

   to:

   ei {(tc th) (d_\)} i: [.pau] ei tc [th]

Dynamic Recognition

You have learned how to specify the recognition vocabulary for a given state by either typing your entries, phrase by phrase, into the Word space of a Vocabulary dialogue box's Tree recognition type, or by creating a grammar in a Vocabulary dialogue box's Grammar recognition type. Both types of recognisers, Tree and Grammar, can be created dynamically. In this exercise you will learn to dynamically create tree recognisers.

Dynamically creating a recogniser is required when the recognition vocabulary for the state involved is not known in advance. For example, the students enrolled on a course, or the set of modules available, may change over time. This information would normally be kept in a database, which would be regularly updated. A static recognition vocabulary is created in advance and would be difficult to update every time the database is changed. A better solution is to dynamically create the recognition vocabulary at run-time by consulting the most recent entries in the database. Two processes are involved:

1. Connecting to a database to retrieve a list of words to be modelled.
2. Creating the pronunciations of these words dynamically using the functions provided in RAD.

Tutorial 12 will show how to connect RAD to a database. In this tutorial a simpler approach will be used in which a text file is prepared that simulates the list of words retrieved from the database. The pronunciation models are then created using this file.

Exercise 19: Dynamic Recognition

1. Create a small text file "students.txt", which represents the words that are to be recognised dynamically. The words should be listed on separate lines. Save the file in c:\.rad\

John

David

Rosemary

Jennifer

2. Create a dialogue system with one state called "names". (*Note*: Lines preceded by the "#" symbol are comments.)

Insert the following prompt in the "names" state:

```
who do you want to speak to?
OnEnter:
set f [open c:/.rad/students.txt r]
#opens your text file in read mode
set words [read $f]
#reads in the words in the file
close $f
#closes the file
set pron [createTreeVocab $words]
#creates pronunciations for the words and stores them in the variable $pron
set state "names"
#sets the name for the state for the tree recogniser as "names"
buildTreeRecognizer $state $pron
#builds a tree recogniser using the pronunciations stored in $pron at the state
"names"

OnExit code:
tts "so you want to speak to $names(recog)"
#confirms the recognised name
```

Save your program as "dynamicrecognition.rad". Test your program using the names included in your file "students.txt".

Tutorial 12: Linking a RAD Application to a Database Using TclODBC

TclODBC is an extension to Tcl which allows access to databases created by many types of database management software. The implementation relies on the standard ODBC interface. In this tutorial MS Access will be used for the database. For further information about TclODBC, see: http://sourceforge.net/projects/tclodbc.

querydetails					
ID	studentid	firstname	lastname	coursecode	stage
1	96050918	john	scott	dk003	1
2	96069783	david	wilson	dk005	award
3	96317159	rosemary	blackburn	dk003	1
4	96416781	jennifer	black	dk003	award

Figure 7.21. The table "querydetails" from the database "student.mdb".

Getting Started

Before you begin this tutorial you need to do the following:

1. Download and install TclODBC (see Appendix 2).
2. Create a database called student.mdb, with a table called "querydetails" as shown in Figure 7.21. Store the database in c:\databases\. (*Note*: This application was developed using MS Access. Many other ODBC compliant database systems could be used.) (Consult the TclODBC documentation for details.)
3. Set up the data source (see Appendix 2).

Exercise 20: Testing TclODBC in the CSLUsh Window

This exercise implements the "View details" function in the student informa-tion application. The system prompts for a student ID, then looks up the data-base to retrieve the relevant record. The connections to the database can be tested separately in the command window, before integrating the code into a RAD program. In the instructions below CSLUsh 2.0b2% is the system prompt in the CSLUsh window. Comments on the commands are in parentheses.

1. Start -> CSLU Toolkit -> CSLUsh
2. CSLUsh 2.0b2% package require tclodbc
(invoke TclODBC package).
3. 2.3
(system confirmation that TclODBC has been loaded).
4. CSLUsh 2.0b2% database db student
(connect to the data source).
5. db
(system confirmation).
6. CSLUsh 2.0b2% set get_student_id 96050918
(this assigns the value 96050918 to get_student_id – in the real application this would be elicited from the user.)

7. CSLUsh 2.0b2% `set   details   [db  "select  firstname,last-`
   `name,coursecode,stage  from  querydetails  where  stu-`
   `dentid = '$get_student_id' "]`
(this command contains the SQL query to return the details (firstname, lastname, coursecode and stage) from the table "querydetails" where student_id = 96050918. The results are stored in the variable "details". Note the format of the command, including the function "db", all of which is enclosed in square brackets.)

For this query, the response is:

{john scott dk003 1}

In order to extract the relevant items from this string, we need to put it into a format which will allow us to use the "lindex" function.

```
regsub {\{} $details {} details
# removes the opening {
regsub {\}} $details {} details
# removes the closing }
set firstname [lindex $details 0]
# extracts the first element and assigns to firstname
set lastname [lindex $details 1]
# extracts the second element and assigns to lastname
set coursecode [lindex $details 2]
# extracts the third element and assigns to coursecode
set stage [lindex $details 3]
# extracts the fourth element and assigns to stage)
```

Once these functions have been tested successfully with a few variations, we can proceed to create a spoken dialogue application in RAD.

Exercise 21: Viewing Student Details in RAD

In this exercise you will build an application to retrieve student details from the database. To keep it simple, we will assume that there are no problems with recognition of the digits representing the student ID. A more comprehensive application that takes account of various problems that could arise is specified as a project below. The dialogue graph for this example is shown in Figure 7.22.

1. Create an application as shown in Figure 7.22.
2. Insert the following in each state:

```
GENERIC: initial
OnExit:
package require tclodbc
database db student

GENERIC: get_student_id
Prompt:
what is the student id?
```

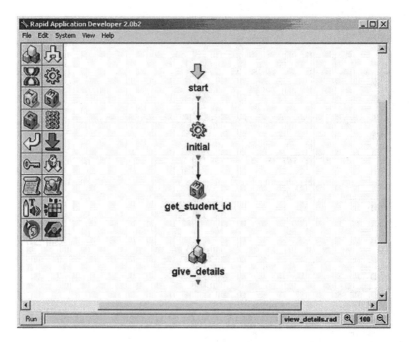

Figure 7.22. Dialogue graph for "view_details.rad". (Reprinted with permission from the Center for Spoken Language Understanding. Copyright 2003, OHSU.)

```
OnExit
set get_student_id(recog) [words2numbers $get_student_id(recog)]
#converts the string of words returned by the digit recogniser into a number to
match the studentid field in the database

GENERIC: give_details
OnEnter
set details [db "select firstname,lastname,coursecode,stage from querydetails
where studentid = '$get_student_id(recog)'"]
regsub {\{} $details {} details
regsub {\}} $details {} details
set firstname [lindex $details 0]
set lastname [lindex $details 1]
set coursecode [lindex $details 2]
set stage [lindex $details 3]

Prompt:
the details are:
Student
$firstname
$lastname
The course code is $coursecode
This student is at stage $stage
```

Save your application as "view_details.rad" and test the application. (*Note*: If you have difficulties with recognition of the digit string, you could incorporate a facility for DTMF input as shown in Tutorial 6.)

Summary

In this chapter the essential elements of RAD for developing speech-based interfaces have been introduced. The following topics have been covered:

- Creating states and linking them to form a dialogue graph.
- Creating prompts for the TTS system.
- Modifying the speech output.
- Creating recognition vocabularies and recognition grammars.
- Modifying pronunciation models.
- Dynamic recognition.
- Dealing with silence and poor recognition in the default repair subdialogue.
- Creating and saving subdialogues.
- Digit and alpha-digit recognition.
- Simulating DTMF input.
- Linking RAD to a database using TclODBC.

Chapter 8 will build on this foundation and will introduce some additional elements that support multimodal input and output in RAD.

Further Reading

RAD

RAD tutorials at CSLU.

The most recent documentation at CSLU is the set of tutorials listed at: http://cslu.cse.ogi.edu/toolkit/docs/2.0/apps/rad/tutorials/index.html

Documentation of an older version of RAD, which includes much of the material in the current RAD tutorials as well as some additional ideas, can be found at: http://cslu.cse.ogi.edu/toolkit/old/old/documentation/cslurp/wincslurp/newmanual.html

CSLR tutorial. This is an introductory tutorial with animation, which is provided with the CSLU Toolkit. It can be found at: Start → Speech Toolkit → RAD Documentation → CSLR Tutorial.

RAD User Guide. This is a good introductory tutorial developed by Alice Tarachow at the Tucker–Maxon Oral School, Portland, Oregon. It can be found at: Start → Speech Toolkit → RAD Documentation → RAD User Guide.

Course on Design and Implementation of Spoken Dialogue Systems by Saturnino Luz at: http://www.it-uni.sdu.dk/mmp/slds/
Includes RAD tutorial at: http://www.it-uni.sdu.dk/mmp/slds/tutorial/

Tcl

For further information on Tcl, consult the Tcl Manuals at: http://www.tcl.tk/doc/, as well as the book (Ousterhout, 1994). See also the Rad Tcl tutorial at: http://cslu.cse.ogi.edu/toolkit/docs/2.0/apps/rad/tutorials/tutorial006/index.html

TclODBC

Information on downloading and installing TclODBC can be found at: http://sourceforge.net/projects/tclodbc

Ideas for Further Projects

1. Combine dynamic recognition with a database to get information about a student. The system should extract names from the database and create a recognition vocabulary dynamically, then prompt the user for a name. The system should consult the database, retrieve the record for that name and read out the details.

2. Viewing student details in RAD – A more advanced application.

The application created in Exercise 21 needs to be further developed to address the following cases:

Case 1. No record is returned because the system has not recognised the correct number of digits.

Case 2. No record is returned because the digits recognised by the system are incorrect.

Case 3. No record is returned because an incorrect digit string has been submitted for which there is no match in the database.

Case 4. The wrong record is returned because the user has input an incorrect digit string which happened to match a record in the database.

Develop a system that will address each of these cases.

3. Improving recognition in RAD.

Recognition can be improved in RAD by adjusting the speech recognition parameters listed in the preference menu. Consult the on-line tutorial on adjusting recognition parameters (RAD Tutorial 19, see Web page reference below).

4. Complete the Student System application, as presented in Chapter 6.

5. Implement the system that you specified in Chapter 6.

6. Voice Banking system.

This system is specified as an assignment at Macquarie University. For details, see: http://www.comp.mq.edu.au/courses/comp349/Assignments-2002/Assignment2/

7. Room booking system.

This system is specified as an assignment at Macquarie University. For details, see: http://www.comp.mq.edu.au/courses/comp349/Assignments-2002/Assignment3/

Developing Multimodal Dialogue Systems Using the CSLU Toolkit

8

The Centre for Spoken Language Understanding (CSLU) toolkit has been used successfully at the Tucker–Maxon Oral School in Portland, Oregon, to improve children's listening and speaking skills, and to increase their vocabulary and enable them to review concepts (Connors et al., 1999).

This chapter explores some additional features of the toolkit that are particularly applicable to interactive learning. The toolkit includes a number of multimodal features, such as an animated talking head and the facility to include images in which clickable areas can be defined. The tutorials in this chapter will show how to configure the toolkit's animated character, how to display images and create image maps, and how to create sequences of recurrent interactions, such as question–answer–feedback. Other features that will also be introduced are the use of a Tool Command Language (Tcl) variable to keep scores in a game, and the use of a database to maintain information about the learner's performance in a game.

The tutorials develop a series of interactive spoken language games for young children aged 5–7 years[1] (Murphy, 2001). The games involve concepts that are taught in the UK National Curriculum Key Stage 1. In each game the system greets the learner and asks them to log in by clicking on their name from a list. The system establishes if the learner has played before. If so, the learner is greeted and the game starts. Their previous score is retrieved and they are encouraged to try to beat that score on this occasion. If not, a brief introduction to the game is given. At the end of the game the learner is told their score and the database is updated. The following tutorials are included in this chapter:

Tutorial 1: Setting up the animated character.

Tutorial 2: Login dialogue.

Tutorial 3: Exploring emotions.

Tutorial 4: Identifying two-dimensional shapes.

Tutorial 5: Improving the interface.

---

[1] These games were developed by Angela Murphy as part of the requirements for the MSc Computing and Information Systems dissertation at the University of Ulster.

In the final part of the chapter the CSLU Vocabulary Tutor will be briefly introduced along with some other ongoing projects in the area of spoken language interactive tutors.

Tutorial 1: Setting Up the Animated Character

Earlier versions of the CSLU toolkit used Baldi as the animated character (for further details on Baldi, see the web site at: http://mambo.ucsc.edu/). Baldi was launched by default when the Rapid Application Developer (RAD) was started. In the most recent version there is a choice of animated characters that can be viewed by selecting File → Preferences and then viewing the options in the drop-down menu box for animated face, as shown in Figure 8.1.

There is a choice between CUAnimate, Fluent and NullFace. The characters in CUAnimate are provided by the Centre for Spoken Language Research (CSLR), University of Colorado (http://cslr.colorado.edu/index.html), while the characters in Fluent are provided by Fluent Animated Speech™ (http://www.sensoryinc.com/). The choice NullFace will result in no animated character being used. This option could also be selected by unchecking the Animated Face box.

Note: The option for the Baldi character may also be shown. In some installations the system will attempt to launch with Baldi and will report an error. In this case, the Animated Face box should be unchecked, or one of the options from the drop-down menu should be selected. If CUAnimate is selected, the character Gurney (also known as Ms ReadWrite) will appear, as shown in Figure 8.2. This is the neutral version of the character, as no emotions have been selected yet.

Clicking on File → Preferences in the CUAnimate Window will bring up the CUAnimate Preferences box shown in Figure 8.3. Here the slider for the "happy" emotion has been moved to a setting of 0.50, resulting in the happy version of the character, as shown in Figure 8.4.

Other available characters – Lilly, Percy, Rowdy and Zach – can be selected from the drop-down menu under the label Configuration, as well as other configurations that have been created and saved. Various modifications can be

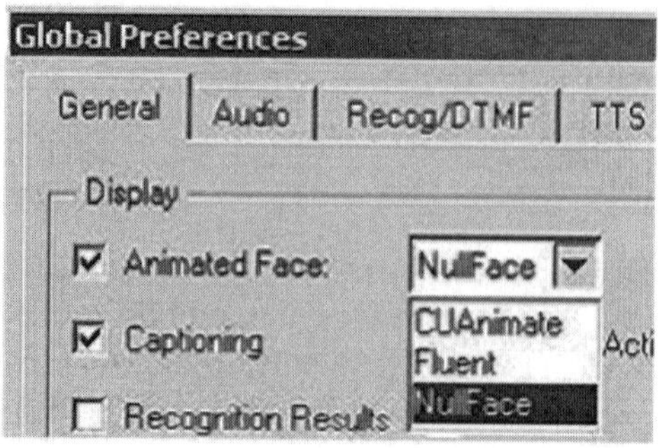

Figure 8.1. Menu for animated characters. (Reprinted with permission from the Center for Spoken Language Understanding. Copyright 2003, OHSU.)

Figure 8.2. The character "Gurney". (Reprinted with permission from the Center for Spoken Language Research.)

Figure 8.3. The CUAnimate preferences box. (Reprinted with permission from the Center for Spoken Language Research.)

Figure 8.4. The character "Gurney" in "happy" mode. (Reprinted with permission from the Center for Spoken Language Research.)

made to the character by making selections in the Preferences box. The use of the Emotions options will be explored in Tutorial 3.

Selecting the Fluent character brings up a version of the Rowdy character with head, arms and body down to waistline. By clicking on File → 3D Model other characters – Lilly, Percy and Zach – can be selected. Clicking on Options will bring up a wide range of options for manipulating the character, as shown in Figure 8.5.

Exercise 1

Experiment with the various configurations and options available in the CUAnimate and Fluent characters.

Tutorial 2: Login Dialogue

This application allows the user to log in from a visually displayed list of users. The system then consults the user profile to retrieve information about the user. In this example the system will check whether the user has played the game "emotions" before.

Exercise 2: Developing a Login Dialogue

1. Select a character. Ensure that there is a matching voice by selecting from the text-to-speech (TTS) Global Preferences, as shown in Figure 8.6. Select one

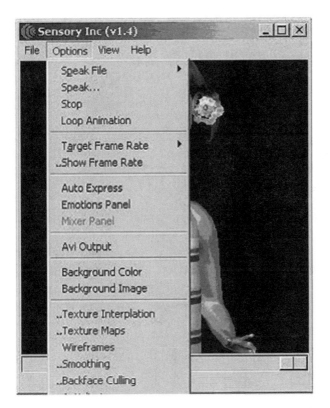

Figure 8.5. Sensory Inc. options for animated characters. (Reprinted with permission from Sensory Inc.)

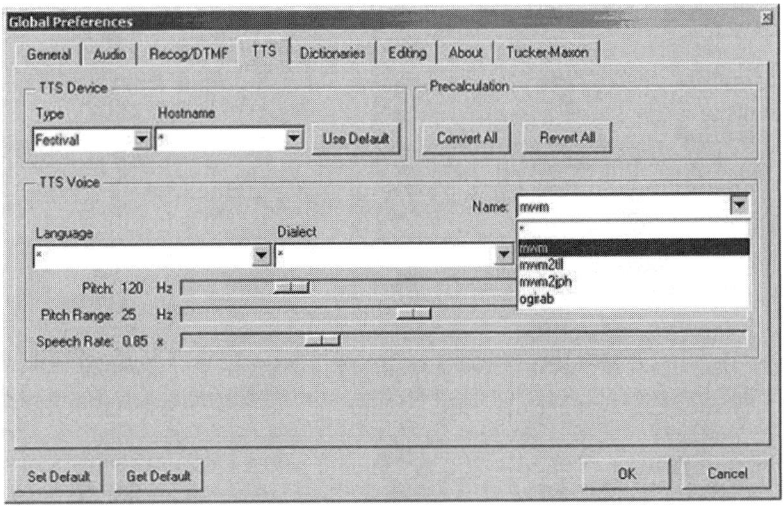

Figure 8.6. TTS preferences. (Reprinted with permission from the Center for Spoken Language Understanding. Copyright 2003, OHSU.)

ID	name	emotions_played	emotions_score	shapes_played	shapes_score
1	John	Yes	4	No	0
2	Mary	Yes	3	Yes	3
3	Gillian	Yes	3	No	0
4	Rosemary	No	0	Yes	3
5	David	No	0	No	0
6	William	No	0	No	0

Figure 8.7. Database table for the interactive games.

of the options from name: mwm, mwm2tll or mwm2jph. The option "ogirab" seems to result in an error. Option "mwm2tll" is a female voice, the others are male.

2. Create a database entitled "rad_games.mdb" with a table entitled "User_Profile" to hold the user profiles, as shown in Figure 8.7.

3. Set the database up in ODBC Data Sources with Data Source Name "games" (see Appendix 2).

4. Create a dialogue graph as shown in Figure 8.8.

5. Edit the states as follows:

GENERIC: sign_in
TTS:
Hello there. Please sign in by clicking on your name from the list.

LOGIN (shaped like a key, row 7, column 2): login
See below for instructions on how to enter data into the LOGIN object

ACTION Tcl: check_database
OnExit:
package require tclodbc
database db games
set played_before [db "select emotions_played from User_Profile where name = '"$user'"]
checks whether user has played the game "emotions" before – this can be set to check other games, as required

CONDITIONAL: state6
Left output port: $played_before == "yes"
Right output port: 1

GENERIC: experienced_player
TTS: Hello $user. I see you have played before.

GENERIC: new_player
TTS: Hello $user. My name is (insert name of the character you selected). Welcome to Games Galore. Each game has instructions at the start and a score at the end.

The Login Object

The login object allows you to create a list of users. The list is presented on the screen and the user chooses their name by clicking on one of the names in the list. As a result the variable "user" is set to the value of the name selected. Double

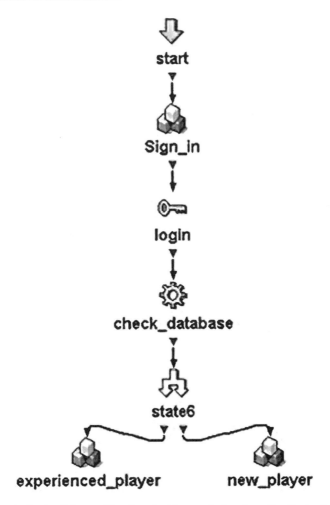

start

Sign_in

login

check_database

state6

experienced_player   new_player

Figure 8.8. The login dialogue. (Reprinted with permission from the Center for Spoken Language Understanding. Copyright 2003, OHSU.)

clicking opens the login object. Enter the names from the "games" database. If you need help, click on the Help tab for instructions.

Save your application as "log_in.rad" and test it. In this tutorial the login dialogue has been developed as a standalone application. Normally the functions of logging in and consulting the user profile would be incorporated as a subdialogue within an application.

Tutorial 3: Exploring Emotions

This application is the first of a series of games. Each game has a similar structure. The user is asked if they want instructions. Then the game is played. During the game if the answer is correct, the system gives praise and increments the score. If the answer is incorrect, the user is given another chance with some help. If it is still incorrect, the system moves on. At the end of the game the final score is spoken to the user and they are asked if they want to play again.

The game "emotions" is concerned with the task of exploring emotions that are conveyed by facial expressions. The point of the game is to encourage children to explore emotions and to express themselves within a controlled dialogue structure. During the game the animated character's facial expression changes, indicating a change in emotions. The main feature of RAD to be covered in this tutorial is the configuration of the animated character. Configuring the animated character is introduced in Exercise 3, while Exercise 4 develops the application.

Exercise 3: Configuring the Animated Character

Start RAD and select the CU Animate character from the File → Preferences menu. Click on File → Preferences in the animated character's window, as described in Tutorial 1. This will bring up the configuration menu, shown in Figure 8.3. The default character is Gurney, but you can select other characters from the drop-down list for Character, if you wish. For this tutorial select the character Percy.

The animated character can be configured differently for every prompt and can be made to display different emotions. The character can also be shown in a transparent mode in order to demonstrate articulation by moving the Opaqueness slider under Rendering. You can also display the character in wireframe mode by checking the Wireframe box. In this tutorial we will explore the parameters in the Emotions section and show how the resulting configurations can be saved and used as required at different dialogue states.

Increase the "Happy" slider in the Emotions section and note the reaction. Decrease the neutral slider and note the reaction. The neutral slider amplifies or reduces the intensity of the emotion tags. Experiment with combinations of emotions. To save a configuration, select Save as, type the name of the face into the Configuration box and hit the Enter key.

To use this configuration in an application, close the Configuration menu, open the Preferences menu of a generic dialogue state where you wish to use the configuration, and select the required option from those available in the Face drop-down menu at the bottom of the menu, as shown in Figure 8.9.

Create and save additional configurations for the following emotions: sad, angry, surprised, disgusted.

Exercise 4: Putting It Together in an Application

In this application (shown in Figure 8.10) the user is asked to log in by clicking on their name on a list presented on screen. The system checks if they have played the game before. If they have, their previous score is retrieved and they

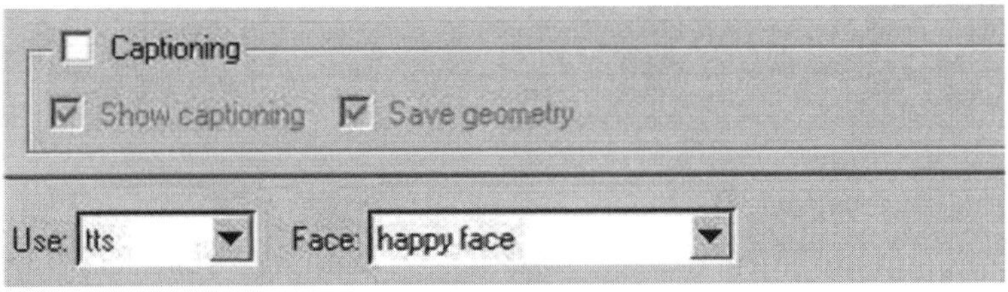

Figure 8.9. Selecting a configuration. (Reprinted with permission from the Center for Spoken Language Understanding. Copyright 2003, OHSU.)

are asked if they wish to hear the instructions again. New players are greeted with a brief statement about the game and asked if they would like to hear the instructions. The instructions present an overview of the game in which the different emotions are displayed. In the main part of the game the animated character (Percy) explains how his emotions are displayed in his facial expressions and then asks how he is feeling now. The dialogue proceeds through a series of different emotions and visual displays of Percy's face. If the player says the correct answer, the score is incremented, otherwise some help is provided and they get another chance. If they are still unsuccessful, Percy moves on. At the end of the game Percy announces the score and asks them if they want to try again. If not, the database is updated with the most recent score. In the current exercise only the first emotion will be presented. Further emotions can be added as an additional exercise.

1. Create a dialogue graph as shown in Figure 8.10. The main part of the application will be within the subdialogue "start_game". This subdialogue will contain further subdialogues for each emotion. For present purposes only the subdialogue "happy" will be developed.
2. Create a login subdialogue as described in Exercise 2.
3. For the main screen, edit the states as follows:

GENERIC: instructions?
OnEnter:
set Oldscore [db "SELECT emotions_score FROM User_Profile WHERE name = '$user';"]
#retrieve previous score, if any, for this game
if {$Oldscore == 0} {tts "In this game we are going to talk a little about our emotions. Would you like instructions?"}
#new player
if {$Oldscore != 0} {tts "The last time you played this game, your score was $Oldscore. Why don't you try to beat it. Would you like to hear the instructions again?"}
#experienced player

Recognition: Left output port: no
Recognition: Right output port: yes

Goodbye
TTS: I hope you enjoyed the game. Try again another time.

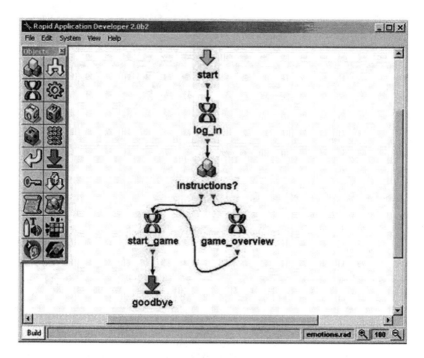

Figure 8.10. Dialogue graph for "emotions.rad". (Reprinted with permission from the Center for Spoken Language Understanding. Copyright 2003, OHSU.)

OnExit:
db "UPDATE User_Profile SET emotions_score = '$score' WHERE name = '$user' ";
#update the database with new score

SUBDIALOGUE: start_game

Create the following states as shown in Figure 8.11.

Note: In the complete application there should be a link from "happy" to "sad" to begin the chain of different emotions. The link from "happy" to "again?" should also be removed. The current links are for the simplified exercise involving only the subdialogue "happy".

ACTION Tcl: set_score
OnExit:
set score 0
#sets the score for this run of the game

GENERIC: how_am_I_feeling
TTS:
You can tell by my face how I am feeling. Sometimes I am angry, sometimes I am sad. Sometimes I am happy. I can also be surprised and disgusted.
Let's begin.

GENERIC: again?
TTS: Congratulations. Your score is $score. Would you like to play again?

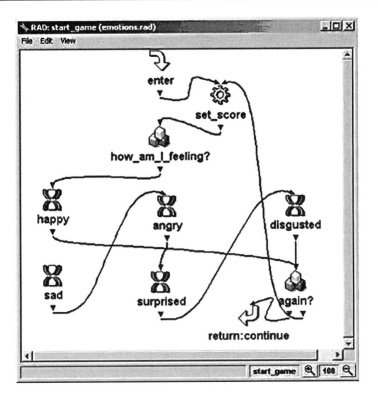

Figure 8.11. Developing emotions.rad. (Reprinted with permission from the Center for Spoken Language Understanding. Copyright 2003, OHSU.)

Recognition:
Left output port: no
Right output port: yes

SUBDIALOGUE: "game_overview".

Create and link together a series of states using GENERIC objects. Name the states "happy", "sad", "angry", "surprised", "disgusted". Include in each state an appropriate prompt such as "sometimes I am happy", and set the face to the appropriate emotion.

Add the following states, as shown in Figure 8.12.

SUBDIALOGUE: happy

GENERIC: happy_face
TTS:
How do I look? Am I happy, sad, surprised, angry, or disgusted?
Face: happy
Recognition:
Left output port: happy
Right output port: *any

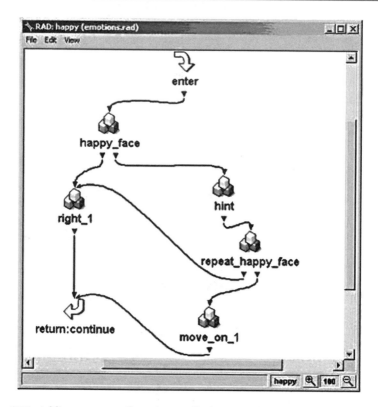

Figure 8.12. Adding states to "emotions.rad". (Reprinted with permission from the Center for Spoken Language Understanding. Copyright 2003, OHSU.)

GENERIC: right_1
TTS: That's right. I am happy.
You get one star.
OnExit: incr score

GENERIC: hint
TTS: To help you, look at my face again. Everything is fine today.
Face: happy

GENERIC: "repeat_happy_face"
TTS: How do you think I am feeling?
Face: happy face
Recognition:
Left output port: happy
Right output port: *any

GENERIC: "move_on_1"
TTS: Oh no, nearly but not there yet. I was feeling happy.

Save and test your application.

Exercise 5: Adding Further Subdialogues

In its present form there is only one question about the "happy" emotion. Add further subdialogues for the other emotions described by Percy in the "game_overview" subdialogue. Save and test your application.

Tutorial 4: Identifying Two-dimensional Shapes

In this tutorial the user is asked to identify two-dimensional shapes. A visual aid is presented with different shapes on it. The animated character describes the shapes using mathematical terms and asks the user to identify the shapes by clicking on the correct shape. If the answer is correct, then the animated character confirms. If the answer is wrong, then a repair subdialogue is begun in which the user is given two more chances. After that the system continues with the next question. The score is given at the end of the game and the database is updated.

This application introduces some additional features provided in RAD. The Listbuilder function is used to loop through a series of exchanges with the same structure, for example, question, answer, feedback. This is a useful alternative to having to plot each exchange separately on the dialogue graph. The Media Object is used to present pictures, in which clickable regions can be defined.

Exercise 6: Using Listbuilder

In this exercise we will create a simple application ("listshapes.rad") that asks six questions. Along with these questions there are six correct answers and six corresponding phrases expressing praise. The system will loop through the question–answer–praise sequences and will then exit. No pictures are involved in this exercise, so the answers will be elicited using speech. Figure 8.13 shows the dialogue graph for this exercise.

Two new objects are the LISTBUILDER object (labelled "Build_Descriptions"), and the GENERIC List object (labelled "Ask_Descriptions"). LISTBUILDER has two output ports. The right-hand port (coloured red), is for looping through the list elements and should be connected to the GENERIC List object, where the list values are recognised. The left-hand output port (coloured blue) is taken when the end of the list element loop is reached.

Double clicking on the LISTBUILDER object will open the LISTBUILDER dialogue box in which the elements of the list are specified. An example is shown in Figure 8.14. Three lists have been specified – description, name and praise – and the entries for "description" are shown in the right-hand pane, beginning at zero. These elements are referenced using the variable $description. Similar entries are specified for the variables "name" and "praise" (see below for

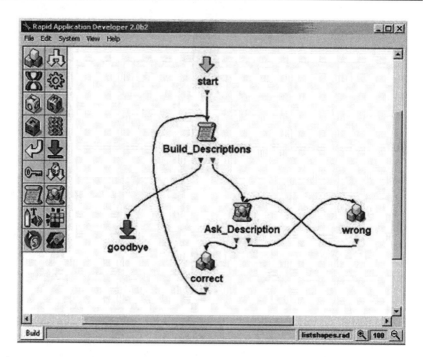

Figure 8.13. Dialogue graph for the Listbuilder dialogue. (Reprinted with permission from the Center for Spoken Language Understanding. Copyright 2003, OHSU.)

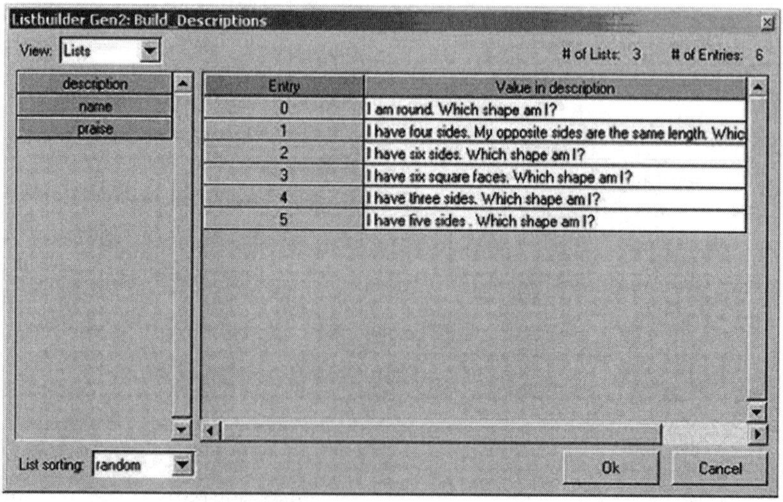

Figure 8.14. Listbuilder dialogue box. (Reprinted with permission from the Center for Spoken Language Understanding. Copyright 2003, OHSU.)

listings). List sorting, at the bottom left-hand corner, has been set to random, so that the system will present the items in random sequence. The alternatives are "order" (sequence as listed), and "reverse".

The GENERIC List object is where the values of the list elements are retrieved. To have values of the "description" items spoken, simply insert the variable $description in the TTS window of this object. To have the values of the "name" items recognised, (i.e., the answers), insert the variable $name into the left-hand output port. The values of "praise" are spoken at the state "correct" by inserting the variable $praise in the TTS window of this object. With this set of dialogue objects in place, the system will take the list elements specified in "Build_Descriptions" in random order, ask a question, listen for an answer and, if the answer is correct, speak the specified feedback. In the example shown there is also a path for incorrect responses, which in this case simply loops back to ask the question again. When all the list elements have been processed, the system exits to the Goodbye state.

The following are the entries for each state (these will also be useful for the next exercise):

To add a new list, right click in the Lists column.

To add a new entry, right click in the Entry column.

LISTBUILDER: Build_Descriptions

description:
0 I am round. Which shape am I?
1 I have four sides. My opposite sides are the same length. Which shape am I?
2 I have six sides. Which shape am I?
3 I have six square faces. Which shape am I?
4 I have three sides. Which shape am I?
5 I have five sides. Which shape am I?

name:
0 circle
1 rectangle
2 hexagon
3 cube
4 triangle
5 pentagon

praise: (insert your favourite praise, if you wish)
0 Good. It's a circle. That was an easy one.
1 Well done. It's a rectangle. Keep up the good work!
2 That's right, a hexagon. Give yourself a pat on the back!
3 Well tickle me, you got it! It's a cube. That was a hard one.
4 Super, it's a triangle. You are doing well.
5 You got it, a pentagon. Brilliant!

GENERIC List: Ask_Description
TTS: $description
Recognition:
Left-hand output port: $name
Right-hand output port: *any

GENERIC: correct
TTS: $praise

GENERIC: wrong
TTS: try again

Save and test your application.

There are several ways in which this application can be improved. It would be useful to show pictures of the shapes to help the player. It would also be a good idea to ensure that the game does not go into a continual loop if the answers are incorrect. These improvements will be incorporated in the next two exercises.

Exercise 7: Adding Clickable Pictures ("mediashapes.rad")

In this exercise a picture will be presented in which each of the shapes is represented. Each shape is defined as a clickable area. The system loops through the list elements, as in Exercise 6. However, this time the player does not say the name of the shape but clicks on the appropriate shape on the displayed image. The media object is used to present and remove the picture and to specify the clickable areas. A conditional object is used to determine if the area clicked is the correct one. The dialogue graph for this exercise is shown in Figure 8.15. To specify the behaviours of media objects, double click on the media object to bring up the media object box, as shown in Figure 8.16.

The following is a brief explanation of the options in the Media object box:

Window Placement. Clicking on the "Modify" tab will present a set of choices for the placement of the picture. Experiment with these in your application.

Text. Any text that you insert here will be used as a caption for the picture.

Image. Select "Browse" to locate the picture that you wish to use. (In this exercise, we will not insert a picture using this option, as we wish to define an image map with clickable areas.)

Image Map. Click "Edit" to bring up the Image map editor, and then "Open" to load a picture into the editor. (See below for instructions on using the Image map editor.)

Recording. This allows you to record or insert sound files.

The Image map editor is used to edit pictures and to define behaviours. Figure 8.17 shows an example using a picture containing the shapes used in this exercise. The drawing tools can be used to specify an area in the image as clickable. In this case the square tool was used. As each area is specified, right clicking on the area brings up a box in which the properties of the area can be defined, for example, a name such as "circle", along with behaviours such as

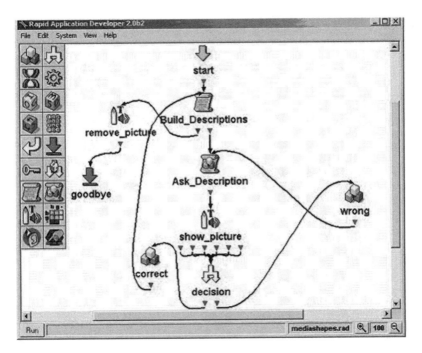

Figure 8.15. Dialogue graph for "mediashapes.rad". (Reprinted with permission from the Center for Spoken Language Understanding. Copyright 2003, OHSU.)

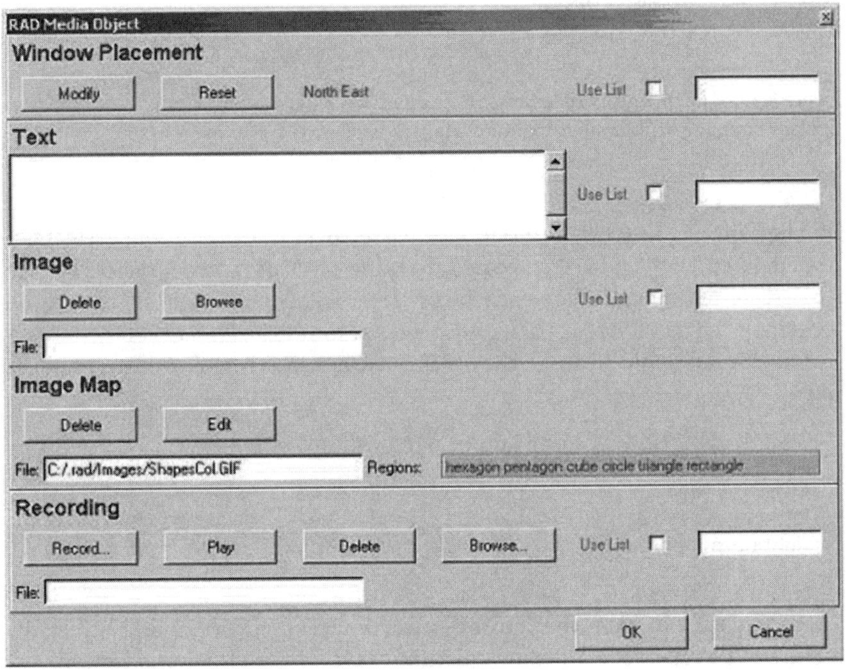

Figure 8.16. The Media Object box. (Reprinted with permission from the Center for Spoken Language Understanding. Copyright 2003, OHSU.)

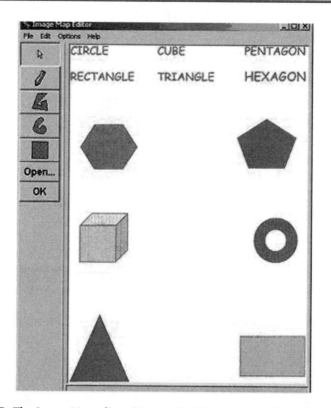

Figure 8.17. The Image Map editor. (Reprinted with permission from the Center for Spoken Language Understanding. Copyright 2003, OHSU.)

highlighting the area when the mouse passes over it. Once all the areas have been defined, click on the Options tab and select "One port per region", which will create output ports for each target area, with labels such as "clicked on 'pentagon'". The variable holding the value of the clicked area is $target.

Develop an application as shown in Figure 8.15. The following should be noted:

"Ask_Description" has one output port with no content.

CONDITIONAL: Decision
left output port: $target == $name
right output port: 1

remove_picture
Right click on "remove picture", select Remove Media and select the picture to be removed, i.e., "show_picture". Save and test your application.

Note: A fairly detailed tutorial on using image maps in the media object is provided in RAD Tutorial 5 at: http://cslu.cse.ogi.edu/toolkit/docs/2.0/apps/rad/tutorials/tutorial005/index.html

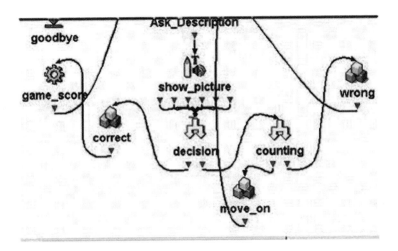

Figure 8.18. Adding decisions and counting. (Reprinted with permission from the Center for Spoken Language Understanding. Copyright 2003, OHSU.)

Exercise 8: Using Counters to Provide Alternative Behaviours ("counting.rad")

This exercise introduces the use of Tcl variables to monitor the number of times a particular behaviour takes place, for example, a state is visited or a question is asked. The purpose of this is to avoid continuous loops if the player fails to select the correct answer. For this exercise you can use the application developed in Exercise 7 (see Figure 8.15). We will add a mechanism to keep count of the number of times a player gets the wrong answer. If this exceeds two, then the system will move on rather than asking them to repeat. There will also be a counter for the score, which will only be incremented if an answer is correct.

1. Insert a Tcl object after Start, entitled "set_score".

   OnExit:
   Set score 0

2. Insert a Tcl object to connect "set_score" and "Build_Descriptions", entitled

   "set_counter".
   OnExit:
   set count 0

   There will be a loop back to this state from "move_on".

3. Create the states at the bottom part of the dialogue graph, as shown in Figure 8.18.

   The state "counting" is entered if the player's answer is incorrect. If the value of $count is less than 3, then the question is asked again – the system loops back to the state "Ask_Description". Otherwise the state "move_on" is entered and the next question is asked, as the system loops back to the state "Build_Descriptions". If the answer is correct, the system moves on to the next question by looping back to "Build_Descriptions", but passes first through "game_score" where the score is updated.

Create the states with the links as illustrated, and edit the states as follows:

```
"counting"
OnExit: incr count
left hand output port: $count == 3
right hand output port: 1

"move_on"
TTS: The shape is a $name. Let's continue

"game_score"
OnExit:
TTS "you get a star"
incr score
```

Save and test your application.

Exercise 9

Complete the application by integrating a login subdialogue and instructions. The system should check if the player has played the game before and, if so, what their previous score was. At the end of the game there should be an opportunity to try again. On exiting, the database should be updated with the new score. Experiment by making any other improvements to the application, as you see fit.

Tutorial 5: Improving the Interface

There are a number of ways in which the interface can be improved and these will be covered briefly in this tutorial. These improvements include making adjustments to the animated character's speech output and setting different background colours.

Exercise 10: Modifying the TTS Parameters

The simplest way to adjust speech output is to modify the TTS parameters. To do this, click on File → Preferences and select the TTS tab. Three sliders are available for adjusting pitch, pitch range and speech rate. Create a simple prompt in a GENERIC object and modify the speech output by moving the bars on the sliders. If the modified output is required only for a particular dialogue state, then double click on that state to open the Properties box, click in the box TTS parameters, and the sliders will become available for modification.

Exercise 11: Recording and Aligning Speech

You can also use a recorded voice instead of the synthetic speech generated by the TTS component. The recorded speech can be aligned with the animated agent so that the lip and face movements are synchronised. To create a natural speech prompt, do the following:

1. Click on File → Preferences and select an animated character, such as CUAnimate.
2. Drag a generic icon onto the canvas.
3. Enter a prompt as text into the TTS prompt box.
4. Save the file.
5. Click on the tab Rec in the TTS box.
6. Click on Edit. This will bring up a window entitled "bsync – Baldi with natural speech", which contains your prompt, a set of buttons to record the prompt and play it back, and a visual representation of the waveform and spectrogram that represent the spoken prompt. This tool is called "Baldi Sync" and it can also be called from the Speech Toolkit menu at Start → Speech Toolkit. The visual representation is part of the Speech Viewer tool, which is also available from the Speech Toolkit menu.
7. Click on the red button to record the prompt. The red button is also used to stop recording.
8. Click align.
9. Click on the black arrow to see and hear the animated character speaking with your voice.
10. If you are satisfied with the recording, click on File → Save Sob. (Sob is the extension for a speech object, which is an aligned recording.)

By default, sobs are saved with a name such as "queryone_24.sob" in a folder entitled "recorded_speech_prompts". You can give the file a more meaningful name and save it in the folder of your choice.

Further details on using speech objects to provide more natural prompts can be found in RAD Tutorial 13 at: http://cslu.cse.ogi.edu/toolkit/docs/2.0/apps/ rad/tutorials/tutorial013/index.html The use of recorded speech, including .sob and .wav files, is also illustrated in some detail in the *RAD User Guide* provided with the toolkit documentation.

Setting Background Colours

If an application is played with the canvas deselected and an animated character selected (in File → Preferences), the animated character will appear on the normal Windows desktop. You can set a background colour for an application using some code in a file "background.rad" which is provided with the toolkit within the CSLU folder in: \Toolkit\2.0\apps\rad\examples\RAD User Guide\

Exercise 12: Setting a Background Colour

1. Create an application with one or two states containing prompts. Right click on the canvas area to bring up the option Insert file, which can be used to locate and load the file "background.rad" as a subdialogue.
2. Incorporate this subdialogue in your application after the Start state and before your first generic state.
3. Build and run the application. The background will be white.

You can change the background to another colour by opening the subdialogue, then opening the state "create_background", and modifying the first line "set colour white" to some other colour. A list of available colours can be found in the file "colors_background.doc", which is also to be found in the *RAD User Guide* folder. To remove the background, include the following in the Goodbye state:

```
OnExit
catch {destroy.background}
```

This method sets up a background colour for a complete application. It is not possible with this method to change background colours within an application.

Exercise 13: Changing Background Colours within an Application

This exercise provides code that is not part of the standard download that will allow background colours to be changed as often as you wish during an application.[2]

1. Create an application consisting of the subdialogue "Background" followed by a Tcl state entitled "background_white", followed by a generic state entitled "white".
2. Add further pairs of Tcl and generic states, labelled with the appropriate colours.
3. In the generic states create a prompt such as "The background is white" and so on, for each of your colours.

---

[2] The code for this example was supplied by Jacques de Villiers at CSLU. Permission to use the code is gratefully acknowledged.

4. In the Tcl states, enter the following:

```
background White
# or Coral, or CornflowerBlue, as appropriate
```

The main modification will be in the state "create_background", where you should enter the following Tcl code:

```
proc background {{colour ""}} {
set b .background
catch {destroy $b}
if {![llength $colour]} return

toplevel $b -bg $colour -height [expr [winfo screenheight .]-28] -width [winfo
screenwidth .]
wm overrideredirect $b 1
wm geometry $b +0+0
raise $b
button $b.quit -text "Exit" -command [list destroy $b] -width 12
pack propagate $b 0
pack $b.quit -side bottom -anchor e
bind $b <ButtonPress> [list raise $b .]
}
background
```

Save and run your program. The background colour should change according to the specifications in the Tcl states.

Some Additional Features

There are a number of additional features in the toolkit, which will be mentioned briefly. Interested readers can follow up the references provided for further information.

Dictionaries

By default the toolkit uses an American English dictionary. You can select other dictionaries by clicking on File → Preferences, and then the Dictionaries tab. Within the box entitled Edit Local Dictionary you can select a different dictionary from the drop-down menu at Current Dictionary. The available dictionaries are: American English, Mexican Spanish, Brazilian Portuguese, Italian, North East Italian. Further information on these dictionaries can be found at: http://cslu.cse.ogi.edu/research/

Out of Vocabulary Rejection

Normally the speech recogniser can only choose between words available in the recognition vocabulary. The dialogue will branch to the recognition port that contains the closest matching word or phrase. With Repair turned off, the recogniser is forced to decide between the available vocabulary items regardless of their confidence score.

However, with Repair Mode engaged, the recogniser is allowed to reject all available vocabulary when it is not confident about matching a word or phrase. This is called "out of vocabulary rejection". Selecting Repair provides an automatic connection to a predetermined subdialogue when the user says something that is "out of vocabulary". This is similar to adding *any to a recognition port except that branching to the repair subdialogue is accomplished automatically.

Tucker–Maxon

A number of options are available if you select Tucker–Maxon from File → Preferences. This includes a method for Dynamic Recognition Adjustment and other options such as providing a "Pause" button. Dynamic Recognition Adjustment allows you to change the "out of vocabulary rejection median" setting during a dialogue based on recognition performance. This is used primarily for applications that teach speech production. Selecting Dynamic Rejection makes the recognizer more forgiving of misrecognitions while successful recognitions make the recognizer more discriminating. For additional features see: http://cslu.cse.ogi.edu/toolkit/docs/2.0/apps/rad/prefs/index.html

Data Capture and Playback

You can record interactions with your applications and then play them back by selecting Data Capture and Playback from the File → Preferences box.

Data Capture

Load your program.

1. Click on File → Preferences and select Data Capture and Playback.
2. To record data, select capture directory. A default directory will be specified for your data. Close the Preferences dialogue box and run your program.

Playing a Recorded File

To run a recorded data file, click on File → Preferences, and within Data Capture and Playback click on Playback from file and Browse. You will see a list of the data files with extension .log. Select a file and close the dialogue boxes. Click on Run and your recorded dialogue will be played.

Current Developments

There are a number of developments that build on the CSLU toolkit and its application in educational contexts. These are described briefly below and some references are provided in the notes for further reading.

CSLU Vocabulary Tutor

The Vocabulary Tutor, which supports the teaching of vocabulary, is the result of a joint effort between CSLU, the Tucker–Maxon Oral School, and the Perceptual Science Laboratory at the University of California, Santa Cruz (UCSC). The tutor provides children who are deaf and hard-of-hearing with increased opportunities to learn and practise vocabulary.

The Vocabulary Tutor facilitates some of the functions provided in the tutorials in this chapter by providing a form-based interface that allows you to create a student log-in facility and put together a lesson consisting of pictures and sounds. There is also a facility for reviewing student performance in the lesson. References to further information on the Vocabulary Tutor are included below.

The CSLR Reading Tutor

The CSLR Reading Project is a part of a collaborative project between schools in Colorado and CSLR at the University of Colorado, Boulder. The aim of the Reading Tutor component of the project is to develop educational software that will help students to learn to read and comprehend text using human communication technologies such as animated agents that speak and engage learners in natural face-to-face conversations in learning tasks. The project involves integrating research in the areas of speech recognition, natural language understanding, computer vision, and computer animation in order to provide learning tools for specific application domains.

Further Reading

CSLU Vocabulary Tutor

The vocabulary tutor editor is now available as part of the standard CSLU toolkit download.

Download information and reference to other materials: http://cslu.cse. ogi.edu/toolkit/docs/2.0/apps/vocabulary/

A brief tutorial is also available at: http://www.tmos.org/tech/vocabulary_ tutor/vt.html

Slide show demonstration: http://www.tmos.org/tech/vocabulary_tutor/ vt1.html

Lessons on various topics: http://mambo.ucsc.edu/vocabtutor/

BALDI

Information about BALDI and the UCSC Perceptual Science Laboratory: mambo.ucsc.edu/

CSLR Reading Tutor

Information on the CSLR Reading Tutor: http://cslr.colorado.edu/beginweb/reading/reading.html

CU Animate

Information on CU Animate: http://cslr.colorado.edu/beginweb/cuanimate/cuanimate_paper.html

Ideas for Further Projects

Develop an interactive tutorial system in an area of your own choice and using the techniques covered in this chapter. Examples could include lessons in geography, history, pronunciation, and using a computer. The program should include images and an animated character.

Developing a Directed Dialogue System Using VoiceXML

9

The next two chapters follow the format of Chapters 7 and 8 by presenting a series of linked tutorials that progressively introduce the main features of VoiceXML. The tutorials are based on the Student System described in Chapter 6 and developed in the Rapid Application Developer (RAD) in Chapter 7. The present chapter will focus on directed dialogues, in which the system controls the dialogue and the user responds to prompts spoken by the system (also described as finite state- or graph-based dialogues). Chapter 10 will discuss mixed-initiative dialogues in which the user can, in a limited way, introduce additional material that is not determined by the system prompt. Some of the more advanced features of VoiceXML will also be presented in Chapter 10. Chapter 10 will also deal with dynamic aspects of VoiceXML, such as connecting to Web servers, accessing databases, and creating dynamic VoiceXML documents.

This chapter begins with a brief introduction to VoiceXML. It will not be possible to cover all aspects of VoiceXML within the scope of these two chapters, and interested readers are referred to a number of specialist books on VoiceXML that are listed at the end of the chapter. These books provide a comprehensive reference to the language, illustrated with examples.

VoiceXML: A Language for Voice Enabling the World Wide Web

VoiceXML is a relatively new language that brings together the public telephone network and the World Wide Web. Applications developed in VoiceXML will enable users to access information and services on the Internet using speech rather than through a graphical user interface (GUI). Until recently, the development of Interactive Voice Response (IVR) applications using Computer–Telephone Integration (CTI) technology involved mastering intricate details of voice cards, application programming interfaces (APIs), circuit provisioning, and hardware configuration. With VoiceXML the developer can build on the

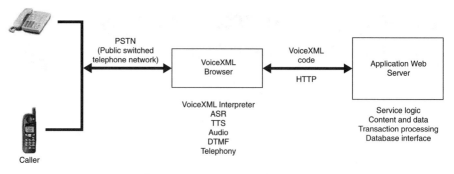

Figure 9.1. VoiceXML architecture.

existing Web infrastructure, using standard Internet protocols and without the need for specialised APIs.

Figure 9.1 presents a simplified view of a VoiceXML architecture. The key element is the VoiceXML browser. A voice browser answers telephone calls and interacts with the user using dialogue elements that include spoken prompts and grammars to recognise the user's spoken input. The core element of a voice browser is the VoiceXML interpreter, which interprets documents that are marked up using VoiceXML tags. Other essential components are a text-to-speech (TTS) engine to handle spoken output and an automatic speech recognition (ASR) engine to process the user's spoken input. In this architecture the VoiceXML browser is a client that interacts with an Application Web Server. The Application Web Server stores VoiceXML files as well as other files, such as Active Server Pages (ASP) or Java Server Pages (JSP) files that are used to interact with external data sources, as in a traditional Web-based environment.

The following sequence illustrates a typical call flow in a VoiceXML application from the perspective of a user:

1. The caller dials a telephone number that accesses a VoiceXML application on a Voice Server.
2. The Voice Server launches the application, usually beginning with a greeting and a prompt asking the caller to state what information they require.
3. The caller responds either using speech or using the Dual Tone Multiple Frequency (DTMF) telephone keypad.
4. The application takes some action depending on the caller's response, such as retrieving or updating information in a database, or storing or retrieving a voice message.
5. The application then asks the caller what they want to do next.
6. The caller or the application can terminate the call. If the caller hangs up during the call, the Voice Server will detect the hang-up and disconnect itself. Alternatively, the caller may explicitly terminate the action by using a word such as "exit" or "goodbye".

VoiceXML: The Language

VoiceXML is an XML-based language. It includes tags for specifying prompts and recognition vocabularies, and for describing dialogues. In this sense it is a declarative language, as the developer is only required to specify the dialogue. The details of how the script is interpreted and executed – for example, activating the speech recognition engine to listen for input and activating a TTS synthesis engine to speak system prompts – are hidden from the developer. Similarly the details of how the dialogue control is implemented do not need to be specified explicitly as they are implicit in the dialogue control algorithm (known as the Form Interpretation Algorithm, or FIA). The developer marks up the required elements, such as forms and fields, and the interpreter processes the VoiceXML document and instantiates a spoken dialogue using the FIA.

However, there is also a procedural element to VoiceXML. ECMAScript (also known as JavaScript) is used for various client-side tasks such as assigning values to variables, passing values, and validating user input, thus avoiding the need for repeated trips back to the server. VoiceXML is also event-driven and includes extensive event model to capture commonly occurring events, such as the user requesting help or the system failing to recognise the user's spoken input. Finally, there is an object-oriented flavour to VoiceXML. For example, there is a set of "shadow variables" that contain various types of information and that are referenced using the "dot" notation used commonly in object-oriented languages. One example is "x$.utterance", which references a string representing the actual words recognised by the speech recognition engine.

Tutorials

This chapter consists of the following tutorials:

Tutorial 1: Prompts, responses, verification.

Tutorial 2: Repair in VoiceXML.

Tutorial 3: Subdialogues.

Tutorial 4: Digit recognition.

Tutorial 5: DTMF.

Tutorial 6: Alphadigit recognition.

Tutorial 7: Modifying speech output.

Tutorial 8: Navigation and global commands.

Most of these constructs have parallels in RAD and, as far as possible, the tutorials will follow the structure of the tutorials in Chapters 7 and 8 in order to allow comparisons between RAD and VoiceXML. Instructions for running VoiceXML applications are to be found in Appendix 3.

Tutorial 1: Prompts, Responses and Verification

The main features to be covered in this tutorial are:

1. How to specify exchanges consisting of prompts and responses in VoiceXML.
2. How to deal with simple verification.

Part 1: Prompts and Responses

This part of the tutorial shows how to create a form in VoiceXML consisting of a system prompt and a recognition grammar for the user's response.

Exercise 1

Load and run the file "studentsystem1a.vxml". The system will prompt you to say one of: "students", "courses", "details".

Explaining the Application

This application consists of one system prompt to elicit a response, then the program terminates. Such an exchange would be handled in RAD within a dialogue state in which the prompt and recognition vocabulary are specified. In VoiceXML a prompt–response exchange is handled using either a form or a menu. As in a graphical Web interface a form specifies a dialogue that consists of one or more fields to be filled. Each field contains a prompt that asks the user to provide some input. In this application the user is prompted to make a choice from a set of options.

The following VoiceXML code will produce this exchange. (*Note*: The numbers at the beginning of each line are not part of the program but are included for ease of reference. These numbers should not be included in a running program.)

File listing: studentsystem1a.vxml

```
1 <?xml version="1.0"?>
2 <vxml version="1.0">
3 <form id = "mainmenu">
4 <field name="choice">
5<prompt>
6. Welcome to the Student System Main Menu.
7 The system provides details on students, courses and reports. To begin say one of
the following: students, courses, reports.
8 </prompt>
9 <grammar type="application/x-jsgf">
10 students | courses | reports
11 </grammar>
12 </field>
```

```
13 </form>
14 </vxml>
```

Explaining the Program

This program is a VoiceXML document that consists of one form, which contains one field. The form begins at line 3 and ends at line 13. Within the form there is a field beginning at line 4 and ending at line 12. The field contains a prompt which, unless otherwise indicated, will be spoken by the TTS component. The field also contains a grammar that specifies the words that can be recognised as a response to the prompt. Once the form has been completed, as no other actions have been specified, the application terminates.

Points to Note

1. Tags in VoiceXML conform to XML syntax. Thus an opening tag, such as `<form>` must have a corresponding closing tag, i.e., `</form>`.

2. A VoiceXML document has header tags. Line 1 specifies that VoiceXML is an XML-based language. This line may optionally include a link to a standard XML `<DOCTYPE>` element definition, which can point to a specific VoiceXML document type definition (DTD) that the interpreter should use. In many cases a default DTD is assumed. Line 2 indicates the version of VoiceXML. Additional parameters that can be included will be introduced later.

3. The `<form>` tag can have a name (using the parameter "id"). The `<field>` tag uses the parameter "name". Other parameters will be introduced later.

4. A form may consist of a number of fields. For example, an application may need to elicit a series of values using a sequence of prompts and responses. The most straightforward way to implement this would be to use a form consisting of a sequence of fields, where each field asks for a specific item of information.

5. The grammar format used in the examples in Chapters 9 and 10 is the Java Speech Grammar Format (JSGF), which is the default grammar format used in the IBM WebSphere VoiceServer SDK (Software Development Kit) and in the IBM WebSphere Voice Toolkit. When using the SDK or the Toolkit it is not necessary to specify the grammar type for JSGF grammars and the simple tag `<grammar>` is sufficient. Grammars are explained in greater detail in Chapter 10. For further information on alternative grammar formats, see Appendix 1.

Some Terminology

So far, terms such as "application", "document" and "dialogue" have been used rather loosely. In fact, some of these terms are used with a special meaning in VoiceXML, particularly with reference to the scope of variables and grammars. To avoid confusion, the following terms are defined.

Session

A session begins when a caller dials into the system and ends when the call is completed. The VoiceXML interpreter creates a group of read-only variables that are not defined within a document. These are called "session variables" and they have session scope. Examples of these variables are:

- session.telephone.ani – stores the caller's phone number.
- session.telephone.dnis – stores the phone number the caller dialled.

Whether such session variables have a valid value depends on whether the relevant telephone service is supported.

Application

An application is made up of one or more documents. One of these documents can be the root document to which a number of leaf documents are attached. The use of a root document will be illustrated in Tutorial 8.

Document

A document is a file that begins with the <vxml> element and terminates with the </vxml> element. Thus the file "studentsystem1a.vxml" is known technically as a document.

Dialog

Dialog (with this spelling) is the technical term for the interaction that takes place within a form or menu. This term will be used with this meaning in the chapters dealing with VoiceXML, while the term "dialogue" will be used, as elsewhere in this book, with the more general meaning describing a spoken interaction between two parties. These terms will be particularly relevant when variable scope and grammar scope are introduced in Chapter 10.

Exercise 2

Extend the example with fields to elicit a student's name and the name of a course. You will need to construct grammars in each field containing a few names of students and courses.

Part 2: State Transitions and Branching

Normally an application would not just elicit some information from the user and then terminate. Once all the information has been collected, the next step is usually to submit that information to a server and to retrieve some information back from a database that can be communicated to the user. This process will be illustrated in Chapter 10. Many real-world examples are structured in this way – the system asks for one or two items of information and then accesses a database to find the required information.

Some applications, such as the dialogue example presented above, will require the user to make choices that involve transitions to different dialogue states and possibly to subdialogues. As we have seen in Chapters 7 and 8, RAD enables the developer to construct a graphical representation of a dialogue consisting of transitions and loops and then to compile and run the dialogue without any further effort. While the analogy of a dialogue graph can be applied to the specification of a VoiceXML application, the developer has to specify transitions and loops within the code as well as considering issues such as how to handle variables. It is also necessary to understand the dialogue control process (known as the FIA) in order to appreciate what actually happens when a dialogue script is executed. These details will be explained gradually during the course of the next two chapters. The remainder of this tutorial will deal with a simple example of state transitions.

After collecting some information from the user, the system might transition to another form within the same document or to another document. Here we will illustrate with transitions to another set of documents. For example, if "students" is selected from the options presented, the transition will be to a document dealing with student details.

The following code extends "studentsystem1a.vxml" which consisted of a single form containing one field called "choice" in which the user had to choose between the options "students", "courses" and "reports". In this example, depending on which choice is made, the system will transition to another document – in this case, one of the following: "studentdetails.vxml", "coursedetails.vxml" or "reports.vxml".

```
<filled>
  <if cond="choice == 'students'">
  <goto next="studentdetails.vxml"/>
  <elseif cond="choice == 'courses'"/>
  <goto next="coursedetails.vxml"/>
  <else/>
  <goto next="reports.vxml"/>
  </if>
</filled>
```

Explaining the Code

The code specifying this transition is represented as a conditional statement within the `<filled>` tag. The `<filled>` tag specifies what action to take when one or more fields have been filled. In this example the action is to transition to another document. Other actions might involve submitting the details that have been collected to a server (see Chapter 10), or checking that the information elicited is compatible and, if not, outputting some error message.

Exercise 3

Save the file "studentsystem1a.vxml" as "studentsystem1b.vxml". Insert the additional code after the end of the field </field> and before the end of the form </form>, i.e., at line 13 in the original "studentsystem1a.vxml".

Note: To make this example work, it will be necessary to create dummy files for "studentdetails.vxml" and the other options for the transitions specified in the <filled> element. The following is an example of a dummy file for "studentdetails.vxml".

```
<?xml version="1.0"?>
<vxml version="1.0">
<form>
<block>
This is student details
</block>
</form>
</vxml>
```

Create similar dummy files for "coursedetails.vxml" and "reports.vxml". Put the code together to create the application. Test your application with suitable responses.

Part 3: Using a Menu Instead of a Form

A menu is an alternative way of getting the user to make a choice from a list and then getting the system to take some appropriate action. A menu is a simplified form with a single field. A menu presents the user with a list of choices that determine transitions to different places depending on which choice is made. The following is an example of a menu that performs the same functions as the form in "studentsystem1b.vxml".

File listing: examplemenu1.vxml

```
<?xml version="1.0"?>
<vxml version="1.0">
<menu id = "mainmenu">
<prompt>
Welcome to the Student System Main Menu.
The system provides details on students, courses and reports.
To begin say one of the following:
</prompt>
<enumerate/>
    <choice next="studentdetails.vxml"> students </choice>
    <choice next="coursedetails.vxml"> courses </choice>
    <choice next="reports.vxml"> reports </choice>
</menu>
</vxml>
```

Exercise 4

Load, run and test the file "examplemenu1.vxml".

Explaining the Program

The main work in a menu is done in the `<choice>` elements which include the following:

- A speech grammar element is specified, e.g., "students".
- An action is specified that is to be taken depending on which grammar element has been recognised, e.g., "next = studentdetails.vxml".
- The `<enumerate />` element gathers together the items listed within the `<choice>` elements and uses them to create a prompt (or in this case to add the choices to the text of the prompt).

Additional Background Information

The `<enumerate>` element is a shorthand method for specifying the options to be spoken in the prompt as well as dynamically constructing the items for the recognition grammar. If more control is required over the prompts and recognition grammar, the `<enumerate>` element can be omitted but then the prompts and grammars have to be specified for each choice, as shown in the following code segment:

```
<prompt>You can say students or student details </prompt>
<choice next="studentdetails.vxml">
<grammar> students | student details </grammar>
</choice>
<prompt>For course details say courses or course details </prompt>
<choice next="course details.vxml">
<grammar> courses | course details</grammar>
</choice>
```

Part 4: *Implementing Verification*

In this part of the tutorial we will examine the document "viewdetails.vxml" in which the system will ask for a student name and then verify that name. If the user confirms that the name is correct, the application will terminate, otherwise it will ask for the name again.

File listing: viewdetails.vxml

```
1 <?xml version="1.0"?>
2 <vxml version="1.0">
3 <form id = "student_details">
4 <block>
5 Welcome to Student Details.
6 </block>
```

```
 7 <field name = "student_name">
 8 <prompt> Please say the student name </prompt>
 9 <grammar>
10 john | david | rosemary | jennifer
11 </grammar>
12 </field>
13 <field name="confirm" type="boolean">
14 <prompt>
15 you want details on <value expr="student_name"/>
16 </prompt>
17 <filled>
18 <if cond="confirm">
19 <prompt> looking up details on <value expr="student_name"/>
20 </prompt>
21 <else />
22 let's try again
23 <clear namelist = "student_name confirm" />
24 </if>
25 </filled>
26 </field>
27 </form>
28 </vxml>
```

Explaining the Program

The Fields

In the first field, entitled "student_name", the system asks for a name, using a prompt and grammar as usual. The system then continues to the next field, called "confirm". This field is declared as being a particular field type, in this case it is "boolean". This means that the response has to be either "yes" or "no" (with variants such as "okay", "sure" and "true" for "yes", and "false" or "negative" for "no" – this will vary according to the VoiceXML platform you are using). When a built-in field type is used, a grammar does not have to be defined for that field. There are a number of other built-in grammars, for example, for digits, some of which will be encountered later.

Referencing a Variable

Note how to reference a variable in VoiceXML that has been elicited within a field. For example, the value of the field "student_name" is referenced in lines 15 and 19 by the expression `<value expr="student_name"/>`.

The Conditional Expression in the `<filled>` Element (lines 18–24)

`<if cond = "confirm">` means that if the response was "yes", the action `<clear>` will clear all the values that have been elicited. In this case, a list of variables to be cleared is specified in `<clear namelist = "student_name confirm" />` referring to the variables "student_name" and "confirm". These values are set to "undefined", which means that those fields will have to be revisited. This is a way of implementing a loop back to re-elicit a value. The details of how this works will be explained when we examine the FIA in Chapter 10.

Exercise 5

Load and run the file "viewdetails.vxml". In response to the prompt "Please say the student name", you can say one of: John, David, Rosemary, Jennifer. In response to the prompt asking for confirmation, you can say either "yes" or "no". Try both options.

Exercise 6: Adding Verification to studentsystem1b.vxml

Using the file "viewdetails.vxml" as a basis, amend the file "studentsystem1b.vxml" so that the system confirms the choice (students, courses or reports). If the user confirms, then the application transitions to the appropriate next document, otherwise it goes back to elicit the value again.

Test and run your application, making sure that it executes as expected following user confirmations and disconfirmations.

Tutorial 2: Repair in VoiceXML

Part 1: Testing for Repair Events

In RAD there were two events that were handled by the default repair subdialogue:

1. The system does not detect any speech (i.e., silence is detected).
2. The speech that is detected does not match the recognition vocabulary.

VoiceXML browsers provide methods for handling these (and other) events, although the specifics of how they are handled may differ from one browser to another. If no specific behaviours are specified (by the programmer), then the events are handled according to the default specifications provided by the browser.

In VoiceXML silence is handled as a <noinput> event. This event is thrown when the timeout interval is exceeded, i.e., the system has not detected any input. The default behaviour for this event is <reprompt>. In the case of the IBM WebSphere Voice Server SDK the system reprompts after the default timeout interval of 7 seconds. In the case of the BeVocal Café, the system outputs the message "I am sorry. I could not hear you." with no reprompt.

Failure to match the recognition vocabulary is handled as a <nomatch> event. The default behaviour for this event is to output a message and then reprompt. In the case of the IBM WebSphere Voice Server SDK the default output message is "Sorry, I didn't understand", followed by a reprompt. BeVocal Café outputs the message "I am sorry. I did not understand you." with no reprompt.

Exercise 7: Testing `<noinput>` and `<nomatch>`

Run one of your applications and test how it behaves when:

1. You do not say anything.
2. You say something that is not in the specified recognition vocabulary.

Part 2: Modifying the Default Behaviours for `<noinput>` and `<nomatch>`

Events such as `<noinput>` and `<nomatch>` are thrown by the platform and caught by the corresponding event handler. These events are predefined but can be modified by the developer. Other events that are not predefined can be defined and used as required. The following example shows how VoiceXML provides ways of modifying the default behaviours for predefined events such as `<noinput>` and `<nomatch>`. Different prompts and actions can be specified, and the "count" attribute can be used to indicate different behaviours if the event is repeated. In this example two different prompts are defined for each of the events.

```
<field name="choice">
<prompt>
Welcome to the Student System Main Menu.
The system provides details on students, courses and reports.
To begin say one of the following: students, courses, reports.
</prompt>

<noinput count="1">
<prompt>I didn't hear anything. Please try again.
</prompt>
</noinput>

<noinput count="2">
<prompt>Please say students, courses, or reports.
</prompt>
</noinput>

<nomatch count="1">
<prompt>Sorry I didn't understand that
</prompt>
</nomatch>

<nomatch count="2">
<prompt>I still don't understand. Please say students, courses or reports.
</prompt>
</nomatch>
```

```
<grammar>
students | courses | reports
</grammar>

</field>
```

Exercise 8: Modifying the Default Behaviours for `<noinput>` and `<nomatch>` in: studentsystem1b.vxml

1. Save the file "studentsystem1b.vxml" as "studentsystem2.vxml".
2. Add the code listed above to your new file.
3. Run and test your application.

Note: Specifying behaviours for events such as `<noinput>` and `<nomatch>` is a question of design. The examples given here are merely for illustration and may not represent the optimal strategies for good voice user interface design. Consider carefully what behaviours to define to handle events such as these. You will find alternative ways of handling these events and of how to manage reprompts in many of the VoiceXML texts cited at the end of this chapter.

Tutorial 3: Subdialogues

As in RAD, a subdialogue is a new interaction that is launched within an ongoing dialogue in a document. All current variables and grammars in the launching context are saved and the subdialogue executes in a new execution context. When the subdialogue is completed, its execution context is deleted and the program returns to the point in the document from which the subdialogue was launched using the `<return>` tag. The `<subdialog>` element is used to invoke subdialogues. Some VoiceXML browsers provide a library of reusable subdialogues that can be shared among documents in an application and also across applications. *Note*: The spelling "subdialogue" will be used to refer to the generic concept of subdialogues, while the spelling "subdialog" will be used to refer specifically to the VoiceXML construct of `<subdialog>`.

Values can be passed between the launching dialogue and a subdialog in the following ways:

1. Passing values back from a subdialog following some computation within the subdialog (Part 1).
2. Passing values into a subdialog to be referenced in that subdialog (Part 2).
3. Passing values in both directions (Part 3).

Part 1: Passing Values Back from a Subdialog

In this example, following a welcome statement, control is passed to a subdialog in which user validation is performed. When the subdialog is completed, execution is returned to the main document and the user is greeted by name.

File listing: studentsystem3a.vxml

```
1. <?xml version="1.0"?>
2. <vxml version="1.0">
3. <form id="main_menu">
4. <block>
5. Welcome to the Student System Main Menu
6 </block>
7 <subdialog name="result" src="#validation">
8 </subdialog>
9 <block>
10 <prompt>
11 hello <value expr = "result.username" />
12 </prompt>
13 </block>
14 </form>
15 <!-- subdialog -->
16 <form id="validation">
17 <field name="username">
18 <grammar>
19 liz | margaret | mike | guest
20 </grammar>
21 <prompt> Please say your user name. </prompt>
22 </field>
23 <filled>
24 <return namelist="username" />
25 </filled>
26 </form>
27 </vxml>
```

Exercise 9

Load and run the file "studentsystem3a.vxml". You can say one of the usernames (Liz, Margaret, Mike, Guest) in response to the system prompt.

Explaining the Program

There are several points to note in this example. The `<subdialog>` is launched in line 7 with a name ("result") and a src ("validation") – this is the name of the form that constitutes the subdialog (beginning at line 16). The field in the subdialog is called "username" (line 17). The value elicited in this field is returned using the element `<return>` and namelist, which specifies a list of values to return (in this case only one). Looking now at line 11, it can be seen

how the value for the name elicited in the subdialog is referenced using the
name of the subdialog and the name of the value (result.username).

Part 2: Passing Values into a Subdialog

In this example a value is elicited in the main document and passed into the
subdialog where it is referenced. The system asks for the user name and then
passes this information to the subdialog where the user is greeted by name.
   File listing: studentsystem3b.vxml

```
1 <?xml version="1.0"?>
2 <vxml version="1.0">
3 <form id="main_menu">
4 <block>
5 Welcome to the Student System Main Menu
6 </block>
7 <field name="username">
8 <grammar>
9 liz | margaret | mike | guest
10 </grammar>
11 <prompt>Please say your user name </prompt>
12 </field>
13 <subdialog name="result" src="#validation">
14 <param name = "name" expr = "username" />
15 </subdialog>
16 </form>
17 <!-- subdialog -->
18 <form id="validation">
19 <var name = "name" />
20 <block>
21 <prompt>
22 hello <value expr = "name" />
23 </prompt>
24 <return />
25 </block>
26 </form>
27 </vxml>
```

Exercise 10

Load and run the file "studentsystem3b.vxml". As before, you can say one of the
usernames (liz, margaret, mike, guest) in response to the system prompt.

Explaining the Program

In line 14 the <param> element is used to pass a value from the calling document to the subdialog. The value to be passed is the value elicited in the field
called "username". Each parameter with values passed into the subdialog has

to be declared within the subdialog using the element <var> (line 19). The value of this parameter is referenced in the subdialog in line 22 using the name of the parameter.

Part 3: Passing Values in Both Directions

The final example combines both types of parameter passing by eliciting a value in the main document, sending the value to a subdialog for validation, and returning a result. Normally validation would involve execution of some code, such as making a calculation or looking up a record in a database. In this case, a conditional statement is used to simulate the process of making a check against a database. Obtaining results from a database will be covered in Chapter 10.

File listing: studentsystem3c.vxml

```
1 <?xml version="1.0"?>
2 <vxml version="1.0">
3 <form id="main_menu">
4 <block>
5 Welcome to the Student System Main Menu
6 </block>
7 <field name="studentname">
8 <grammar>
9 john | david | rosemary | jennifer
10 </grammar >
11 <prompt> Please say name of the student. </prompt>
12 </field>
13 <subdialog name="result" src="#validation">
14 <param name = "name" expr = "studentname" />
15 </subdialog>
16 <block>
17 <prompt>
18 hello <value expr = "studentname" />
19 the student number is <value expr = "result.studentid" />
20 </prompt>
21 </block>
22 </form>
23 <!-- subdialog -->
24 <form id="validation">
25 <var name = "name" />
26 <var name = "studentid" expr="""" />
27 <block>
28 <if cond= "name=='john'">
29 <assign name = "studentid" expr = "'96050918'" />
30 </if>
31 <return namelist = "studentid" />
32 </block>
33 </form>
34 </vxml>
```

Exercise 11

Load and run the file "studentsystem3c.vxml". This time you have to say the student name "John" for the conditional statement in the subdialog to evaluate correctly.

Explaining the Program

As in the previous examples a name is elicited in the main document and passed to the subdialog using <param> (line 14). This parameter is declared using <var> (line 25) along with a parameter for the value to be assigned within the subdialog (line 26). The value of this parameter is set initially to "empty". The conditional statement assigns a student ID to the user "john" (lines 28–30), and this value is returned in line 31 to be used in a prompt in the main document at line 19.

Exercise 12

Add further conditions in the subdialog for the names "David" and "Rosemary". Amend the code in the main dialog so that if the user says the name "Jennifer", the system responds "Sorry that student is not listed in the database".

Note: Names that are not in the database will still have to be included in the recognition vocabulary to be recognised and passed on to the subdialog.

Tutorial 4: Digit Recognition

Earlier we encountered the "boolean" built-in grammar type. Another built-in type is digits. The user can say one or more digits between 0 and 9 and the result will be a string of digits. Digit recognition is performed in VoiceXML by using a built-in grammar for digits that is declared as a field type. For example:

```
<field name="pin" type ="digits">
```

If the field value is used in a prompt, it will be spoken as a sequence of digits. To illustrate the use of a digit grammar, the validation dialogue presented in "studentsystem3a.vxml" will be modified as follows:

1. Instead of saying a name the user will say a four-digit pin.
2. The system will check that four digits have been recognised.
3. If not, it will ask the user to say the digits again, otherwise it will confirm the pin.
4. If the user confirms the pin, the system will say "welcome" followed by the pin.
5. If the user does not confirm the pin, the system will ask them to say the pin again.

File listing: studentsystem4.vxml

```
1 <?xml version="1.0"?>
2 <vxml version="1.0">
3 <form id="main_menu">
4 <block>
5 Welcome to the Student System Main Menu
6 </block>
7 <subdialog name="result" src="#validation">
8 </subdialog>
9 <block>
10 <prompt>
11 welcome <value expr = "result.pin" />
12 </prompt>
13 </block>
14 </form>
15 <!- subdialog ->
16 <form id="validation">
17 <field name="pin" type="digits">
18 <prompt> Please say your four digit pin. </prompt>
19 <filled>
20    <if cond="pin.length != 4">
21       your pin must have four digits.
22       <clear namelist="pin"/>
23    </if>
24 </filled>
25 </field>
26 <field name="confirm" type="boolean">
27 <prompt>
28 Please confirm:
29 your pin is <value expr="pin"/>
30 </prompt>
31 <filled>
32    <if cond="confirm">
33    <return namelist="pin" />
34    <else />
35    let's try again
36    <clear namelist = "pin confirm" />
37    </if>
38 </filled>
39 </field>
40 <block>
41 <return />
42 </block>
43 </form>
44 </vxml>
```

Explaining the Program

The four-digit pin is elicited in line 12. In lines 14–19 the system checks if four digits have been recognised and, if not, sets the value of "pin" to undefined so that the system will loop back and elicit the value again. Once four digits have been recognised, the system moves on to the next field where the user is asked to confirm the digit string. If the user does not confirm, then "pin" is set to undefined and the system will loop back and try to elicit the value again. If the pin is confirmed, execution returns to the main dialogue where the user is greeted.

Note that you can also parametrise the digit built-in grammar as follows:

```
digits?minlength=n - a string of at least n digits
digits?maxlength=n - a string of at most n digits
digits?length=n - a string of exactly n digits
```

For example,

```
<field type="digits?minlength=3;maxlength=5">...</field>
```

If the input does not match the specified parameter, the system will throw a `<nomatch>` event.

Exercise 13

Modify the example so that different prompts are given to help the user when either the digit string does not contain four digits or the user disconfirms the digit string. After three unsuccessful attempts the system should go to a file called "exit.vxml" where the system states that there is some technical problem and exits.

Experiment with the parameters for specifying the length of the digit string in combination with different prompts as opposed to using the conditional statement in the example provided.

Tutorial 5: DTMF

DTMF (or touch-tone) entry is used in VoiceXML as an alternative to speech input, particularly when speech recognition is unreliable or problematic. Normally DTMF entry requires the use of a telephone keypad. However, some standalone platforms, such as the IBM WebSphere Voice Server SDK, include a DTMF simulator so that users can type in a sequence of DTMF input using the simulator.

The `<dtmf>` element is used to specify a DTMF grammar for a field item. For example, the following DTMF grammar specifies the key sequence "1 2 3":

```
<dtmf>
1 2 3
</dtmf>
```

DTMF is used for numeric input in forms and menus. It can be used as an alternative to speech, where only DTMF input is possible, or it can be combined with speech to give the user a choice of input mode.

Part 1: Using DTMF Instead of Speech

File listing: studentsystem5a.vxml

```
<?xml version="1.0"?>
<vxml version="1.0">
<form id = "mainmenu">
<field name="choice">
<prompt>
Welcome to the Student System Main Menu.
The system provides details on students, courses and reports.
For students press 1, for courses press 2, for reports press 3
</prompt>
<dtmf>
1 {students} | 2 {courses} | 3 {reports}
</dtmf>
</field>
</form>
</vxml>
```

Explaining the Program

In this example there is no grammar for voice input. Instead a DTMF grammar is used in which the keystrokes 1, 2 and 3 are assigned to the choices "students", "courses" and "reports", respectively. The meanings assigned to the keystrokes are declared in the words enclosed in braces, e.g., {students}.

An alternative is to allow the user a choice of either voice or DTMF input. This would require a prompt such as:

```
For students say students or press 1, for courses say courses or press 2, for reports
say reports or press 3.
```

It would also require a grammar for the words to be recognised, as in the following code:

```
<grammar>
students | courses | reports
</grammar>
<dtmf>
1 {students} | 2 {courses} | 3 {reports}
</dtmf>
```

Exercise 14

Save the file: "studentsystem5a.vxml" as "studentsystem5b.vxml".

Amend the file so that the user can either say the required words or use DTMF.

Part 2: Using DTMF with Prompt Counts

One way to use DTMF is to combine it with prompt counts, as in the following example, where the user is given two opportunities to make a choice using speech, and is then advised to use the keypad.

```
<field name="choice">
<grammar>
students | courses | reports
</grammar>
<dtmf>
1 {students} | 2 {courses} | 3 {reports}
</dtmf>
<prompt count="1">
Welcome to the Student System Main Menu.
The system provides details on students, courses and reports.
Please say students, courses or reports.
</prompt>
<prompt count="2">
Say students, courses or reports.
</prompt>
<prompt count="3">
Perhaps you should use your telephone keypad.
Press 1 for students; 2 for reports; or 3 for reports
</prompt>
<noinput>
<reprompt/>
</noinput>
<nomatch>
<reprompt/>
</nomatch>
</field>
```

Exercise 15

Save the file: "studentsystem5b.vxml" as "studentsystem5c.vxml". Amend the file as shown above so that the user is given two opportunities to make a choice using speech, and is then advised to use the keypad. Run and test your program.

Part 3: DTMF in Menus

DTMF can also be used in menus by incorporating the <dtmf> element within the <choice> elements, as shown in the following example in which only DTMF input is permitted.

File: examplemenu2.vxml

```
<?xml version="1.0"?>
<vxml version="1.0">
```

```
<menu id = "mainmenu">
<prompt>Welcome to the Student System Main Menu.
      The system provides details on students, courses and reports. For students
press 1, for courses press 2, for reports press 3 </prompt>
            <choice dtmf="1" next="studentdetails.vxml" />
            <choice dtmf="2" next="coursedetails.vxml" />
            <choice dtmf="3" next="reports.vxml" />
</menu>
</vxml>
```

Other variants on using DTMF in forms and menus can be found in the VoiceXML specification and in VoiceXML textbooks.

Exercise 16

Save the file: "examplemenu2.vxml" as "examplemenu3.vxml". Amend the file so that it will accept either spoken or DTMF input.

Part 4: DTMF and Built-in Grammars

All built-in grammar types support DTMF input. Behaviour may differ according to platform.

boolean – 1 = "yes", 2 = "no".
In the IBM WebSphere SDK the return value is "true" or "false". If the field name is used in a value attribute within a prompt, the TTS engine will speak "yes" or "no", respectively.

date – Four digits for the year, followed by two for the month and two for the day. The result is a string in the format yyyymmdd. If the field name is used in a value attribute within a prompt, the TTS engine will speak the date.

digits – Strings of digits. If the field name is used in a value attribute within a prompt, the TTS engine will speak the string as a sequence of digits.

currency – The "*" key acts as a decimal point. The result is a string with the format UUUmm.nn, where UUU is the character standard for currency (e.g., USD for US dollars, GBP for British pounds, EUR for euros). If the field name is used in a value attribute within a prompt, the TTS engine will speak the currency value.

number – Includes numbers entered using digits and "*" to represent the decimal point. Entry may have to be terminated using the "#" key. If the field name is used in a value attribute within a prompt, the TTS engine will speak the string as a natural number.

phone – A string of digits, where "*" represents extension. If the field name is used in a value attribute within a prompt, the TTS engine will the string as a phone number, including the extension.

time – The first four digits represent the 24 hour clock. The return value is hhmmx, where "x" represents either "h" (meaning 24 hour format) or "?"

(meaning ambiguous). If the field name is used in a value attribute within a prompt, the TTS engine will speak the time.

Exercise 17

Create some sample applications to test DTMF with the various built-in grammar types. For example, an application for currency should prompt for a currency amount (with the field type set to "currency"), and should include a field with a prompt to verify the user's input. You may find some variation across platforms in how built-in grammars are used in combination with DTMF. For this you will need to consult the documentation for the platform you are using.

Note: Deciding whether DTMF input is appropriate as an alternative or complement to speech is a design issue and was discussed in Chapter 6. These exercises are intended only to test the facilities for DTMF input provided in VoiceXML.

Tutorial 6: Alphadigit Recognition

Alphadigit (or alphanumeric) recognition is useful for input that requires combinations of letters and numbers such as course codes, flight numbers or items in a catalogue. Alphanumeric recognition is not defined as a built-in grammar in the VoiceXML Version 1.0 specification, although a document submitted to the World Wide Web Consortium (W3C) sets out a specification for Speech Objects that includes alphadigit strings along with a number of other reusable dialogue components (Burnett, 2000). IBM provides VoiceXML subdialogs for alpha strings, consisting of sequences of alphabetic characters, and for alphanumeric strings, consisting of sequences of alphabetic and numeric characters. These subdialogs are part of the IBM Reusable Dialog Components that are used in conjunction with the IBM WebSphere VoiceServer, Voice Toolkit, and Voice Server SDK (http://www-3.ibm.com/software/pervasive/products/voice/reusable_dialog.shtml). Other subdialogs are available for selecting elements from a list: confirmation, processing input for credit card numbers/expiration dates, currency, dates, directions, durations, email addresses, numbers, social security numbers, street types, telephone numbers, time, URL, major cities of the United States, US states and time zones. Scansoft's OpenSpeech DialogModules (www.scansoft.com/openspeech/dialogmodules/) and Nuance's SpeechObjects (www.nuance.com) provide similar facilities.

It would also be possible to write a grammar for a specific application. The following example shows how to create a simple grammar to recognise the strings required for the Student System to specify course codes. The grammar is required to recognise a combination of the letters "d" followed by "k" then followed by three digits. This can be implemented using the following grammar, which is saved as an external grammar file (called "alphadigit.gram"):

```
#JSGF V1.0;
grammar alphadigit;
public <code> = <alpha> <alpha> <digit> <digit> <digit>;
<alpha> = d | k;
<digit> = 0 | 1 | 2 |3 | 4 | 5 | 6 | 7 | 8 | 9;
```

Explaining the Grammar

The rule named "code" requires that a valid input consists of two alpha words followed by three digit words. The alpha words are the letters "d" and "k" and the digits are the digits 0–9. The grammar is sourced within an application, as shown in the following example "coursedetailsalphadigit.vxml":

```
<?xml version="1.0"?>
<vxml version="1.0">
<form>
<field name="code">
<prompt>
what is the course code
</prompt>
<grammar src = "alphadigit.gram" />
</field>
<block>
that was <value expr="code" />
</block>
</form>
</vxml>
```

Exercise 18

1. Run and test the program "coursedetailsalphadigit.vxml".
2. Create a similar grammar to recognise some alternative alphanumeric strings, such as DGT346Z or LVO55CG.

   Grammars will be discussed in more detail in Chapter 10.

Tutorial 7: Modifying Speech Output

Speech output is important in a spoken dialogue application from the perspectives of acceptability and usability. Current TTS systems are not capable of producing completely natural human speech and some users may find synthesised speech difficult to understand or simply annoying. Speech output can be improved either by using prerecorded files or by employing speech markup to render the synthesised speech more acceptable. Audio (prerecorded) files are referred to by a URI (Uniform Resource Indicator). The VoiceXML language does not specify a required set of audio file formats, but platforms may differ regarding which formats they support. For TTS a number of different speech markup languages have been proposed, including:

- JSML: Java API Speech Markup Language.
- SABLE: A consortium developing standards for speech markup (used, e.g., in the CSLU toolkit, see Chapter 7).
- SSML: The W3C Speech Synthesis Markup Language (http://www.w3.org/TR/speech-synthesis/).

Part 1: Adding Markup

It is important to determine which markup standard is supported by a particular VoiceXML platform as well as which attributes and values of particular tags are realised. The following section provides broad guidelines, but currently there is considerable variation in how speech output and markup are handled across platforms so that the relevant documentation should be consulted for details.

Markup is used to indicate emphasis, breaks and prosody in prompts. Table 9.1 shows some common tags as defined in the VoiceXML Version 1.0 Specification based on the Java Speech Markup Language, along with changes specified in VoiceXML Version 2.0.

The following is an example of a prompt that contains speech markup based on the VoiceXML Version 1.0 specification:

```
<prompt><pros rate = "+5%">
Welcome to Student System Main Menu.
<break size = "large"/>
The system provides details on students, courses and reports.
<break size = "large"/>
The commands <emp level="strong">help</emp>, <emp level="strong">quit
</emp> and <emp level="strong">main menu</emp>are always available.
<break size = "large"/>
</prompt>
```

Exercise 19

Create an application with a similar prompt and experiment with the different speech markup tags and their attributes and values. The tags and attributes that you use will depend on the platform you use and on which version of VoiceXML is supported.

Part 2: Prompts with Barge-in and Audio Prompts

Prompts with Barge-in

A prompt can be set to allow barge-in, if this is supported by the implementation platform. Users can interrupt a prompt if its "barge-in" attribute is "true". In some platforms this is the default setting as specified by the value of the

Table 9.1. Mark-up tags for TTS synthesis

Tag	VoiceXML V1.0	VoiceXML V2.0
⟨break⟩	Specifies a pause in the speech output. Attributes of ⟨break⟩ are: ms – the number of milliseconds to pause. size – a relative pause duration, with possible values "none", "small", "medium", "large".	The attribute "time" is used instead of "ms" to indicate the absolute time in seconds or milliseconds, e.g., "250ms", "2.5 s".
⟨div⟩	Identifies the enclosed text as a sentence or paragraph.	⟨div⟩ is not used. Instead the tags ⟨paragraph⟩ and ⟨sentence⟩ are provided.
⟨emp⟩	Specifies that the enclosed text should be spoken with emphasis, with values "strong", "moderate" (default), "none" or "reduce".	⟨emphasis⟩
⟨pros⟩	Specifies prosodic information for the enclosed text, with attributes "rate", "vol", "pitch", "range". More specific details can be found in the Java API. Speech Markup Language Specification	⟨prosody⟩ replaces ⟨pros⟩ with the attributes: pitch-values: high, medium, low, or default. contour – sets the actual pitch. Contour for the contained text. Range-values: high, medium, low or default. rate-values: fast, medium, slow or default. duration – specifies the duration in seconds or milliseconds for the desired time to take to read the element contents. volume-values: silent, soft, medium, loud or default.
⟨sayas⟩	Specifies how a word or phrases should be spoken. The attributes of ⟨sayas⟩ are: phon – representation of the Unicode International Phonetic Alphabet (IPA) to be spoken instead of the text. sub – defines substitute text to be spoken instead of the contained text. class – the possible values are "phone", "date", "digits", "literal", "currency", "number", "time".	⟨say-as⟩ replaces ⟨sayas⟩, and "type" replaces "class" with an increased set of types, including "acronym", measure, net (email or url), and address (postal).
⟨phon⟩		⟨phoneme⟩ replaces ⟨phon⟩ with the following attributes: ph – required attribute which specifies the phonetic string. alphabet – optional attribute which specifies the alphabet to use from one of: IPA (International Phonetic Alphabet), worldbet (Postscript) phonetic alphabet, or xsampa phonetic alphabet. ⟨voice⟩ – specifies voice characteristics, with attributes including "gender" and "age".

"barge-in" property. Barge-in can be set to "false" so that the user cannot interrupt the prompt, as follows:

```
<prompt bargein="false">
welcome to the Student System Main Menu
</prompt>
```

Audio Prompts

Prompts can consist of audio clips and can also contain a mixture of audio clips and synthesised speech. The audio is usually specified using a URI, but it can also be an audio variable that was previously recorded. The following are some examples:

Audio Only

```
<prompt>
<audio src="http://www.myserver.com/welcome.wav"/>
</prompt>
```

Recorded Audio Variable

```
<prompt>Your recorded greeting is <value expr="greeting"/>
</prompt>
```

In this case the system has recorded the user saying something in the field called "greeting".

Audio and TTS (e.g., where the audio plays a jingle)

```
<prompt>
Welcome to the Student System Main Menu
<audio src="http://www.myserver.com/welcome.wav"/>
</prompt>
```

Audio with Alternative Text in Case the Audio Sample Is Not Available

```
<prompt>
<audio src="http://www.myserver.com/welcome.wav"/>
Welcome to the Student System Main Menu
</prompt>
```

Exercise 20

Make some recordings to use in prompts and experiment with the different combinations of audio and TTS described above.

Tutorial 8: Navigation and Global Commands

A VoiceXML application will usually consist of a number of documents that are linked together in a variety of ways. Documents may contain subdialogues, and within documents there may be several forms and/or menus, and forms may contain several fields. In a VoiceXML application there are likely to be transitions to items within the same document, to subdialogues, and to other URLs. This tutorial deals with two aspects of navigation:

1. Transitions within and between documents.
2. Global commands to support the user's navigation within a VoiceXML application.

Part 1. Transitions Within and Between Documents

`<subdialog>`

The `<subdialog>` element provides a way of transitioning to another place (either within the same document or in another document) and then returning to the original document when the subdialogue has been completed. All local variables, grammars and other information are saved before execution passes to the subdialogue and restored when it returns.

`<goto>`

`<goto>` is another way to direct execution to another dialog, either within the current document or in another document. Some examples of the transitions to another document were illustrated earlier, as shown in the following code sample:

```
<if cond="choice == 'students'">
    <goto next="studentdetails.vxml"/>
    <elseif cond="choice == 'courses'"/>
    <goto next="coursedetails.vxml"/>
    <else/>
    <goto next="reports.vxml"/>
</if>
```

Note that when transitioning to another document, the attribute "next" is used in conjunction with a URI (or, as in this case, a document located in the same directory). If execution is to pass to a particular form (e.g., "getdetails") in that document, the symbol "#" is used, as follows:

```
<goto next="coursedetails.vxml#getdetails"/>
```

This symbol is also used to transition to another dialog (form or menu) within the same document:

```
<goto next="#getdetails"/>
```

To transition to another item within a form the attribute "nextitem" is used:

```
<goto nextitem="confirm"/>
```

It is important to note that transitioning to another dialog or document using `<goto>` will cause the old dialog's variables to be lost. If the variables are to persist across multiple documents, they should be stored with application scope (see Chapter 10 for further details on variables).

`<submit>`

`<submit>` is used to submit values to the document server via an HTTP GET or POST request. As with `<goto>` a new document is obtained. The following is an example in which the "next" attribute specifies the URL to which the values are submitted and the "namelist" attribute specifies which values are being submitted:

```
<submit next="http: www.myserver.com/myscript.jsp" namelist = "username coursename" />
```

Control will not necessarily return to the calling document. For example, the script specified in the "next" attribute might generate a VoiceXML document dynamically and execution will continue with this document.

`<link>`

`<link>` is another way of specifying transitions to a new dialog or document. The `<link>` element specifies a grammar so that when the user's input matches the grammar, execution will transition to the destination specified, or an event specified by the event attribute is thrown. The following is an example of the use of the `<link>` element to cause transition to a new document if the word "help" is spoken or "9" is pressed:

```
<link next="http://www.myserver.com/help.vxml">
<grammar type="application/x-jsgf"> help </grammar>
<dtmf> 9 </dtmf>
</link>
```

`<link>` is particularly useful for the specification of global navigational commands (see the next section).

Part 2. Global Commands to Support the User's Navigation Within a VoiceXML Application

Navigational support for the user in VoiceXML involves global navigational commands and links that are analogous to a visual navigational bar in a graphically based application. Commands, such as "help", "main menu" and "exit" can be made globally available, so that they can be used to throw events at any time during a session or to enable the user to go to a particular function within the application without having to navigate back to the top-level menu.

Global commands can be created in a root document (here entitled "studentsystemroot.vxml") which is referenced by all the leaf documents in the application, as follows:

```
<vxml version="1.0" application = "studentsystemroot.vxml">
```

The root document will contain links to leaf documents, global commands and global events. The following is an example of a link to a form entitled "main-menu" in a leaf document entitled "mainmenu.vxml" that will be activated if the user says either "main menu" or "start":

```
<!– provides a link from any document to the Main Menu –>
<link next="mainmenu.vxml"#mainmenu">
<grammar>
main menu | start
</grammar>
</link>
```

Exercise 21

Assuming that you have separate documents for the main elements in the Student System – student details, course details, view student details, reports and main menu – create a root document with links to these documents. Run and test your application to ensure that the links work from each document.

Notes on ECMASCRIPT

ECMAScript (European Computer Manufacturer's Association), the standard version of JavaScript, is the scripting language of VoiceXML. ECMAScript can be used in VoiceXML documents for client-side processing, for example, to validate user input, without requiring access to the server.

Some examples of ECMAScript have already been presented in the code samples in this chapter. For example, the VoiceXML variables that have been used are completely equivalent to ECMAScript variables. ECMAScript objects were used as the parameter passing mechanism for elements such as `<subdialog>` and `<object>`, while the "expr" and the "cond" attributes reference ECMAScript expressions.

Although ECMAScript can be used within a VoiceXML document in the ways mentioned, there are some characters that need to be escaped in order to conform to the rules of XML. For example, characters used in boolean expressions, such as ">", "<" and "&&" need to be escaped to ">", "<" and "&&", respectively, as in this example:

```
<if cond = "age &gt; 21" >
```

The `<script>` element can be used to specify a block of ECMAScript code, as follows:

```
<SCRIPT>
<![CDATA[
... ECMAScript code ... ]]>
</SCRIPT>
```

It is also possible to define reusable script libraries by placing ECMAScript in external files and referencing them using the "src" attribute of the script element. For example, a file called "mylib.js" in a scripts directory would be referenced as:

```
<script src="scripts/dtlib.js"/>
```

Further Reading

Books on VoiceXML

Abbott K (2001). *Voice Enabling Web Applications: VoiceXML and Beyond.* APress L. P. Berkeley, CA. (Book and CD-ROM.)

Andersson EA et al. (2001). *Early adopter VoiceXML.* Wrox Press, Birmingham UK.

DreamTech Inc. (2002). *VoiceXML 2.0 Developer's Guide.* McGraw-Hill, New York.

Edgar BC (2001). *The VoiceXML Handbook.* CMP Books Gilroy, CA.

Hocek A, Cuddihy D (2003). *The definitive reference guide to VoiceXML.* Prentice Hall, Upper Saddle River, NJ.

Larson JA (2002). *VoiceXML: Introduction to Developing Speech Applications.* Prentice Hall, Upper Saddle River, NJ.

Miller M (2002). *VoiceXML: 10 Projects to Voice Enable Your Web Site.* Wiley, New York.

Sharma C, Kunins J (2001). *VoiceXML: Strategies and Techniques for Effective Voice Application Development with Voicexml 2.0.* Wiley, New York. (Book and CD-ROM.)

VoiceXML Resources

VoiceXML forum: http://www.voicexml.org

List of resources at Jim Larson's Larson Technical Services site: http://www.larson-tech.com/bookres.htm

Ken Rehor's World of VoiceXML: http://www.kenrehor.com/voicexml/

W3C Voice Browser Activity: http://www.w3.org/Voice/

Developer.com (voice): http://www.developer.com/voice/

VoiceXML Central – A VoiceXML search engine and community: http://www.voicexmlcentral.com/

More Advanced VoiceXML

10

In Chapter 9 the basic elements of VoiceXML were introduced. This chapter examines some more advanced aspects, such as mixed-initiative dialogue and the generation of dynamic VoiceXML in Web server applications. Some important aspects of VoiceXML are explained, such as the Form Interpretation Algorithm (FIA), the structure and use of recognition grammars, and the issue of scope in relation to variables and grammars. This chapter consists of the following tutorials:

Tutorial 1: Mixed-initiative dialogue.

Tutorial 2: The Form Interpretation Algorithm (FIA).

Tutorial 3: Recognition grammars.

Tutorial 4: Variable and grammar scope.

Tutorial 5: Dynamic VoiceXML and Web Server Applications.

Tutorial 6: Dynamic grammars.

Tutorial 1: Mixed-initiative Dialogue

The examples developed in Chapter 9 all involved directed dialogues, in which the system controls the dialogue and prompts the user for one or more items, one at a time, in a predetermined order. A mixed-initiative dialogue allows greater flexibility as the items do not need to be elicited in a set sequence and an utterance can include more than one item at a time. If some of the values required by the application are not elicited in mixed initiative mode, the system can prompt for the missing values by reverting to directed dialogue mode.

Two additional features are required to make VoiceXML documents mixed-initiative:

1. An <initial> element.
2. A form level grammar.

An <initial> element is similar to a field. A form can have one or more <initial> elements, which are listed before any other fields in the form. The

263

<initial> element has prompts and event handlers, but it cannot contain its own grammars or <filled> elements.

A form-level grammar, which is declared as a child of <form> (i.e., following the <form> element as shown in lines 3 and 4 below) is required with the <initial> element to interpret the user's input. Form-level grammars are similar to the recognition grammars used in the Rapid Application Developer (RAD) to process strings of words (see Chapter 7). In the example below the grammar will only contain two elements but, as we will see later, more complex grammars can be written to recognise much longer strings and more complex combinations.

The following is an application (studentsystem6a.vxml) in which the user can speak two values – a student's name and the name of a course – in either order:

```
1 <?xml version="1.0" ?>
2 <vxml version="1.0">
3 <form id="getdetails">
4 <grammar src="studentsystem6a.gram"/>
5 <initial name="get_alldetails">
6 <prompt>
7 Say a student's name and the name of a course
8 </prompt>
9 </initial>
10 <field name="studentname">
11 <grammar src="studentsystem6a.gram#studentname"/>
12 <prompt>What is the student's name?
13 </prompt>
14 </field>
15 <field name="coursename">
16 <grammar src="studentsystem6a.gram#coursename"/>
17 <prompt>What is the name of the course?</prompt>
18 </field>
19 </form>
20 </vxml>
```

The <initial> element (lines 5–9) is where the user is prompted for the student's name and the name of the course. The subsequent fields entitled "studentname" and "coursename" will only be visited if these values are not elicited in the <initial> element.

The following grammar (studentsystem6a.gram) is used in conjunction with this document. In this grammar the top level rule "getdetails" will accept either a "studentname" followed by a "coursename", or a "coursename" followed by a "studentname". The code in braces, for example {this.studentname=$}, assigns the value elicited to the name of a field (in this case, the field entitled "studentname"). The tokens (or words) for "studentname" and "coursename" are defined in the second and third rules, respectively:

```
#JSGF V1.0;
grammar studentsystem6a;
```

```
public <studentsystem6a> = <studentname> {this.studentname=$} <course-
name> {this.coursename=$} | <coursename> {this.coursename=$} <studentname>
{this.studentname=$};
<studentname> = john | david | rosemary | jennifer;
<coursename> = communications | algorithms | programming | databases;
```

Exercise 1

1. Load and run the application "studentsystem6a.vxml". You will notice that both "studentname" and "coursename" are required, in either order. If one or the other is not spoken, the input will not match the grammar and a `<nomatch>` event will be thrown.

2. Test the program by saying the two items in either order, and also by saying one of the items only.

Exercise 2: Developing the Mixed-Initiative Application

To allow for the case where only one of the items is spoken, and to allow the system to go on to elicit the missing value in directed-dialogue mode, we need to modify the grammar to make one of the items in the top-level rule optional.

1. Save the file "studentsystem6a.vxml" as "studentsystem6b.vxml".

2. Save the file "studentsystem6a.gram" as "studentsystem6b.gram" and make the following changes:

```
public <studentsystem6b> = <studentname>
{this.studentname=$} [<coursename>
{this.coursename=$}] |
<coursename> {this.coursename=$} [<studentname>
{this.studentname=$}];
```

This rule now says that you can either have `<studentname>` and optionally `<coursename>`, or `<coursename>` and optionally `<studentname>`.

It is also necessary to make the rules "studentname" and "coursename" public. What this means is that the rules can be used by the speech recognition engine when called from outside the grammar, as would be the case in studentsystem6b.vxml at lines 11 and 16. Rules that are not public, as in the first version of the grammar, can only be called by other rules within the grammar.

Note that the "#" symbol, as in `<grammar src="studentsystem6b.gram#studentsystem6b" />` denotes the particular rule within studentsystem6b.gram that is to be applied. This rule applies in the mixed-initiative form "getdetails". Other rules from the grammar are required for the fields "studentname" and "coursename". Amend the code in "studentdetails6b.vxml" accordingly.

The rule "studentsystem6b" will allow input such as:

john databases
databases john
john
databases

3. Amend the grammar. Make any necessary changes to "studentsystem6b.vxml" to reference the grammar file "studentsystem6b.gram".

4. Test your application with a variety of valid and invalid inputs according to your grammar.

Tutorial 2: The Form Interpretation Algorithm (FIA)

The Form Interpretation Algorithm (FIA) specifies the actions that the VoiceXML browser should take when interpreting a document. It is possible to create dialogue scripts declaratively in VoiceXML and leave the FIA to interpret the code and control the dialogue flow implicitly. However, some appreciation of the FIA will be useful, particularly in order to understand the dialogue flow when it does not seem to follow the anticipated sequence.

At a broad level the FIA processes a form by proceeding sequentially through the fields to elicit values, unless transitions are specified to other elements. At the end of the form, if all the fields have assigned values, and unless there is a transition specified to another form or document, the FIA terminates.

The FIA consists of the following phases:

1. An initialisation phase that occurs once when a form is entered.
2. A loop consisting of selection, collection and processing phases that repeat as long as the form remains active.

The following is a high-level account of these phases. For a more complete account, see the VoiceXML specification.

Initialisation Phase

In this phase variables are set to "undefined" unless they have been assigned values by an "expr" attribute. Prompts are created for each field and <initial> item with values set to 1. Grammars for link tags with document scope are activated, followed by grammars for link tags with dialog scope.

Selection Phase

In this phase the next item in the form is chosen for execution. Usually this will be the next field whose value is "undefined". If no item is found – normally because the fields have all been visited and their values have been set to "true" – the FIA exits the form with an implicit <exit>.

Collection Phase

This phase starts by choosing the prompts to be spoken to the user. All the grammars to be used in the current scope are activated and the user input is matched to a grammar or an event such as `<noinput>` or `<nomatch>` is thrown. If the item is a block, the code specified in the block is executed and the block's implicit variable is set so that the block will not be visited again.

Processing Phase

This phase determines what actions are to be taken based on the user input or on events that were thrown. If the user input matches a grammar, one or more variables are set. In a field-level grammar one field variable will be set, while in a form-level grammar variables for more than one field may be set. Finally, any `<filled>` handlers will be executed.

Understanding How the Value "Undefined" Is Used in a Loop

The role of the value "undefined" in a loop can be examined by revisiting the application "viewdetails.vxml" that was introduced in Chapter 9. In this example, reproduced below, the system collects a student's name and then confirms the name. The code in the `<filled>` element speaks out a prompt if the user confirms, otherwise the values for the fields "student_name" and "confirm" are cleared, i.e., set to "undefined".

```
<?xml version="1.0"?>
<vxml version="1.0">
<form id = "student_details">
<block>
Welcome to Student Details.
</block>
<field name = "student_name">
<prompt> Please say the student name </prompt>
<grammar>
john | david | rosemary | jennifer
</grammar>
</field>
<field name="confirm" type="boolean">
<prompt>
you want details on <value expr="student_name"/>
</prompt>
<filled>
<if cond="confirm">
<prompt> looking up details on <value expr="student_name"/>
</prompt>
<else />
let's try again
<clear namelist = "student_name confirm" />
```

```
</if>
</filled>
</field>
</form>
</vxml>
```

In terms of the FIA, if all the fields are processed as expected and the user confirms, then all the values will have been set to "true". When the FIA loops through the form again, there will be no items left for selection and so an implicit <exit> will occur. However, if some of the values are reset to "undefined" as a result of <clear>, then those items will be revisited on the next loop.

Exercise 3

1. Save the file "viewdetails.vxml" as "newviewdetails.vxml".
2. Delete the line <clear namelist = "student_name confirm" /> and see what happens.
3. Insert the line but delete the value "confirm".
4. Try again, this time with "confirm" included and "student_name" deleted.

Exercise 4

Save the file "studentsystem6b.vxml" as "studentsystem7a.vxml", using the grammar "studentsystem6b.gram" as before. Modify the application so that the system confirms both values at once (e.g., "was that John and databases"). If the user says "no", the system should ask which item they wish to change (e.g., "say which item you wish to change: the student name or the course name"), and should then clear the item requested. Observe carefully the behaviour of the application using different inputs.

The following code extract should be inserted after the fields in which the "studentname" and "coursename" have been elicited:

```
<field name="confirm" type="boolean">
<prompt>
you want details on <value expr="studentname"/> taking <value
expr="coursename" />
</prompt>

<filled>
<if cond="confirm">
<prompt> looking up details on <value expr="studentname"/> and <value
expr="coursename"/>
</prompt>
<assign name="change" expr="true" />
<else />
```

```
<goto nextitem = "change" />
</if>
</filled>

</field>

<field name="change">
<prompt>
which item do you wish to change: the student or the course
</prompt>
<grammar>
student | course
</grammar>

<filled>
   <if cond="change == 'student'">
   <clear namelist="studentname confirm"/>
   <else/>
   <clear namelist="coursename confirm"/>
   </if>

</filled>

</field>
```

Note the line `<assign name="change" expr="true" />`. This prevents the FIA going on to the field "change" if the user confirms the values for studentname and coursename by assigning the value for the field "change" to "true" so that this field is not visited by the FIA (see also the next section).

Understanding Mixed Initiative Forms in Terms of the FIA

When applied to mixed initiative forms the same principles apply as in directed forms regarding the setting of field variables, except that one or more variables can be set within the `<initial>` element, whereas in a directed dialogue only one variable is set at a time as each field is processed sequentially. In a mixed-initiative dialogue the system first tries to elicit user input within the `<initial>` element and matches any input to a form-level grammar. During this matching process tags are encountered within the grammar that assigns values to field items. If one or more tags are matched, then the fields corresponding to those tags will be matched and all `<initial>` form item variables will be set to true. This will cause the FIA to leave the `<initial>` field and to move to those fields whose values are undefined. If all the required values are elicited within a single utterance, then none of the fields within that form will need to be visited as all the values will have been set to "true". In this way, the FIA in conjunction with mixed-initiative forms allows an application to elicit multiple values but also to fall back on a directed mode if not all of the values are successfully elicited.

Exercise 5

1. Save the grammar "studentsystem6b.gram" as "studentsystem7.gram" and include a further slot for the level of the course, which can be 1, 2 or 3.
2. Amend "studentsystem7a.vxml" to prompt for the course level and save as "studentsystem7b.vxml".
3. Run and test with different combinations of input.

Manipulating the `<initial>` Form Item Variable: Getting the System to Move On

It is possible to disable the `<initial>` form item variable so that the system can move on to the next form item and not loop round continuously in an attempt to fill slots. For example, after a number of attempts the system could give up on mixed-initiative input and move to directed mode. The following code shows how this would be done on the second failure to match:

```
<nomatch count="2">
<prompt> Sorry I still don't understand that.
Let's take this step by step
</prompt>
<assign name="get_alldetails " expr="true"/>
</nomatch>
```

Once this `<nomatch>` event is thrown the `<initial>` element will be set to "true" and so `<initial>` will not be selected anymore by the FIA. Conversely, the form item variable in an `<initial>` element could be cleared, causing the `<initial>` element to be selected again by the FIA, for example, if on confirmation the items recognised within the `<initial>` element are not confirmed by the user and the system goes back to start over again.

Exercise 6

Develop simple applications that test these different possibilities.

Tutorial 3: Recognition Grammars

Recognition grammars are the key to successful performance of the speech recognition component of a spoken dialogue system. Currently a number of different grammar formats are available on different VoiceXML platforms, and for specific details it will be necessary to consult the documentation provided with each platform (see Appendix 1 for further information on grammar formats).

Inline Grammars

Grammars that are specified within a VoiceXML document are called "inline" grammars. Most of the examples provided so far have been inline grammars, in which the words or phrases that the system can recognise are listed inside the elements to which they apply, as in:

```
<field name = "student_name">
<prompt> Please say the student name </prompt>
<grammar>
john | david | rosemary | jennifer
</grammar>
</field>
```

The items in the grammar are enclosed within the <grammar> tags.

Inline grammars can be enclosed within a CDATA section. This is required if they include XML terms or nonterminals. The following is an example of the use of a CDATA section:

```
<grammar>
<![CDATA[
(
john |
david |
rosemary |
jennifer
)
]]>
</grammar>
```

External Grammars

A grammar that is saved as a separate file is referenced in a document using the <grammar> element and the "src" attribute, as follows:

```
<grammar src="studentsystem7.gram"/>
```

The "type" attribute can be used to specify which grammar format (or MIME type) is to be used. In the following example the Java Speech Grammar Format (JSGF) is specified:

```
<grammar src="studentsystem7.gram" type="application/x-jsgf"/>
```

Whether the "type" attribute is required will depend on the VoiceXML platform being used. In some cases a default type is assumed. The <grammar> element can also have a "scope" attribute. This attribute will be discussed later.

Grammar Header

VoiceXML grammars are preceded by a grammar header and a declaration, for example:

```
#JSGF V1.0;
grammar studentdetails;
```

which are followed by the grammar rules.

Grammar Concepts

VoiceXML grammars are similar to other grammars such as the recognition grammars used in RAD (see Chapter 7). There are rules for individual words or phrases (usually referred to as "tokens" in VoiceXML grammars), as in:

```
<studentname> = john | david | rosemary | jennifer;
```

and there are rules that may consist of further rules and/or tokens on the right-hand side of the rule, as in:

```
<studentdetails> = <studentname> <coursename>;
```

Operators

Grammars make use of operators to indicate optional elements, groupings of items, and recurring items:

```
| means "or": e.g. john | david;
[ ] means "optional": e.g. [firstname] lastname; (lastname is required, firstname is
optional)
* indicates zero or any number of applications of a rule e.g. firstname*
+ indicates at least one application
```

Semantic Tags

As seen already in the grammar "studentsystem6a.gram" a grammar may include tags, which specify how the results are returned to the application. For example:

```
public <studentsystem6a> = <studentname> {this.studentname=$};
```

Here the tag {this.studentname=$} indicates that whatever is recognised by the item <studentname> should be instantiated as the value of the variable "studentname". Normally this variable would be the name of a field and in this way a field will receive a value through the process of recognition using a recognition grammar.

Using Tags for Alternative Phrasings

Tags can be used within rules to allow alternative phrasings and to ensure that each of the alternatives is matched on to the same concept (or variable). The following example shows how the words "comms" and "communications" are alternative words for the name of a course. Furthermore, the values that are returned are course codes. A grammar such as this would allow items to be recognised by their natural language names rather than by less intuitive code names:

```
<coursename> = (comms | communications) {this.$value="01"} | algorithms
{this.$value="02"} | programming {this.$value="03"} | databases {this.$value="04"};
```

Exercise 7

Integrate this rule and the grammar into an application that takes in the name of a student and the name of a course and outputs the student's name along with a course code.

Using Recognition Grammars for Keyword Spotting

In Chapter 7 a grammar was introduced that allowed two keywords – words matching a pizza size and words matching a pizza type – to be recognised and any other words to be discarded. For example, given the input

(I'd like a) small pepperoni (pizza please)

we may wish the words in parentheses to be ignored and only the words "small" and "pepperoni" to be retained. In the following grammar the keywords are defined and other extraneous words are indicated as optional:

```
#JSGF V1.0;
grammar pizza;
public <pizza> = [I'd like a] <size> <type> [pizza] [please];
<size> = small | medium | gigantic | large;
<type> = vegetarian | pepperoni | cheese;
```

This grammar is rather inflexible as it still requires the extraneous words to be matched exactly. Further rules could be provided to cover a wide range of alternatives to "I'd like a", as well as alternatives to the other optional elements.

Exercise 8

Devise a set of such rules that will permit a wider range of sentences while still only retaining the "size" and "type" keywords.

Exercise 9: A More Extensive Grammar

Consider the following grammar rules which were used in Chapter 7, Exercise 12, in connection with extended recognition grammars in RAD:

```
viewdetails -> (give me details on) (student) studentname (on) coursecode (on | at)
(stage) coursestage
studentname -> john scott | david wilson | rosemary blackburn | jennifer black
```

coursecode -> diploma in applications and support | dk003 | diploma in software development | dk004
coursestage -> 1 | award

Recall that these rules allow the user to speak sentences such as:

1 Give me details on student john scott on dk003 at stage award.
2 john scott dk003 award.

Specify a VoiceXML grammar that uses these rules and that will accept these sentences. Construct an application that incorporates this grammar. Test your application and grammar with a variety of inputs.

Tutorial 4: Variable and Grammar Scope

In Chapter 9 we saw that a VoiceXML application can consist of a number of documents, which in turn can consist of a number of dialogs (forms or menus). This hierarchical structure is important to understand when considering the scope of variables and grammars in VoiceXML applications.

Variables

Declaring Variables and Assigning Values to Variables

The element <var> is used to declare variables. Variables are declared with a name and may also be assigned a value. For example:

```
<var name = "studentname" />
<var name = "studentid" expr = "590609181" />
```

A value can be assigned at a later stage to a variable, or a value that was assigned can be updated, as in:

```
<assign name = "studentname" expr = " 'john' " />
```

Note that in this example the "expr" attribute includes two sets of quotes. The outer quotes surround the attribute value, as in the earlier example, while the inner quotes indicate to the JavaScript interpreter that the value is a literal string that must be a valid JavaScript expression.

Variable Scope

Variables can be declared in the following scopes: session, application, document, dialog and anonymous, as follows:

Session – These are read-only telephony related variables that are declared and set by the interpreter context and that are valid for an entire user session. New session variables cannot be declared by VoiceXML documents. Examples of session variables are "session.telephone.ani" (automatic number identification), which is set to the caller's telephone number, when available, and "session.telephone.dnis" (dialed number identification service), which is set to the number the caller dialed. This information is provided by the telephony interface and may or may not be available, depending on the service provider.

Application – These variables are declared using `<var>` elements that are children of the application root document's `<vxml>` element. These variables are initialized when the application root document is loaded and are visible to the application root document and any loaded application leaf document.

Dialog – Each dialog (`<form>` or `<menu>`) has a scope that exists while the FIA is visiting that dialog. Variables within a dialog are visible to that dialog.

Anonymous – Variables declared with a `<block>`, `<filled>` or catch element have anonymous scope and are only visible within the scope of that element.

If two variables in different scopes are declared with the same name, the one with narrower scope will be used.

Consider the following example (variabletest1.vxml):

```
1 <?xml version="1.0"?>
2 <vxml version="1.0">
3 <form>
4 <var name="student" expr="'john'" />
5 <block>
6 <prompt>
7 The student name is <value expr="student" />
8 </prompt>
9 </block>
10 </form>
11 </vxml>
```

In line 4 the variable "student" is assigned the value "john" and in line 7 this value is retrieved in the prompt. The variable has been declared with dialog scope.

Now consider this example (variabletest2.vxml):

```
1 <?xml version="1.0"?>
2 <vxml version="1.0">
3 <form>
4 <var name="student" expr="'john'" />
5 <block>
6 <var name="student" expr="'jennifer'" />
7 <prompt>
8 The student name is <value expr="student" />
9 </prompt>
10 </block>
11 </form>
12 </vxml>
```

As before, the variable "student" is assigned the value "john" with dialog scope in line 4. However, within the `<block>` beginning at line 5 the variable "student" is assigned the value "jennifer" at line 6 with anonymous scope. The prompt at line 8 is within this block, so that the variable that is referenced is the one that has anonymous scope, i.e., with the value "jennifer". As anonymous scope is narrower than dialog scope, it is the variable with anonymous scope that is used.

Exercise 10

Work out the system prompts if the following additional block is inserted into "variabletest2.vxml":

```
<block>
<prompt>
The student name is <value expr="student" />
</prompt>
</block>
```

1. Between lines 4 and 5.
2. Between lines 10 and 11.
3. Both between lines 4 and 5 and between lines 10 and 11.

Note that if we wish to access a variable from a different scope, we need to attach a prefix to the variable. So, for example, in the file "variabletest2.vxml" if we changed line 8:

```
The student name is <value expr="student" />
```

to

```
The student name is <value expr="dialog.student" />
```

then the prompt would be "The student name is john".

Some further examples are provided in the book *Early Adopter VoiceXML* (Andersson et al., 2001), on which these examples are based. Using the files provided here as a basis, experiment with further examples of variable scope including variables declared with application and document scope.

Grammar Scope

The scope of a grammar is declared using the "scope" attribute, as in:

```
<grammar scope = "document"> ---- </grammar>
```

Grammars can have the following values for scope:

Document – A grammar with document scope will be active in all dialogs of the current document (and any relevant application leaf documents).

Dialog – Form grammars have dialog scope and are active throughout the current form. Form grammars are given dialog scope by default, but they can also be assigned document or application scope, if required.

Menu – Menu grammars are also by default given dialog scope, and are active only within the menu, unless a different scope is assigned.

Field – A grammar that is scoped to a field is only active when the FIA is visiting that field. Grammars contained within fields cannot specify a scope.

Link grammars have the scope of the element that contains the link. For example, if they are defined in the application root document, then the links will be active in any loaded leaf application. Grammars contained in links cannot specify a scope.

A grammar that is defined within a form or menu can be given document scope by defining the scope of the form, as follows:

```
<form scope = "document" >
<grammar> ---- </grammar>
</form>
```

Here the grammar will be assigned document scope by default.

To specify a grammar with dialog scope within such a form the grammar would have to be explicitly assigned dialog scope, as follows:

```
<form scope = "document" >
<grammar> grammar1 </grammar>
<grammar scope = "dialog"> grammar2 </grammar>
</form>
```

In this example "grammar1" has document scope while "grammar2" has dialog scope. Generally it is preferable to restrict the scope of grammars in order to limit the possibility of overlapping grammars as well as in the interests of recognition performance.

Properties

The <property> element is used to control various behaviours such as barge-in, timeout, and caching and fetching policies. A <property> can be defined at the different levels specified earlier – application, document, dialog and child of form. The following are some examples of <property> definitions:

Confidence level of the speech recogniser – The "confidencelevel" property can be set to a value so that any recognition results falling beneath that level are rejected. For example:

```
<property name = "confidencelevel" value = "0.7" />
```

Bargein – If barge-in is set to false, the user is not allowed to interrupt system prompts. For example:

```
<property name = "bargein" value = "false" />
```

Timeout – This specifies how long the system should wait for input before throwing a <noinput> event. For example:

<property name = "timeout" value = "15s" />

Voice/DTMF – Both voice and DTMF are allowed by default. If one or the other is to be used, the "inputmodes" property can be set accordingly. For example:

<property name = "inputmodes" value = "dtmf" />

Caching – Caching can be set to "safe" or "fast". With "fast" a document is fetched when the document has expired. With "safe" the document is fetched when it has expired or is modified. For example:

<property name = "caching" value = "safe" />

It is essential to examine the documentation for each platform to determine which behaviours are supported by the <property> element and what the default values are.

Tutorial 5: Dynamic VoiceXML and Web Server Applications

The VoiceXML applications developed so far in this book have involved static content in which the system has elicited some input from the user and then the dialogue has terminated. Some of the applications also involved client-side processing, using ECMAScript to validate the input or perform other computations without requiring trips back to a Web Server. In these applications VoiceXML was used simply as a language for scripting standalone spoken dialogue systems.

However, VoiceXML can be used in a much more powerful way. As VoiceXML is an XML-based language, it is able to make use of the technologies and architectures that are used to build and deploy Internet-based applications, in which server-side logic is used to dynamically create VoiceXML code and manage interactions with backend applications such as database servers. This feature distinguishes VoiceXML from other proprietary spoken dialogue environments that require special languages and appilication programming interfaces (APIs) to access Web servers and external databases and applications. The basic VoiceXML architecture is illustrated in Figure 10.1. The main component that has not been considered so far is the Application Server, which runs the application logic, and may contain a database or interfaces to an external database or transaction server.

VoiceXML is used in the same way as HTML to interact with Web servers and backend applications. As with HTML applications the application server receives an HTTP request consisting of a URL and some input parameters, and processes the request using application server software, such as Microsoft Active Server Pages (ASPs) or Java Server Pages (JSPs). This involves mapping

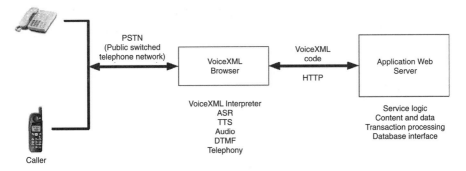

Figure 10.1. VoiceXML architecture.

the request to scripts that may communicate with back-end systems to retrieve information and then format the information into a dynamically generated document that can be output to the user – either on the screen, as with HTML, or, as spoken output, as with VoiceXML.

One of the main advantages of VoiceXML over proprietary alternatives is that Web developers will be familiar with this architecture and the processes involved, so that developing a VoiceXML application boils down to becoming familiar with the VoiceXML language and the processes involved in developing interactive speech systems. All of the backend logic and processes can be assumed.

There is a wide variety of technologies that can be used to build dynamic Web applications. It is beyond the scope of this book to describe all these technologies. Some simple applications that integrate VoiceXML with Web servers and backend applications will be presented. Readers who require more background in the basics of Web servers and scripting languages are referred to the texts listed at the end of the chapter.

For the purposes of the present tutorial, two additional components are required:

1. A Web server.
2. A scripting language.

Apache Tomcat will be used as the Web server here and JSPs will be used as the scripting language. The files are compiled automatically within Apache Tomcat, but a Java development environment, such as Forte, might be useful to check the JSP code. Some information on obtaining and setting up these components is presented in Appendix 3.

Example: Getting Information from a Database Using JSPs

This example will make use of the scenario presented in Chapter 7, in which RAD and TCLODBC were used to retrieve information about the student. To recap, the following steps were involved:

1. The system elicits a student ID in the form of a digit string.
2. The system retrieves a record from a database and speaks out a student name, course code and stage.

The files that will be used are "viewdetails.vxml", which will be amended slightly to include a <submit> element, and "student.mdb", the student database that was used in Chapter 7 for the same purposes. A JSP script "getstudentdetails.jsp" will be required to perform the Web server functions of communicating with the backend database and generating dynamic VoiceXML code to present the results to the user.

The following processes are involved:

1. The system submits the digit string to a Web server using <submit>.
2. The Web server invokes a JSP script.
3. The script makes a connection to a database using the JDBC–ODBC bridge.
4. A record is retrieved from the database.
5. Items from the retrieved database record are incorporated into dynamically generated VoiceXML code.

As far as the launching VoiceXML file "viewdetails.vxml" is concerned, the only modification is within the <filled> element where, if the student ID has been elicited and confirmed, the application submits the details to the server along with the script "getstudentdetails.jsp" which, for the purposes of this example, is located in the Apache Tomcat directory in Apache Tomcat 4.0\webapps\studentsystem\:

```
<filled>
<if cond="confirm">
<prompt> please wait while I look up the details
</prompt>
<submit next= "http://localhost/studentsystem/getstudentdetails.jsp" />
<else />
let's try again
<clear namelist = "getstudentid confirm" />
</if>
</filled>
```

Note that in the <submit> statement the "namelist" attribute has not been used. This means that all values elicited within the scope of the element in which <filled> occurs, in this case the field "getstudentid", are submitted. Here only one value is involved. If several values had been involved and it was necessary to specify which ones to include, the <submit> statement would have read something like:

```
<submit next= "http://localhost/getstudentdetails.jsp" namelist = "getstudentid" />
```

Save the file "viewdetails.vxml" as "viewdetailsdb.vxml", including these modifications.

The main work is done in the file "getstudentdetails.jsp". This file is presented below with some comments for those unfamiliar with Web server applications.

Parts of the code that may need to be changed in the exercises are indicated in bold.

Note: Single line comments use the symbol "//" at the beginning of each line, as in:

```
// set up variable to obtain and store the student id
```

Longer comments are preceded by the symbol "/*" and terminated by the symbol "*/", as in:

```
/* This is a longer comment
*/
    <?xml version="1.0"?>
    <vxml version="1.0">
    <%@page contentType="text/xml"%>
    <%@page import="java.sql.*"%>
    <%@page import="java.util.*"%>
    <%@page import="java.io.*"%>
    <form>
    <block>
    <%
    /*
    Set up a variable to obtain and store the student id that has been submitted from
    the document "view_details.vxml"
    */
    String getstudentid;
    String values[];   // array to store the student id
// Get the student id data from the form
// Initialise "studentid"
    getstudentid="";
/*
    Call the method "request.getParameterValues" to obtain the "studentid" data
    from the VoiceXML document and store it in the values array
    */
    values=request.getParameterValues("getstudentid");
    /*
    Associate the variable "studentid" with the value in the first place of the values
    array
    */
    if(values!=null)
    {
    getstudentid=values[0];
    }
    //create the SQL query
    String sqlStatement = ("SELECT * FROM querydetails WHERE (studentid)='"
    +getstudentid+"';");
    //specify that the JDBC-ODBC bridge is being used
    String driverName ="sun.jdbc.odbc.JdbcOdbcDriver";
    //identify the student database as the connectionURL
    String connectionURL ="jdbc:odbc:student";
    //initialise connection, statement and result set variables
    Connection con = null;
```

```
Statement stmt = null;
ResultSet rs = null;
//connect to the database, pose the query and obtain the results
try
{
//make a new instance of the JDBC-ODBC driver
Class.forName(driverName).newInstance();
//make a connection to the Opensesame database
con = DriverManager.getConnection(connectionURL);
//create a statement object to interface with the SQL engine
stmt = con.createStatement();
//execute the SQL query and place the results in the variable rs
rs = stmt.executeQuery(sqlStatement);
}
catch (Exception e)
{
out.println(e);
}
//format and present results
try
{
//If there is data in the ResultSet, get the ResultSet's metadata,
if(rs.next())
{
//set up variables to contain the database fields data
String firstname;
String lastname;
String coursecode;
String stage;
// obtain and print out the record of the database.
   do
   {
   firstname = rs.getString(3);
   lastname = rs.getString(4);
   coursecode = rs.getString(5);
   stage = rs.getString(6);
   //set up dynamic vxml
   out.println("The details are Student " + firstname + " " + lastname);
   out.println("The course code is " + coursecode);
   out.println("This student is at stage " + stage);
   }while (rs.next());
   } // end of if
// else statement will tell user that student does not exist or the student id is
invalid
      else
         {
out.println("There is no such student in the student database. Please double
check your database manually");
         }
}
catch(Exception e)
```

```
{
out.println(e);
}
out.flush ();
//close the connection to the database
try{
if (con != null){
con.close();
}
}
catch(Exception e) {
out.println(e);
}
%>
</block>
</form>
</vxml>
```

This program does the following:

1. It makes a connection to the student database via the JDBC–ODBC bridge.
2. It poses the SQL query "SELECT * FROM query_details", where query_details is the table containing the relevant information.
3. It retrieves the query results.
4. It formats the results as a dynamic VoiceXML document.
5. It closes the connection to the database.

It will be noted that this code consists of a mixture of VoiceXML code and Java code, which is preceded by the symbols "<%" and terminated by the symbols "%>", e.g.,

```
<%@page contentType="text/xml"%>
```

This file can be used as a template for similar applications, where the elements marked in bold are those which would need to be changed, for example, to take in a variable with a different name, to connect to a different database, to modify the SQL statement and the fields from which values are to be retrieved, and to create the dynamic VoiceXML code for output.

Exercise 11

Test this program using some of the student IDs that are in the student database. Try with some student IDs that are not listed in the database. In this case the error message should be returned telling you that this student is not listed in the database.

Note: For this application to work, your web server should be running.

Exercise 12

1. Adapt the application so that the VoiceXML document "viewdetailsdb.vxml" elicits the student's first and last name in mixed initiative mode (i.e., attempt to elicit the complete name initially, then use directed dialogue mode to elicit the two elements separately if this does not work).

2. Adapt the JSP program "getstudentdetails.jsp" to take in the two variables and to query the database to return and speak out the student ID. To do this, you will need to do the following:

   (a) Set up variables to take in the two values: firstname and lastname, for example:

```
String firstname;
String lastname;
String values1[];
String values2[];
```

   (b) Make appropriate adjustments elsewhere in the program to reflect these changes.

   (c) Amend the SQL query.

   (d) Amend the dynamically generated VoiceXML to output the student ID.

Tutorial 6: Dynamic Grammars

A dynamic grammar is required when the recognition vocabulary relevant to a prompt is not known in advance. For example, the students enrolled on a course, or the set of modules available, may change over time. This information would normally be kept in a database, which would be regularly updated. A static grammar that is created in advance would be difficult to update every time the database is changed. A better solution is to dynamically create the grammar at run-time by consulting the most recent entries in the database. We saw in Chapter 7 how dynamic recognition vocabularies could be created in RAD by linking to a database to retrieve a list of items to be inserted into a recognition vocabulary. VoiceXML grammars can also be created dynamically by retrieving lists of words from a database. However, while RAD provided built-in functions for creating recognition grammars, given a list of words to be recognised, in VoiceXML this process has to be coded. The following processes are required:

1. Connecting to a database to retrieve a list of words to be modelled.

2. Creating an external grammar file that contains these words.

Retrieving the list of words involves the use of a JSP file to access a database and retrieve the required words. This process is already familiar from the previous tutorial. Creating an external grammar file will require a procedure to write the words to a named file with the appropriate grammar format. This process can be included with the same JSP file used to access the database.

In the file "dynamicgrammar.vxml" the system tells the user that they can ask for information by student name, student ID or coursecode. Only the function for student name is implemented in the file. If the user responds with the words "name" or "student name", the system submits this information to the Web server with the file "dynamicgrammar.jsp". The student first and last names are retrieved from the database "student.mdb" and an external grammar file is created with the following rules:

```
#JSGF V1.0;
grammar names;
public <names> = <firstname> <lastname> ;
public <firstname> =
john | david | rosemary | jennifer ;
public <lastname> = scott | wilson | blackburn | black;
```

Control is then passed back to a file "namescontinued.vxml", which asks "Which student do you want information on?" and uses the dynamically created grammar file to recognise the user's response.

The following is the listing for "dynamicgrammar.jsp". This file is similar to the file "getstudentdetails.jsp" listed above except for the section, indicated in bold, where the grammar file is dynamically generated.

File listing: dynamicgrammar.jsp

```
<?xml version="1.0"?>
<vxml version="1.0">
<%@page contentType="text/xml"%>
<%@page import="java.sql.*"%>
<%@page import="java.util.*"%>
<%@page import="java.io.*"%>
<form>
<block>
<%
// set up variable to obtain type of search i.e. by name
String info;
String values[];// array to store records
int numMatches = 0;
Vector matches = new Vector();
int numMatches2 = 0;
Vector matches2 = new Vector();
//Get the records
info="";
values=request.getParameterValues("info");
if(values!=null)
{
info=values[0];
}
//create the SQL query
String sqlStatement =("SELECT * FROM querydetails;");
```

```
//specify that the JDBC-ODBC bridge is being used
String driverName ="sun.jdbc.odbc.JdbcOdbcDriver";
//identify the student database as the connectionURL
String connectionURL ="jdbc:odbc:student";
//initialise connection, statement and result set variables
Connection con = null;
Statement stmt = null;
ResultSet rs = null;
//connect to the database, pose the query and obtain the results
try
{
//make a new instance of the JDBC-ODBC driver
Class.forName(driverName).newInstance();
//make a connection to the Opensesame database
con = DriverManager.getConnection(connectionURL);
//create a statement object to interface with the SQL engine
stmt = con.createStatement();
//execute the SQL query and place the results in the variable rs
rs = stmt.executeQuery(sqlStatement);
}
catch (Exception e)
{
out.println(e);
}
//format and present results
try
{
//If there is data in the ResultSet, get the ResultSet's metadata,
   if(rs.next())
   {
   //set up variables to contain the database fields data
   String firstname;
   String lastname;
   int num = 0;
   // obtain and print out the records of the database.
   do
   {
      num = num + 1;
      firstname = rs.getString(3);
      lastname = rs.getString(4);
      matches.addElement(firstname);
      numMatches ++;
      matches2.addElement(lastname);
      numMatches2 ++;
      //set up dynamic vxml
      out.println(firstname +" " +lastname);
boolean success;
   File    outFile   =   new    File("C:\\Program    Files\\Apache    Tomcat
4.0\\webapps\\studentsystem\\names.gram");
   success = outFile.createNewFile();
     if (outFile.canWrite()) {
```

```
        PrintWriter     fos    =    new     PrintWriter(new     BufferedWriter(new
FileWriter(outFile)));
     // Write data to the disk file
     fos.println("#JSGF V1.0;");
     fos.println("grammar names;");
     fos.println("public <names> = <firstname> <lastname> " +";");
     fos.println();
     fos.println("public <firstname> = ");
     if(num == 1)
     {
     for (Enumeration e = matches.elements(); e.hasMoreElements();)
     fos.println(e.nextElement());
     }
     else
     {
     for (Enumeration e = matches.elements(); e.hasMoreElements();)
     fos.println(" | " + e.nextElement());
     }
     fos.println(";");
     fos.println();
     fos.println("public <lastname> = ");
     if(num == 1)
     {
     for (Enumeration e = matches2.elements(); e.hasMoreElements();)
     fos.println(e.nextElement());
     }
     else
     {
     for (Enumeration e = matches2.elements(); e.hasMoreElements();
     fos.println(" | " + e.nextElement());
     }
     fos.println(";");
     fos.close();
     } else {
     out.println("Cannot write to file");
     return;
     }
   }while (rs.next());
   }//end of if
//else statement will tell user their contact does not exist or is invalid
   else
   {
   out.println("There is no such student in the student database. Please double
check your database manually");
   }
}
catch(Exception e)
{
out.println(e);
}
out.flush ();
```

```
//close the connection to the database
try{
if (con != null){
con.close();
}
}
catch(Exception e) {
out.println(e);
}
%>
<goto next="namescontinued.vxml" />
</block>
</form>
</vxml>
```

Exercise 13

Set up the required files for this example and test them. Note that the dynamic grammar file "names.gram" should be written to the same directory within your Web server to which the file "dynamicgrammar.jsp" has been submitted. The file "namescontinued.vxml" should also be in the same directory. Examine the sample files carefully to see how the directory is specified and use this as a basis for your own set-up.

Further Reading

Web Server Technology

Apache Web Server. Extensive information about the Apache Web Servers can be found at the Apache Software Foundation web site at: http://www.apache.org/

The O'Reilly online bookstore has a large number of references to books on Web technologies: http://www.oreilly.com/

JSP

For extensive information about JSPs, see: http://java.sun.com/products/jsp/

See also the JSP Resource Index at: http://www.jspin.com/

The following book is recommended: Bergsten H (2002). *JavaServer Pages*, 2nd ed. O'Reilly, Location.

Ideas for Further Projects

1. Develop the example further so that the system takes the student name, looks up the required information, speaks it out to the user, and asks if they want any further information.

2. Develop the example further so that the user can request information by student ID and by course code.

3. Implement the system that you specified in the exercises in Chapter 6.

4. Voice Banking system. Implement the voice banking system specified as an assignment at Macquarie University in VoiceXML. See: http://www. comp. mq.edu.au/courses/comp349/Assignments-2002/Assignment2/

5. Room booking system. Implement the room booking system specified as an assignment at Macquarie University in VoiceXML. See: http://www. comp. mq.edu.au/courses/comp349/Assignments-2002/Assignment3/

Multimodal Web-based Dialogue: XHTML + Voice and SALT

11

VoiceXML was designed with telephone-based interaction in mind. VoiceXML supports recognition of spoken and Dual Tone Multiple Frequency (DTMF) input, output of synthesised and recorded prompts, and interaction with back-end applications on the web. An extension to VoiceXML supports multimodal interaction with web-based applications on devices such as advanced mobile (cellular) phones and Personal Digital Assistants (PDAs). This extension, known as XHTML + Voice, allows developers to speech-enable visual web pages by incorporating and linking VoiceXML code with the visual markup code written in XHTML. An alternative to XHTML + Voice is SALT (Speech Application Language Tags). SALT is a set of extensions that add speech recognition, speech synthesis, and telephony capabilities to existing markup languages, such as HTML and XHTML, to enable multimodal and telephony access to web-based applications from PCs, telephones, tablet PCs and wireless PDAs.

In this chapter the main characteristics of XHTML + Voice and SALT will be examined and some simple examples will be presented. Both of these languages are still in the process of development, and environments in which applications can be created are just beginning to emerge. For this reason the examples in this chapter will not be presented as tutorials but rather as illustrations of the new technologies. Up-to-date information on the languages and development environments can be found at the sources listed at the end of the chapter. Advanced multimodal interfaces incorporating spoken dialogue will be discussed in Chapter 14.

XHTML + Voice

Introduction

XHTML + Voice (or X + V) is designed to enable multimodal access to web-based information and services by allowing users to combine several modes within the same session. For example, input modes may include speech recognition, keyboard, touch screen and stylus, while output modes include visual as well as spoken display of information. This combination of input and output modes will facilitate interaction with small internet-enabled devices such as advanced mobile phones and PDAs. Input is limited on both types of device due to their size, while output is limited on mobile phones but less so on PDAs. Ideally, the interface should make up for the limitations of a device and play to its strengths. For example, as speech is transient and not suitable for data such as tables or spatial information, a visual display on a PDA would be more appropriate for output of this type. In this way the different modalities can be treated as being complementary.

XHTML + Voice is a language specification that has been submitted to the World Wide Web Consortium (W3C) as part of the W3C Speech Interface Framework by IBM, Motorola, and Opera Software ASA. IBM's Multimodal Tools include the Multimodal Toolkit for WebSphere Studio and the WebSphere Everyplace Multimodal Browser (developed in a strategic relationship with Opera Software ASA). The Multimodal Toolkit enables the creation of multimodal dialogues using X + V while the Multimodal Browser includes an Opera browser enhanced with IBM's automatic speech recognition and text-to-speech (TTS) technology and integrated support for testing X + V applications (for download information, see Appendix 4). Documentation includes a *Getting Started Guide*, which introduces and explains a simple multimodal application. The Multimodal Toolkit currently supports most, though not all, of the functionality described in the XHTML + Voice Profile 1.0 Specification.

An Example: Ordering a Pizza

The following example, which enables a user to order a pizza, is provided as one of the sample applications for the IBM Multimodal Toolkit ("pizza.mxml"). In this example the user is presented with the visual dialogue box shown in Figure 11.1. The system speaks the initial prompt and the user can speak the required responses into a microphone by pressing the Scroll Lock key as a Push-to-Talk button. The user's responses are inserted into the visual dialogue box and the system confirms the order when the "Submit Pizza Order" button is pressed. The following is an example of an interaction with this application:

> System: How many pizzas would you like?
> User: Two.
> System: What size of pizza would you like?
> User: Large.
> System: Would you like extra cheese?
> User: No.
> System: What vegetable toppings would you like?
> User: Mushrooms, onions and peppers.
> System: What meat toppings would you like?
> User: Chicken, sausage and ham.
> System: Your pizza order is: 2 large pizzas with mushrooms, onions, peppers, chicken, ham and sausage.

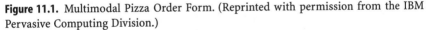

Quantity:

Size:
○ Small 12" ○ Medium 16" ○ Large 22"

Toppings:
□ Extra Cheese

Vegetable Toppings:
□ Olives □ Mushrooms
□ Onions □ Peppers

Meat Toppings:
□ Bacon □ Chicken □ Ham
□ Meatball □ Sausage □ Pepperoni

[Submit Pizza Order]

Figure 11.1. Multimodal Pizza Order Form. (Reprinted with permission from the IBM Pervasive Computing Division.)

Note that the grammars to collect the vegetable and meat toppings are sufficiently flexible to allow the user to enter the toppings in any order, as shown in the response to the prompt for meat toppings, in which the order of the items spoken does not correspond to the order presented visually. A mixed-initiative version of this application is also supplied as a sample with the Multimodal Toolkit ("pizza_order_form.html"). In this example, if the user's initial input is "Two medium pizzas with pepperoni and mushrooms" the fields for quantity, size, and toppings will be filled and the system will prompt for the extra cheese field.

Developing Applications with XHTML + Voice

A multimodal web-based application written using XHTML + Voice consists of a visual component, written in XHTML, and a voice component, written in VoiceXML. XHMTL (eXtensible HypetText Markup Language) is an XML-based markup language that has replaced HTML as the next generation of languages for creating visual applications for desktop and wireless devices.

In the Multimodal Toolkit the visual and voice components are linked together using the XML Events Handler. For example, a VoiceXML element, such as a form, has a unique ID that is activated by an XML-event using a handler that references the ID of the VoiceXML form. The VoiceXML form is executed by the Form Interpretation Algorithm (FIA), as explained in Chapter 10. Results are shared between the speech and visual components of the application using JavaScript and the XML-events syntax. Note that not all of the elements of VoiceXML are available in XHTML + Voice. For example, nonlocal transfer using "goto", "exit", "link", "submit" and "script" is not possible.

Developing an Application Using the Multimodal Toolkit

It is possible to develop X + V applications in a text editor and then test them in the Multimodal Browser. However, the Multimodal Toolkit automates some of the process of creating X + V applications and makes available a number of additional facilities, such as validating the XML code, testing grammars and building pronunciations. This section will briefly outline some of these features. Specifics of how to use these features in building an application can be found in the *Getting Started Guide* provided with the download of the toolkit.

Building an X + V application with the Multimodal Toolkit involves first creating a multimodal project and then, within this project, creating an X + V file. When this has been done, a skeleton of the file is opened, including the heading and namespace declarations, and some empty tags, as follows:

```
<?xml version="1.0" encoding="iso-8859-1"?>
<!DOCTYPE html PUBLIC "-//W3C/DTD XHTML+Voice 1.0/EN" "xhtml+voice.dtd">
<html xmlns="http://www.w3.org/1999/xhtml"
xmlns:ev="http://www.w3.org/2001/xml-events"
xmlns:vxml="http://www.w3.org/2001/vxml" xml:lang="en_US" >
  <head>
    <title> </title>
  </head>
  <body>
  </body>
</html>
```

A number of additional files and folders that are required for the project are added automatically when a project is created.

Adding content to the file is facilitated by the use of "Content Assist", which indicates the tags that are legal at a specific location within the file (see Figure 6.8). Once the file has been created, running the command "Validate the current state of the XML file" will verify if the file is valid and, if not, will return an error message indicating the location and description of the error. When the application is ready to run, clicking on "Execute" launches the Multimodal Browser so that the application can be tested.

There is a wide range of features that are also provided in the Voice Toolkit to aid the developer, including a Grammar Development Tool, Grammar Test

Tool, Pronunciation Builder Tool and Reusable Dialog Components. For further details, see Appendix 4. The following examples illustrate how some of the applications developed in Chapters 9 and 10 can be adapted to include some multimodal functionality.

Example 1: Getting Student Details (getstudentdetails.mxml)

This example is based on the application "viewdetailsdb.vxml" discussed in Chapter 10 and on the exercise extending this application in Exercise 11 of that chapter. In this example the user is presented with a web form asking for a student's first and last name. The user can enter the name either by using the keyboard or by using speech. Clicking the "Submit" button sends the elicited information to the database where the information is retrieved and then displayed on the user's screen. Clicking on "Reset" causes the application to start over. Figure 11.2 shows the visual interface for the application.

Creating the Visual Component

The first step is to create the visual component. If an existing HTML page is to be used, then it needs to be revised to comply with XHTML conventions. This can be done by changing the heading to incorporate the code shown above, and then renaming the file with an .mxml extension. Alternatively, the main body of the code can be added to the empty .mxml file shown above. The following additional code, inserted between the <body> and </body> tags above will produce the visual form shown in Figure 11.2.

```
<form id="names" method="get"
action="http://localhost:8080/studentsystem/mmgetstudentdetailsbyname.jsp">
<center>
<h3>STUDENT DETAILS </h3>
<br/>
<b>Student's First Name:</b>
<input type="text" size="17" value=""
id="firstname" name="getstudentfirstname"
```

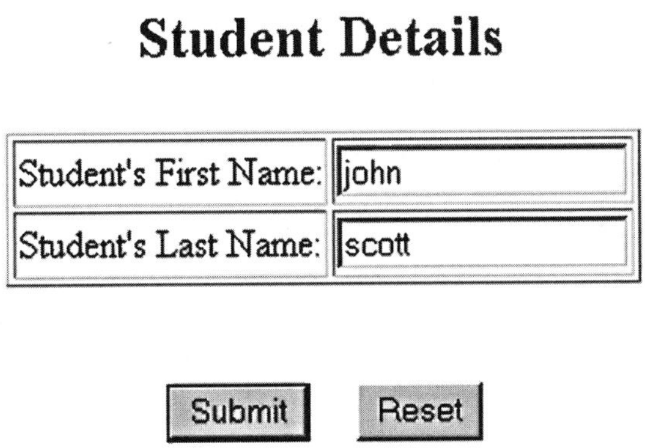

Student Details

| Student's First Name: | john |
| Student's Last Name: | scott |

Submit   Reset

Figure 11.2. Student details: Visual interface.

```
ev:event="focus" ev:handler="#getstudentfirstname_vform" />
<br/><br/>
<b>Student's Last Name:</b>
<input type="text" size="17" value=""
id="lastname" name="getstudentlastname"
ev:event="focus" ev:handler="#getstudentlastname_vform" />
<br/><br/>
<input type="submit" size="6" value="Submit" />
<input type="reset" id="reset" name="reset" ev:event="focus" ev:handler=
"#getstudentfirstname_vform" />
</center>
```

Using the same setup with Apache Tomcat as was used in Chapter 10, and substituting the required address for the file "**mmgetstudentdetailsbyname.jsp**" in the action highlighted in bold in the above code, the visual component can be tested with input such as "john" (Student's First Name) and "scott" (Student's Last Name), according to the names listed in the database "student.mdb". (*Note*: "mmgetstudentdetailsbyname.jsp" is the same as the original "getstudentde-tailsbyname.jsp" with a slight modification that presents the results of the data-base search as a visual table rather than as a message to be spoken.)

Adding the Voice Component

The two fields in the visual web form can be voice-enabled by adding VoiceXML code, including prompts and grammars, to the existing X + V file. The VoiceXML tags to be used in the X + V file take the form of `<vxml:tag>`, for example:

```
<vxml:form>, <vxml:prompt>, </vxml:form>.
```

The VoiceXML code should be added within the `<head>` element of the X + V file. The following code consists of a VoiceXML form to elicit the field "Student's First Name" by voice. The form includes field elements, grammars, prompts and filled elements, just as in VoiceXML documents:

```
<vxml:form id="getstudentfirstname_vform">
<vxml:field name="getstudentfirstname">
   <vxml:grammar src="firstnames.jsgf" />
     <vxml:prompt>What is the first name</vxml:prompt>
     <vxml:filled>
     <vxml:assign name="document.getElementById('firstname').value"
expr="getstudentfirstname" />
     </vxml:filled>
</vxml:field>
</vxml:form>
```

The main difference from VoiceXML forms as presented in Chapters 9 and 10 is the "assign" statement within the `<vxml:filled>` element:

```
<vxml:assign name="document.getElementById('firstname').value"
expr="getstudentfirstname" />
```

This statement assigns the value elicited in the field "getstudentfirstname" to the value of the element "firstname" in the visual version of the form. The following code asks for the student's last name and assigns the value elicited to the value of the element "lastname" in the visual version of the form:

```
<vxml:form id="getstudentlastname_vform">
<vxml:field name="getstudentlastname">
  <vxml:grammar src="lastnames.jsgf" />
    <vxml:prompt>What is the last name</vxml:prompt>
    <vxml:filled>
    <vxml:assign name="document.getElementById('lastname').value"
expr="getstudentlastname" />
    </vxml:filled>
</vxml:field>
</vxml:form>
```

A simple confirmation can be implemented by adding the following code before the `</vxml:filled>` element, as follows:

```
<vxml:prompt>you would like information on
<vxml:value expr="document.getElementById('firstname').value"/>
<vxml:value expr="document.getElementById('lastname').value"/>
Press submit to continue or reset to change
</vxml:prompt>
```

In this case the user is asked to press the "submit" button to submit the elicited information or the "reset" button to clear the fields and start over.

Linking the XHTML and VoiceXML Components

In Version 1.1 of the XHTML + Voice specification, XHTML and VoiceXML components are linked using a declarative synchronisation element <sync> (Raman et al., 2003). In the current version of the Multimodal Toolkit (4.1) the interface between the XHTML and VoiceXML components involves specifying event types and handlers in the XHTML part that defines the input for the fields. For example, the `<input>` element for "firstname" was defined as follows:

```
<input type="text" size="17" value=""
id="firstname" name="getstudentfirstname" />
```

This should now be extended with an event type and an event handler, as follows:

```
<input type="text" size="17" value=""
id="firstname" name="getstudentfirstname"
ev:event="focus" ev:handler="#getstudentfirstname_vform" />
```

The event specified by `ev:event="focus"` means that an event will be executed when the cursor enters the field identified by "getstudentfirstname". The handler for this event is specified as the VoiceXML form with the ID "getstudentfirstname_vform". In other words, when the user clicks on the field entitled "Student's First Name" in the visual form, the voice enabled component will be executed with a prompt asking for the student's first name and a grammar defining the set of legal responses that can be recognised by the speech recognition engine. Whatever the system recognises will then be assigned to the value of the field "getstudentfirstname" in the VoiceXML component and of the field "firstname" in the XHTML component. A similar code is added to the "lastname" field to produce the same effects.

The "reset" input is also amended to get the system to reprompt for the First Name field if the user clicks on "reset":

```
<input   type="reset"   id="reset"   name="reset"   ev:event="focus"   ev:handler=
"#getstudentfirstname_vform" />
```

The flow of events in this program together with the relevant code are displayed in Figure 11.3.

Logic   ## Code

Logic	Code
Event: click on field **"firstname"**. Set focus to vxml form "getstudentfirstname_ **vform"**.	`<input type="text" size="17" value=""` `id="firstname" name="getstudentfirstname"` `ev:event="focus"` `ev:handler="#getstudentfirstname_vform" />`
Prompt: first name. Event: recognition in vxml field "getstudentfirstname". Assign result to "firstname".	`<vxml:assign` `name="document.getElementById('firstname').value"` `expr="getstudentfirstname" />`
Event: click on field **"lastname"**. Set focus to vxml form "getstudentlastname_ **vform"**.	`<input type="text" size="17" value=""` `id="lastname" name="getstudentlastname"` `ev:event="focus"` `ev:handler="#getstudentlastname_vform" />`
Prompt: last name. Event: recognition in vxml field "getstudentlastname". Assign result to **"lastname"**.	`<vxml:assign` `name="document.getElementById('lastname').value"` `expr="getstudentlastname" />`
Event: click on "reset" button. Set focus to vxml form "getstudentfirstname_ **vform"**.	`<input type="reset" id="reset" name="reset"` `ev:event="focus"` `ev:handler="#getstudentfirstname_vform" />`

Figure 11.3. Flow of events in "getstudentdetails.mxml."

Creating the Grammar Files

Grammar files can be created using the Java Speech Grammar Format (JSGF) editor in the Multimodal Toolkit, which provides a skeleton into which the grammar rules can be inserted. Grammar files should have the extension ".jsgf". The following is the grammar file "firstnames.jsgf":

```
#JSGF V1.0;
grammar firstname;
public <firstname> = john | david | jennifer | rosemary;
```

A similar file is required for "lastnames.jsgf".

The TTS engine creates default pronunciations for all the words in the grammars. Pronunciations can be customised by creating pronunciation pool files (see the *Getting Started Guide* for further details).

Testing the Application

The complete application, listed in the file "getstudentdetails.mxml" and including the grammar files, can be tested using the Multimodal Browser as follows:

1. Open the file in Opera.
2. Click in a voice-enabled field and listen for the prompt.
3. Press the Scroll Lock key as a Push-to-Talk button and listen for the beep.
4. Pause briefly, then speak the response into a microphone.
5. Pause again before releasing the button.
6. The spoken selection should appear in the field.

If the response is not recognised, it might be necessary to hold the Scroll Lock key slightly longer after the response has been spoken in order to ensure that the complete acoustic signal has been captured. (*Note*: When using the Multimodal Toolkit, the file can be tested by clicking on the "Execute" tab and selecting "Launch Multimodal Browser".)

Example 2: Extending the Application ("getstudentdetailsextended.mxml")

There are a number of ways in which this example can be extended. In the current application the user has to click on each field to set the focus and thus activate the voice component. The focus can be set automatically by setting the focus of the first field when the document is loaded, so that the system will execute the prompt without requiring the user to click on the field. When a field has received a value, the focus can then move automatically to the next field where the next prompt is executed. The following code shows how the focus can be set automatically to achieve these effects.

The following addition to the <body> tag will set the focus to the first field when the document is loaded:

```
<body onload="document.getElementById('firstname').focus()">
```

The focus can be changed when a specified event has occurred by using the "listener" attribute, as shown below:

```
<ev:listener  ev:event="vxmldone"  ev:handler="#lastnamefocus"  ev:observer=
"firstname" ev:propagate="stop" />
```

The "listener" attribute waits for a specified event to happen. In this case the event is "vxmldone" specified for the observer of the input field "firstname". When this event occurs, the handler executes the script "lastnamefocus", which sets the focus to the input field "lastname". In this way the focus shifts from the field entitled "firstname" to the field entitled "lastname" when "firstname" is filled using a VoiceXML form. (*Note*: All listener events must be included within the <head> tag.)

Scripts

The final element is a set of scripts that execute the change of focus, assuming that the document has been loaded (see first script). Scripts must be included within the <head> tag:

```
<script type="text/javascript">docIsDoneLoading = true;
</script>

<script id="firstnamefocus" type="text/javascript">
   if(docIsDoneLoading ) { document.getElementById('firstname').focus();
   }
</script>

<script id="lastnamefocus" type="text/javascript">
   if(docIsDoneLoading ) { document.getElementById('lastname').focus();
   }
</script>
```

Additionally, some extra code is added to the <input> element entitled "reset" so that the focus is returned to the first field "firstname" via the script "firstnamefocus" if the user presses the "reset" button to start over:

```
<input  type="reset"  id="reset"  name="reset"  ev:event="focus"  ev:handler=
"#firstnamefocus" />
```

The flow of events for the first part of this program together with the relevant code are displayed in Figure 11.4.

Example 3: Confirming the Input ("confirm1.mxml")

Confirmation of the voice input can be done in a variety of ways. In this example a new form is added "confirm_vform" in which the system attempts a simple confirmation, such as "Was that John Scott?". If the user replies "yes", they are asked to press the "submit" button, otherwise they are asked to press "reset" to start over.

```
<vxml:form id="confirm_vform">
   <vxml:field name="confirm" type="boolean">
```

Logic   ## Code

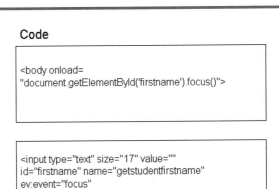

Logic	Code
Event: on load. Set focus to the field "firstname".	`<body onload=` `"document.getElementById('firstname').focus()">`

Set focus to vxml form
"getstudentlastname_
vform".
	`<input type="text" size="17" value=""`
	`id="firstname" name="getstudentfirstname"`
	`ev:event="focus"`
	`ev:handler="#getstudentfirstname_vform" />`

Prompt: first name.
Event: recognition in
vxml field
"getstudentfirstname".
Assign result to
"firstname".
	`<vxml:assign`
	`name="document.getElementById('firstname').value"`
	`expr="getstudentfirstname" />`

Event: vxml done.
Call script
"lastnamefocus".
	`<ev:listener ev:event="vxmldone"`
	`ev:handler="#lastnamefocus"`
	`ev:observer="firstname" ev:propagate="stop" />`

Set focus to
"lastname".
	`<script id="lastnamefocus" type="text/javascript">`
	`        if(docIsDoneLoading ) {`
	`document.getElementById('lastname').focus();`
	`        }`
	`</script>`

Figure 11.4. Part of the flow of events for "getstudentdetailsextended.mxml".

```
<vxml:prompt>Was that <vxml:value expr = "document.getElementById('first-
name').value" />
<vxml:value expr="document.getElementById('lastname').value"/>
  </vxml:prompt>
  <vxml:filled>
    <vxml:if cond ="confirm ==true">
      <vxml:prompt>
      Please press the submit button
      </vxml:prompt>
      <vxml:return />
    <vxml:else/>
      <vxml:prompt>
      Please press the reset button
      </vxml:prompt>
```

```
        <vxml:return />
      </vxml:if>
    </vxml:filled>
    </vxml:field>
</vxml:form>
```

Note the use of <vxml:return /> which causes the voice handler to end its execution and return the application to the XHTML. The listener event for the input field "getstudentlastname" should also be amended to include a handler that points to "confirm_vform":

```
<ev:listener ev:event="vxmldone" ev:handler="#confirm_vform" ev:observer="last-
name" ev:propagate="stop" />
```

Example 4: An Alternative Type of Confirmation ("confirm2.mxml")

The disadvantage of the confirmation in the previous example is that the user has to start over if one of the items is incorrect and supply both items again, including the item that was correct at the first attempt. A better solution would be to ask the user which item was incorrect and then to elicit a new value for just that item. One way to do this is to throw an event that causes the system to re-elicit one or both of the values if the user disconfirms. The system will ask: "Which would you like to change: the first name, the last name, or both names?" and according to the user's response the elicited value(s) will be "cleared" so that the FIA will revisit the field(s). The following is the conditional statement used in the confirmation:

```
<vxml:if cond="confirm == true">
<vxml:prompt>Please press the submit button</vxml:prompt>
<vxml:return />
<vxml:else />
<vxml:throw event="change.name" />
</vxml:if>
```

A field called "change_name" is required along with code to catch the "change.name" event:

```
<vxml:field name="change_name" modal="true" cond="changeName == true">
    <vxml:grammar src="change_name.jsgf" />
    <vxml:prompt>Which would you like to change: the first name, the last name, or
both names?</vxml:prompt>

    <vxml:filled>
    <vxml:assign name="changeName" expr="false" />
      <vxml:if cond="change_name == 'both'">
      <vxml:clear namelist="getstudentfirstname getstudentlastname confirm" />
      <vxml:elseif cond="change_name == 'first'" />
      <vxml:clear namelist="getstudentfirstname confirm" />
      <vxml:else />
      <vxml:clear namelist="getstudentlastname confirm" />
      </vxml:if>
```

```
    </vxml:filled>
  </vxml:field>

  <vxml:catch event="change.name">
    <vxml:assign name="confirmName" expr="false" />
    <vxml:assign name="changeName" expr="true" />
  </vxml:catch>
```

Note: For this example to work, the forms from the previous example were amalgamated into one form "getstudentnames_vform" with fields "getstudent-firstname", "getstudentlastname", "confirm" and "change_name". A grammar "change_name" is also required, as follows:

```
#JSGF V1.0 iso-8859-1;
grammar change_name;
public <change_name> = [change][the] <which> {$.change_name = $which}
[name | names];
<which> = both | first | last;
```

Note that this grammar permits alternative input such as "change the first name", "the first name", "first", "both names", and so on, and that semantic tags based on the Semantic Interpretation for Speech Recognition (SISR) specification are used so that the output of the grammar is one of "both", "first" or "last" only (see reference at end of chapter).

Example 5: A Mixed-initiative Example ("getstudentdetailsmixed.mxml")

In this section a mixed-initiative version of the previous example is developed. The main change is the incorporation of a form-level grammar and a `<vxml:initial>` element:

```
<vxml:form id="names_form">
<vxml:grammar src="names.jsgf" />
<vxml:initial>
<vxml:prompt>First and last names</vxml:prompt>
</vxml:initial>
```

The grammar "names.jsgf" also makes use of semantic tags:

```
#JSGF V1.0 iso-8859-1;
grammar names;
public <names> = <firstname> {$.getstudentfirstname=$firstname} [<lastname>
{$.getstudentlastname=$lastname}]
| [<firstname> {$.getstudentfirstname=$firstname}] <lastname> {$.getstudentlast-
name=$lastname};
<firstname> = john | david | rosemary | jennifer;
<firstname> = john | david | rosemary | jennifer;
```

and gives the option of both names being spoken, or either the first or last name. If only one of the names is spoken, the system prompts for the other name.

SALT

Introduction

Like XHTML + Voice, SALT is designed to enable multimodal as well as telephony access to web-based information and services by allowing users to combine several modes within the same session. SALT consists of a small set of XML elements for applying a speech interface to web pages. SALT was developed by the SALT Forum (www.saltforum.org/), founded by Cisco, Comverse, Intel, Microsoft, Philips and SpeechWorks in 2001, and currently consisting of about 70 companies interested in developing speech technologies for multimodal and telephony applications. The SALT Forum produced the SALT 1.0 specification, which is under consideration within the W3C.

A number of platforms are emerging that support application development with SALT. These include the following:

The Microsoft .NET Speech SDK (Software Development Kit)

Microsoft has developed the Microsoft .NET Speech SDK Version 2.0 Beta, a set of development tools based on the SALT specification that enable developers to incorporate speech functionality into Web applications. The SDK is integrated with Microsoft's Visual Studio.NET developer environment, and includes speech extensions for the Microsoft Internet Explorer browser. Included along with the download of the SDK are a wide range of sample applications and tutorials (see Appendix 4).

Voice Web Solutions

Voice Web Solutions has developed Voice Web Studio, an extension for Macromedia Dreamweaver™ MX. Voice Web Studio provides tools for building speech-enabled Web and telephone applications based on SALT 1.0 (http://www.voicewebsolutions.net/products/vweb/).

OpenSALT

An open-source browser based on SALT 1.0 is being developed at Carnegie Mellon University (CMU) in the OpenSALT project. This browser, which is based on the open source Mozilla web browser, will use CMU's open source Sphinx recognition and Festival synthesis software (www.speech.cs.cmu.edu/OpenSALT/).

Information about other development environments for SALT can be found at the SALT Forum web pages.

An Example: Booking a Flight

The following is a sample application that has been provided with Microsoft .NET Speech SDK Version 2.0 Beta. This application, which is called "Margie's

Travel", allows users to book a flight using a visual, voice-only, or multimodal interface.

Voice-only Interface

The following is an interaction with the voice-only interface:

> System: Welcome to Margie's Travel. Where are you flying from?
> User: Boston.
> System: Flying from Boston. Where are you flying to?
> User: Miami.
> System: To Miami. On what date would you like to depart?
> User: May the tenth.
> System: Flying out on May tenth. At what time would you like to depart?
> User: Early morning.
> System: Flying out early morning. On what date would you like to return?
> User: May the twentieth.
> System: Returning on May twentieth. At what time would you like to return?
> User: Early evening.
> System: Returning early evening. Searching for flights. I have found two flights. (System lists details of the first flight.)
> System: Say next or select.
> User: Select.
> System: Would you like smoking or nonsmoking?
> User: Nonsmoking.
> System: A nonsmoking seat. Please select window or aisle, or say no preference.
> User: Window.
> System: A window seat. Please select a meal type from standard, vegetarian, diabetic or low cholesterol.
> User: Vegetarian.
> System: A vegetarian meal. Please select buy or hold.
> User: Buy.
> System: Your credit card will be charged shortly. Enjoy your trip.

This is a system-directed dialogue similar to those encountered in Chapter 9. The system detects "no input" and "no match" events and prompts accordingly, as in VoiceXML. Implicit verification is used following each user input. If the user corrects, then the system attempts to deal with the correction. The following is one example of how this is done:

> System: Returning early evening.
> (User interrupts.)
> User: No, early morning.
> System: Am I right with returning early morning?

Multimodal Interface

The multimodal interface, shown in Figure 11.5, allows the user to proceed through each field by either clicking on the microphone icon to speak the input or by selecting an option from the drop-down list. Alternatively, the complete flight specification can be spoken within a single input by clicking on the microphone icon next to the "Speak All" prompt. For example, "from Boston to Miami

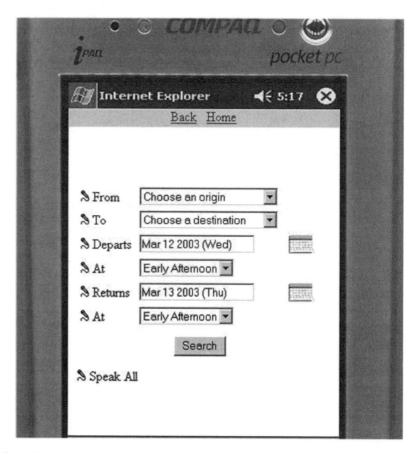

Figure 11.5. Margie's Travel. (Screen shot from Microsoft .NET Speech Application SDK Version 2.0 Beta, reprinted with permission.)

on May the tenth leaving early morning and returning on May the twentieth early evening". The fields in the visual form are updated according to the system's recognition of the spoken input. If some fields have not been filled, the user can click on the microphone icon next to those fields to speak the required values, or can enter them using the drop-down menus. There are no spoken system prompts, and information and instructions are displayed in text form, as in a traditional visual interface. Clicking on "Search" leads to a second screen in which flights are displayed, from which the user selects by clicking. This leads to a third screen in which further details of the flight are elicited, for example, whether smoking or nonsmoking, the type of seat, and the type of meal. These details can all be spoken in one input, for example, "nonsmoking", "window seat", "vegetarian meal". If any recognised input is incorrect, it can be corrected either by using speech or by using the drop-down menus. This is particularly useful if the date is not recognised correctly. In this case, if the user clicks on the input field for the date, a calendar appears from which the correct date can be selected by clicking.

Overview of SALT

SALT and VoiceXML

SALT uses some of the key components of the VoiceXML 2.0 specification, such as the XML-based grammar specification and the speech synthesis markup tags. Some aspects of SALT are similar to those of XHTML + Voice. SALT uses a small set of XML elements that are embedded within a page written in a host markup language such as XHTML, HTML + SMIL or WML. An object-oriented event-driven model is used to integrate multiple input methods. For example, user actions, such as mouse clicks and speech input, are reported as events that are handled by objects containing methods, such as the speech object <listen> that has a "start" method to collect acoustic samples and perform speech recognition. SALT differs from VoiceXML, which has a larger set of XML elements and is intended to be used as a complete, standalone markup language with its own built-in dialogue control flow – the FIA. Dialogue control in SALT, including the sequencing and coordination of speech events such as system prompts and recognition of user input, is coded explicitly in the host language. Furthermore, whereas in VoiceXML values acquired during an interaction are assigned automatically to field attributes, in SALT the assignment of values has to be coded explicitly. This is similar to the method used in XHTML + Voice.

SALT Elements

There are four main top-level elements in SALT:

<prompt> – Used to specify system output, which may be in the form of simple text, speech output markup, variable values, links to audio files or a mix of these forms.

<listen> – Used for speech recognition.

<dtmf> – Used for DTMF input in telephony applications.

<smex> – Used for sending and receiving messages from other local and remote components, for example, sending and receiving emails, or submitting data to a back-end server.

In the applications to be developed in this chapter we will focus mainly on the <prompt> and <listen> elements. Note that each element has an "ID" so that it can be referenced by code elsewhere.

<prompt>

The following is a simple example of a <prompt> element in SALT:

```
<salt:prompt id="Welcome">
Welcome to Student Details.
</salt:prompt>
```

Prompt elements can also contain values of XHTML elements, for example:

```
<salt:prompt id="confirm">
So you want details on
<salt:value targetElement="firstname" targetAttribute="value" />
<salt:value targetElement="lastname" targetAttribute="value" />
</salt:prompt>
```

The `<prompt>` element also contains methods to start, stop, pause and resume the playback of a prompt, and to adjust speed and volume. Its handlers include events such as user barge-in.

```
<listen>
```

The `<listen>` element is used to specify recognition grammars using `<grammar>` and to deal with the assignment of speech recognition results using `<bind>`. It is also used to record spoken messages using `<record>`. `<listen>` also has methods to activate and deactivate grammars, and to start and stop recognition. The following is a simple example of the use of the `<listen>` element which calls on a remote grammar of student first names and uses a bind statement to process the recognition result:

```
<salt:listen id=" recoFirstName">
<salt:grammar src="firstnames.xml" />
<salt:bind targetElement="txtBoxFirstName" value="/result/first_name" />
</salt:listen>
```

As in VoiceXML, the `<grammar>` element is used to specify grammars, which can be either inline or external. The `<bind>` element is a method for processing recognition results and assigning values to the relevant slots in a page.

`<listen>` has handlers for events such as successful recognitions, misrecognitions, timeouts and other speech events, and each recognition turn can be configured to specify timeout periods, confidence thresholds and other parameters.

Event Wiring

As explained above, each of the SALT elements contains methods, properties and event handlers. For example, there are methods to begin and end execution of the elements, properties for configuration, and event handlers for events associated with speech. One example of a speech event is an "onReco" event, which is fired when recognition results have been returned. Another example is "onBargein", which is fired if the user interrupts a system prompt. Although these events are also handled in VoiceXML, they have to be explicitly coded in SALT. The following example shows how the start method for `<listen>` is wired to the event of clicking on an input field in a visually displayed form and how a grammar is activated according to the field that is clicked:

```
<input name="txtFirstName" type="text" onclick="recoFirstName.Start()" />
<salt:listen id="recoFirstName">
```

```
<salt:grammar src="firstnames.xml" />
<salt:bind targetElement="txtBoxFirstName"value="/result/first_name" />
</salt:listen>
```

Dialogue Flow

The dialogue flow can be managed in SALT through explicit sequencing, using events such as "onComplete" to transfer control when an event such as a prompt has been executed, and "onReco" to transfer control when successful speech recognition has occurred. These events will be illustrated in some of the examples below. Alternatively, a script can be used, as in the following example in which the speech objects <prompt> and <listen> are controlled by the RunAsk() script, which references these objects by their names ("askFirstName" and "recoFirstName", respectively).

```
<script>
function RunAsk() {
if (getStudentDetails.txtBoxFirstName.value=="") {
askFirstName.Start();
recoFirstName.Start();
}
}
</script>
```

In this script the prompt called "askFirstName" is executed if the field called "txtBoxFirstName" is empty, then the recogniser is called according to the <listen> object entitled "recoFirstName" to process the user's input.

Developing Applications in SALT

Two different ways of developing SALT applications will be illustrated in this chapter:

1. Using the Microsoft Internet Explorer Speech Add-in.
2. Using the Microsoft .NET Speech SDK.

Using the Microsoft Internet Explorer Speech Add-in

The Microsoft Internet Explorer Speech Add-in enables developers to create SALT applications in a text editor such as WordPad and run them in Internet Explorer using the Speech Add-in. The advantage of this approach is that it is useful for tutorial purposes to be able to examine the SALT code and the associated control elements in a simple application developed in this way compared with the more complex code created within an integrated development environment such as Visual Studio.NET, which is used in association with the .NET Speech SDK to create SALT applications. This method is useful for those who do not have access to the Visual Studio.NET environment.

The Speech Add-in is available on the CD that contains the .NET Speech SDK (see Appendix 4). The add-in can be selected during the installation process without having to install the complete SDK.

Running Applications

Once the Speech Add-in has been installed and a SALT file has been created with a ".htm" or "html" extension, the file can be run by clicking on the file to load Internet Explorer. This will cause the application to start. At the point where input is expected in a multimodal application, a small Audio Meter will appear on the screen. The Audio Meter, which is linked to the microphone, is a visual aid that provides feedback on how well the system is capturing the speech. If the Audio Meter feedback is flat during speech input, the microphone should be configured. Instructions are provided at the Start Page for the Speech Add-in.

Example 1: A System Prompt (welcome.htm)

In this application a form is displayed for Student Details and the system speaks out the prompt "Welcome to Student Details". User input to the fields and the use of the "Submit" and "Reset" buttons will be introduced in subsequent examples. The code for this application is listed below. Note that the line numbers are not part of the program code.

```
1 <html xmlns:salt="http://www.saltforum.org/2002/02/SALT">
2 <body onload="welcome.start();">
3 <head>
4 <!– SALT Add-in to Internet Explorer object –>
5 <object id="SpeechTags"
    CLASSID="clsid:DCF68E5B-84A1-4047-98A4-0A72276D19CC"
    VIEWASTEXT>
6 </object>
7 <!– salt: Importing the namespace for the implementation –>
8 <?import namespace="salt" implementation="#SpeechTags" />
9 </head>

10 <!– HTML form –>
11 <center>
12 <h2>Student Details</h2>
13 </center>
14 <br />
15 <center>
16 <form id="getStudentDetails">
17 <table border="1">
18 <tr>
19 <td>Student's First Name:</td>
20 <td>
21 <input type="text" size="17" value="" id="txtBoxFirstName"
22 </td>
23 </tr>
24 <tr>
```

```
25 <td>Student's Last Name:</td>
26 <td>
27 <input type="text" size="17" value="" id="txtBoxLastName"
28 </td>
29 </tr>
30 </table>
31 </form>
32 </center>
33 <br />
34 <center>
35   <table align="center">
36   <tr>
37   <td>
38   <input type="submit" size="6" value="Submit" />
39   </td>
40   <td></td>
41   <td></td>
42   <td></td>
43   <td></td>
44   <td>
45   <input type="reset" size="6" value="Reset" onClick="askFirstName.start();"/>
46   </td>
47   </tr>
48   </table>
49 </center>
50 </body>
51 <!- SPEECH OUTPUT ->
52 <salt:prompt id="welcome">
53 Welcome to Student Details
54 </salt:prompt>
55 </html>
```

The code in lines 1–9 contains namespace declarations and references to the Speech Add-in that are required to run a SALT application using the Speech Add-in.[6] Line 2 is required to start the application when the document is loaded. In this case, control is passed to the object entitled "welcome", which in this case is the SALT prompt entitled "welcome". Lines 1–9 will be required for all the following examples and will not be repeated, although the command to start the application in line 2 may change, as indicated in the examples. Lines 10–50 contain the HTML code for the visually displayed form. As this will not change throughout the examples, it will not be repeated. The SALT prompt is in lines 52–54.

Note that the interface to the Web Server is not implemented in the SALT examples, so that pressing the "submit" will not cause information to be sent to the Web Server. Implementing this aspect of the examples is left as an exercise for the reader.

---

[6] The assistance of Jim Larson in providing the correct code for namespace declarations and references to the Speech Add-in is gratefully acknowledged.

Example 2: An Interactive Application ("getstudentdetails.htm")

The next example illustrates an interactive application in which the system outputs a welcome prompt, as before, and then goes on to elicit input from the user to fill the two text boxes called "txtBoxFirstName" and "txtBoxLastName". Two additional prompts (lines 55–57 and 58–60) and two <listen> objects (lines 62–65 and 66–69) are required, along with grammars (lines 63 and 67), and functions for control flow and assignment. The code for this application is as follows:

```
51 <!– SPEECH OUTPUT –>
52 <salt:prompt id="welcome" onComplete = "askFirstName.start();">
53 Welcome to Student Details
54 </salt:prompt>
55 <salt:prompt id="askFirstName" onComplete = "recoFirstName.start();">
56 What is the first name?
57 </salt:prompt>
58 <salt:prompt id="askLastName" onComplete = "recoLastName.start();">
59 What is the last name?
60 </salt:prompt>

61 <!– SPEECH INPUT –>
62 <SALT:listen id="recoFirstName" onreco="askLastName.start();" >
63 <salt:grammar src="firstnames.xml"/>
64 <salt:bind targetelement = "txtBoxFirstName" value="//"/>
65 </salt:listen>
66 <SALT:listen id="recoLastName" >
67 <salt:grammar src="lastnames.xml" />
68 <salt:bind targetelement = "txtBoxLastName" value="//"/>
69 </salt:listen>
```

The following is the XML grammar "firstnames.xml":

```
<grammar version="1.0" xml:lang="en-US"
xmlns="http://www.w3.org/2001/06/grammar" root="firstnames">
<rule id="firstnames" scope="public">
 <one-of>
   <item>john</item>
   <item>david</item>
   <item>rosemary</item>
   <item>jennifer</item>
 </one-of>
 </rule>
 </grammar>
```

The flow of events for the first part of the application is shown in Figure 11.6.

Example 3: Confirming Values ("getstudentdetailsconfirm.htm")

The following addition allows an implicit confirmation of the values that have been elicited. This requires transfer of control following the recognition of the last name in line 66 to a prompt entitled "confirm", as follows:

Logic	Code

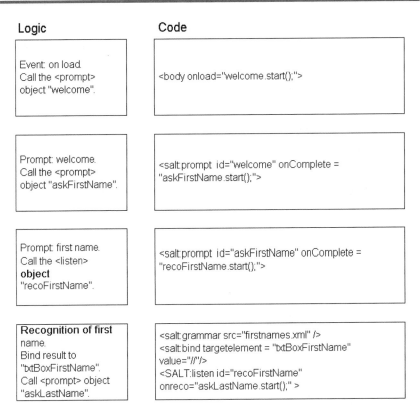

Figure 11.6. Flow of events for first part of "getstudentdetails.htm."

66 <SALT:listen id="recoLastName" onreco="askConfirmNames.start();" >

The prompt object "askConfirmNames" is added to the list of prompts:

```
<salt:prompt id="askConfirmNames" >
 So you want details on
<salt:value targetelement="txtBoxFirstName" targetAttribute="value" />
<salt:value targetelement="txtBoxLastName" targetAttribute="value" />
Click on submit to continue or reset to start over.
</salt:prompt>
```

This prompt retrieves the values assigned to "txtBoxFirstName" and "txtBoxLastName" using "targetelement" and "targetAttribute". If the values are correct, the user presses the "submit" button, or clicks on the "reset" button to start over, passing control back to the prompt "askFirstName".

Example 4: Extending the Confirmation Function ("getstudentdetailsconfirmextended.htm")

The application can be extended to allow the user to respond to an explicit confirmation request. This involves adding a further <listen> object to recognise the user's response and a script to process the response. Two further prompts are added to instruct the user what to do next. The following are the required additions:

1. The prompt entitled "askConfirmNames" is extended to include control transfer to a `<listen>` object entitled "recoConfirmNames":

```
<salt:prompt id="askConfirmNames" onComplete = "recoConfirmNames.start();">
```

2. The `<listen>` object entitled "recoConfirmNames":

```
<SALT:listen id="recoConfirmNames" onreco = "processConfirmNames();">
  <salt:grammar src="yes_no.xml" />
</salt:listen>
```

3. A script entitled "processConfirmNames()" called by "recoConfirmNames":

```
<script>
  function processConfirmNames() {
    if (recoConfirmNames.text == "no") startOver.start();
    if (recoConfirmNames.text== "yes") submitDetails.start();
  }
</script>
```

Note that the values of the `<listen>` object are referenced using the object name and ".text".

4. The two additional prompts are:

```
<salt:prompt id="submitDetails">
Click on the submit button to continue
</salt:prompt>
```

```
<salt:prompt id="startOver">
Click on the reset button if you wish to try again
</salt:prompt>
```

5. Grammar for "yes/no" responses:

```
<grammar version="1.0" xml:lang="en-US"
xmlns="http://www.w3.org/2001/06/grammar" root="firstnames">
<rule id="firstnames" scope="public">
<one-of>
  <item>yes</item>
  <item>no</item>
  </one-of>
</rule>
</grammar>
```

Example 5: Using a Script for Dialogue Control ("getstudentdetails_script.htm")

As an alternative to control transfer being attached to each `<prompt>` and `<listen>` object, a dialogue control script can be used. This solution is preferable when there are a number of dialogue exchanges, as it is easier to add a new exchange to the script. The following script "RunDialogue", which is called following the "welcome" prompt, is used in this example:

```
<script>
function RunDialogue() {
if (getStudentDetails.txtBoxFirstName.value=="") {
askFirstName.Start();
recoFirstName.Start(); }
else if (getStudentDetails.txtBoxLastName.value=="") {
askLastName.Start();
recoLastName.Start();}
else {
confirmNames.Start();
}
}
</script>
```

If the field entitled "txtBoxFirstName" is empty, the prompt and listen objects to fill this field are called. Similarly with the field entitled "txtBoxLastName". Once these fields are filled, the prompt entitled "confirmNames" is called.

Other changes in this example include functions to process the recognition events, which include the assignment of the recognised values. Each <listen> object calls a procedure, as follows:

```
<salt:listen id="recoFirstName" onreco="procFirstName()">
```

This is the function "procFirstName()":

```
function procFirstName() {
getStudentDetails.txtBoxFirstName.value = recoFirstName.text;
RunDialogue();
}
```

This function sets the value of the field "txtBoxFirstName" to the value recognised by the object "recoFirstName". This is an alternative to the use of the <bind> element within the <listen> object. Control is passed back to the RunDialogue() function. A similar function processes the recognition of the last name.

Finally, if the user clicks on the "reset" button, a function is called to reset the values and to start the dialogue over again:

```
function resetValues() {
getStudentDetails.txtBoxFirstName.value = "";
getStudentDetails.txtBoxLastName.value = "";
RunDialogue();
}
```

This function is called from the input event specified for the "reset" button:

```
<input type="reset" size="6" value="Reset" onClick="resetValues();"/>
```

Developing Applications Using the Microsoft .NET Speech SDK

The .NET Speech SDK is a development environment that is integrated into Visual Studio .NET, offering a complete set of tools for the creation of SALT applications and their deployment on an ASP.NET Web Server. The SDK includes a number of development tools – a Grammar Editor, Prompt Editor, ASP.NET Speech Control Editor and the Speech Debugging Console. The SDK also includes a comprehensive set of tutorials and documentation together with a range of sample applications.

Developing a SALT application with the SDK involves a higher-level application programming interface (API) compared with the method presented so far in this chapter. Much of the processing detail encountered in the SALT examples in this chapter is shielded from the developer. For example, by using the ASP.NET Speech Controls provided with the SDK, SALT and Jscript code is generated automatically to supplement other codes produced by existing .NET class libraries.

In the remainder of this section some of the key features of the .NET Speech SDK will be introduced. Readers who are interested in working with the SDK should follow the comprehensive tutorial provided. This tutorial shows how to build a pizza ordering application that demonstrates the use of multimodal and voice-only input and shows how to use the Grammar Editor to construct complex recognition grammars; the Speech Control Editor to link the grammars to speech controls and Web page controls; the Prompt Editor to create a prompt database for the application; and the Speech Debugging Console to monitor and manipulate speech data, events and errors.

Grammar Editor

The Grammar Editor is a graphical tool that is used to create grammar files that are bound to a QA (Question/Answer) control. The resulting grammar is an XML file with the extension .grxml. The Grammar Editor can also validate a grammar file to verify that the XML code is valid. On the left-hand side of Figure 11.7 the graphical display of the grammar "lastnames.grxlm" is shown. At the top of the figure is the dialogue box for the grammar validator. Typing in a word or phrase to be recognised by the grammar produces the grammar editor output shown in the main part of Figure 11.7. The output includes the SML (Semantic Markup Language) results which, in this example, show that the input has been recognised with 1.0 confidence. The Grammar Editor supports the development of complex grammars to process sentences in which items can be marked as optional and rules can refer to further subrules, as in a context-free grammar. The SML is the result returned by the recogniser. In this example, the SML was the same as the input term. SML can be used more generally to return a single value for synonymous expressions, similar to grammar tags in VoiceXML (see Chapter 10).

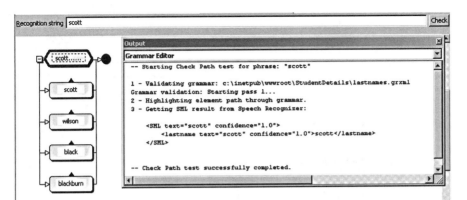

Figure 11.7. The Grammar Editor tool. (Screen shot from Microsoft .NET Speech Application SDK Version 2.0 Beta, reprinted with permission.)

Speech Control Editor

The Speech Control Editor is used to develop a speech-enabled Web application in Visual Studio .NET. One of the main Speech Controls is the QA control, which defines a single interaction consisting of a prompt, the recognition of the user's response using a grammar, and the binding of elements of the recognition results to other controls on the page, such as form input boxes. Several QA controls and grammars can be combined within a Speech Application Control to create common reusable components for scenarios such as eliciting a date, providing a zip code or selecting an item from a list. Another type of Speech Control is Command. Command controls are used in voice-only mode. Command controls allow the user to speak global commands such as "help", "repeat" or "main menu".

To illustrate with an example: In Figure 11.8, QA controls have been added to a visual Web page to process the user's speech when completing the form. The QA controls "FirstNameQA" and "LastNameQA" contain grammar files, answers and events. The grammar files "firstnames.grxml" and "lastnames.grxml" are used to recognise the user's spoken input and to generate SML – the semantic result returned by the recogniser. The Answers part of the control processes the SML and links it to a Semantic Item that will update the relevant text boxes on the page. This is achieved through the Semantic Map control. Events that are set for these QA controls determine when recognition should start and stop, in this case, recognition starts when the user clicks in one of the text input boxes. More complex controls, including QA controls to confirm the user's answers, are provided for voice-only applications and illustrated in the tutorial.

Prompt Editor

The Prompt Editor is used to create a database of prompts for voice-only applications. The Prompt Editor includes a graphical Wave Editor for recording and

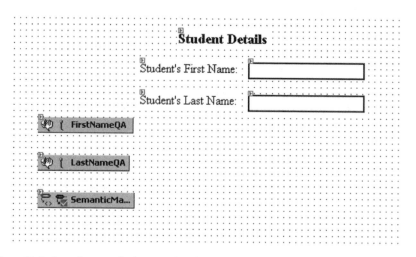

Figure 11.8. Speech controls. (Screen shot from Microsoft .NET Speech Application SDK Version 2.0 Beta, reprinted with permission.)

amending .wav files. The Wave Editor displays the wave form and allows the developer to edit word boundaries, copy and paste individual sound segments within and across .wav files, and play back the edited .wav files. A Prompt Validate Tool is provided to check for prompt coverage within an application. Prompt elements that are not recorded will be synthesized by the TTS engine.

Speech Debugging Console

The Speech Debugging Console can be used within the Visual Studio.NET environment to debug .NET Speech Applications, and it can also be used as a stand-alone debugging application outside Visual Studio. The tool monitors recognition events and can display the list of grammar rules that are active during a recognition event. The SML returned from a recognition event can be viewed and modified before it is sent back to the application. The Speech Debugging Tool also allows the developer to simulate exceptions, such as when the user says a phrase that is not recognised with sufficient confidence by the speech recogniser.

Summary

This chapter has introduced XHTML + Voice (X+V) and SALT as approaches to creating multimodal applications for platforms such as wireless PDAs. Multimodal applications are understood as web-based applications that permit more than one mode for input and output, in particular, where the traditional

Graphical user Interface (GUI) mode has been supplemented or complemented by speech. Both X+V and SALT are still in the process of development. There are some development environments that support the creation of applications of multimodal applications, such as the IBM WebSphere Multimodal Toolkit and the Microsoft .NET Speech SDK. Developers learning X+V and SALT can also use the speech extensions to browsers such as Opera and Internet Explorer, as shown in the examples presented in this chapter.

Further Reading

IBM Multimodal Toolkit: http://www.ibm.com/pvc/multimodal

This page describes IBM's approach to multimodal applications, with links to white papers, the XHTML + Voice specification, and the download page for the Multimodal Toolkit.

XHTML + Voice

XHTML + V Specification: http://www-3.ibm.com/software/pervasive/multimodal/x+v/11/spec.htm
A useful set of X+V and SALT links: http://www.voiceingov.org/x_plus_v.htm

Semantic Interpretation for Speech Recognition (SISR) Specification: http://www.w3.org/TR/2003/WD-semantic-interpretation-20030401/

SALT

SALT Forum: http://www.saltforum.org/
Microsoft SDK: www.microsoft.com/speech/getsdk/
Voice Web Solutions (Voice Web Studio):
http://www.voicewebsolutions.net/products/vweb/
The CMU Open SALT Browser: http://www.speech.cs.cmu.edu/OpenSALT/
Tutorials by Hitesh Seth on SALT:
http://www.developer.com/voice/article.php/1565431

CMU Pronunciation Tool

This tool is useful as an aid for customising pronunciations: http://www.speech.cs.cmu.edu/cgi-bin/cmudict

Ideas for Further Projects

1. Extend the functionality of the student system using X+V. Develop the scripts so that the system can speak out the information or display it in tabular form, according to the user's request.

2. Create a mixed-initiative version of the application that allows the user to fill several fields with one utterance, such as first and last names, course name and level.

3. Develop a connection between the SALT version of the student system and the web-based database. Develop the functionality of the system as in Exercise 1.

Part III
Advanced Applications

Advanced Dialogue Systems: Some Case Studies

12

Most current spoken dialogue systems support a limited type of dialogue, in which the system controls the interaction and the user responds to carefully designed system prompts. These dialogues are suitable for simple, well-structured tasks. Chapters 6–11 showed how this type of system can be implemented using a number of different toolkits and development environments.

This chapter presents case studies of some advanced spoken dialogue systems that involve more complex tasks and require more robust, mixed initiative dialogue, in which both system and user can initiate the interaction, ask for clarification, signal nonunderstanding, change the topic and interrupt the other participant. These systems are often described as "spoken dialogue agents" or "conversational agents", although here the latter term will be reserved for systems that include animated agents, also known as "embodied conversational agents" (see Chapter 14). The systems to be described in this chapter are:

- The DARPA Communicator systems, in particular, the CU Communicator, developed at the Center for Spoken Language Research (CSLR) at the University of Colorado, Boulder.
- The TRAINS and TRIPS systems developed within the Conversational Interaction and Spoken Dialogue Research Group at the University of Rochester.
- The Conversational Architectures Project at Microsoft.

The focus of the case studies will be mainly on the dialogue management components of these systems, although in each case a key element of the research has been enhancement of the overall system through the integration of the different system components.

DARPA Communicator

The goal of the DARPA Communicator programme is to develop robust spoken dialogue systems that support complex conversational interaction. As well as supporting full mixed-initiative dialogues, these systems should also address multidomain problems, such as travel planning, that require access to several data sources such as flight and hotel booking, car rental, weather information, and email and voice-mail access. The systems should also support multiple modalities, ranging from speech-only interfaces to those that include graphics, maps, pointing and gesture. One example scenario for the deployment of such a system involves a traveller driving to the airport and talking to an intelligent agent to obtain information on traffic patterns, flight information, and the weather at the traveller's destination (Aberdeen et al., 1999). Another scenario involves a soldier using a wearable computer and carrying on a complex dialogue with a computer to obtain military-related information (Aberdeen et al., 1999).

The Communicator programme involved a number of development teams at several research institutes and universities in the United States, including: MITRE, Bolt Beranek and Newman (BBN), Carnegie Mellon University (CMU), IBM, Microsoft, MIT, Stanford Research Institute (SRI), and University of Colorado (CU). There was an affiliated European Communicator programme involving NISLab (Denmark) together with Philips Speech Research, Daimler–Chrysler Research, KTH, Stockholm and Nijmegen University, Holland. In the United Kingdom there is an Edinburgh Communicator at the University of Edinburgh and, more recently, the Queen's Communicator at the Queen's University of Belfast.

Galaxy Communicator Architecture

At the core of the Communicator programme is the Galaxy Communicator architecture, which is designed to support a plug-and-play approach to dialogue systems development. The Galaxy architecture is based on MIT's Galaxy II distributed architecture (Seneff et al., 1998), which has been developed by the MITRE Corporation and made available under an open source license (http://communicator.sourceforge.net/). Figure 12.1 shows the CU DARPA Hub compliant version of the Galaxy architecture, in which a number of servers interact with each other through the DARPA hub (Pellom et al., 2001). The servers pass messages, in the form of frames, to the hub and the hub acts as a router, sending frames to the receiving server. The actions of the hub are controlled by a simple script.

The following is a brief description of the servers in the CU version of the Galaxy architecture, as described in Pellom et al. (2001). Some of the components will be described in greater detail later.

- The **audio server** answers incoming calls, plays prompts and records incoming user input. The original MIT/MITRE audio server that was supplied to DARPA Communicator program participants has been replaced by the CSLR Dialogic audio server that supports up to four phone lines and barge-in.
- The **speech recogniser** used in the original system is the CMU Sphinx-II system. The acoustic samples are sent to three recognisers with models for speaker independent analog telephone, female adapted analog telephone,

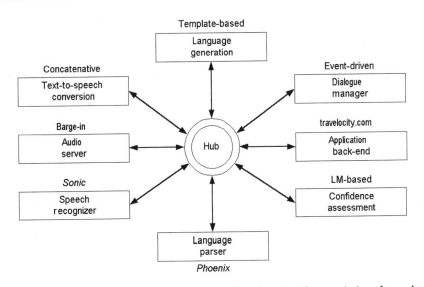

Figure 12.1. CU Communicator architecture. (Reprinted with permission from the Center for Spoken Language Research.)

and cellular telephone adapted acoustic model sets. The most likely word string from the three decoders is passed to the natural language component. The language model is a class-based and grammar-based language model for the domains of air travel, and hotel and car rental information. In a more recent version of the system the CSLR Sonic Speech Recogniser is being used for acoustic and language modelling. A key feature of the speech recognition component is the use of knowledge integration to enhance performance.

- The **confidence server** detects and rejects misrecognised units at the concept level using language model features and acoustic features from the recogniser. Confidence features are combined to compute word-level, concept-level and utterance-level confidence scores.

- The **language understanding** component uses a modified version of the Phoenix parser, which analyses the string output by the speech recogniser and produces a sequence of semantic frames consisting of a named set of slots that represent pieces of information gathered within the dialogue.[7] The values for the slots are determined by context-free semantic grammars that specify the strings of words that can fill each slot and that map on to the concept structures of the task. For example, the utterance "show fares of flights from Denver to Boston on United" is parsed as:

Frame: Air
[Field](show [_fares](fares of flights))
[Origin](from [City](Denver))

---

[7] Phoenix was developed by Wayne Ward at CMU. Wayne Ward is currently at the CSLR. Updates to Phoenix that are used in the CU Communicator were made by Wayne Ward while at the CSLR.

[Destination](to [City](Boston))
[airline](on [AirlineName](United))

- The **dialogue manager** in the CU Communicator system is "event driven". This means that it does not use an explicit script, like a finite-state dialogue manager. Instead, it uses a hierarchical set of frames that represent the information to be discussed by the system and user as a basis for deciding what to do next in the dialogue. This is similar to the frame-based architectures discussed in Chapter 5 (see further below).

- The **Database/Backend** component receives SQL queries from the Dialogue Manager and queries the database, using domain-specific Perl scripts to retrieve live data from the web.

- The **Language Generator** uses templates to generate text based on dialogue speech acts, such as "prompt" (to prompt for required information), "summarise" (to summarise retrieved information about flights, hotels and cars, and "clarify" (to clarify ambiguous information, such as departure and arrival cities with the same name).

- The **Text-to-Speech (TTS) Synthesiser** synthesises the word strings from the Language Generator and sends them to the audio server to be spoken out. A domain-dependent concatenative synthesiser is used.

One of the benefits of the Galaxy architecture is that it supports rapid configuration, plug and play, and portability, as developers can insert their own components, such as a speech recogniser or a dialogue manager, into the architecture. Normally it can be a major challenge to combine such diverse components into a robust interface. The initial Galaxy architecture included components for speech recognition, speech synthesis, dialogue management, language understanding, context tracking and language generation. In the future it is planned to add additional components for handling graphics as well as gestural input and output modalities. The Mitre Web site contains detailed information about the Galaxy architecture and the Communicator programme (http://fofoca.mitre.org).

The CU Communicator in Action

The CU Communicator, developed at the CSLR at the University of Colorado, is a telephone-based spoken dialogue system that acts as an automated travel agent. The agent accesses the internet for live information about flights, hotels and car rentals. Users can access and try out the system by registering at the CU Communicator website (http://communicator.colorado.edu). The Communicator system along with extensive documentation can be downloaded from the same site. The following example, adapted from an example provided on the web site, is an extract from an interaction with the CU Communicator.

12.1
1 System: What are your travel plans?

2 User: I'm interested in a flight from Denver to Boston on August third on United Airlines.

3 System: What time do you want to leave Denver?

4 User: In the morning.

5 System: Let's see then. I have you going from Denver to Boston on August third. Is that correct?

6 User: Yes it's correct.

7 System: Please let me check availability and see what I can find. I found five flights meeting your requirements. Option one: United flight seventeen sixty two departs Denver at eight oh one a.m. and arrives in Boston at one fifty p.m. Is that ok?

8 User: How about a later flight.

9 System: Please let me check availability and see what I can find. I found four flights meeting your requirements. Option one: United flight twelve twenty departs Denver at ten thirty a.m. and arrives in Boston at four sixteen p.m. Is that ok?

10 User: Yes that's fine.

11 System: Will you return to Denver from Boston?

12 User: The next afternoon.

13 System: Let's see then. I have you going from Boston to Denver on August fourth. Is that correct?

14 User: Yes you got it.

15 System: Please let me check availability and see what I can find. One option was returned. Option one: United flight five twenty one departs Boston at two thirty p.m. and arrives in Denver at six thirty eight p.m. Is that ok?

16 User: Yes that's fine.

16 System: Hold on while I price your itinerary. Your total airfare is five hundred and forty four dollars. Would you like a hotel in Boston?

17 User: No thanks.

18 System: Would you like a rental car in Boston?

19 System: Yes I'd like to get a car from Budget.

20 System: Please let me check availability and see what I can find. Thirteen options were returned. Option one: Budget has a compact pickup automatic with conditioning with unlimited miles for twenty four dollars a day. Is that ok?

21 User: Next option.

22 System: Option two Budget has an economy car automatic with air conditioning with unlimited for thirty four dollars a day. Is that ok?

23 User: uh I'll take the first option.

Some of the key features of the CU Communicator system can be seen in this example (see Pellom et al. (2001) for a full discussion of these issues). The system has a sophisticated natural language understanding component that can handle relative reference, for example, "a later flight" (line 8), "the next afternoon" (line 12) and "the first option" (line 23). Dialogue control is frame-based (see Chapter 5). For example, the user provides some parameters for the flight in line 2 in response to an open-ended system prompt, and the system picks up on any parameters that need to be elicited in order to be able to make a database query (3).

Data Collection and Evaluation

Data collection and evaluation have been a key focus of the DARPA Communicator programme. Data of user interaction with the CU Communicator was collected through a toll-free dial-up system at CSLR. In addition to this the National Institute of Standards (NIST) organized a multisite data collection project involving the nine DARPA Communicator participants. The users of the systems were native speakers of American English who had to perform a number of tasks, including fixed scenarios for booking one-way and return flights as well as open-ended scenarios for business or vacation bookings. The following is an example of one of the scenarios that were used (Walker et al., 2002).

You are in Denver, Friday night at 8 p.m. on the road to the airport after a great meeting. As a result of the meeting, you need to attend a group meeting in San Diego on Point Loma on Monday at 8:30 a.m., a meeting Tuesday morning at Miramar at 7:30 a.m., then one from 3–5 p.m. in Monterey; you need reservations (car, hotel, air). You pull over to the side of the road and whip out your Communicator. Through spoken dialog (augmented with a display and pointing), you make the appropriate reservations, discover a conflict, and send an email message (dictated) to inform the group of the changed schedule. Do this in 10 minutes.

The CU Communicator received 72 calls in the NIST evaluation. In total 53 (73.6%) of the tasks were completed successfully. Most of the failures (42%) were due to problems with the audio server, in particular, with failure to detect the end of user speech and to return control to the dialogue manager. The second main problem involved speech recognition of city names, for example, confusable pairs such as Boston versus Austin. Finally, a number of inattentive users confirmed incorrect information so that the system was unable to retrieve the data required to complete the transaction. Word-error rate overall was 26%. Other metrics, for which the median scores are given, were task to completion (260.3 s), total turns to completion (37.6), response latency (1.9 s), user words to task end (39.4), system words to task end (331.9) and number of reprompts (2.4) (see also Pellom et al. (2000); San-Segundo et al. (2000)).

Dialogue Management in the CU Communicator

The CU Communicator has been a test-bed for research into the different components of a spoken dialogue system and, as mentioned earlier, how these components can be integrated in such a way as to enhance the overall performance of the system. The most recent development is the CSLR Conversational Agent Toolkit, which builds on the original Galaxy architecture. In the new system a server has been added for animation, in order to support interaction with animated agents in a number of applications, such as reading tutors. The following description of the dialogue management component of the Conversational Agent Toolkit is based on a number of sources, including documentation provided at the 2002 short course at CSLR (http://communicator.colorado.edu).

The Dialog Manager in the CU Conversational Agent Toolkit fulfils the same basic functions as dialogue managers in other systems: it receives input from the parser, sends prompts and other output to the natural language generator, and communicates with a database or other backend application. The input that is received from the parser has to be interpreted and integrated into the evolving dialogue context, and the system has to decide how to manage the interaction with the user in terms of what to do or what to say next.

As mentioned earlier, dialogue management in the CU Conversational Agent Toolkit is event-driven rather than scripted. The system uses a frame to represent the domain for the dialogue. The aim of the dialogue is to fill the slots in the frame. The following is a frame for air travel:

```
Frame: Air_Travel
   [Travel_Time]
      [Depart_Time]
         [Start_Time]
         [End_Time]
      [Arrive_Time]
         [Start_Time]
         [End_Time]
```

The domain ontology is defined in a *task* file which contains frame information as well as templates for prompts, verifications, and for generating SQL queries. The following is an example of part of a task file:

```
[Arrive_Loc]+
   Prompt: "what is your destination"
   [City_Name]*
   Prompt: "what city $(in [Arrive_Loc].[State]) would you like to go to?"
   Confirm:   "I    have    you    arriving    in    $([Arrive_Loc].[City_Name])
$([Arrive_Loc].[State]) .
   Have I got that right?"
   Sql: "arr_cd_$[leg_num] in (select airport_code from airport_codes where city
like '!%'
   $(and state_province like '[Arrive_Loc].[State]'))"
   [State]
   [Airport_Name]*
   Confirm: "I have you arriving in $([Arrive_Loc].[Airport_Name]) .
   Is that correct?"
   Sql:  "arr_cd_$[leg]  in  (select  airport_code  from  airport_names  where
airport_name like '!%')
```

This is a frame for air travel with a slot for an arrival location [Arrive_Loc] that can be either a city name or an airport name. The + indicates that this is a mandatory field. The prompt string is used to elicit the value for the field, the confirm string is used to confirm the values, and the SQL string is a template for a query to the database. The "*" after [City_Name] and [Airport_Name] indicate that if either of them is filled, then the parent node [Arrive_Loc] is filled. Users can provide information in any order and the system will prompt for all the mandatory nodes until the frame is complete.

The user's input is passed from the parser as a sequence of parsed extracts to the Dialog Manager and is integrated into the frames. Processing the input involves the following steps:

1. Mapping to canonical form, e.g., resolving relative dates such as "tomorrow".
2. Resolving ellipsis, e.g., determining whether a user response such as "Boston" maps on to a departure or an arrival location.
3. Executing context functions, e.g., clarifying whether a time such as "8" is a.m. or p.m.
4. Merging into context frames, e.g., updating frames and creating new frames.

Once the information from the user has been extracted and merged into the context, the system determines the next system action based on a prespecified set of priorities, as follows:

1. Check for global system actions, set by functions, e.g., Hang Up, Reset, Repeat.
2. Check if prompt pending for output, e.g., to clarify extracted information.
3. Check if pending data to present.
4. Check whether db request should be generated.
5. Check whether frame in focus is complete, if not, prompt for data.
6. Check other active frames for completion.
7. Create closing frame if one doesn't exist, set focus to closing, fill if not complete.
8. End, i.e., say "goodbye" and hang up.

These actions deal with high-level dialogue events and should generalize across applications. Using the task file and frames in conjunction with this set of action priorities, the Dialog Manager can produce a fairly flexible and natural dialogue that does not have to be scripted in the way that a finite-state dialogue system would be.

Dialogue Management in the CMU Communicator

In the CMU Communicator the task of creating an itinerary is viewed as a case of complex problem solving that involves searching over different solutions and taking account of competing constraints (Rudnicky and Xu, 1999; Rudnicky et al., 1999, 2000). In this view the problem cannot be reduced to a sequence of predetermined steps, nor can it be modelled with form-filling since the trip is negotiable during the course of the dialogue and so the structure of the form is not known in advance. The following is an example of a dialogue involving the CMU Communicator:

12.2
1 System: Hello. You've reached the CMU Communicator. Tell me your full name.
2 User: Hi I'd like to fly to Seattle Tuesday morning.
3 System: Travelling to Seattle on Tuesday, August eleventh in the morning. Your full name?
4: User: Wei Xu.
5: System: Hello, Wei, I'm glad to hear from you again. You can now ask me for help.
6 System: OK. Let's see I have a United flight departing Pittsburgh at ten forty five a.m. arriving into Seattle at one fifty seven p.m. Is that OK?

7 User: Yes.
8 System: Will you return to Pittsburgh from Seattle?
9 User: No I will go to Los Angeles.
10 System: Travelling to Los Angeles. On what date?
11 User: Sorry can we go back to talk about the previous leg again?

In utterance 2 the user does not respond to the system's first query, however the system accepts this implicit change of topic and then returns to its agenda which involves eliciting the user's name. The system then continues to elicit the required information about the return flight but is interrupted at 11, when the user asks to go back to the topic of the first leg.

As can be seen in this example, handling topic shift is a key element in the more open-ended dialogue management addressed in the CMU system. Although the system has the goal of eliciting the required information for the domain of travel and will have specific questions to ask and slots to fill, the structure of the activity is not predetermined. Thus instead of a form containing slots to be filled, the CMU Communicator creates a product tree representing the itinerary dynamically. For example, when the user mentions flying to Seattle, a tree is creating containing the outbound and return legs. However, the return leg might later be pruned if the user does not request a return trip, or a further subtree can be added if the itinerary is extended (e.g., "and then go on to Vancouver"). Although the system has an agenda with a default ordering for the traversal of the itinerary tree, there is always the opportunity for the user to change the focus or introduce a new topic, in which case the focus of the dialogue can shift and the elements in the tree or subtrees can be rearranged.

Dialogue Management in the Queen's Communicator

The focus of the Queen's Communicator is on the use of object-oriented development techniques to create a spoken dialogue manager (DM) that encapsulates generic and domain-specific dialogue management strategies, such as when and how to verify information elicited from the user (O'Neill and McTear, 2002; O'Neill et al., 2003). In the Queen's Communicator the DiscourseManager determines the system's generic dialogue behaviour in response to the user's utterances. Domain-specific experts, which inherit from the DiscourseManager, each have rules that develop the dialogue in a manner specific to their own business domain. Currently strategies are being developed that will allow domain experts to volunteer relevant dialogue handling expertise, either in direct response to a user's utterance, or as a result of another expert's own request for supporting expertise (e.g., credit card processing abilities). Thus there is a possibility of several frames being used in the course of a single session as each domain-specific expert takes over its part of the transaction.

Typically, new information from the user is confirmed implicitly. However, other factors may affect this strategy, such as the status of the information supplied by the user. In order to assess how to proceed, the DiscourseManager makes use of a DiscourseHistory that maintains a record of the evolving dialogue in terms of a stack of DialogFrames, each of which comprises a set of Attribute objects relevant to the transaction. These DialogFrames are similar to the frames used in the CU Communicator, in that they represent the slots that need to be filled in order to complete a transaction. However, in the Queen's Communicator these slots contain the following additional information:

- The "confirmation status" of attributes – This is a measure of the status of the attributes within the dialogue (Heisterkamp and McGlashan, 1996). For example, information can be "new for system", "inferred by system", "repeated by user", "modified by user", "negated by user", "modified by system", "negated by system".
- The discourse peg of attributes – This is a score that is used to ensure that every attribute has been adequately confirmed before it is used to further a transaction.

Completion of a transaction requires that key information is reconfirmed. To ensure that this is the case, the discourse pegs for key pieces of information have to be set greater than 1. Every attribute uttered by the user must be repeated once or explicitly confirmed by the user to be considered confirmed by the system. Attributes that are negated or changed by the user are queried, before they are considered adequately confirmed. Only confirmed attribute values are considered for use with the system's request templates and associated rules. To achieve this, discourse pegs are incremented by 1 when the user repeats a value, zeroed if the value is modified, and set to -1 if the value is negated.

The confirmation status and discourse peg are used to determine the system's intentions. The principal intentions are "confirm" (for new values), "repair confirm" (for a modified value), "repair request" (for a negated value) and "specify" (to have the user specify a required value). Once a particular level of confirmation has been reached (a "confirmedness threshold"), the system can decide how to use information supplied by the user, for example, to complete or to further the transaction.

TRAINS and TRIPS

Since the early 1990s the Conversational Interaction and Spoken Dialogue Research Group at the University of Rochester has been engaged in spoken dialogue research. The main focus of this work has been to develop an intelligent planning assistant that is conversationally proficient in natural language. The initial system, called TRAINS, involved a planning and scheduling domain for a railroad freight system, in which a human manager and the system communicated in order to solve problems by developing and executing plans. More recently the TRIPS system has extended this work within a more complex logistics and transportation world. The TRAINS and TRIPS projects have supported a wide range of doctoral research in the areas of natural language processing, speech interpretation, discourse processing, planning and reasoning under uncertainty. The ultimate goal of the research is a fully integrated system incorporating online spoken and typed natural language together with graphical displays and Graphics User Interface (GUI)-based interaction. In the following discussion, rather than presenting a single system, the major elements of the Rochester spoken dialogue systems will be presented, drawing on a number of published sources, in particular, Allen et al. (2000, 2001a, b).

The conversational capacity of the Rochester systems goes beyond the form-filling and extended topic and context switching approaches used in the various Communicator projects. In the Communicator systems, the dialogue centres on eliciting values to fill slots in the forms. In the Rochester systems, the participants engage in dialogue in order to develop plans to cooperatively solve a task. Solving the task requires communication, as neither participant is able to solve the task on their own. Additionally, however, the participants have to be able to reason about the task and about the plans that they each develop. Consequently, the architecture of the TRAINS and TRIPS systems requires additional components to perform this problem-solving and reasoning. The following extract, which was discussed briefly in Chapter 1, illustrates some features of the dialogue as well as the problem-solving capabilities of the TRIPS system (Allen et al., 2001a, p. 30):

12.3
1 User: We need to get the woman in Penfield to Strong.
2 System: OK.
3 User: What vehicles are available?
4 System: There are ambulances in Pittsford and Webster.
5 User: OK. Use one from Pittsford.
6 System: Do you know that Route 96 is blocked due to construction?
7 User: Oh. Let's use the interstate instead.
8 System: OK. I'll dispatch the crew.

This example shows how in TRIPS the system and user engage in dialogue to solve a real-world task that involves moving an injured woman from the town of Penfield to a hospital called Strong. Pittsford and Webster are names of other towns.

The dialogue is described as being "limited mixed-initiative" in that it supports clarifications and corrections, as in utterance 6, but does not allow the shifting of task-level initiative, for example, the user cannot propose switching to another task during the course of a dialogue in which the current task is being resolved.

The example demonstrates the reasoning that is required to participate in such a dialogue. The system must be able to reason that the blocking of Route 96 constitutes a possible impediment to the plan proposed by the user. At a more subtle level the system has to interpret words such as "vehicles" in utterance 3 according to the appropriate context. In this context "vehicles" is interpreted as meaning "ambulances", whereas in another context the vehicles could be some other form of transport, such as electric utility trucks.

TRIPS Architecture

Figure 12.2 (based on Allen et al., 2001b, p. 3), shows the main components of the TRIPS architecture and how they relate to each other. Like the DARPA Communicator, TRIPS consists of a set of loosely coupled components that pass messages to one another through a hub, using the Knowledge Query and Manipulation Language (KQML). The system has three main components: the Interpretation Manager, which processes the user's input, the Behavioral Agent, which plans the system's behaviour, and the Generation Manager, which generates the system's output. The following sections describe these components in greater detail.

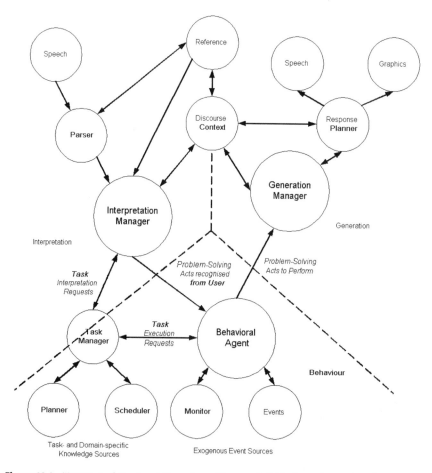

Figure 12.2. TRIPS Architecture. (Based on Allen et al. (2001b, p. 3), reprinted with permission of the authors.)

Interpretation Manager

The user's input, which can be in the form of speech or GUI events, is processed and passed to the Interpretation Manager (IM) for interpretation. Speech input is processed by the speech recogniser, which passes a set of word hypotheses to the parser. The parser also processes GUI user input and produces a sequence of speech acts. The IM interprets the speech acts in terms of how they relate to the current plan and identifies the system's discourse obligations that have arisen as a consequence of the speech acts. For example, an utterance such as "Do you know that Route 96 is blocked due to construction?" might be interpreted in one context as a problem statement with the intention of initiating a change of plan (as in utterance 6 above). In another context the utterance might simply be interpreted as an attempt to update the user's knowledge. The Task Manager may be used to help with the interpretation of intended speech acts and problem solving acts, by relating what the user is saying or doing to the task at hand. Taking the example under discussion, the Task Manager considers objects and their role in the task or domain. Thus, if Route 96 is the route that the ambulance from Pittsford would take and if Route 96 is blocked, then the utterance can plausibly be interpreted as an attempt to ask the user to replan.

The IM works in close collaboration with the Discourse Context, which provides information about the state of the dialogue (see Chapter 13 for a fuller discussion of Information State Theory, which develops the functions of the TRIPS Discourse Context). The Discourse Context contains the following information:

- A model of the salient entities in the dialogue – this supports the interpretation of reference. For example, in Dialogue 12.3 the expression "the woman in Penfield" is interpreted as referring to the discussed entity WOM1, which identifies the injured woman in Penfield who was mentioned earlier in the dialogue. A discourse history keeps track of the entities discussed in the dialogue.
- A representation of the structure and interpretation of the immediately preceding utterance.
- The current status of the turn – whether it has been assigned to one participant or is open.
- A discourse history of the speech acts so far, and whether they have been grounded.
- The current obligations, for example, whether the system has an obligation to respond to the user's last utterance.

Following each utterance the Discourse Context is updated.

Behavioural Agent

The Behavioural Agent (BA) is responsible for problem solving within the system. There are three aspects to this task:

- Interpreting user utterances and actions in terms of problem solving acts.
- Keeping track of the system's goals and obligations during the course of problem solving.
- Dealing with changes in the world state, for example, incoming news of Route 96 being blocked, which may affect a plan previously developed or currently under discussion.

The problem solving model that is used in TRIPS is a general abstract model that is applicable to all dialogues involving practical problem solving. This model includes concepts such as "objectives" (goals, subgoals, constraints), "solutions" (plans), "resources" (available objects for the solutions), and "situations" (how the world is currently). Agents can perform a number of actions when solving problems, for example, they can "create" new objectives and solutions, they can "select" a particular objective, and they can "evaluate", "compare", "modify", "repair" and "abandon" objectives, solutions, resources and situations. Dialogue will often be used to communicate with the other agent about these concepts and actions. In addition, there are communicative acts, such as "describe", "explain" and "identify", which are used in conjunction with the problem solving concepts during the course of collaborative problem solving.

The BA works in conjunction with the Task Manager. Whereas the behaviours of the BA are defined in terms of a general and abstract problem solving model, the Task Manager is concerned with objects and actions in a specific domain. For example, in the emergency rescue scenario illustrated in Dialogue 12.3, an ambulance is considered as a "resource" and moving the injured woman to a hospital is part of a "solution" within the scenario.

The second aspect of the BA's task is to consider its goals and obligations. The dialogue agent will have a set of goals to pursue, such as getting information from the user. At the same time the agent will have a number of obligations, such as responding to the user's utterances. A simple example is when an agent is attempting to elicit the various items of information for a flight booking and the user interrupts with a query about hotels. The agent has to decide whether to continue with its own agenda or whether to allow the user to shift the topic. Even when the agent decides to pursue its own agenda, it must at least fulfil the conversational obligation of acknowledging the user's attempt to shift topic (e.g., by saying something like "I'll come back to hotels in a minute".

Discourse obligations are an important element of the conversational agent. In earlier plan-based models of dialogue the dialogue agent constructed a model of a speaker's intentions, inferred the speaker's goals, and adopted a goal to achieve these goals. However, this model assumed that dialogue agents would always want to behave cooperatively by following the user's intentions blindly. This strategy failed to explain why an agent would still respond when it did not know an answer or when it did not wish to adopt the user's goals. Thus a distinction was made between the agent's goals and intentions when performing a task and the obligations that arise as part of the conventions of dialogue

(Traum and Allen, 1994). These obligations are generally addressed before task-related goals and intentions. For example, if the user makes a request, then there is a discourse obligation on the dialogue agent to acknowledge the request, though not necessarily to fulfil it.

More generally, in the TRAINS and TRIPS projects a reactive-deliberative model of dialogue agency has been developed in which the agent reasons about its discourse obligations and domain goals (Traum, 1996). Where there is a conflict, the agent displays a "relaxed" conversational style in which discourse obligations are addressed before the agent's own goals. This gives rise to an interaction in which the initiative of the other agent is followed. However, in a less cooperative situation, the agent can continue to address its discourse obligations but can respond in different ways, for example, by rejecting requests and refusing to answer questions. Finally, the system can take the initiative, for example, in a situation where the other agent does not take a turn, by taking the turn and using this opportunity to address its own goals. Thus depending on the flow of the dialogue and on the behaviour of the other agent, the dialogue agent can shift its focus from the obligation-driven process of following the other's initiative to the goal-driven process of taking the lead in the conversation.

Finally, there are occasions when the dialogue agent's strategy is determined by exogenous events, such as incoming news that might affect how the current task can be solved. The agent must decide whether to interrupt the ongoing dialogue to inform the user of this event and whether to adopt an intention to propose a solution or leave the solution to the user. In utterance 6 above, the agent informed the user of some important new information but left it to the user to formulate a new plan.

Generation Manager

The Generation Manager (GM) is responsible for the system's output. In deciding what to say, GM takes two sources of information into account:

- Problem solving goals provided by BA that require generation.
- Discourse obligations from the Discourse Context.

The GM constructs discourse acts for generation and sends these with their associated context to the Response Planner, which produces a surface representation for generation. Earlier versions of the GM used templates for generation but, recently, more sophisticated methods are being developed, such as rhetorical relations expressed as schemas. The GM works asynchronously from the IM, so that it can be continuously planning its output before receiving information from the IM or BA. So, for example, if there is no available information from the IM or BA to communicate at a particular point in the dialogue, the GM can use basic dialogue rules to acknowledge the user's utterance and perform some basic grounding. When the GM has successfully produced a discourse act, the Discourse Context is updated.

An Example

This example, which draws on a more extended example presented in Allen et al. (2001a, pp. 34–36), shows in an informal series of steps how the various components of the system architecture come into play in relation to utterance 3 "What vehicles are available?" from Example 12.3 presented earlier:

1. Speech recogniser notices that user has started speaking.
2. IM interprets this as a turn-taking event in which the user has the turn.
3. When the turn is complete, IM interprets this as a turn-releasing event.
4. GM begins planning a response.

5. IM receives the logical form of the user's utterance and interprets it in context by interacting with the Task Manager, in this case, to determine that "vehicles" is to be interpreted as "ambulances", as these are the appropriate resources in this context. The term "available" also has to be interpreted. In this context an ambulance is available if it has not been assigned to another task, if a crew is ready, and if it is reasonably close to the emergency location in Penfield.

6. IM updates the Discourse Context with a representation of the user's utterance and with a message that the system has an obligation to respond to the user's question.

7. When the Discourse Context receives notification of the new discourse obligation, it notifies other components such as GM.

8. GM cannot answer the question without a response from BA. GM adopts the goal of answering and waits for further information from BA. GM might produce an acknowledgement of the question while it is waiting.

9. In the meantime, IM sends a message to BA that the user has initiated a problem solving act.

10. BA initiates the problem solving act of identifying suitable ambulances (in the towns of Pittsford and Webster).

11. BA determines which action to take in response to the user's initiation of a problem solving act. BA has a number of choices:

- "Do the Right Thing" – Try to answer the question and send the answer to GM. This should satisfy its problem solving goal as long as IM confirms that the user has understood the response.

- Request clarification – For example, if BA cannot determine which is the most suitable ambulance, it might ask GM to request a clarification.

- Failure – BA may fail to identify a resource and so may need to ask GM to report this to the user.

- Ignore – BA may decide that some other information, such as an urgent message, is more important, in which case GM is asked to communicate the message to the user and BA keeps the obligation to return to the postponed task later. In the current example BA chooses the first action and sends a message to GM.

12. GM constructs a message, which is sent to the Response Planner to produce text suitable for TTS output (and possibly graphical display).

13. GM informs the Discourse Context that the discourse obligation to respond to the user's question has been met.

14. The Discourse Context is updated with any obligations that the system's utterance has put on the user.

15. IM uses these expectations to support subsequent interpretation, for example, the user will have an obligation to acknowledge the system's response.

16. On receiving utterance 5 "OK, use one from Pittsford", the system interprets the utterance as an acknowledgement and notifies the Discourse Context that the user's obligation has been discharged.

17. IM interprets utterance 5 in terms of the current task, for example, "one" is resolved to mean an ambulance, and the utterance can be interpreted as contributing to the plan under development to get an ambulance to the location of the emergency.

TRAINS and TRIPS as Working Spoken Dialogue Systems

One of the main goals in the Rochester research was to produce systems that would work in near real-time, that would perform robustly, and that could be evaluated in terms of end-to-end performance.

Robustness is achieved in the Rochester systems by using a combination of the following:

- statistical post-correction of speech recognition errors;
- syntactically and semantically driven robust parsing;
- extensive use of dialogue context.

The speech recognition system is the SPHINX-II system from CMU that was trained on acoustic models from data collected in the Air Travel Information System (ATIS) domain. Using SPHINX-II on the TRAINS domain utterances word accuracy was 58.7%. A higher rate of accuracy was achieved by building a language model for the TRAINS utterances. However, the main innovation was to make use of a speech post-processor (SPEECHPP), which corrected speech recognition errors using a statistical model of the recogniser's past performance in the TRAINS domain. The types of errors that SPHINX-II made in the TRAINS domain were modelled in terms of a channel model that accounted for the errors made by the speech recogniser, and a language model that predicted likely sequences of words. The channel model included typical substitutions that had occurred as errors in the past, whereas the language model was a word-bigram model based on transcribed dialogues with TRAINS. Results of experiments indicated an improvement on the base performance of SPHINX-II when the language model was modified to include bigrams from the TRAINS dialogues. However, accuracy was enhanced even further when the post-processor was used to correct errors produced by the speech recogniser.

Parsing in the Rochester systems involves a bottom-up parser with a grammar in which the constituents in each rule specify both a syntactic and a semantic category. The output of the parser is a sequence of speech acts that provides the "minimal covering" of the input, i.e., the shortest sequence that accounts for the input. The rules are robust as they can match at different levels of specificity with partial or ill-formed input. The following is an example (Allen et al., 2000, pp. 368–369):

Spoken sentence:
Okay let's take the train from Detroit to Washington.

Recognised sentence:
Okay let's send contain from Detroit to Washington.

Speech act sequence:
1. CONFIRM / ACKNOWLEDGE ("Okay").
2. TELL (involving some interpretable words: "let's send contain").
3. TELL (mentions a route: "from Detroit to Washington").

The parser has not been able to interpret the complete input from the user, but has extracted enough information to allow the IM to perform some interpretation, involving identification of objects mentioned, before passing on the acts to the BA to perform verbal reasoning. In particular, the third speech act could be a suggestion to move from Detroit to Washington. To check if this is plausible, the BA needs to check that there is an engine at Detroit. As this is the case, the interpretation is accepted and the Discourse Context is updated. More generally, the system uses its knowledge of the domain to make a reasonable interpretation of the user's input. A clarification subdialogue might be required to elicit any further information that was missing in the information received from the speech recogniser and parser. Generally, however, the system was designed in such as way as to avoid clarification subdialogues, where possible. For example, when faced with an ambiguous expression, the system chooses what it considers to be the most likely interpretation, even at the risk of making a mistake. This strategy is used to avoid the problem of lengthy and, sometimes, unnecessary, clarification subdialogues. Of course, the strategy relies on the system's ability to recognise and interpret any subsequent corrections by the user in order to keep the dialogue on track.

Evaluation has played an important role in the Rochester systems. An evaluation of one of the earlier versions of TRAINS contrasted the effectiveness of speech input versus keyboard input. Two measures were used to evaluate task performance: the amount of time taken to arrive at a solution, and the quality of the solution, in terms of the amount of time required to travel the planned routes. Subjects were undergraduate students who had not seen the system before. The experiment showed that the plans generated using speech input were of a similar quality to those produced using the keyboard. However, the time required to complete the task was significantly lower when speech input was used. These results indicate that the system is robust and can be used without any prior user training.

Conversational Architectures Project

The aim of the Conversational Architectures project at Microsoft Research is to build natural, human-like spoken dialogue systems. A key assumption of the research is that a dialogue system should be robust enough to be able to conduct a conversation despite imperfect speech recognition, language understanding, or models of the user's goals and attention. Participating in conversation is modeled as a process of decision making under uncertainty, in which the system reasons about sources of misunderstandings and engages in a costs/benefits analysis to determine what actions to take, if any, to resolve miscommunication. Dialogue is viewed as a joint activity, in which participants aim to achieve mutual understanding of their intentions and actions through "grounding" (Clark, 1996; see also Chapter 3). A major focus of much of the work within the Conversational Architectures project is to develop a computational model of grounding, using Bayesian models to represent dependencies between uncertainties, and decision theory to identify the most useful actions to be taken to resolve miscommunication. This approach to dialogue has been developed within an architecture called Quartet, in which several prototype dialogue systems have been developed, including Presenter, a system for navigating PowerPoint presentations, and the Bayesian Receptionist, a system that simulates front-desk receptionists at the Microsoft corporate campus. The following description of the Conversational Architectures project is based on a number of sources, in particular, Paek and Horwitz (1999, 2000).

Quartet

Quartet is a platform for building multimodal dialogue applications. In Quartet key uncertainties in dialogue are represented using Bayesian networks, and local expected utility and value-of-information analyses are used to determine actions that will maximize mutual understanding.

There are four levels of representation in Quartet that support inference and decision making under uncertainty in conversation. Each level of representation requires coordination between a speaker (S) and a listener (L), so that each participant is assured that the other(s) are attending, hearing, understanding and cooperating with what is being said. Thus grounding is required at each level. More specifically, the representations at each level involves the following:

- **Channel.** This level is concerned with the channel of communication between S and L. In order to communicate, S will attempt to open a channel of communication with L by displaying some behaviour, such as an utterance or a gesture. For communication to be successful at this level, L must attend to S.

- **Signal.** This level is concerned with the signal that is presented from S to L. S and L have to agree that a behaviour was intended as a signal, as some behaviours, such as adjusting spectacles, are not normally intended as signals.

- **Intention.** The intention level involves the semantic content of signals. At this level S signals some message to L, and L has to determine the intentions behind this message.

- **Conversation.** At the conversation level S proposes a joint activity for L to consider and take up.

Actions at all four levels of representation involve uncertainty. At the lowest level S may not be sure whether L is attending, while at the signal level the signal may not have been identified clearly. There are costs associated with actions that are carried out to resolve uncertainty at each level. For example, at the channel level the cost of asking for a repeat because L has not been attending is likely to be low compared with the cost of continuing the dialogue without ensuring mutual understanding. These levels of interpretation are incorporated within the Quartet architecture, as shown in Figure 12.3.

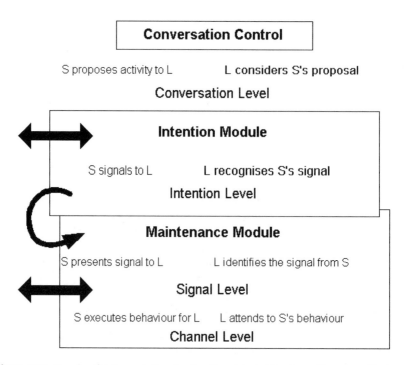

Figure 12.3. Levels of interpretation in the Quartet architecture. (Based on Paek and Horwitz (2000), reprinted with permission of the authors.)

The architecture consists of two modules within a larger controlling module. One of these modules, the Maintenance Module, handles uncertainty at the channel and signal levels, while the second module, the Intention Module, deals with uncertainty at the intention level. The controlling module, Conversation Control, exchanges information with the Maintenance and Inference modules. Conversation Control assesses the status of key variables in all of the modules and decides how to resolve uncertainties by assessing likely costs and benefits. This module also maintains a dialogue history that includes information such as the number of questions asked and the number of times repair actions have been carried out in the dialogue. This enables the system to adjust its uncertainties and utilities in the light of evidence provided by the dialogue history.

Representing Uncertainty

Bayesian networks are used to model dependencies between uncertainties within each of the modules in the Quartet architecture. Figure 12.4 shows part of the networks used in the Maintenance Module (based on Paek and Horwitz, (2000)). These networks show relationships between different elements of uncertainty over time. The node "User's Focus of Attention" is concerned at the channel level with whether the user is attending to the dialogue system, to another person, or to something else. This element is important when attention shifts, for example, in the Presenter system the user is sometimes addressing an audience using a Powerpoint presentation, in which case the words spoken do not have to be interpreted by the system. When the user's attention shifts to the system, then the user's commands – for example, to move to the next slide –

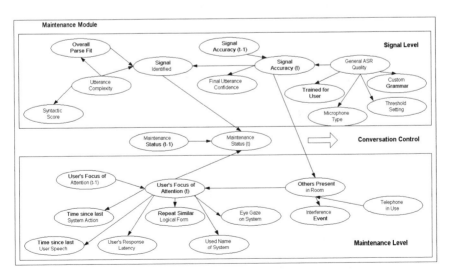

Figure 12.4. Bayesian networks in the Maintenance Module. (Based on Paek and Horwitz (2000), reprinted with permission of the authors.)

have to be interpreted and acted upon by the system. As can be seen from the network, there are several sources of evidence that contribute to the estimate of the user's focus of attention, including time since the last system action, time since the last user speech, the user's response latency, and whether the user has looked at the system, called the system by name or repeated an utterance.

Beliefs about the signal level are encoded in the node "Signal Identified". This node summarises information from the automatic speech recognition (ASR) engine and the natural language parser. Information from ASR includes signal accuracy over time, which is influenced by factors such as whether the system has been trained for this user, the microphone type, the language model and the threshold setting. The factors contributing to the natural language parser element are shown on the left-hand side of the diagram within the signal level.

All of the information from the channel and signal levels is combined in the "Maintenance Status" node to produce a probability distribution over four different grounding states: NO CHANNEL, CHANNEL BUT NO SIGNAL, SIGNAL BUT NO CHANNEL and CHANNEL AND SIGNAL.

The grounding strategies used in Quartet depend on the type of user utterance that the system is responding to. The following are some of the strategies that are available:

1. No repair.
   1.1. Do an action that is relevant to the preceding turn.
   1.2. Assume speech is overheard and so ignore.
   1.3. Wait for further information before deciding.
   1.4. Give positive feedback (acknowledgement).
2. Display confusion (and attempt to elicit repair by user).
   2.1. In a general way.
   2.2. By specifying the grounding level.
3. Confirm understanding.
   3.1. Seek clarification.
      3.1.1. In a general way.
      3.1.2. By specifying the grounding level.
   3.2. Declare intention before action.
4. Consider combinations of repair actions.
5. Other repairs.

For example, a general repair might be something like "So you want a shuttle?", while a repair specifying the grounding level (in this case, signal) might be "I'm not sure I heard you correctly – did you want a shuttle?"

Each of the grounding strategies is associated with an expected utility. For example, requesting repetition of an utterance has a high expected utility if NO CHANNEL is suspected, as L will not have attended to the utterance, whereas repetition has low expected utility if CHANNEL AND SIGNAL OPEN, as the utterance will have been heard and the problem is more likely to be located at a higher level, such as Inference or Conversation Control. Decisions as to which strategy to select are encoded in Decision-based Transition Networks (DTNs), in which transitions are set by decision-theoretic functions. DTNs represent conversational structures such as "adjacency pairs" and the transitions model the probabilities associated with different choices of next response.

Taking Decisions

The following example illustrates how decisions about grounding are taken at the Intention Level. Goals cannot be observed directly, so the system infers a probability distribution over all possible goals given the different types of evidence – linguistic, contextual and nonlinguistic – that it has available. If the probability of a particular goal given the evidence $p(\text{Goal}|E)$ does not exceed a given threshold, the system has to decide between two different strategies: Inquire_Goal and Ask_Repair (these strategies are encoded in a DTN). Inquire_Goal asks the user to state their goal explicitly, while Ask_Repair uses an embedded sequence (clarification request) to obtain more information.

Considering the strategy of Ask_Repair, probability thresholds are used to decide which version of this strategy to use. Problems at lower levels, such as signal and channel problems, can also affect grounding at the Intention level, so a probability distribution is obtained over the states represented at the Maintenance Level that are concerned with problems due to channel and signal. Taking this information into account results in selection of the following strategies:

- Ask_Repair (elaboration) – This is used if the probability of channel and signal exceeds a threshold. In other words, it is assumed that the misunderstanding is at the intention level, but a maintenance level problem such as an incorrect parse is not excluded.
- Ask_Repair(repeat) – This is used if the most likely maintenance level state is channel and no signal, as the system may not have received a sufficiently clear signal from the user.
- Ask_Repair(specify) – This strategy uses value-of-information analysis to identify the best signals to observe given the inferred probabilities of different goals. For example, if it is recommended that the word "shuttle" should be observed, the system can make the repair more specific by asking if the request has anything to do with getting a shuttle.

Example: The Bayesian Receptionist

The following example is taken from Paek and Horwitz (1999), where a fuller description can be found. Several more examples can be found in other papers, such as Paek and Horwitz (2000). The Bayesian Receptionist simulates front-desk receptionists at the Microsoft corporate campus. Observational studies of the receptionist domain were used to obtain values for the Bayesian Receptionist application. These involved interviews as well as video-tapes of interactions with receptionists, looking at linguistic signals as well as various visual cues. Prior distributions for each variable were obtained by eliciting conditional probabilities from the receptionists. Utilities were gathered by estimating costs for various states. For example, for people the cost of looking to display attention is low, whereas elaborating on a concept may have a higher cost. Utilities for the different transitions in a DTN were obtained through a study involving imaginary scenarios in which a receptionist who did not understand a request would respond using different strategies. Each strategy was rated on a Likert scale and on the basis of this the utilities were estimated.

The components of the Bayesian Receptionist are similar to those used in other spoken dialogue systems, with the addition of a face-pose tracker from Microsoft Research, which is used to gauge the user's attention. The Microsoft Whisper system is used for speech recognition. This system has a trigram language model of about 60,000 words. No customized grammars from the application domains are used to support speech recognition. Natural language understanding is performed using the Microsoft NLPWin parser, which outputs syntactic and logical structures derived from the recognized speech.

In the current example the user approaches the Bayesian receptionist and says "I uh . . . I need . . . how do I get to building 25?" The utterance consists of hesitations and false starts, so it is likely to cause problems for the speech recognition and language understanding components. The system has to try to infer the user's goals using, among other things, the evidence provided from its analysis of the user's utterance. In so doing, the system needs to recognise and resolve uncertainties that occur across several levels.

The system computes a probability distribution over the goals of the user and finds that the most likely goal is a "request for a shuttle" at $p(\text{Shuttle}) = 0.478$. The probability of a "request for directions" is 0.413, and there are a number of other possible goals with low probabilities, such as "request for pickup", "request for entry" and "request for drop-off". $p(\text{Shuttle})$ fails to exceed the probability threshold $p(\text{guess}) = 0.7$ for Inquire_Goal in the Intention Module DTN. The maximum goal probability is less than a threshold for checking the maintenance level set at $p(\text{min}) = 0.5$, so the system initiates a check in the Maintenance Module. Taking into account further information from the vision and other components, the state "request for directions" is recommended.

Inference within the Maintenance Module takes into account various observations, such as the noisy message and attention-getting attempts. The probabilities for the states are estimated as:

$p(\text{ChannelAndSignal}) = 0.294$,

$p(\text{ChannelAndNoSignal}) = 0.575$,

$p(\text{NoChannel}) = 0.131$.

Accordingly, the state ChannelAndNoSignal is selected, which is appropriate given the noisy input.

The Conversation Control subsystem passes this information to the Intention Module, which evaluates the costs and benefits of different types of repair. Value-of-information analysis considers what would be the best observations to make and recommends asking a question that will elicit an observation about "directions", so that the system can decide between the two most likely goals: "request for shuttle" and "request for directions". Given that the most likely maintenance state is ChannelAndNoSignal, the system's next question uses a query frame that indicates that the problem may have been at this level as well as asking explicitly about the user's goal: "I'm sorry, I may not have heard you properly. Did you want directions?"

Thus in order to resolve misunderstandings and to determine the user's intentions the system reasons about uncertainties at several different levels of analysis.

Summary

In this chapter case studies of three spoken dialogue systems have been presented that involve complex tasks and require more advanced techniques for dialogue management.

Each of the Communicator projects addresses the same basic task, but there are differences in the ways in which dialogue management is achieved. The CU and Queen's systems employ a form-filling approach, while the CMU system uses a dynamic data structure that changes during the course of the interaction. Flexibility is achieved in the CU system through an event-driven dialogue manager and a set of action priorities that allow the system to respond flexibly to the user's input. The Queen's system achieves flexibility in verification strategies through the use of confirmation statuses and discourse pegs, while the CMU system is the most flexible system, using an agenda to keep the system on track but allowing the user to shift topic and modify the structure of the itinerary.

The Rochester spoken dialogue systems involve a close integration between the dialogue and the task being performed. Whereas in most other dialogue systems the domain is hard-coded, usually in the form of a frame with slots to be filled, in the Rochester systems the domain is a task to be solved in a dynamically changing world. Problem solving involves explicit reasoning about the domain and this reasoning is reflected in the dialogue, in which utterances are interpreted in relation to the task at hand and to the elements of the abstract problem solving model – objectives, solutions, resources and situations.

The Microsoft Conversational Architectures project has been concerned with mechanisms for resolving uncertainties in dialogues. These uncertainties can occur at different levels and the system has to reason about possible sources of misunderstanding, using Bayesian reasoning and expected value decision making to determine the most appropriate actions to take to achieve mutual understanding.

A number of important research issues have been touched on in the discussion of these case studies, including error detection, dialogue systems that adapt dynamically during the course of an interaction, systems that learn optimal dialogue strategies, and systems that maintain a comprehensive record of their information state to guide their interpretation of the user's utterances, as well as to assist in their choice of the next action to take in the dialogue. These research issues will be considered further in Chapter 13.

Further Reading

Extensive references, including lists of publications and demos, can be found at the following project web sites:

CMU Communicator: http://www.speech.cs.cmu.edu/Communicator/
Conversational Architectures: http://research.microsoft.com/adapt/
    conversation/
CU: Communicator http://communicator.colorado.edu/
TRAINS: http://www.cs.rochester.edu/research/trains/
TRIPS: http://www.cs.rochester.edu/research/cisd/projects/trips/

Research Topics in Spoken Dialogue Technology

13

Spoken dialogue technology is an exciting and active interdisciplinary research area, attracting researchers from disciplines such as computational linguistics, artificial intelligence, speech technology, linguistics and educational technology. This chapter presents a selection of current research issues in spoken dialogue technology beginning with Information State Theory, an influential approach to the representation of dialogue context that can play an important role in dialogue management for advanced dialogue systems. Following this the issue of error handling is discussed. This is an important issue in spoken dialogue technology, due to the pervasiveness of errors at all levels of analysis when interacting with a spoken dialogue system. The discussion will focus mainly on methods for error detection, including the use of machine learning techniques to predict the circumstances in which errors are likely to occur.

The third research area to be discussed is adaptivity in spoken dialogue systems. An "intelligent" system should be able to adapt itself to the needs of different users and to the current state of the dialogue. Several different approaches to adaptivity are discussed, including adaptations as a means of handling problems detected in the ongoing dialogue. The final area is the use of machine learning to optimise dialogue system performance. Reinforcement learning has been used to enable dialogue systems to learn the best dialogue strategies, for example, whether to elicit input from the user with open-ended rather than more constraining prompts, or whether to verify the system's interpretation of the user's utterances. The results of research using reinforcement learning suggest that fine-grained choices in dialogue strategy can be learned by a dialogue system on the basis of experience of interaction with users.

Information State Theory

Information State Theory was introduced briefly in Chapter 3. Information State Theory is concerned with representing information about the state of the dialogue, which may include information about what has been discussed so far, what information is part of the common ground between the dialogue participants, and what obligations a dialogue participant has at a particular stage in the dialogue.

The development of Information State Theory and its application to the design of dialogue systems was the main focus of the EU-funded TRINDI (Task oriented Instructional Dialogue) project (www.ling.gu.se/projekt/trindi/). A number of different versions of the theory were developed and implemented. These are discussed in detail in the TRINDI book (TRINDI Consortium, 2001). However, in addition to this theoretical work a toolbox was implemented – TRINDIKIT – that can be used to experiment with different kinds of information states and with rules for updating the states (Larsson, 2002; www.ling.gu.se/projekt/trindi/trindikit/). This section will examine the version of Information State Theory developed by Poesio and Traum (1997, 1998), which focuses among other things on the role of dialogue obligations in dialogue management. This approach also builds on Traum's work on a computational model of grounding (Traum, 1994) that was developed as part of the TRAINS project (see Chapter 12).

Key Concepts in Information State Theory

An information state represents information about a dialogue that provides a means for the dialogue manager to interpret the user's utterances and to decide what action to take next. The information state is continually updated as the dialogue progresses. Other terms that have been used in the literature include "discourse context", "conversational score" and "mental state". The information state can be used to model the knowledge of the dialogue participants, including their beliefs, intentions, desires and obligations, as well as information that is shared (common ground). In some approaches the information states of both participants are modelled in order to provide a view of the dialogue from the perspective of an external observer. Generally, in spoken dialogue systems the information state represents the perspective of the system, including the system's beliefs, desires, intentions and obligations, and often the system's beliefs about the user's information state. However, given that the system is not omniscient, it cannot be certain that its representation of the user's information state is accurate. For this reason establishing information as common ground is an important part of attempting to ensure that the participants' information states concur.

Information State Theory involves the following components (Larsson and Traum, 2000; Traum and Larsson, 2001, to appear):

1. A description of the items to be represented in the information state.

There are many different items that can be represented in the information state, including the mental states of the participants (beliefs, desires, intentions, obligations and commitments), as well as information about the dialogue (utterances spoken, dialogue moves generated by the utterances, information that is common ground, information that is not part of the common ground).

Some of the information may be static and so unlikely to change during the course of the dialogue, such as domain knowledge and knowledge of dialogue conventions. Other information, such as the mental attitudes of the participants and the status of the dialogue is dynamic and changes as the dialogue progresses.

2. A formal representation of the information.

There are a number of ways to represent the items in the information state. These include lists and sets as well as more complex representations, such as typed feature structures, Discourse Representation Structures, and modal operators from a logic, which can be used to support more sophisticated processes of reasoning.

3. A set of dialogue moves that will trigger the update of the information state.

Dialogue moves describe the functions of utterances in the dialogue, as well as providing a basis for update of the information state. One major issue, as discussed in Chapter 3, is how to recognise these moves on the basis of the user's utterances.

4. A set of update rules that specify how the information state is updated.

The update rules define formally how the information state is updated. Update rules consist of applicability conditions, which define the circumstances in which the rule applies, and effects, which define the consequences of applying the rule.

5. A control strategy.

The control strategy is used to decide which update rule to apply if a number of rules are applicable at a given point in the dialogue. There are several ways to do this. The simplest strategy is to select the first rule that applies. Other strategies include selection of the most applicable rule based on probabilistic information or on utility theory.

Information State Theory: The Poesio–Traum Approach

This description is based on the Poesio–Traum model of information states as presented in Matheson et al. (2001). The model is formalised using the notation of Discourse Representation Theory (Kamp and Reyle, 1993). A simplified version of the model and of the processes involved will be presented here. Interested readers can consult the original document for details of the more formal version of the model.

As mentioned earlier, the Poesio–Traum model focuses on Traum's computational model of grounding in dialogue and emphasises the social effects of dialogue acts, such as obligations and commitments, rather than mental states, such as beliefs and intentions. The information state for each participant consists of the following parts:

- A private part that includes information known to the participant but not introduced into the dialogue, such as private beliefs and intentions.

- A public part that includes information assumed to be part of the common ground (G). This includes obligations and commitments, as well as facts about what has been said in the dialogue.
- A semipublic part that includes information introduced into the dialogue but not yet grounded. This information is contained in Discourse Units (DUs).

The application of the model can be illustrated using the dialogue presented in Matheson et al. (2001, p. 78):

13.1
1 A: There is an engine at Avon.
2 B: Okay.
3 A: It is hooked to a boxcar.

When a new utterance is produced, the current discourse unit is updated with this act, i.e., that A has uttered "there is an engine at Avon". Assuming that the utterance is interpreted as an Assert act (i.e., that the utterance has generated the speech act Assert), an obligation is placed on the recipient of this act to acknowledge the assertion and to address it. This is performed by B in 2 with the utterance "okay", which also fulfils the function of grounding the assertion in utterance 1. The dialogue continues with a further assertion (3), where one requirement for the model is to find a referent for the anaphoric pronoun "it" – in this case the engine at Avon mentioned in 1.

Update rules are a crucial part of how the dialogue is processed in Information State Theory. Update rules are triggered by certain conditions occurring. In the simplest cases this might be that an utterance has been perceived or that an assertion has been made. The effects of the update rule often involve adding obligations for one of the participants (e.g., to produce an acknowledgement), or to cause an item to be moved to the common ground (G). Obligations are generally imposed by forward-looking acts, such as assertions, while grounding is achieved by backward-looking acts, such as acknowledgements (see Chapter 3 for a discussion of forward- and backward-looking acts). The following are some examples of update rules involving forward-looking acts:

Name:	Utterance.
Condition:	A utters the utterance P.
Update:	Add to Current Discourse Unit (CDU) that A uttered P.
Name:	Statement.
Condition:	G (common ground) contains a Statement K addressed by A to B.
Update:	Add to G that A is conversationally committed to K with regard to B (i.e., A is committed to B that K is the case, whether A believes K or not).
Name:	Assert.
Condition:	G contains an Assert K addressed by A to B.
Update:	Add to G that: if A asserts K, then A is trying to get B to believe K, and that, if B believes K, then B is also conversationally committed to K.

Backward-looking acts remove the obligation to address an act. The backward-looking acts presented in Matheson et al. (2001) are Agreement, Accept, Answer and Reject. For example, B's utterance in Dialogue 13.1 is an Accept act and once it has been recognised by A, B's obligation to address A's assertion has been removed. Acknowledgements are a different type of backward-looking act that perform grounding. Following an acknowledgement the DU that is acknowledged is added to the common ground (G).

The following is a simplified account of how the first two utterances of Dialogue 13.1 are processed within the Poesio–Traum model (see also Pulman (2002), for a similar description of the dialogue using a slightly different notation).

A: There's an engine at Avon.

1. The utterance "there's an engine at Avon", spoken by A to B and denoted as u1, is perceived and added to the common ground (G).
2. The utterance u1 is interpreted as an assertion ce1 by A to B.
3. Recognition of u1 as an assertion triggers the following updates:

   B is conversationally committed to an act of understanding with reference to ce1.

   B is conversationally committed to addressing ce1.

These commitments are added to G.

B: Okay

1. The utterance "okay", spoken by B to A and denoted as u2, is perceived and added to G.
2. The utterance u2 is recognised both as an acknowledgement and as an acceptance of ce1 and is denoted as ce2.
3. The acknowledgement ce2 causes ce1 to be grounded.
4. The grounding of ce1 by ce2 triggers the update rule for acknowledgements which removes B's obligation to address ce1 to be removed.

Although this is a simple example it gives some indication of the power of Information State Theory. Readers interested in finding out more about the theory and its applications can consult the references listed under Further Reading at the end of the chapter.

Error Handling in Spoken Dialogue Systems

Errors can occur at every level of a dialogue, from the recognition of what words were spoken to the understanding of the intentions behind the words. Most work to date has addressed speech recognition errors. However, as speech recognition accuracy improves, errors at other levels – syntactic, semantic, discourse and pragmatic – will also need to be addressed.

Error handling can be viewed in terms of the following stages (see also Turunen and Hakulinen (2001a), for a more detailed set of stages):

1. Error prevention.
2. Error detection.
3. Error recovery.

Error prevention occurs at the design stage, where the designer predicts potential errors, and designs the system so as to avoid these errors occurring (see Chapter 6). For example, careful design of prompts will help to constrain the user's input to words that the system will be able to understand, while recognition grammar design can ensure that words that are easily confused and words that are frequently misrecognised are avoided. Similarly, dialogues can be designed to direct the user to the sorts of input that the system can handle and, where problems occur, appropriate use of verification strategies can help in recovery from the errors. However, given the fact that speech technology is error-prone and indeed that communication, even between humans, often involves misunderstandings, nonunderstandings and misinterpretations (McRoy, 1998), methods are required to detect errors that occur in interactions with spoken dialogue systems and to provide ways of recovering from these errors. The remainder of this section will examine a number of methods that are being developed for the detection of errors. Some approaches to error recovery will be described in the following section on adaptive dialogue systems, where one aspect of adaptation is to change the dialogue strategy to address communication problems that have arisen in the dialogue.

Error Detection

In order to detect errors the system needs to be able to monitor the ongoing dialogue for features that indicate that some problem has occurred in the dialogue. Errors are normally understood as failures by the system to interpret correctly the user's utterances. Detection of errors has focussed mainly on speech recognition errors, although there has also been some research on errors in spoken language understanding. Approaches to errors at other levels have been investigated extensively for natural language interfaces with keyboard input but have not been addressed to any great extent in spoken dialogue systems (Reilly, 1987).

The following example, taken from Litman et al. (1999), involves a dialogue with Annie, an agent for voice dialling and messaging (Table 13.1). The actual dialogue is shown in column 1, while column 2 shows the interpretation produced by the speech recogniser, and column 3 shows the recognition confidence score. Interpretations that fall below a threshold defined for the system are rejected. Error detection occurs at a number of points in this dialogue. On analysing U1, U2 and U3, the system rejects the user's utterances because the acoustic confidence scores fall below the given threshold. Skantze (2003a)

Table 13.1. Dialogue with the "Annie" system. (© 1999, Association for Computational Linguistics. All rights reserved. Reprinted by permission of ACL and the author.)

Actual Dialogue	ASR Interpretation	ASR Confidence
A1: Annie here.		
U1: Hello Annie, could you give me the information on the meeting I have tomorrow?	REJECT	−4.84
A2: What was that?		
U2: I need to find out uh a meeting time and place. Kim sent me a message on it.	REJECT	−4.20
A3: For all options say help me out.		
U3: Help me out.	REJECT	−6.35
A4: Annie here.		
U4: Help.	help	−1.74
A5: Help. Say call or say send a message, followed by a label or a number. Or say get my messages. . . .		
U5: Get messages (user interrupts A5).	get me sips	−3.33
A6: Speech and Image Processing Lab.		
U6: Help.	help	−1.78
A7: Help. Say the first and last name.		
U7: Kim.	annie	−3.81

describes this as early detection, as the system detects that something is wrong in the user's current utterance and takes immediate steps to address the problem.

A spoken dialogue system can respond in several different ways to a user's utterance:

1. It can accept the utterance and continue the dialogue. This strategy may be used when the system is confident in its interpretation of the user's utterance, but carries the danger that the system may have misinterpreted the utterance. Misinterpretations are often only detected later in the dialogue, if at all (McRoy, 1998).

2. It can accept the utterance and attempt to verify it, either with an explicit verification or, as in this example, with an implicit verification, in which some or all of the user's utterance is repeated (A5, A6, A7). This strategy gives the user an opportunity to reject the system's interpretation and to make a correction. Detection of an error following a system verification is known as a late detection (Skantze, 2003a).

3. It can reject the user's utterance and ask the user to repeat or rephrase the utterance, or the system can restart the dialogue (A2, A3, A4). Rejections in current spoken dialogue systems usually occur when the acoustic confidence scores for the user's utterance fall below a given threshold (U1, U2, U3).

The system's choice of strategy can also be erroneous. A false rejection, in which the system wrongly rejects a user's utterance, is less serious, as it leads to a request for repetition or confirmation, or a reprompt. A false acceptance, in which the system adopts an interpretation of a user's utterance, in which the confidence score exceeds the threshold (see U5 and U7), is more problematic as it may not be easy for the user to correct the system and put the dialogue back on track. For example, in U5 the user says "get messages" which the system interprets as "get me sips", the acronym for the Speech and Image Processing Lab, while in U7 the user says "Kim" which is interpreted as "Annie".

Another possibility is error prediction, in which the system decides on the basis of the current state of the dialogue that problems are likely to occur. The following sections describe some studies that have investigated these different types of error detection.

Early Error Detection

The most commonly used measure for early detection of errors is the acoustic confidence score. However, acoustic confidence scores are not entirely reliable, as there is no one-to-one mapping between low confidence scores and recognition errors, nor between high confidence scores and correct recognitions (Bouwman et al., 1999). For this reason attempts have been made to find additional features that can be monitored automatically within the dialogue and that might indicate whether a speech recognition hypothesis is likely to be correct.

Litman et al. (2000) investigated the use of prosodic cues to predict automatic speech recognition performance. They examined the prosodic features of correctly and incorrectly recognised speaker utterances in interaction with the TOOT system, a spoken dialogue system used to access train schedules from the Web using the telephone. Following this, machine learning experiments were conducted to explore the predictive power of prosodic features on their own as well as in combination with other measures such as confidence scores. The results indicated significant prosodic differences between correctly and incorrectly recognised utterances, suggesting that prosodic features could be used to predict whether an utterance has been misrecognised.

In this study misrecognitions were defined as utterances in which there was either a speech recognition error or a speech understanding error. Comparing the transcriptions of the dialogues with the string produced by the speech recogniser produced a word error rate (WER) for each utterance. Those utterances in which WER was greater than 0 (i.e., there were speech recognition errors in the recognised string), were classified as misrecognitions. Misrecognitions also included utterances which were semantically incorrect. This was determined using the measure of concept accuracy (CA), in which each of the concepts in the user's utterance (such as time, departure and arrival cities) was compared with the concepts produced in the recognised string. Those utterances where CA was less than 1 (i.e., one or more concepts was missing or had been misrecognised), were classified as misrecognitions. The CA metric is important, as an utterance can be understood sufficiently well for the purposes of the transaction, even if not all of the words have been correctly recognised.

The prosodic features used in this study included features associated with hyper-articulated speech, such as wider pitch excursions (measured in terms of maximum and mean fundamental frequency values), louder speech (measured in terms of maximum and mean energy values), and slower speech, as well as features such as total duration of the utterance, the length of pause preceding the utterance, the speaking rate, and the amount of silence within the turn. Utterances rejected on account of either WER or CA were characterised by significantly higher fundamental frequency and energy maxima, longer durations and longer preceding pauses. Furthermore, the results applied to relative differences for speakers, so that for a given speaker utterances that were higher in pitch, louder, longer or that followed longer pauses, were less likely to be recognised correctly than utterances by the same speaker that were lower in pitch, less loud, shorter and following shorter pauses. Thus it was possible to identify misrecognitions in terms of these prosodic features.

The purpose of the machine learning experiments was to determine whether a particular utterance would be recognised correctly or not. For these experiments the machine learning program RIPPER (Cohen, 1996) was used to develop a classification model that could predict the class of future examples, i.e., whether correct or incorrect recognitions.

The input to RIPPER was:

- A set of classes to be learned – In this case, either correct or incorrect recognition.
- A set of features and possible values – These included the prosodic features discussed earlier, various speech recognition features, such as automatic speech recognition (ASR) grammar, ASR confidence, and ASR string, and a number of additional features, including dialogue strategy, task number, subject, gender and whether the speaker was a native speaker.
- Training data specifying the class and feature values for each training example.

The output of RIPPER was a classification model in the form of an ordered set of if–then rules.

The best results were achieved when examining misrecognitions involving WER (speech recognition). Trained on the acoustic confidence score the algorithm had an accuracy of 77.77%, but adding the prosodic features increased the accuracy to 87.24%. Even greater accuracy (93.47%) was achieved by including the words from the recognised string and the recognition grammar as features. In this way, adding prosodic as well as contextual features yielded a much greater error detection accuracy than would be achieved using acoustic confidence scores on their own. As far as recognitions involving CA (concept accuracy) were concerned, there were only minor improvements over traditional rejection methods using acoustic confidence scores.

There are a number of explanations for these results. In the first place utterances with extreme prosodic values (wider pitch excursions, higher degrees of loudness) will differ considerably from the utterances used in the training of the speech recogniser, so it should be expected that utterances containing these features will be less likely to be correctly recognised. Second, utterance duration, which featured strongly in many of the rules, can be explained as a factor in that longer utterances provide more opportunities for errors. Finally, the feature involving pauses before the utterance contributes to greater disfluency, which will tend to degrade recognition performance.

In a study using the same machine learning techniques, Walker et al. (2000a) developed a classifier for distinguishing utterances containing spoken language understanding (SLU) errors from correctly interpreted utterances. The data in this study were taken from the How May I Help You? (HMIHY) corpus. HMIHY is a call routing system under development at AT&T, in which one of the main tasks for the system is to identify from the user's utterance which task from a set of 14 categories (such as person-to-person dialling or call billing) the utterance refers to. In this case, speech recognition accuracy is less important than concept accuracy. A number of features were used, including:

- Speech recognition – Output of the recogniser, number of words, duration, recognition grammar and tempo.
- Natural language processing (NLP) – Parsing confidence, recognised task, amount of context shift and salience.
- Dialogue management and discourse history – Content of preceding prompt, whether a reprompt, subdialogue or confirmation.

These features are defined and explained in more detail in the original paper.

The best performance (86.16%) was achieved using all the components. However, a high level of performance (84.8%) was achieved using the NLP features, indicating that a classifier based on NLP features could be integrated into the NLP module of the system to reliably distinguish errors in spoken language understanding.

In summary, there is evidence to support the claim that speech recognition and spoken language understanding errors can be reliably and automatically identified within a dialogue, by detecting the relevant features online and applying the rules produced by the classifiers. Some of these features are to be found within the utterance (in particular, the prosodic and NLP features), while others are derived from information outside the utterance (dialogue context and discourse history). More advanced conversational systems will need to be able to make use of this sort of information in order to support natural interaction that avoids the problems associated with misrecognitions and, in particular, false acceptances.

Late Error Detection

Most work on late detection has examined how the user responds to the system's attempt to verify the user's previous utterance, although of course the detection of the error could also occur later than this in the dialogue. In the following example (cited in Krahmer et al. (2001)) the user U is interacting with a Dutch spoken dialogue system S that provides train timetable information. The dialogue is translated from the original Dutch dialogue.

13.2
1 System: Good morning, this is the talking computer. From which station to which station do you want to travel?
2 User: From Eindhoven to Reuver.
3 System: On what day do you want to travel from Eindhoven to Winsum?
4 User: I want to travel at 8 o'clock from Eindhoven to Reuver.
5 System: On what day do you want to travel from Eindhoven to Utrecht CS at 8 o'clock in the morning?
6 User: No, in the evening at 8 o'clock I want to travel from Eindhoven to Reuver.

In this example the system attempts to verify the user's utterances using an implicit form of verification (3, 5). Following each verification, the user tries to correct the system, but without much success (4 is an attempt to correct 3, 6 is an attempt to correct 5). However, there are cues in the user's responses to the system's verifications that indicate that the system had misinterpreted the user's previous utterances and that could be used in a spoken dialogue system to predict potential system misinterpretations. For example, although this is not indicated in the transcript, it is likely that in 4 the word "Reuver" was spoken with stronger emphasis to indicate a correction, while in 6 the use of the word "no", as well as more unusual (or marked) word order, would also indicate that the user is making corrections.

Krahmer et al. (2001) carried out a descriptive analysis of a corpus of 120 dialogues between users and two versions of a Dutch spoken dialogue system for train timetable enquiries to investigate how users responded to system verifications. They distinguished between positive and negative signals, finding that users employed negative signals more often when the preceding system utterance contained a problem, particularly when this utterance was an implicit verification. In contrast, they found that positive signals were used when there was no problem.

Table 13.2 lists the different types of signals (or cues). Some of these cues are obvious, such as "confirm" as a positive cue, and "disconfirm", "repetitions" and "corrections" as negative cues. The other features relate to the general desire of dialogue participants to conclude the dialogue as quickly and efficiently as

Table 13.2. Positive and negative cues. (Reprinted with permission from Krahmer et al. (2001, Table 1, p. 23).)

Positive ("go on")	Negative ("go back")
Short turns	Long turns
Unmarked word order	Marked word order
Confirm	Disconfirm
Answer	No answer
No corrections	Corrections
No repetitions	Repetitions
New information	No new information

possible. For this reason, short turns, which do not include corrections and repetitions, but do include new information, are likely to further the dialogue, while dialogues with longer turns, including corrections, repetitions and no new information, will prolong the dialogue. "No answer", in which the user either fails to answer or pauses before responding, is an example of a dispreferred response that indicates some problem in the preceding utterance (see Chapter 3). Marked word order is where an unusual word order has been employed, for example, to emphasise a correction, as in U3 above.

Krahmer et al. (2001) also investigated the predictive capacity of these cues and whether it would be possible to automatically decide whether a preceding system utterance contained an error. They conducted a series of machine learning experiments in which they used features to be found in the system's verification utterance as well as the positive and negative cues in the user's response, finding that the best results (almost 97% accuracy) were obtained when all the features were used in combination. In a companion study they also examined prosodic information in the user's utterance, finding that user utterances that corrected a system verification often contained a high boundary tone, high pitch, as well as a relatively long delay between the end of the system's question and the beginning of the user's answer (Krahmer et al., 2002). Similar results were reported in a study of American English human–machine dialogues (Swerts et al., 2000).

Error Prediction

Error prediction is concerned with predicting potential problems on a dialogue based on features monitored in the dialogue so far. Once such problems have been detected, steps can be taken to prevent the errors, for example, by changing the dialogue strategy.

Litman et al. (1999) applied machine learning techniques (similar to those described earlier) to develop a classifier that could detect dialogues with poor speech recogniser performance. The features included acoustic confidence scores as well as features concerning dialogue efficiency and quality. The best classification involved the use of all the available features. In this study the features were collected over the complete dialogues and so the rules learned by the classifier could not be applied within the dialogues during runtime.

In a subsequent study, Walker et al. (2000b) used a corpus of 4774 dialogues from the HMIHY (How May I help you?) corpus to train the system to be able to predict problems that were likely to occur in a dialogue. In this case the aim was to make the predictions early on so that adaptation could occur within the ongoing dialogue. Predictions were based on information available to the system in the form of features extracted automatically from the log files of the dialogues. The results showed that rules could be learned to predict problematic dialogues using the fully automatic features with an accuracy ranging from 72% to 87%, depending on how much of the dialogue the system had seen so far. The features used included speech recognition features, such as confidence scores, utterance duration and number of recognised words, as well as natural language understanding (NLU) features and dialogue features. The NLU features included confidence features for the parse (which involved assigning the utterance to one of the 15 tasks of the HMIHY system), as well as measures indicating inconsistency and context shift. Inconsistency was an intra-utterance measure that indicated discrepancy between tasks that the system appeared to be requesting, while context-shift was an inter-utterance measure that detected if the user's subsequent utterance was in conflict with a previous utterance, suggesting that the system's interpretation of either utterance may have been erroneous. Dialogue measures included a number of features concerned with prompts and confirmations, including keeping running tallies for these features.

Prediction accuracy was investigated based on the system having seen only the first exchange in the dialogue compared with predictions made after seeing the first two exchanges, as well as identification accuracy after having seen the whole dialogue. Accuracy using the set of automatically available features was 72% after seeing just the first exchange, and after the second exchange it was 79%, while identification of problems after the complete dialogue was 87%. Thus the rules learned by the classifier to predict potential problems could be employed automatically in a dialogue system to contribute to improvements in system performance.

Error Recovery

There are several ways in which a spoken dialogue system can attempt error recovery. The most straightforward way to get the dialogue back on track is to simply ask the user to repeat or rephrase the problematic utterance. Different verification strategies, based on different levels of acoustic confidence scores, have also been employed (Sturm et al., 1999). Another method, as suggested by Krahmer et al. (2001), is to use information available in the detection of the error, such as the different negative cues discussed earlier, and indicators such as heavier emphasis on the corrected word, to construct a more suitable follow-up question for the system to ask, rather than simply asking the user to repeat or confirm all of the information that had been elicited, especially when some of it was probably correct. Dialogue 13.2 is an example where such a strategy would have been more useful compared with a blanket confirmation of all the values.

The most radical strategy for error recovery has been proposed by Skantze (2003b), based an analysis of human error handling strategies. In this study 40 dialogues were collected using a modified version of the Wizard of Oz (WoZ) method, in which the user's utterances were processed by a speech recognizer and passed to the operator (or Wizard) so that reactions to realistic speech recognition errors could be investigated. The domain was a direction-giving task in which both user and operator used landmarks and relative directions to solve the task. Different strategies were used by the operator following nonunderstandings. In addition to signals of nonunderstanding, as discussed above, other strategies were to continue with the route description or to ask a task-related question about the user's current location. The following are examples of these strategies (items in parentheses indicate the operator's possible interpretation of the user's utterance):

> 13.3
> *Continuation of route description*
> 1 Operator: Continue a little bit forward.
> 2 User: Street that there house (Past the wooden house?)
> 3 Operator: Now walk around the wooden house. Take left and then right.

> 13.4
> *Task-related question about position*
> 1. Operator: Do you see a wooden house in front of you?
> 2. User: Yes crossing address now (I pass the wooden house now).
> 3. Operator: Can you see a restaurant sign?

In both of these cases there was probably partial understanding of the user's utterance, which the operator supplemented with domain information to provide a reasonable dialogue continuation. Skantze proposes that this is a more natural strategy that avoids the traditional strategy of signaling nonunderstanding, which tends to lengthen the dialogue and make it appear problematic in the user's perception. Other methods for handling and recovering from errors will be discussed in the next section.

Adaptive Dialogue Systems

One approach to handling errors involves the system adapting its dialogue strategies to address the problems that have been detected in the ongoing dialogue. For example, the system could shift from mixed initiative to system initiative if speech recognition performance is poor, and could also employ other strategies such as explicit confirmation, leading prompts, and the option of an alternative input mode, such as the keyboard.

Adaptation is hand-crafted in current dialogue systems. For example, in VoiceXML applications, alternative prompts and help messages can be scripted to be output when "noinput" and "nomatch" events are detected, and the system can shift from mixed-initiative to system-initiative to complete the collection of information that was not elicited in the user's initial utterance (see Chapters 9 and 10).

It is important to distinguish between different approaches to adaptation. On the one hand, we can make a distinction between adaptable and adaptive interfaces. An adaptable interface allows the user to control changes in the system's dialogue strategies, whereas an adaptive interface responds automatically to problems detected within the dialogue. A second distinction concerns when the adaptation takes place. Adaptation can occur either within the ongoing dialogue or over time. In the latter case the system engages in a number of dialogues and uses machine learning techniques to acquire an optimal dialogue strategy (see section below on learning dialogue strategies).

An Adaptable Dialogue System

An adaptable interface requires the user to detect when problems are occurring within a dialogue and to request adaptations of the system's dialogue strategy in order to improve performance. Litman and Pan (1999) report an empirical evaluation of the effectiveness of an adaptable spoken dialogue system, in which two aspects of dialogue strategy were involved: initiative (mixed, system or user), and confirmation (explicit, implicit, none). The system began with the most open strategy, which involved no confirmation and user initiative. This strategy corresponds most closely to human–human dialogue and results in shorter transaction times provided that there are no problems with speech recognition. The most conservative strategy involves explicit confirmation and system initiative. This strategy results in longer transaction times but is more reliable in terms of task success when speech recognition is poor. Between these extremes there are various combinations, such as implicit confirmation and mixed initiative.

The following extract is taken from a dialogue with the adaptable version of the TOOT system, a spoken dialogue system for retrieving online train schedules. The extract illustrates how the user was able to modify the system's dialogue strategies to improve the dialogue.

13.5
1 User: I would like to go from Baltimore to Chicago on Saturday at 8 o'clock.
2 System: Do you want me to find the trains from Baltimore to DC on Tuesday around 11:45 a.m. now?
3 User: No.
4 System: How may I help you?
5 User: Change strategy.
6 System: You are using the user initiative. Which initiative do you want to change to? System –
7. User: System initiative please. (*User interrupts*).
8 System: You are using the no confirmation strategy. Which confirmation do you want to change to? No confirmation, implicit confirmation, or explicit confirmation?
9 User: Implicit please.

Following these changes of strategy the system elicited the required parameters one by one and confirmed each parameter implicitly. The dialogue reached a successful conclusion.

In their evaluation of the adaptable system Litman and Pan (1999) asked 20 novice users to carry out four tasks with two versions of the system (adaptable and nonadaptable), and found that the adaptable version performed better than the nonadaptable version in terms of measures such as user satisfaction and task success. However, as can be seen from the example, requiring users to change the strategy involves the use of terms that are likely to be obscure and unnatural for everyday users (such as different types of initiative and confirmation). For this reason it might be preferable to develop systems that can adapt automatically (and thus more naturally) to the user's needs and the problems arising during the dialogue. Nevertheless, there is some scope for systems in which the user can make choices to control the interaction, for example, in the case of users with impairments that make interaction with a standard spoken dialogue system problematic. To date there has been little work on spoken dialogue systems that cater for the needs and preferences of different users in this way.

An Adaptive Version of TOOT

In a subsequent study Litman and Pan (2002) investigated the effectiveness of an adaptive version of the TOOT system that modified its strategies automatically. The dialogue strategy at the beginning of a dialogue was a combination of user initiative and no confirmation, but if problems were detected, the system moved to more conservative strategies, in the first instance to implicit confirmation, and on subsequent adaptations to more directed questions with explicit confirmations. Speech recognition performance was used as a basis for detecting problems, using rules learned from a set of training dialogues. Prediction was made incrementally over the course of a dialogue and the system adapted to a more conservative strategy if the user model indicated that dialogue problems had exceeded a given threshold. For example, one of the rules that had been learned in the training phase for classifying dialogues as "good" or "bad" (i.e., problematic) stated that if the percentage of user utterances that are predicted to be misrecognitions (based on a confidence score threshold of −4) exceeds 3%, then the dialogue is to be classified as problematic. Given this rule the system will adapt if there is at least one misrecognition in a window of four utterances. The following example, extracted from the dialogue presented in Litman and Pan (2002, p. 113) illustrates these adaptations. (Results from the speech recogniser, including confidence scores, are indicated in bold, and comments on the system's behaviour are in parentheses.)

13.6

1 System: How may I help you?
(System begins with open-ended question)
2 User: I need to find a train going to New York City.
DC I don't care on Thursday. −5.293949
3 System: Which city do you want to leave from?
(Initial setting is "no confirmation", so System asks the next question despite the misrecognition – score exceeds threshold of −4.)
4 User: Baltimore.
5 System: Do you want me to find the trains from Baltimore to DC on Thursday at anytime now?
6 User: No.
. . . . .
7 User: I need to leave on Sunday.
DC between 1 night and 8. −4.916628
8 System: I heard you say go to DC between 1 night and 8. Do you want me to find you the trains from Baltimore to DC on Thursday between 1 night and now?

(System adapts its strategy as there has been at least one misrecognition within the previous four utterances. System uses implicit confirmation "I heard you say . . ." combined with mixed initiative.)
9 User: No.
. . . . .
10 User: I need to go to New York City from Baltimore on Sunday at 8.30 p.m.
To Chicago Tuesday 8.45 am. −5.948381
11 System: I heard you say go to Chicago on Tuesday around 8.45 a.m. Do you want me to find the trains from Baltimore to Chicago on Tuesday around 8.45 a.m. now?
12 U: No.
13 System: Which city do you want to go to?
(Given detection of further problematic features, the System adapts to the strategy of a system directed dialogue, asking a series of directed questions to elicit each value separately and asking the user to explicitly confirm each utterance.)
14 User: New York City.
15 System: Do you want to go to New York City?
16 User: Yes.
17 System: Which city do you want to leave from?
18 User: Baltimore.
19 System: Do you want to leave from Baltimore?
(The System uses the same strategies to elicit the day and time of departure. As a result of adapting to the most conservative dialogue strategy misrecognitions are eliminated and the dialogue is completed successfully.)

As with the earlier study an empirical investigation was conducted in which the adaptive version of the system was compared with a nonadaptive version. The results showed a significant improvement in task success rate for the adaptive version.

Adaptivity in the Finnish Interact Project

Adaptivity in TOOT was based on rules learned from a set of training dialogues that enabled TOOT to determine whether the user was having speech recognition problems during the course of a dialogue. A different approach has been developed within the Finnish Interact project (Jokinen et al., 2002), in which adaptivity includes taking account of the needs and abilities of different groups of users as well as learning and adapting the system's behaviour to changing situations. An example of adaptivity to different user groups is an intelligent bus-stop that allows spoken and text interaction about city transportation and that includes a sign language help facility. The system should learn appropriate interaction strategies based on its interactions with different users and adapt to different user needs and preferences. Adaptation to the current dialogue situation involves similar changes in strategies for initiation and confirmation as discussed with reference to the TOOT project, but also includes adaptations that affect the system's output through the language generation component.

Interact uses the Jaspis adaptive speech application architecture, developed by Turunen and Hakulinen (2001b). In this architecture, as shown in Figure 13.1, information about the system state, such as the dialogue history and user

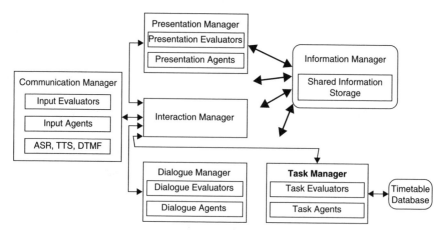

Figure 13.1. The Jaspis architecture. (Kerminen and Jokinen (2003), reprinted with permission of the authors.)

profiles, is kept in a shared knowledge base (Information Storage), which can be accessed by each module through the Information Manager. Interaction is coordinated by the Interaction Manager, using managers, agents and evaluators. Within each module there is a Manager that coordinates the module's agents and evaluators. The agents handle all the different dialogue situations that might arise, such as generation of explicit or implicit confirmations and selection of system- or user-initiative dialogue, while the evaluators determine the best agent for each dialogue situation. Using the Information Storage and this method of selecting agents, the system can adapt to different situations and can choose the most suitable dialogue strategy to handle different dialogue situations. Agents are specialised for particular tasks, such as handling speech recognition errors or presenting information in a particular way. There can also be different agents for the same task, for example, to provide speech output in different languages. This feature enables the system to adapt dynamically to the situation and the user.

The selection of a specific agent is made dynamically based on scores calculated by the evaluators, which score each agent according to their applicability within a given dialogue situation. Each evaluator gives a score for each agent and the agent that receives the highest score is selected to deal with the current dialogue situation, which includes information about the current input, the dialogue context and user preferences. Since the choice of the appropriate agent is a combination of different evaluations, based on information in the Information Storage, the system can adapt appropriately to different dialogue situations. Thus the architecture produces a flexible system that is capable of learning and adapting itself to new tasks, situations and users.

As well as modifying dialogue strategy, the system is also able to modify its generation strategies. The following example, taken from Jokinen and Wilcock (to appear), illustrates this point:

13.7
1 When will the next bus leave for Malmi?
2a 2.20 p.m.
2b It will leave at 2.20 p.m.
2c The next bus to Malmi leaves at 2.20 p.m.

Within the generation component there are three generation agents that operate with different degrees of explicitness, depending on changing levels of confidence in speech recognition accuracy. The first agent, illustrated in utterance 2a, is used for quick, informal interactions involving high-speech recognition confidence, whereas the second agent, illustrated in 2b, is suitable for more polite interactions with good speech recognition. In cases where speech recognition confidence is low, a more explicit utterance is generated, as in 2c, in which the topic is displayed for implicit confirmation.

Adaptivity in the Kyoto City Bus Information System

The Kyoto City Bus Information System determines which bus a user wants to take and then tells the user how long it will take before the bus arrives (Komatani et al., 2003). Users are asked to speak the bus stop where they want to get on (or a famous place or public facilities nearby), the destination, or the bus route information. There are 652 bus stops in Kyoto and 85 bus routes. The following is an example of a dialogue with the system:

13.8
System: Please tell me your current bus stop, your destination, or the specific bus route.
User: Shijo-Kawaramachi.
System: Do you want to take a bus from Shijo-Kawaramachi?
User: Yes.
System: Where will you get off the bus?
User: Arashiyama.
System: Do you want to go from Shijo-Kawaramachi to Arashiyama?
User: Yes.
System: Bus number 11 bound for Arashiyama has departed Sanjo-Keihammae, two bus stops away.

As bus information changes every minute, it is important that information is communicated quickly. On the other hand, it is also important that the user is supplied with the most appropriate information. In this system, the system adapts the information it provides as well as its dialogue management strategies based on user models. More specifically, users are modelled according to three dimensions:

1. Skill level – The degree of skill the user has in speaking to the system. Users who demonstrate a low level of skill are given more guidance in using the system, for example, with explicit requests for "yes/no" answers and more extensive instructions (e.g., "now I will ask for each item in order"). Users who

demonstrate a high skill level are provided with a user-initiated dialogue strategy.

2. Domain knowledge level – The extent of the user's knowledge of the domain. For example, if the user is a stranger to Kyoto, it is not appropriate to provide information that is too detailed, while for inhabitants of the city it is inappropriate to provide obvious information, but more detailed information can be given such as proposal of a different route.

3. Degree of hastiness – The extent to which the information is urgent and, thus, concise information is required. In the case of urgency a dialogue management strategy is adopted that supports a short transaction with no confirmations. If the measure of hastiness is low, then the system generates additional information according to the user's skill and knowledge levels.

The user models were implemented as classifiers, using a decision tree and features derived from single utterances as well as from the complete session. Some examples of the features are shown in Table 13.3.

The following is an example of the system's behaviour based on its use of the user models. The system begins with an open prompt that allows for user initiative, but the user's skill level is classified as low because the user's first utterance contains only one content word. Accordingly, the system shifts to system-directed control. The hastiness is classified as low by the decision tree so the system provides some instructions on how the user should respond and adopts the strategy of eliciting the required information one item at a time.

Table 13.3. Features used to classify the user models. (From Komatani et al. (2003).)

Features obtained from a single utterance:
- dialogue state (defined by already filled slots)
- presence of barge-in
- elapsed time of current utterance
- recognition result
- recogniser score
- number of slots filled by current utterance

Features obtained from complete session:
- number of utterances
- dialogue state of previous utterance
- elapsed time from beginning of session
- average number of repetitions of same question
- ratio of time of user utterances to complete elapsed time
- ratio of occurrence of barge-in to all utterances
- recognition result of previous utterance
- ratio of something recognised

Features obtained from complete session (used only to classify knowledge level):
- attribute of specified bus stops
- how bus stop specified (whether correct name used or not)
- ratio of each attribute to specified bus stops
- ratio of each way of specifying bus stops

13.9
System: Please tell me your current bus stop, your destination, or the specific bus route number.
User: Maruyama Park.
System: Let me confirm one by one.
<Explanation added according to [skill level:low]>
   Will you get off at Maruyama Park?
<Content confirmed according to [hastiness:low]>
   Please reply with yes or no.
<Instruction added according to [skill level:low]>
User: Yes.
System: Where will you get off the bus? Please specify by a bus stop name or a well-known landmark.
<Explanation added according to [skill level:low]>
User: Tofukuji temple.
System: Will you get off at Tofukuji temple?
   Please reply with yes or no.
User: Yes.
System: The following buses are located.
<Explanation added according to [skill level:low]>
The nearest bus stop to Maruyama Park is Gion.
<Domain information added according to [knowledge level:low]>
Bus number 202 bound for Nishioji-Kujo has departed Higashiyama-Sanjo, which is two stops away.

Evaluation of the system involved 20 novice subjects interacting with the system to obtain bus information according to a set of scenarios. Half of the subjects performed the tasks first with the user models active then without the user models. The other group performed the tasks in the opposite order. Results showed that incorporation of the user models helped the novice users to complete the tasks more quickly and that the user models helped the novice users to get accustomed to the system more quickly as they were given explicit instructions when their skill level was diagnosed as low. On the other hand, as users became more familiar and more competent with the tasks, the user models prevented the system from generating redundant information for skilled users. Thus dynamic user modelling, based on the dimensions of skill level, domain knowledge level and hastiness, and automatically derived by decision tree learning, were able to generate user-adaptive responses and dialogue management strategies.

Strategies for Selective Use of Verification

Verification strategies are required to reduce miscommunication in spoken dialogue systems. However, if verification is used selectively, there are two problems. On the one hand, the system might use verifications unnecessarily to verify utterances that have been correctly understood (over-verification). In this case the dialogue becomes longer and possibly irritating for the user. On the other hand, a failure to verify can lead to misunderstandings, where the system and user have different interpretations of what has been said (under-verification).

Smith (1998) conducted a series of experiments using the Circuit Fix-It Shop system (see Chapter 2) to evaluate different strategies for deciding whether to verify or not. The aim was to find strategies that would require the system to verify its interpretation of the user's utterance only if the accuracy of the interpretation was in doubt or if a correct understanding was essential to the success of the dialogue. A number of strategies were evaluated, including the following.

Use of Parser Confidence Score

Parser confidence in the Circuit Fix-It Shop system was calculated in terms of a parse cost that was associated with each utterance. Parse cost was determined on the basis of the number of operations performed by an error-correcting parser. Utterances with a low parse cost were an indication that the system had high confidence in its interpretation. A further measure, which was used in the rules for each strategy, was the Verification Threshold. This was a measure of how important the meaning of the utterance was for the success of the dialogue. The rule for using the parser confidence score was:

If the Parser Confidence Score > the Verification Threshold
Then do not verify.

Use of this rule in the experiments raised the rate of understanding from 81.5% to 97.4%, due to a decrease in the rate of under-verifications, but at the cost of verifying utterances that had been correctly understood in the first place.

Using Context

The second strategy involved the use of context, defined in terms of the expectation of what should come next in the dialogue, i.e., what the user should say in response to a question or command from the system. For example, in response to a command to carry out an action on an object in which the value of some property of the object should be changed (e.g., a switch should be moved to the "up" position), the following user responses are expected:

- An assertion that the object's property now has the desired value.
- An acknowledgement that the action has been completed.
- A question about the location of the object.
- A question about how to do the action.

A subset of these expectations was defined as the main expectation, giving rise to the rule:

If the utterance meaning is in the Main Expectation
Then do not verify.

Use of this strategy reduced under-verification but increased over-verification.

Parse Cost/Context Combination

In this strategy the two strategies were combined, resulting in a large reduction in over-verifications but with a rise in under-verifications. On the basis of a number of further experiments involving, among other things, using alternative thresholds, it was concluded that in general the context-dependent strategy is effective at reducing over-verifications and keeping under-verifications to a minimum. However, when the word recognition rate is low then the Parse Cost strategy should be used to avoid under-verifications.

Learning Optimal Dialogue Strategies

Adaptive strategies, such as switching from mixed initiative to system initiative or using different verification strategies when problems are encountered in the dialogue are determined in advance by the dialogue designer. The choice of these strategies is based on best practice guidelines as well as experience, and can be amended as a result of a process of iterative design and testing.

An alternative approach is to have the dialogue system automatically learn an optimal dialogue strategy using reinforcement learning (Levin et al., 2000; Walker, 2000; Young, 2000). This section will present the approach adopted in one particular set of experiments, in which strategy choices discussed earlier – choice of dialogue initiative and choice of confirmation type – are explored (Singh et al., 2002). The system involved is the NJFun system, a spoken dialogue system developed at AT&T that provides users with information about leisure activities in New Jersey.

Reinforcement Learning

Reinforcement learning, as applied to dialogue management design, involves a systematic exploration of all the different actions that the system can take in a dialogue, and determines the best choice of actions (or policy) that will optimise the system's performance as measured by a utility function, such as the user's evaluation of the system. Exploration of the different action choices to obtain training data involved collecting a corpus of interactions between the NJFun system and human users. An alterative method would be to simulate user interactions in order to obtain the training data (Levin et al., 2000; Scheffler and Young, 2002).

In order to explore the different action choices that are available at different states within a dialogue, it is necessary to define an explicit representation of all of the dialogue states and of the action choices available at each state. Each state incorporates information that is relevant to the choice of actions, such as the acoustic confidence scores and the dialogue history. Due to the nature of the learning algorithms involved, this information has to be summarised in terms of the values of a small set of features, rather than in terms of the much richer set of features used in the Information State Theory approach presented earlier.

Thus dialogue management is formalised as a sequential decision process involving a state space consisting of all the possible dialogue states, a set of possible actions at each state and a dialogue policy. The dialogue policy is a mapping between the state space and the action set that prescribes for any given state what should be the next action to perform. Thus transition from one state to the next state is determined by the system's choice of action at that first state. For example, in a flight information system, the system starts in an initial uninformed state about the values of certain parameters that form the basis of the user's information request – such as the destination, origin, date and time of the flight. Over the course of the dialogue the system elicits values for these parameters and eventually arrives at a state in which it can access a database and offer one or more flights that satisfy the user's requirements. The system may have a choice of actions at a given state. For example, it might ask the user questions about the values of unknown attributes, ask questions to verify known attributes, clarify some misunderstanding, or access a database. To behave optimally, the system must select an action in each state that has the maximum expected utility.

The final component of this representation is a reward (or reinforcement) that is associated with each state. The reward captures the immediate consequences of executing an action in a state. For example, each user interaction may incur a small negative reward, while successfully concluding the dialogue may result in a large positive reward. Other costs and rewards may include the number of corrections, the number of accesses to a database, speech recognition errors, dialogue duration and user satisfaction measures. In some studies the PARADISE dialogue evaluation methodology has been used to learn a performance function that covers a variety of measures (Walker, 2000). Capturing the long-term consequences of an action involves a utility function. The utility of taking an action a in state s is the expected reward for that action plus the sum of the long-term rewards over the complete transaction, assuming the agent acts using the best policy.

The representation as described here is known as a Markov Decision Process (MDP). The MDP is generally constructed from sample dialogues and models the possible user interactions with the system. Given such an MDP, learning the optimal dialogue policy from data is a matter of computing the best policy for choosing actions in an MDP. With multiple action choices at each state, reinforcement learning (RL) is used to explore the choices systematically and to compute the best policy for action selection based on rewards associated with each state transition. The RL algorithms calculate the utility values of each state in terms of the value of a successor state. If the value of the final state is known, the utility values for all earlier states can be calculated.

Reinforcement Learning Applied to the NJFun System

The NJFun system provides users with information about leisure activities in New Jersey. The system asks the user for the values of activity, location and time attributes and retrieves activities from a database. Dialogues ranged from 1 to 12 user utterances before the database query.

Three different types of dialogue initiative were used, based on the type of system prompt and the type of grammar used to recognise the user's response:

- System initiative: Directive prompt and restrictive grammar.
- User initiative: Open prompt and nonrestrictive grammar.
- Mixed initiative: Directive prompt and nonrestrictive grammar.

With system initiative the user's response is constrained to providing the values requested, so that a restrictive grammar that permits a limited range of utterances can be used. System initiative is a safe strategy that maximises the likelihood of successful recognition of the input, but at a cost of an inflexible and potentially longer dialogue. User initiative, on the other hand, provides an open-ended prompt with a nonrestrictive grammar (e.g., How may I help you?), that permits a wider range of user responses but with a greater potential for recognition errors requiring subsequent correction. Mixed initiative, as defined in this system, is a compromise between system and open initiative.

As far as confirmations were concerned, the choice was between the use of explicit confirmation or no confirmation. Confirmations are the main mechanism for establishing whether information is grounded. However, explicit confirmation of each item of information may result in a longer dialogue. Thus the choice of action in terms of dialogue initiative and confirmation strategy has consequences in terms of a number of measures of dialogue performance, such as transaction success, dialogue duration, proportion of turns required for correction and user satisfaction.

The formal state space used for learning in the NJFun system contained seven variables, as shown in Table 13.4 (taken from Singh et al. (2002, p. 115)). There were 62 states in the formal system, of which 42 were choice states with two actions each. Thus the number of unique policies for the system to explore was 242. Each state along with the action choices available was listed in a matrix (policy class), from which the following two rows are an example (Table 13.5).

Table 13.4. State features and values for the NJFun system. (From Singh et al. (2002, p. 115).)

Feature	Values	Explanation
Greet (G)	0, 1	Whether the system has greeted the user.
Attribute (A)	1, 2, 3, 4	Which attribute is being worked on.
Confidence/ Confirmed (C)	0, 1, 2, 3, 4	0, 1, 2 for low, medium and high ASR confidence. 3, 4 For explicitly confirmed, and disconfirmed.
Value (V)	0, 1	Whether value has been obtained for the current attribute.
Tries (T)	0, 1, 2	How many times the current attribute has been asked.
Grammar (M)	0, 1	Whether nonrestrictive grammar was used.
History (H)	0, 1	Whether there was any trouble on any previous attribute.

Table 13.5. States with action choices. (Based on Figure 8, Singh et al. (2002, p. 117).)

Choice States

G	A	C	V	T	M	H	Action Choices
0	1	0	0	0	0	0	GreetS, GreetU
1	1	0	1	0	0	0	NoConf, ExpConf1

Table 13.6. States generating Dialogue 13.10. (From Singh et al. (2002, p. 118).)

State

G	A	C	V	T	M	H	Action	Turn	Reward
0	1	0	0	0	0	0	GreetU	S1	0
1	1	2	1	0	0	0	NoConf	–	0
1	2	2	1	0	0	1	ExpConf2	S2	0
1	3	2	1	0	0	1	ExpConf3	S3	0
1	4	0	0	0	0	0	Tell	S4	1

The first row states that the system has a choice between a system-directed prompt ("Please say an activity name or say 'list activities' for a list of activities I know about") and a user initiative prompt ("How may I help you?"). The second row states that the system had acquired a value for the first attribute and has a choice between no confirmation and an explicit confirmation.

The following is an example of a dialogue with NJFun (from Singh et al. (2002, p. 106)):

> 13.10
> S1: Welcome to NJFun. How may I help you?
> U1: I'd like to find um winetasting in Lambertville in the morning.
>   (ASR: I'd like to find out wineries the in the Lambertville in the morning.)
> S2: Did you say you are interested in Lambertville?
> U2: Yes.
> S3: Did you say you want to go in the morning?
> U3: Yes.
> S4: I found a winery near Lambertville that is open in the morning. . . .

Table 13.6 shows how this dialogue is generated from the dialogue policy class. Taking the row for S2 as an example: This row states that the system has acquired a value for the second attribute with medium ASR confidence and a history of previous difficulties in the dialogue. An explicit confirmation strategy was selected.

Training an Optimal Dialogue Policy

In order to train an optimal dialogue policy, a corpus of experimental dialogues was obtained to train and test the system. A version of NJFun was implemented that would choose randomly between two available actions at any state where there was a choice of actions. This system was used with 54 subjects to obtain training data. The subjects carried out dialogues with the system according to a set of six tasks, such as:

You are thirsty and want to do some winetasting in the morning. Are there any wineries close to your home in Lambertville?

After completing the tasks the users filled out a survey and rated the system on a number of measures. These ratings were used to calculate the reward.

The training phase resulted in 311 dialogues in which there was a fairly balanced distribution of action choices at each state. These dialogues were used to construct an empirical MDP in which the reward function was based on a binary measure of task completion. Finally, the optimal dialogue policy in this learned MDP was computed.

The learned policy stated that the best use of initiative is to begin with user initiative and to back off to either mixed or system initiative if it was necessary to reprompt for an attribute. The specific back-off method differed according to the attribute involved, for example, system for the first attribute and mixed for the second. For confirmation, the best strategy was to confirm at lower acoustic confidence levels, although the levels differed across different attributes. The dialogue presented earlier and represented in Table 13.6 is an example of a dialogue generated by the optimal policy.

The system was reimplemented to use the optimal policy. In this case there were no action choices. The same tasks were performed by 21 test subjects and results for the training and test versions of the systems were compared, showing improvement in the various objective measures, such as task completion. The learned policy also performed better than a number of standard policies based on design guidelines proposed in the literature.

These experiments involving the NJFun system show that it is possible to optimize the performance of a dialogue system using reinforcement learning. The combination of task-related and dialogue-quality-related variables produced interesting strategies that suggest that the system's action choices are determined partly by what is being asked and partly by the system's assessment of the success of the dialogue so far. Some of these choices provide a more fine-grained basis for decision making compared with those investigated in traditional empirical studies. Thus the use of RL to explore dialogue strategy based on such combinations of variables is a promising way ahead.

There are some limiting factors in this approach, however, relating to the size and nature of the state space. A large state space that enables the exploration of an interesting range of variables would require a large and costly sample of dialogues for the learning process. Thus a crucial issue in this work is to design a small enough state space that is sufficiently rich to support the learning of an accurate model while minimising data sparseness.

Summary

A number of active research topics in spoken dialogue technology have been presented, including: Information State Theory, error handling, adaptivity and optimisation of dialogue system performance using reinforcement learning. Various techniques from Artificial Intelligence (AI) have contributed to this research. For example, Information State Theory uses complex representations and reasoning processes, while machine learning techniques have been applied in error handling, adaptivity and dialogue system optimisation.

The topics discussed here are only a selection of the many different approaches being adopted in current research. One example of a promising avenue for development is the application of statistical techniques, previously applied mainly in speech recognition, to all other modules in spoken dialogue systems, such as dialogue management and response generation (Young, 2000, 2002). References to other research topics are included in the section on Further Reading.

Further Reading

Information State Theory

The TRINDI web site is a good starting point for publications on TRINDI, the TRINDIKIT, and Information State Theory. There are also links to people who were involved in the TRINDI project, with further links to their subsequent publications. See: http://www.ling.gu.se/projekt/trindi/

DIPPER is an architecture that extends the TRINDI framework using the Open Agent Architecture (OAA). DIPPER provides a number of agents that represent dialogue system components as well as an information state update language to support dialogue management. DIPPER is described in Bos et al. (2003). See also the DIPPER web site at: http://www.ltg.ed.ac.uk/dipper

Error Handling

Gabriel Skantze provides a comprehensive set of references to error handling in spoken dialogue systems. See: http://www.speech.kth.se/~gabriel/presentations/felhantering_referenser.htm

Error Handling was the topic of an ISCA Workshop in August 2003: ISCA Workshop on Error Handling in Spoken Dialogue Systems. See: http://www.speech.kth.se/error/

Adaptive Dialogue Systems

Adaptation in spoken dialogue systems was the topic of a special NAACL Workshop in June 2001: Adaptation in Dialogue Systems, NAACL 2001 Workshop, 4 June, 2001, Pittsburgh, PA, USA. See: http://www.cs.utah.edu/~cindi/AdaptDial.html

Jens-Uwe Möller has provided a set of references to learning and adaptation at: http://nats-www.informatik.uni-hamburg.de/~jum/research/dialog/sys.html

Reinforcement Learning

Sutton and Barto (1998) is an excellent introductory text on reinforcement learning. Kaebling, Littman and Moore have provided a survey, which is available online at: http://www.cs.washington.edu/research/jair/volume4/kaelbling96a-html/rl-survey.html

The Reinforcement Learning Warehouse is a useful resource with links to books, tutorials, etc., ranging from introductory to advanced levels. See: http://reinforcementlearning.ai-depot.com/Intro.html

Miscellaneous Research Publications in Spoken Dialogue Technology

The SigDial Workshops focus on computational models of dialogue and discourse. See: http://www.sigdial.org/

Workshops on the Semantics and Pragmatics of Dialogue: http://cswww.essex.ac.uk/semdial/

IJCAI Workshops on Knowledge and Reasoning in Practical Dialogue Systems: 2nd IJCAI Workshop on Knowledge and Reasoning in Practical Dialogue Systems: www.ida.liu.se/labs/nlplab/ijcai-ws-01/ijcai-ws-program.html

The 3rd Workshop dealt specifically with the use of ontologies in dialogue systems. See: http://www.ida.liu.se/~nlplab/ijcai-ws-03/

Special Issue on: Collaboration, cooperation and conflict in dialogue systems (Jokinen K, Sadek D, Traum D (eds.) (2000)). *International Journal of Human Computer Studies* 53(6).

Special Issue on: Detecting, repairing and preventing human–machine miscommunication. (McRoy SW (ed.) (1998)). *International Journal of Human–Computer Studies* 48(5).

Glass JR, Rosenfeld R (eds.) (2000). Special issue on: Language modeling and dialogue systems. *IEEE Transactions on Speech and Audio Processing* 8(1).

Other Relevant Conferences

EACL (European Association of Computational Linguistics): http://www.eacl.org/

ACL (Association of Computational Linguistics): http://www.aclweb.org/

ISCA (International Speech Communication Association): http://www.isca-speech.org/conferences.html

ICASSP (IEEE International Conference on Acoustics, Speech, and Signal Processing): http://www.ieee.org/

Future Directions: The Way Ahead

14

In the preceding chapters of this book the theory and practice of spoken dialogue technology have been reviewed and documented. This chapter examines future directions. The first section reviews some current work on advanced multimodal systems that incorporate spoken language input and output as one of the modalities that may be used in combination with other modalities such as pen, touch, movement, gesture, gaze, and head and body movement. In the second section some areas for future research are identified and the relationship between academic and commercial research and development in spoken dialogue technology is explored.

Advanced Multimodal Systems

Multimodal interfaces using languages such as XHTML + Voice and SALT (Speech Application Language Tags), as described in Chapter 11, support alternative modes of input and output. One of the main advantages of these systems is that the user can select the mode that best fits their current circumstances and preferences. Thus, in a noisy environment, speech input and output can be deselected, whereas in a hands-busy/eyes-busy situation speech is likely to be the preferred mode. Currently these systems require the user to select the required mode. With the more advanced systems to be described here, the selection of modes may be determined dynamically by the system based on the current circumstances. Furthermore, the modes may often be used in combination, so that, for example, a user may convey a message by pointing as well as by speaking. In this case the message can only be interpreted by combining the information acquired from the two different modes. A further advantage of this approach is that the modes can often be used to compensate for each other. In particular, it has been shown that poor speech recognition performance can be compensated for by additional information from a visual mode.

This section will present some recent work on advanced multimodal dialogue systems, looking at issues concerning multimodal input and output, the uses and advantages of multimodal communication, the architectures involved, and the application of these technologies in environments inhabited by animated characters and embodied conversational agents.

Multimodal Input

Combined multimodal input involves the combination of two or more modes, such as speech, pen, touch, movement, gesture, gaze, and head and body movement. A number of early systems combined speech with a graphical interface, in which the user could speak and point, using a fairly limited set of pointing gestures. Typical applications were maps and forms. For example, in the CUBRICON system the user could point to an object in a map and ask "Is this <point> an air-base?" (Neal and Shapiro, 1991). The task for the system was to integrate the referent of the pointing gesture into the spoken query to achieve the overall intended meaning of the query.

More recent systems employ a wider range of gestures that combine with speech as parallel streams conveying rich semantic information. In the Quick-Set system (Cohen et al., 1997), the user can draw on a map using map symbols, editing gestures and spatial features. Similarly, in the MATCH system (Johnston et al., 2002), users interact with a dynamic map using synchronous multimodal combinations of drawing and speech. For example, to ask for cheap Italian restaurants in Chelsea they can circle the relevant area on the map and say "show cheap Italian restaurants in this neighbourhood", or to get information about restaurants they can circle some restaurants on the map and say "phone numbers for these restaurants". These systems involve more complex architectures and processing technologies.

A distinction can be made between systems that involve "active" input modes and those involving "passive" input modes (Oviatt, 2002). The systems described so far involved active input mode, as the user intentionally used a combination of modes to convey a message to the system. With passive input modes the system monitors and interprets the user's behaviours. An example of this is the interpretation of lip movements in conjunction with speech (Benoit et al., 2000). This type of processing requires a detailed classification of visible lip movements that correspond with consonants and vowels in speech (visemes), and a mapping of these visemes on to the phonemes of speech. Manual gestures can also be monitored passively by the system to assist in the interpretation of messages. There is an extensive cognitive science literature on audio-visual perception which, in combination with advances in vision-based technologies, is making passive monitoring more feasible (see McKevitt (1994–1996) for a collection of papers on recent research in this area).

Multimodal Output

Presentation of information often involves the combination of different media, such as text, graphics, charts and tables, taking advantage of the strengths of each media and using the different media effectively in parallel. A number of techniques have been adapted from natural language generation research to support the generation of multimodal presentations (see André (2000) for a recent survey). Some systems, such as COMET (Feiner and McKeown, 1991) and SAGE (Roth et al., 1991), used schemata to describe the contents and structure of multimedia presentations.

More recently, operator-based approaches have been used, for example, in the WIP and PPP systems developed at DFKI (Wahlster et al., 1993; André and Rist, 1996). The multimodal communicative acts within a presentation are treated as operators within a planning system. The system begins with an overall presentation goal and looks for operators whose effect subsumes the goal. This leads to the generation of further subgoals until all the basic generation tasks have been determined. The overall structure is represented as a graph that depicts the discourse structure of the presentation.

Multimedia presentations involve the dynamic allocation and coordination of the different media. Allocation rules may be applied, such as (André and Rist, 1993):

1. prefer graphics over text for spatial information unless accuracy is preferred over speech, in which case text is preferred.
2. use text for quantitative information (i.e., concepts such as "most" and "some").
3. present objects that are contrasted with each other in the same medium.

Following the allocation stage the different media have to be coordinated spatially and temporally. Spatial coordination involves layout issues, such as contrast and geometrical constraints, while temporal issues apply when the information is presented over time. For example, speech may need to be synchronised with the display of graphical elements (André and Rist, 1996).

Uses and Advantages of Multimodal Communication

Multimodal systems provide a more flexible interface for users who can choose the most appropriate interface to meet their requirements and preferences. Users of different age levels, cognitive abilities, and with various impairments, can select the mode that is appropriate to their needs. Mode selection can also be determined by the context of use, for example, speech while driving a car or walking along a street, and other input and output modes when privacy is required or where speech might be intrusive. A number of studies have indicated that users have a strong preference to interact multimodally rather than unimodally (see, e.g., Oviatt (1997)).

Multimodal systems that permit more than one input mode can also provide for better handling of errors, particularly errors produced by the speech recognition component. Several studies have shown how a multimodal architecture can support error suppression and mutual disambiguation. One example from a study involving the QuickSet system involved a user interacting with a dynamic map interface and saying "zoom out" while making a checkmark on the map. The phrase "zoom out" was ranked fourth on the speech recognisers's n-best list behind three other phrases ("zoom in", "show info" and "show all"). However, the semantic information from the checkmark gesture helped the system to discard interpretations from the speech recogniser that were inappropriate in the current context, and to rank the interpretation "zoom out" first on the multimodal n-best list (Oviatt, 1999). Other studies have shown that higher recognition rates can be achieved with a multimodal interface compared with a unimodal speech-based interface with decreases in errors ranging from 19% to 41% (Oviatt, 1999, 2000).

Architectures and Processing Techniques

In the more basic multimodal systems that combined speech and pointing the integration of the pointing gesture was accomplished during the parsing of the spoken utterance by searching for an appropriate gesture when the user spoke an expression such as "here" or "this". More complex multimodal integration is required for advanced systems that process richer combinations of input (Oviatt, 2000). In some cases the integration (or "fusion") involves modalities that are closely synchronised temporally, where one modality influences recognition in the other, as in speech and lip movements. In other cases the input modalities are less coupled temporally. Each modality has its own recogniser and the information from each modality has to be integrated on a semantic level. In this method each module creates partial representations that are fused by a multimodal integration component.

Various methods have been used for modality integration. In the QuickSet system a common semantic representation was created by unifying typed feature structures from the outputs of the different modalities (Johnston et al., 1997). For example, if the utterance was "Is this number <pointing gesture> correct?", only objects of the type "number" would be appropriate as referents of the pointing gesture. In the MATCH system a finite-state approach is used for multimodal integration, in which lattices representing the outputs from the different processors are combined to produce a list of potential multimodal interpretations (Johnston et al., 2002).

Processing multimodal input in this way is generally accomplished using a multiagent architecture, in which the different processing components may be written in different programming languages and on different machines with different operating systems. For example, the MATCH system uses an agent-based architecture similar to the DARPA Communicator hub described in Chapter 12. In MATCH, communication is through a facilitator (MCUBE) which enables messages encoded in XML to be passed either to single agents or to groups of agents. The agents can reside on the client systems or can be distributed across a network (Johnston et al., 2002).

Animated Characters and Inhabited Multimedia Environments

Embodied animated agents that inhabit virtual multimedia environments are becoming an integral part of advanced multimodal interfaces. These characters are endowed with the natural modalities of human face-to-face communication, such as speech, facial expressions, gestures and body stance. One example is a REA (Real Estate Agent), a character on a screen that uses advanced computer vision techniques to interpret the conversational and nonverbal behaviours of humans standing in front of the screen (Cassell et al., 2000). The REA acts as a real estate agent and shows users the features of various models of houses.

A PPP Persona (Personalised Plan-based Presenter) is an animated presentation agent that can explain and comment on textual and visual information on a multimodal interface (André et al., 1996). The domain for PPP is accommodation offers on the Internet. PPP highlights the advantages of the accommodation using verbal annotations, for example, by pointing to part of the picture during an utterance. The Virtual Music Center is another example of a virtual reality environment in which agents assist the user with information about performances or by selling tickets or helping with directions within the building (Nijholt and Heylen, 2002).

SmartKom

SmartKom is a joint research project funded by the German Federal Ministry of Education and Research (Wahlster et al., 2001). The project is concerned with the development of a multimodal interface for applications in three different domains: SmartKom-Public, SmartKom-Mobile and SmartKom-Home. SmartKom-Public is an advanced telephone kiosk which provides tourist and movie information and includes gesture and mimic recognition as well as biometric access control. Users delegate a task, such as finding a cinema and making reservations, to a virtual agent which is visible on the graphic display. The system's output is displayed graphically or spoken using synthesised speech. SmartKom-Mobile involves hand-held devices to support mobile users with route planning and travel information, while the environment of SmartKom-House is a living room in which the user has a tablet PC and uses speech and a touch screen to control entertainment devices and access an electronic programme guide. For example, in a typical interaction, SmartKom-Home greets the user who selects a TV programme on the basis of a spoken dialogue accompanied by a visually presented guide (Portele et al., 2003). The video recorder is programmed to record the show if the user wishes to watch a different programme. The system is user-driven and the user can switch between two different modes: a "lean-forward" mode, in which touch input and visual output are supported, and a "lean back" mode, in which only the speech channel is used for input and output.

Each of the SmartKom applications uses a common interaction module that maintains a model of the interaction (Portele, 2003). About 50 different input sources are used to collect values (indicators) which are used to construct more general values (models). The mimic analysis module, for example, monitors the user's emotional state, while the speech recognition module calculates scores and confidence measures for the user's utterances. One indicator calculates the ratio of words such as "stupid" that may indicate that the system has misinterpreted the user's utterance. This information is all combined and matched with the domain and discourse models to determine which items are most meaningful in the current context and to select the best interpretation from several different hypotheses. Other models assess the user's emotional state as well as the progress of the dialogue. The models are used to support the dynamic help component of the system.

Speech and Multimodal Interfaces in Vehicles

Some currently available cars include a speech-based system with which drivers can perform hands-busy/eyes-busy operations such as controlling the temperature in the car, operating the entertainment system, or making and receiving phone calls. Most current systems require unnatural command sequences and have limited dialogue capabilities (Heisterkamp, 2001), although there are a number of projects in which more conversational interfaces are being developed (Minker et al., 2002; Bernsen and Dybkjaer, 2002).

Pieraccini et al. (2003) describe a multimodal conversational interface that has been implemented on a Ford Model U Concept vehicle. The system allows the user to control the temperature, use the telephone, navigate, use the entertainment system to play MP3s, browse lists and change the volume, and make modifications to the display preferences. In addition to speech input and output the system supports haptic interaction (touch screen) and can output graphical displays. Some of these features would be disabled during driving.

The system supports three models of dialogue: directed, terse commands and natural language commands. Directed dialogue is appropriate for novice users who begin by speaking one of the words displayed on the graphic display, such as "climate control". The system prompts for additional information, such as "driver, passenger, or both?" and "warmer or cooler". Terse commands allow the user who is more familiar with the functionalities of the system to convey more than one item of information within a single utterance, for example, "climate driver seat temperature up". Finally, natural language commands allow more conversational input such as "turn the seat temperature all the way down".

This system incorporates several innovative technologies, including dynamic semantic models (DSMs) and conditional confirmation. DSMs are used to rescore the speech recognition outputs according to how best they fit the current context. For example, if the current context involves determining a contact to call, a recognition hypothesis such as "call her at work" will score more highly than "I'd like to listen to classical music". The final score is used to determine whether to reject, confirm or accept an utterance, with utterances that are within the same semantic model and thus scored as less costly being accepted without confirmation.

Future Directions

Spoken dialogue technology is developing at a rapid pace and a number of new approaches are being adopted and tested, some of which have been described in this chapter and in the preceding chapters in Part III. This final section indicates some potential areas for development, and addresses the issue of the relative contributions of academic, compared with commercially driven, approaches.

As far as research is concerned, there are a number of areas where more effort is likely to be directed, including the following:

- More robust speech recognition, including the ability to perform well in noisy environments. There is an increasing trend to make greater use of additional information in the speech signal, such as prosody. Other external information, such as the relationship of the recogniser's hypotheses to the current context, will also become more important as methods become available for scoring such contextual information.

- Conversational interfaces. Current systems provide a rather limited and inflexible mode of interaction. In some cases this is the most suitable approach, given the potential for increased speech recognition errors with more open dialogue strategies. However, in other cases, dialogue strategies based on conversational interaction may be more appropriate. Research is needed on which features of conversational interaction are suitable for incorporation into currently available technologies. Continuing development and evaluation of the approaches described in Chapter 13 involving adaptivity and machine learning will play an important role in this research.

- Multimodal interfaces. Increasingly multimodal interfaces will become more prevalent. Chapter 11 described current developments with regard to VoiceXML and SALT and some research on advanced multimodal interfaces was reviewed in this chapter. An important area for further investigation is the complementary role of different modalities and how a particular modality that is optimal for the current situation and user can be automatically selected.

- Devices for conversational interaction. To date, most spoken dialogue with automated systems is conducted over the telephone. As hand-held devices become more ubiquitous there will be more opportunities for applications that can be conducted on these devices, using conversational and multimodal technologies. Spoken dialogue technology may also be embedded in many other devices, in the home, in the car, and even on the person in the form of wearable computers. Embedded devices will bring numerous challenges for spoken dialogue technology but also provide potential for wider application of the technology.

- New application areas. To date, most applications for spoken dialogue technology have involved information retrieval and transactions. There is scope for a wider range of applications in areas such as education and entertainment. Spoken dialogue technology could be used to provide on-line tutorials for students on the move, accessing the services through mobile phones and Personal Digital Assistants (PDAs). Similar services could also be developed in the entertainment domain.

Commercial and Academic Approaches: Are They on the Same Wavelength?

Research in spoken dialogue technology is motivated by academic and scientific concerns as well as commercial interests. Academic research ranges from theoretical investigations of the nature of dialogue to computational modelling of dialogue behaviour. In some cases the aim is to model the ways in which humans behave when they engage in dialogue and to test theories of dialogue and, in other cases, the focus is on the application of computational models and algorithms. Commercially driven research and development in spoken dialogue technology is motivated by different concerns. The main aim here is to produce systems that will work in the real world and that will be successful financially. The performance of the system is measured in terms of its efficiency, effectiveness, usability and acceptability under real-world conditions. Factors that determine the successful deployment of a system include marketability, profitability and user acceptance. The details of the technology are of no interest to users of the system who simply want to achieve a task in the most efficient way possible.

Thus there would appear to be a wide gulf between the concerns of academic researchers working on spoken dialogue and those of commercial developers. Two papers presented at a workshop on error handling in spoken dialogue systems illustrate these differences in perspective (http://www.speech.kth.se/error/). Mike Phillips from Scansoft, a company involved in the deployment of a large number of telephone-based dialogue systems, some of which handle more than 100,000 calls per day, presented a commercial perspective (Phillips, 2003). An academic perspective was presented by Herb Clark of Stanford University (Clark, 2003).

It is a commonly held view that the main obstacle to the wider deployment of speech-based systems lies with the unacceptably high rate of errors produced by the speech recognition component, particularly for telephone-based dialogue where performance may be adversely affected by a noisy and unpredictable channel. Yet, as Phillips pointed out, in-grammar speech recognition errors tend not to be the major source of error in commercially deployed systems. Rather the problems lie with false acceptance of out-of-grammar utterances and with mismatches between applications and users' expectations. To deal with these issues typically a system-directed dialogue is recommended with fairly constrained methods for handling errors and for constraining users' expectations. For example, explicit confirmations are used and a lot of attention is paid to the careful design of prompts that should reduce the potential for error. Fine-tuning of the deployed system results in various changes, of which almost 50% involve expanding the grammar to cope with unpredicted user input. Summing up the progress so far, Phillips concluded that we are still a long way from dialogue systems that can produce behaviour similar to human–human interactions.

How humans behave in dialogue was the topic of Clark's presentation. In particular, Clark illustrated how people not only choose what to say but also when to say it. Many so-called errors are in fact complex phenomena that demonstrate how speakers are constrained by issues of timing when they talk. One example of timing involves processing constraints, as speakers cannot speak until they have formulated what they are going to say. However, speakers also attend to other types of timing. Cross-timing requires that speakers place their utterances with respect to their partner's speech (turn-taking). Speakers are also constrained by internal timing, which involves trying to deliver their utterances fluently. Departure from internal timing constraints often signals specific information. For example, fillers (such as "um" and "er"), which are usually factored out in speech recognition grammars as "noise", fulfil the important function of signalling a delay in the production of a fluent utterance that carries the implication that the speaker does not wish to relinquish the turn. Many more examples of such timing phenomena were illustrated in Clark's paper.

Presented in these terms it would seem that these two perspectives on handling spoken dialogue errors are on completely different wavelengths. What could detailed analyses of human–human dialogue have to say to designers of commercial spoken dialogue systems? Interestingly, however, it seems that there is much that is of use, possibly even in the short-term. As Clark showed, humans communicate a lot of information, not only in what they say but also in how they say it. System logs of dialogues contain crucial data in the form of prosodic and paralinguistic cues as well as features associated with timing, and this information could be used by designers of spoken dialogue systems to assist with detecting when things are going wrong in the dialogue. Indeed, many of the other papers presented at the workshop illustrated in detail how issues such as these are being addressed in current approaches to spoken dialogue technology (see also Chapter 13).

Thus rather than concluding that there is a wide gulf between academic and commercial concerns, it is possible to discern areas in which academic research can contribute to the design and development of commercially deployed systems, in some cases in the short-term and in other cases perhaps in the longer term. Conversely, the concerns of commercial developers may help to provide an impetus and focus for academic researchers. For example, as Phillips suggested, one of the main problems for commercially deployed systems is not speech recognition accuracy per se, as is normally assumed, but rather the false acceptance of out-of-grammar utterances. Future scientific research ought to be focusing on developing strategies for handling the problem of false acceptance rather than concentrating on improving accuracy for in-grammar utterances.

Concluding Remarks

Spoken dialogue technology is an exciting area. It deals with one of the major activities that humans engage in – talking to each other – and explores ways in which dialogue with computers can be realised. There are many theoretical issues to be resolved and, at the same time, there are also many practical issues for those who wish to develop spoken dialogue systems for use in real-world applications.

Appendixes

Appendix 1:
Grammar Formats

There are a number of different grammar formats that are currently supported on various VoiceXML platforms. The VoiceXML 1.0 specification used the Java Speech Grammar Format (JSGF) in its examples when illustrating the use of grammars, and JSGF is the format used in the current version of the IBM Web-Sphere Voice SDK (Speech Development Kit). The IBM Voice Toolkit also supports the Speech Recognition Grammar Format (SRG XML) and the Speech Recognition Control Language (SRCL), a variant of the Backus–Naur Form (BNF). Some VoiceXML platforms use proprietary grammar formats. For example, Nuance, Voxpilot and BeVocal support the Grammar Specification Language (GSL) format, which was developed by Nuance and is used widely in several VoiceXML textbooks.

In an effort to arrive at a standard for VoiceXML grammars, the VoiceXML 2.0 specification defines the XML form of the World Wide Web Consortium (W3C) Speech Recognition Grammar (SRG) Format as required for all VoiceXML 2.0 browsers. An alternative format, the Augmented BNF (ABNF) form, is defined as optional. Platforms can support additional formats if they so wish.

The XML form represents a grammar as an XML document with the logical structure of the grammar captured by XML elements. This format is ideal for computer-to-computer communication of grammars, as it is compatible with widely available XML technology, such as parsers and XSLT (Extensible Style Language Transformation).

The ABNF form combines traditional BNF Spoken Dialogue Technology with a regular expression language. This format is familiar to many speech application developers and is a more compact and more human-readable representation than XML. It is also fairly similar to the JSGF. Some platforms allow grammars written in one format to be converted to another format.

The XML and ABNF Grammar Formats

There is a direct mapping between the XML and ABNF grammar formats, so that it is easy to convert a grammar written in one of these formats into the

Table A1.1. XML and ABNF grammar formats

ABNF grammar format	XML grammar format
Expansion involving further rules:	
$viewdetails = $studentname $coursename	⟨rule id = "viewdetails"⟩
	⟨ruleref uri = "#studentname"⟩
	⟨ruleref uri = "#coursename"⟩
	⟨/rule⟩
Expansion involving choice of tokens:	
$studentname = john | david;	⟨rule id = "studentname"⟩
	⟨one-of⟩
	⟨item⟩ john ⟨/item⟩
	⟨item⟩ david ⟨/item⟩
	⟨/one-of⟩
	⟨/rule⟩
Expansion with optional and repeated items:	
Optional:	⟨count number = "optional"
[student]	student
	⟨/count⟩
Zero or more times:	⟨count number = "0+"
coursename*	coursename
	⟨/count⟩
One or more times:	⟨count number = "1+"
coursename+	coursename
	⟨/count⟩

Table A1.2. Semantic tags in XML and ABNF grammars

ABNF grammar format	XML grammar format
$coursename = comms | communications {"01"}	⟨rule id = "coursename"⟩
	⟨one-of⟩
	⟨item⟩ comms ⟨/item⟩
	⟨item⟩ communications
	⟨tag⟩ "01" ⟨/tag⟩
	⟨/item⟩
	⟨/one-fo⟩
	⟨/rule⟩

other format. Table 1 illustrates how different types of rule are expressed in the two formats.

Semantic Tags

Semantic tags can be associated with rules, as described in Chapter 10. Table 2 illustrates semantic tags in the ABNF and XML grammar formats to cater for alternative phrasings. In this example, the coursename can be either "comms" or "communications", and the value to be returned if either word is used is "01".

Headers and Grammar References

Headers that are grammar references and extensions vary slightly from one platform to another.

IBM WebSphere

The XML format is supported on the IBM WebSphere platforms, but requires a header such as the following (note that the root rule has to be specified):

```
<grammar type="application/srgs+xml" root="choice">
```

The following is an inline XML grammar that could be used with the file "studentsystem1a" (see Chapter 9):

```
<grammar type="application/srgs+xml" root="choice">
<rule id = "choice" scope = "public">
<one-of>
<item> students </item>
<item> courses </item>
<item> reports </item>
</one-of>
</rule>
</grammar>
```

There are certain limitations on XML grammars in WebSphere Voice Server Version 3.1. For example, external references to grammars by the Uniform Resource Indicator (URI) and tag-format declarations are not supported. For this reason it is currently not possible to write form-level grammars in XML format for mixed-initiative forms for examples such as "studentsystem6a.vxml" (from Chapter 10) that will run on the WebSphere Voice Server platform.

Bevocal

Bevocal supports the XML grammar format. The required header is:

```
<grammar type="application/grammar+xml" version = "1.0" root="choice">
```

Note that the version number is required.

Form-level grammars are supported for mixed-initiative forms. We can illustrate with the example "studentsystem6a" from Chapter 10, in which the user could state a studentname and a coursename within the same utterance. The following is the XML version of the grammar ("studentdetails.gram"). Note that the extension ".grxml" is required:

```
<grammar type="application/grammar+xml" xml:lang = "en" root="studentsys-
tem6a" version="1.0">

<rule id="studentsystem6a" scope="public">
<ruleref uri="#studentname"/>
<ruleref uri="#coursename"/>
</rule>

<rule id="studentname" scope="public">
<one-of>
```

```
<item> john <tag> studentname="john" </tag> </item>
<item> david <tag> studentname="david" </tag> </item>
<item> rosemary <tag> studentname="rosemary" </tag> </item>
<item> jennifer <tag> studentname="jennifer" </tag> </item>
</one-of>
</rule>

<rule id="coursename" scope="public">
<one-of>
<item> communications <tag> coursename="communications" </tag> </item>
<item> algorithms <tag> coursename="algorithms" </tag> </item>
<item> programming <tag> coursename="programming" </tag> </item>
<item> databases <tag> coursename="databases" </tag> </item>
</one-of>
</rule>
</grammar>
```

This grammar is referenced in the document "studentststem6a.vxml" as follows:

Form-level grammar (calling the top-level rule "studentsystem6a"):

```
<grammar type="application/grammar+xml" version="1.0"
src="studentsystem6a.grxml#studentsystem6a"/>
```

Field-level grammar for "studentname":

```
<grammar type="application/grammar+xml"
src="studentsystem6a.grxml#studentname"/>
```

Field-level grammar for "coursename":

```
<grammar type="application/grammar+xml"
src="studentsystem6a.grxml#coursename"/>
```

Note that JSGF grammars can be used on the Bevocal platform, although they need to be enclosed within a CDATA section, as in the following example:

```
<grammar>
  <![CDATA[
    #JSGF 1.0;
    grammar topping;
    public <topping> =
       ( pepperoni | sausage | mushrooms );
  ]]>
</grammar>
```

Vxml documents also require a reference in the document header to the document type definition (DTD), as in the following example:

```
<?xml version="1.0"?>
<!DOCTYPE vxml PUBLIC "-//BeVocal Inc//VoiceXML 1.0//EN"
"http://cafe.bevocal.com/libraries/dtd/vxml1-0-bevocal.dtd">
<vxml version="1.0">
```

Appendix 2:
The CSLU Toolkit and Related Software for Chapters 7 and 8

In order to run and develop the exercises in Chapters 7 and 8 the following software is required:

1. CSLU toolkit.
2. TclODBC.

You will also need to set up data sources using the ODBC Data Source Administrator.

CSLU Toolkit

The CSLU toolkit is available from the following site:
http://www.cslu.ogi.edu/toolkit/
Full installation instructions are provided at the site. The toolkit currently runs under Windows 95, 98, NT, ME, 2000, XP Home and XP Professional on Intel (or compatible) processors only.

TclODBC

TclODBC is required to make a connection between the CSLU toolkit and an ODBC compatible database, such as Microsoft Access, as used in Chapters 7–11. Information on downloading and installing TclODBC can be found at: http://sourceforge.net/projects/tclodbc
Download the Windows version (tclodbc.2.3.1.zip) to a temporary directory. Click on tclodbc.2.3.1.zip and then click on the file "setup.tcl". This will cause tclodbc to be installed in the directory Program Files\CSLU\.

Setting Up a Data Source (ODBC)

ODBC is used to access data from a variety of database management systems. To set up a data source in Windows XP:

Click **Start**, click **Control Panel**, and then click **Performance and Maintenance.** Click **Administrative Tools**, and then double-click **Data Sources (OBDC).** This will bring up the ODBC Data Source Administrator. For further instructions, click on the **Help** tab in the bottom right-hand corner.

Other versions of Windows have slightly different paths to Data Sources (ODBC). There is also a helpful tutorial at
http://support.gfi.com/manuals/en/me56/tosetupanodbcdatasource.htm
for a good set of instructions.

You will need to set up the following data sources:

"students", with a link to the path of the file "student.mdb", for example, "c:\databases\student.mdb".
"games", with a link to the path of the file "rad_games.mdb", for example, "c:\databases\rad_games.mdb".

Appendix 3:
Software for Chapters 9 and 10

In order to run and develop the exercises in Chapters 9 and 10 a VoiceXML browser is required. The IBM WebSphere VoiceServer SDK is recommended, but other platforms listed in Appendix 7 are also appropriate.

Software is also required to create a dynamic link to a database. Apache Tomcat 4.0 and Java(TM) 2 SDK, Version 1.3.1, were used to set up and develop the exercises in Chapters 9, 10 and 11. Other web servers and scripting languages may also be used.

Downloading the IBM WebSphere VoiceServer SDK

The WebSphere VoiceServer SDK can be obtained from the following site: http://www-3.ibm.com/software/pervasive/voice_toolkit/

The IBM WebSphere Voice Server SDK includes a VoiceXML speech browser, speech recogniser, speech synthesiser, sample applications, and other tools for developing and testing VoiceXML applications. A comprehensive manual *VoiceXML Programmer's Guide* as well as the VoiceXML 1.0 Specification are provided as Adobe Acrobat files. The SDK runs in command mode and can be used independently of other software.

The following is an indication of the main requirements for the SDK:

Hardware
Intel® Pentium® 366 MHz processor with minimum of 128 MB RAM and 290 MB disk space.

A Microsoft® Windows® 2000 compatible 16-bit, full-duplex sound card (with a microphone input jack) with good recording quality.

A quality microphone.

Software
Microsoft Windows 2000 Professional or Server Service Pack 2. (*Note*: The SDK will work with Windows XP, although Windows XP is not officially supported.)

Sun Java Runtime Environment (Sun JRE) 1.3.1 (included in the package, but must be installed prior to the IBM WebSphere Voice Server SDK software).

Networking (e.g., an IP network) must be enabled.

Adobe Acrobat Reader, Version 5.0 (included in the package) or later. HTTP 1.1 Client, if desired.

Full installation instructions are provided with the download.

Starting the VoiceXML Browser

To start the VoiceXML browser, use the following command in the DOS command window:

%IBMVS%\bin\batchfile URL

IBMVS is the environment variable containing the location of the IBM Web-Sphere Voice Server SDK installation destination directory.
Batchfile is one of the following:

vsaudio. Generates spoken output and accepts spoken and simulated DTMF input (the language engine needs to be stipulated, e.g., vsaudio_en_US for the US language model).

vstext. Generates text output and accepts text or simulated DTMF input (the language engine needs to be stipulated, e.g., vstext_en_US for the US language model).

URL is the initial URL for your application.

Example:

```
"%IBMVS%\bin\vsaudio" myfile.vxml
```

In order to avoid lengthy path names for files on the computer's hard drive, it is best to change directory to the directory in which the files reside, e.g., `cd c:\voicexml`

Voice Toolkit for WebSphere Studio

The Voice Toolkit for WebSphere Studio works with the WebSphere Voice Server SDK for application development and testing, and with the IBM Reusable Dialog Components for adding VoiceXML components to voice applications. The Voice Toolkit is an integrated development environment for building VoiceXML applications and includes a VoiceXML editor and debugger, a grammar editor and test tool, pronunciation builder, built-in recorder, and VoiceXML reusable dialog components. The hardware and software requirements for the Voice Toolkit are listed at the web site. The Voice Toolkit is available as a free download. However, an important factor is that the Voice Toolkit is integrated into IBM's WebSphere Studio environment and requires either IBM WebSphere Studio Site Developer 5.0 or IBM WebSphere Studio Application Developer 5.0 to be installed. Site Developer and Application Developer are available with a free 60-day license, or professors can sign up for the IBM Scholars Program for WebSphere soft-

ware at the following site:
http://www.ibm.com/software/info/university/products/websphere/

Downloading and Installing Apache Tomcat

Apache Tomcat can be obtained from the following site:
http://jakarta.apache.org/tomcat/

Apache Tomcat 4.0 is the version that was used for the files in Chapters 10 and 11.

Java Server Pages (JSP)

The version of JSP that was used for the files in Chapters 10 and 11 was the Java(TM) 2 SDK, Standard Edition, Version 1.3.1, available at:
http://java.sun.com/j2se/1.3/download.html

Other versions of the SDK, such as 1.4, did not appear to work with Apache Tomcat 4.0.

Appendix 4:
Software for Chapter 11. IBM
Multimodal Tools and Microsoft.NET
Speech SDK

IBM Multimodal Tools

The IBM Multimodal Tools are required to run the XHTML+Voice programs in Chapter 11. The Multimodal Tools can be obtained as a free download from: http://www-3.ibm.com/software/pervasive/multimodal/

The hardware and software requirements for the Multimodal Tools are listed at the web site. As with the Voice Toolkit (Appendix 3), the Multimodal Tools require that either IBM WebSphere Studio Site Developer 5.0 or IBM WebSphere Studio Application Developer 5.0 is installed. Site Developer and Application Developer are available with a free 60-day license, or professors can sign up for the IBM Scholars Program for WebSphere software at the following site: http://www.ibm.com/software/info/university/products/websphere/

Microsoft .NET Speech SDK

The Microsoft .NET Speech SDK is required to run the SALT programs in Chapter 11. (Other environments for running SALT programs were described briefly in Chapter 11.) The SDK is available as a download from: http://www.microsoft.com/speech/

System requirements are listed at the site. The SDK is integrated into the Microsoft Visual Studio .NET 2003 environment which is required for the development and integration of SALT programs such as speech-enabled ASP.NET applications.

Appendix 5:
Spoken Dialogue Technology:
Projects and Links

The following are links to a number of projects and sites involved in research and development in spoken dialogue technology.

Table A5.1. Links for spoken dialogue technology

Companies

Apple Speech Recognition	http://www.apple.com/macosx/jaguar/speech.html
Dialogue Understanding Research Group (NTT, Japan)	http://www.brl.ntt.co.jp/cs/dug/index.html
IBM Pervasive Computing	http://www-3.ibm.com/software/pervasive/multimodal/
Larson Technical Services – VoiceXML resources	http://www.larson-tech.com/bookres.htm
Microsoft Research	http://www.research.microsoft.com/research/projects/
Nuance	http://www.nuance.com
Pipebeach	http://www.pipebeach.com/
Scansoft – leading supplier of imaging, speech and language solutions	http://www.scansoft.com
Telera (VoiceXML community)	http://www.telera.com/devxchange.html
Vocalis – Voice- driven Business Solutions	http://www.vocalis.com/
Voice Web Solutions – Development Tools for VoiceXML and SALT	http://www.voicewebsolutions.net

Universities and Research Centres

Center for PersonKommunikation (CPK), Aalborg, Denmark	http://cpk.auc.dk/smc/index.html

Table A5.1. *Continued*

Centre for Communication Interface Research (CCIR), University of Edinburgh	http://www.ccir.ed.ac.uk/
Centre for Language Technology (Macquarie University, Australia)	http://www.clt.mq.edu.au/Information/Overview.html
Conversational Interaction and Spoken Dialogue Research Group, University of Rochester	http://www.cs.rochester.edu/research/cisd/
CSLR Home Page (Center for Spoken Language Research, University of Colorado)	http://cslr.colorado.edu
CSLU Home Page (Center for Spoken Language Understanding, Oregon)	http://cslu.cse.ogi.edu/
Department of Language and Speech (University of Nijmegen, Netherlands)	http://lands.let.kun.nl/
GoDAG (University of Gotherburg, Sweden)	http://www.ling.gu.se/grupper/GoDAG/
HCRC Dialogue Group (University of Edinburgh)	http://www.hcrc.ed.ac.uk/Site/DIALOGUE.html
KTH – Centre for Speech Technology, Stockholm, Sweden	http://www.speech.kth.se/ctt/
LIMSI: Projects on spoken language (France)	http://www.limsi.fr/Recherche/TLP/projects.html
Natural Dialogue Group (CSLU)	http://www.cslu.ogi.edu/ndg/
Natural Interactive Systems Laboratory (NIS), Odense University, Denmark	http://www.nis.sdu.dk/
Natural Language Processing Group (University of Sheffield)	http://nlp.shef.ac.uk/
NLPLAB (Linköping University, Sweden)	http://www.ida.liu.se/labs/nlplab/

Table A5.1. *Continued*

Speech Media Processing Group (University of Kyoto, Japan)	http://winnie.kuis.kyoto-u.ac.jp/home-e.html
Pattern Information Processing Group (Kyoto Institute of Technology, Japan)	http://www-vox.dj.kit.ac.jp/index-e.html
Speech Media Laboratory (University of Kyoto, Japan)	http://www.ar.media.kyoto-u.ac.jp/home-e.html
Speech-based and Pervasive Interaction Group (Tampere, Finland)	http://www.cs.uta.fi/research/hci/spi/index.html
Spoken Language Systems Group (MIT)	http://www.sls.lcs.mit.edu/sls/sls-green-nospec.html
Tokyo Institute of Technology: Furui Laboratory	http://www.furui.cs.titech.ac.jp/english/index.html
Tutorial Dialogue Group (University of Edinburgh)	http://www.cogsci.ed.ac.uk/~jmoore/tutoring/links.html
University of Pittsburgh	http://www.cs.pitt.edu/~litman/
Projects and Systems	
Amities – Multilingual dialogue systems (University of Sheffield)	http://www.dcs.shef.ac.uk/nlp/amities/
August: A Swedish multimodal spoken dialogue system	http://www.speech.kth.se/august/
BusLine (CMU)	http://www-2.cs.cmu.edu/~aria/BusLine.html
CMU Communicator	http://www.speech.cs.cmu.edu/Communicator/
COMIC – Multimodal interaction (University of Edinburgh)	http://www.hcrc.ed.ac.uk/comic/
Conversational Architectures Project	http://research.microsoft.com/adapt/conversation/
CU Communicator	http://communicator.colorado.edu/
DiaLeague – Forum for the evaluation of dialogue systems	http://dialeague.csl.sony.co.jp/
DINEX – Boston restaurant guide	http://www.sls.lcs.mit.edu/sls/applications/dinex.shtml
DIPPER	http://www.ltg.ed.ac.uk/dipper
DISC Best Practice Guide	http://www.disc2.dk/

Table A5.1. *Continued*

DUG-1 spoken dialogue system (NTT, Japan)	http://www.brl.ntt.co.jp/cs/dug/dug1/
GALAXY (MIT)	http://www.sls.lcs.mit.edu/GALAXY.html
How May I Help You? (AT&T)	http://www.research.att.com/~algor/hmihy/
Japanese dialogue system for an office robot	http://www-csli.stanford.edu/semlab/juno/
Julietta Research Group (Seville, Spain)	http://fing.cica.es/
Jupiter (MIT)	http://www.sls.lcs.mit.edu/sls/whatwedo/applications/jupiter.html
Language and Speech Technology programme (Netherlands)	http://odur.let.rug.nl:4321/
NASA spoken and multimodal dialogue systems	http://www.riacs.edu/research/detail/RIALIST_ver4/projects.htm
Natural Language Research Group (Technical University of Catalonia, Spain)	http://www.lsi.upc.es/~nlp/
OLGA – Multimodal user interfaces and animated characters (Sweden)	http://www.nada.kth.se/~osu/olga/e_index.html
OVIS – Public transport system (Netherlands)	http://lands.let.kun.nl/TSpublic/strik/ovis.html
SMARTKOM – Multimodal dialogue (Germany)	http://www.smartkom.org/start_en.html
Spoken Dialogue for Intelligent Tutoring Systems (University of Pittsburgh)	http://www2.cs.pitt.edu/~litman/why2-pubs.html
Swedish Dialogue Systems	http://www.ida.liu.se/~nlplab/sds/
TRAINS Project Home Page (University of Rochester)	http://www.cs.rochester.edu/research/trains/
TRINDI	http://www.ling.gu.se/projekt/trindi/
TRIPS (University of Rochester)	http://www.cs.rochester.edu/research/cisd/projects/trips/
Universal Speech Interface (CMU)	http://www-2.cs.cmu.edu/~usi/
Verbmobil project (Germany)	http://verbmobil.dfki.de/overview-us.html

Table A5.1. *Continued*

Voyager – Tourist and travel information (MIT)	http://www.sls.lcs.mit.edu/sls/applications/voyager.shtml
Waxholm dialog project (Sweden)	http://www.speech.kth.se/waxholm/waxholm2.html
WITAS – Multimodal conversational interfaces	http://www-csli.stanford.edu/semlab/witas/

Resources

Dialogue Diversity Corpus	http://www-rcf.usc.edu/~billmann/diversity
Dialogue systems links (Dan Bohus)	http://www-2.cs.cmu.edu/~dbohus/SDS/
Dialogue systems links (Emiel Krahmer)	http://fdlwww.kub.nl/~krahmer/usimodule-C4-2001.htm
Dialogue systems links (Gabriel Skantze)	http://www.speech.kth.se/~gabriel/speech.html
Dialogue systems links (Jens-Uwe Möller)	http://nats-www.informatik.uni-hamburg.de/~jum/research/dialog/sys.html
Dialogue systems links (Steffan Larsson)	http://www.ling.gu.se/~sl/dialogue_links.html
List of spoken dialogue systems currently in operation	http://www.disc2.dk/tools/opSLDSs.html
SALT Forum	http://www.saltforum.org/
SIGDIAL – Special interest group of ACL for dialogue and discourse	http://www.sigdial.org/
Spoken Dialogue systems links	http://liceu.uab.es/~joaquim/speech_technology/tecnol_parla/dialogue/refs_dialeg.html
VoiceXML Forum	http://www.voicexml.org
W3C "Voice Browser" activity	http://www.w3.org/Voice/

Appendix 6:
Spoken Dialogue Technology:
Toolkits and Resources

Toolkits and Resources for Spoken Dialogue Technology

Table A6.1. Spoken dialogue technology: Toolkits and resources

CODIAL – Tutorial and tool in support of cooperative dialogue design for spoken language dialogue systems	http://www.disc2.dk/tools/codial/
CSLU toolkit	http://cslu.cse.ogi.edu/toolkit
CU Communicator	http://communicator.colorado.edu/
DRI Shared tools and resources	http://www.georgetown.edu/faculty/luperfos/Discourse-Treebank/tools-and-resources.html
IBM WebSphere Multimodal Tools	http://www-3.ibm.com/software/pervasive/multimodal/
IBM WebSphere VoiceServer SDK	http://www-3.ibm.com/software/pervasive/products/voice/voice_server_sdk.shtml
MATE workbench – A software tool set for multilevel and cross-level annotation of corpora and extraction of information about annotated corpora	http://mate.nis.sdu.dk/
Microsoft Speech Technologies	http://www.microsoft.com/speech/
Mobile Conversay Software Development Kit (SDK)	http://www.conversa.com
Natural Language Speech Assistant (NLSA) (Unisys Corporation)	http://www.unisys.com/
NUANCE Developers Toolkit	http://www.nuance.com
SpeechWorks OpenVXI 2.0.1	http://www.speech.cs.cmu.edu/openvxi
SUEDE: A Wizard of Oz Prototyping Tool for Speech User Interfaces	http://guir.berkeley.edu/projects/suede/
Telera AppBuilder (VoiceXML tool)	http://www.telera.com/appbuilder.html
TRINDIKIT	http://www.ling.gu.se/projekt/trindi//trindikit/

Web Sites for Hosted VoiceXML Applications

Table A6.2. Web sites for hosted VoiceXML Applications

BeVocal Cafe	http://cafe.bevocal.com/
HeyAnita	http://freespeech.heyanita.com/
Tellime Studio	http://studio.tellme.com/
VoiceGenie	http://developer.voicegenie.com/
Voxeo	http://community.voxeo.com/
Voxpilot	http://www.voxpilot.com/

References

Aberdeen J, Bayer S, Caskey S, Damianos L, Goldschen A, Hirschman L, Loehr D, Trappe H (1999). DARPA Communicator Program tackles conversational interface challenges. *The Edge* (Intelligent Human–Computer Interface Issue) **3**:4. MITRE Publications. Available at:
http://www.mitre.org/news/the_edge/december_99/third.html

Alexandersson J, Buschbeck-Wolf B, Fujinami T, Kipp T, Koch S, Maier E, Reithinger N, Schmitz B, Siegel M (1998). *Dialogue Acts in Verbmobil – 2*, 2nd ed. Verbmobil-Report Nr. 226. DFKI GmbH, Saarbrücken.

Allen JF (1983). Recognising intentions from natural language utterances. In: Brady M, Berwick RC (eds.), *Computational Models of Discourse*. MIT Press, Cambridge, MA.

Allen JF (1995). *Natural Language Processing*, 2nd ed. Benjamin Cummings, Redwood City, CA.

Allen JF, Core M (1997). Draft of DAMSL: Dialog act markup in several layers. Available at:
http://www.cs.rochester.edu/research/cisd/resources/damsl/
RevisedManual/RevisedManual.html

Allen JF, Perrault CR (1980). Analysing intentions in utterances. *Artificial Intelligence* **15**:143–178.

Allen JF, Ferguson G, Miller BW, Ringger EK, Zollo TS (2000). Dialogue systems: From theory to practice in TRAINS-96. In: Dale R, Moisl H, Somers H (eds.), *Handbook of Natural Language Processing*. Marcel Dekker, New York, pp. 347–376.

Allen JF, Byron DK, Dzikovska M, Ferguson G, Galescu L, Stent A (2001a). Towards conversational human–computer interaction. *AI Magazine* **22**(4):27–38.

Allen JF, Ferguson G, Stent A (2001b). An architecture for more realistic conversational systems. *Proceedings of Intelligent User Interfaces (IUI-01)*, Santa Fe, NM.

Allwood J (1976). *Linguistic Communication as Action and Cooperation*. Gothenburg Monographs in Linguistics, Vol. 2. Department of Linguistics, University of Göteborg.

Andersson EA, Breitenbach S, Burd T, Chidambaram N, Houle P, Newsome D, Tang X, Zhu X (2001). *Early Adopter VoiceXML*. Wrox Press, Birmingham, UK.

André E (2000). The generation of multimedia presentations. In: Dale R, Moisl H, Somers H (eds.), *Handbook of Natural Language Processing*. Marcel Dekker, New York, pp. 305–327.

André E, Rist T (1993). The design of illustrated documents as a planning task. In: Maybury M (ed.), *Intelligent Multimedia Interfaces*. AAAI Press, Menlo Park, CA.

André E, Rist T (1996). Coping with temporal constraints in multimedia presentation planning. *Proceedings of the 13th National Conference of the American Association on Artificial Intelligence (AAAI'96)*, Portland, OR, pp. 142–147.

André E, Müller J, Rist T (1996). The PPP Persona: A multi-purpose animated presentation agent. In: Catarci T, Costabile MF, Levialdi S, Santucci G (eds.), *Advanced Visual Interfaces*. ACM Press, New York, pp. 245–247.

Androutsopoulos I, Ritchie G (2000). Database interfaces. In: Dale R, Moisl H, Somers H (eds.), *Handbook of Natural Language Processing*. Marcel Dekker, New York.

Androutsopoulos I, Aretoulaki M (2003). Natural language interaction. In: Mitkov R (ed.), *The Oxford Handbook of Computation al Linguistics*. Oxford University Press, Oxford, UK, pp. 629–649.

Aretoulaki M, Ludwig B (1999). Automaton descriptions and theorem-proving: A marriage made in heaven? *Proceedings of the IJCAI'99 Workshop on Knowledge and Reasoning in Practical Dialogue System*, Stockholm, Sweden.

Argyle M (1975). *Bodily Communication*. Methuen, London.

ARPA (1994). *Proceedings of the Speech and Natural Language Workshop*. Morgan Kaufmann, San Mateo, CA.

Atkinson JM, Drew P (1979). *Order in Court: The Organization of Verbal Interaction in Judicial Settings*. Macmillan, London.

Aust H, Oerder M, Seide F, Steinbiss V (1995). The Philips automatic train timetable information system. *Speech Communication* 17:249–262.

Austin JL (1962). *How to Do Things with Words*. Oxford University Press, Oxford, UK.

Balentine B, Morgan DP, Meisel WS (2001). *How to Build a Speech Recognition Application: A Style Guide for Telephony Dialogues*, 2nd ed. Enterprise Integration Group, San Ramon, CA.

Bales RF (1950). *Interaction Process Analysis*. Addison-Wesley, Cambridge, MA.

Batacharia B, Levy D, Catizone R, Krotov A, Wilks Y (1997). CONVERSE: A conversational companion. *Proceedings of the 1st International Workshop on Human–Computer Conversation*, Bellagio, Italy. (Reprinted in: Wilks Y (1999) (ed.), *Machine Conversations*. Kluwer Academic, Dordrecht.)

Benoit C, Martin JC, Pelachaud C, Schomaker L, Suhm B (2000). Audio-visual and multimodal speech-based systems. In: Gibbon D, Mertins I, Moore R (eds.), *Handbook of Multimodal and Spoken Dialogue Systems: Resources, Terminology and Product Evaluation*. Kluwer Academic, Dordrecht, pp. 102–203.

Bergsten H (2002). *JavaServer Pages*, 2nd ed. O'Reilly, Sebastopol, CA.

Bernsen NO (2003). On-line user modelling in a mobile spoken dialogue system. *Proceedings of the 8th International Conference on Speech Communication and Technology (Eurospeech2003)*, Geneva, September, pp. 737–740.

Bernsen NO, Dybkjær L (1997). The DISC project. *ELRA Newsletter* 2(2):6–8. Available at: http://www.disc2.dk/publications/other/INFO-1-Elra.html

Bernsen NO, Dybkjær H, Dybkjær L (1998). *Designing Interactive Speech Systems: From First Ideas to User Testing*. Springer-Verlag, New York.

Bernsen NO, Dybkjær L (2002). A multimodal virtual co-driver's problem with the driver. *Proceedings of IDS02*, Kloster Irsee, Germany, June.

Bilmes J (1988). The concept of preference in conversation analysis. *Language in Society* 17(2):161–182.

Bobrow DG (1968). Natural language input for a computer problem-solving system. In: Minsky M (ed.), *Semantic Information Processing*. MIT Press, Cambridge, MA.

Bobrow DG, Kaplan RM, Kay M, Norman DA, Thompson H, Winograd T (1977). GUS: A frame-driven dialogue system. *Artificial Intelligence* 8:155–173.

Boros M, Eckert W, Gallwitz F, Görz G, Hanrieder G, Niemann H (1996). Towards understanding spontaneous speech: Word accuracy vs. concept accuracy. *Proceedings of the 4th International Conference on Spoken Language Processing (ICSLP96)*, Philadephia, PA, October, pp. 1005–1008.

Bos J, Klein E, Lemon O, Oka T (2003). DIPPER: Description and formalisation of an information-state update dialogue system architecture. *Proceedings of the 4th SIGDial Workshop on Dialogue and Discourse*, Sapporo, Japan, 5–6 July.

Bouwman A, Sturm J, Boves L (1999). Incorporating confidence measures in the Dutch train timetable information system developed in the Arise project. *Proceedings of the International Conference on Acoustics, Speech, and Signal Processing (ICASSP)*, Vol. 1, Phoenix, AZ, pp. 493–496.

Brennan SE, Hulteen E (1995). Interaction and feedback in a spoken language system: A theoretical framework. *Knowledge-Based Systems* 8:143–151.

Brown G, Yule G (1983). *Discourse Analysis*. Cambridge University Press, Cambridge, UK.

Bunt HC (1979). Conversational principles in question–answer dialogues. In: Krallmann D (ed.), *Zur Theorie der Frage*. Narr Verlag, Essen, pp. 119–141.

Bunt HC, Black B (2000a) (eds.). *Abduction, Belief and Context in Dialogue: Studies in Computational Pragmatics*. John Benjamins, Amsterdam.

Bunt HC, Black B (2000b). The ABC of computational pragmatics. In: Bunt HC, Black B (eds.), *Abduction, Belief and Context in Dialogue: Studies in Computational Pragmatics*. John Benjamins, Amsterdam, pp. 1–46.

Burnett DC (2000) (ed.). SpeechObjects Specification V1.0. *W3C Note* November. Available at: http://www.w3.org/TR/speechobjects

Button G, Coulter J, Lee JRE, Sharrock W (1995). *Computers, Minds and Conduct*. Polity Press, Cambridge, UK.

Cahn JE, Brennan SE (1999). A psychological model of grounding and repair in dialog. *Proceedings of the AAAI Fall Symposium on Psychological Models of*

Communication in Collaborative Systems. North Falmouth, MA. AAAI Press, Menlo Park, CA, pp. 25–33.

Carberry MS (1986). The use of inferred knowledge in understanding pragmatically ill-formed queries. In: Reilly R (ed.), *Communication Failure in Dialogue and Discourse.* North-Holland, Amsterdam.

Carbonell J (1981). POLITICS. In: Schank RC, Riesbeck CK (eds.), *Inside Computer Understanding.* Lawrence Erlbaum, Hillsdale, NJ.

Carletta J, Isard A, Isard S, Kowtko J, Doherty-Sneddon G, Anderson A (1997). The reliability of a dialogue structure coding scheme. *Computational Linguistics* **23**:13–31.

Carlson R, Granström B (1997). Speech synthesis. In: Hardcastle WJ, Laver J (eds.), *The Handbook of Phonetic Science.* Blackwell, Oxford, UK, pp. 768–788.

Cassell J, Sullivan J, Prevost S, Churchill E (2000) (eds.). *Embodied Conversational Agents.* MIT Press, Cambridge, MA.

Chin D (1989). KNOME: Modeling what the user knows in UC. In: Kobsa A, Wahlster W (eds.), *User Models in Dialog Systems.* Springer-Verlag, London, pp. 74–107.

Clark HH (1996). *Using Language.* Cambridge University Press, Cambridge, UK.

Clark HH (2003). When to start speaking, when to stop, and how. Invited talk: *Proceedings of the ISCA Workshop on Error Handling in Spoken Dialogue Systems,* pp. 1–4.

Clark HH, Schaefer EF (1989). Contributing to discourse. *Cognitive Science* **13**:259–294.

Cohen PR (1994). Models of dialogue, cognitive processing for vision and voice. In: Nagao M (ed.), *Proceedings of the Fourth NEC Research Symposium.* SIAM, Philadelphia, PA.

Cohen PR, Johnston M, McGee D, Oviatt SL, Pittman J, Smith I, Chen L, Chow J (1997). Quickset: Multimodal interaction for distributed applications. *Proceedings of the Fifth ACM International Multimedia Conference.* ACM Press, New York, pp. 31–40.

Cohen W (1996). Learning trees and rules with set-valued features. *Fourteenth Conference of the American Association of Artificial Intelligence.*

Colby KM (1975). *Artificial Paranoia – A Computer Simulation of Paranoid Processes.* Pergamon Press, New York.

Cole RA, Mariani J, Uskoreit H, Zaenen A, Zue V (1997) (eds.). *Survey of the State of the Art in Human Language Technology.* Cambridge University Press, Cambridge, UK. Available at: http://cslu.cse.ogi.edu/HLTsurvey

Cole R, Massaro DW, de Villiers J, Rundle B, Shobaki K, Wouters J, Cohen M, Beskow J, Stone P, Connors P, Tarachow A, Solcher D (1999). New tools for interactive speech and language training: Using animated conversational agents in the classrooms of profoundly deaf children. *Proceedings of the ESCA/SOCRATES Workshop on Method and Tool Innovations for Speech Science Education,* London, April.

Connors P, Davis A, Fortier G, Gilley K, Rundle B, Soland C, Tarachow A (1999). Participatory design: Classroom applications and experiences. *Proceedings of the International Conference of Phonetic Sciences,* San Francisco, CA.

Cooper R, Larsson S, Matheson C, Poesio M, Traum DR (1999). Coding Instructional Dialogue for Information States Trindi Project Deliverable D1.1. Available at: http://www.ling.gu.se/projekt/trindi//publications.html

Cullingford R (1981). SAM. In: Schank RC, Riesbeck CK (eds.), *Inside Computer Understanding*. Lawrence Erlbaum, Hillsdale, NJ.

Dahlbäck N, Jönsson A (1998). A coding manual for the Linköping dialogue model. Available at: http://www.cs.umd.edu/users/traum/DSD/arne2.ps

DAMSL Dialog Annotation (2001). Available at: http://www.cs.rochester.edu/research/cisd/resources/damsl/

Danieli M, Gerbino E (1995). Metrics for evaluating dialogue strategies in a spoken language system. *Working Notes of the AAAI Spring Symposium on Empirical Methods on Discourse Interpretation and Generation*. AAAI, Stanford, CA, pp. 34–39.

DARPA (1992). *Proceedings of the Speech and Natural Language Workshop*. Morgan Kaufmann, San Mateo, CA.

den Os E, Boves L, Lamel L, Baggia P (1999). Overview of the ARISE project. *Proceedings of the 6th International Conference on Speech Communication and Technology (Eurospeech99)*, Budapest, Hungary, September, pp. 1527–1530.

Eckert W, Nöth E, Niemann H, Schukat-Talamazzan EG (1995). Real users behave weird: Experiences made collecting large human–machine dialog corpora. *Proceedings of the ESCA Workshop on Spoken Dialogue Systems*, Vigso, Denmark, pp. 193–196.

Edgington M, Lowry A, Jackson P, Breen A, Minnis S (1996a). Overview of current Text-to-Speech techniques: Part I – Text and linguistic analysis. *BT Technical Journal* 14:68–83.

Edgington M, Lowry A, Jackson P, Breen A, Minnis S (1996b). Overview of current Text-to-Speech techniques: Part II – Prosody and speech generation. *BT Technical Journal* 14:84–99.

Feiner SK, McKeown KR (1991). Automating the generation of co-ordinated multimedia explanations. *IEEE Computer* 24(10):33–41.

Fillmore CH (1968). The case for case. In: Bach E, Harms RT (eds.), *Universals in Linguistic Theory*. Holt, Rinehart and Winston, New York, pp. 1–88.

Fraser N, Gilbert GN (1991). Simulating speech systems. *Computer Speech and Language* 5:81–99.

Gardner-Bonneau D (1999) (ed.). *Human Factors and Voice Interactive Systems*. Kluwer Academic, Boston, MA.

Giachin E, McGlashan S (1997). Spoken language dialogue systems. In: Young S, Bloothooft G (eds.), *Corpus-based Methods in Language and Speech Processing*. Kluwer Academic, Dordrecht, pp. 69–117.

Gibbon D, Moore R, Winski R (1997) (eds.). *Handbook of Standards and Resources for Spoken Language Systems*. Mouton de Gruyter, New York.

Glass JR (1999). Challenges for spoken dialogue systems. *Proceedings of the IEEE ASRU Workshop*, Keystone, CO, December.

Glass JR, Polifroni J, Seneff S, Zue V (2000). Data collection and performance evaluation of spoken dialogue systems: The MIT experience. *Proceedings of the 6th International Conference on Spoken Language Processing (ICSLP2000)*, Beijing, China.

Glass JR, Weinstein E (2001). SPEECHBUILDER: Facilitating spoken dialogue system development. *Proceedings of the 7th European Conference on Speech Communication and Technology*, Aalborg, Denmark, September.

Goddeau D, Meng H, Polifroni J, Seneff S, Busayapongchai S (1996). A form-based dialogue manager for spoken language applications. *Proceedings of the 4th International Conference on Spoken Language Processing (ICSLP'96)*, Pittsburgh, PA, pp. 701–704.

Graesser AC, VanLehn K, Rose C, Jordan P, Harter D (2001). Intelligent tutoring systems with conversational dialogue. *AI Magazine* **22**:39–51.

Green BF, Wolf AW, Chomsky C, Laughery KR (1963). BASEBALL: An automatic question–answerer. In: Feigenbaum EA, Feldman J (eds.), *Computers and Thought*. McGraw-Hill, New York.

Grice HP (1975). Logic and conversation. In: Cole P, Morgan JL (eds.), *Syntax and Semantics*, Vol. 3: *Speech Acts*. Academic Press, New York.

Grosz BJ (1978). Discourse. In: Walker D (ed.), *Understanding Spoken Language*. Elsevier North-Holland, New York.

Grosz BJ, Sidner CL (1986). Attention, intentions, and the structure of discourse. *Computational Linguistics* **12**(3):175–204.

Hauptmann AG, Rudnicky AI (1988). Talking to computers: An empirical investigation. *International Journal of Man–Machine Studies* **28**(6):583–604.

Heeman PA, Allen JF (1994). Detecting and correcting speech repairs. *Proceedings of the 32nd Annual Meeting of the Association for Computational Linguistics (ACL-94)*, Las Cruces, June, pp. 295–302.

Heisterkamp P (2001). Linguatronic – Product level speech system for Mercedes-Benz cars. *Proceedings of the HLT 2001*. Morgan Kaufmann, San Francisco, CA.

Heisterkamp P, McGlashan S (1996). Units of dialogue management: An example. *Proceedings of the Fourth International Conference on Spoken Language Processing (ICSLP'96)*, Philadelphia, PA, pp. 200–203.

Hirschberg J (2002). Communication and prosody: Functional aspects of prosody. *Speech Communication* **36**:31–43.

Hirschberg J, Litman DJ, Swerts M (1999). Prosodic cues to recognition errors. *Proceedings of the Automatic Speech Recognition and Understanding Workshop (ASRU99)*, Keystone, CO, December.

Hirschman L (1994). The roles of language processing in a spoken language interface. In: Roe DG, Wilpon JG (eds.), *Voice Communication Between Humans and Machines*. National Academy Press, Washington, DC.

Hosom JP, Cole RA, Fanty M, Colton D (1997). Speech recognition using neural networks at the Center for Spoken Language Understanding. Available at: http://www.cslu.ogi.edu/toolkit/old/old/documentation/recog/recog.html

Huang X, Acero A, Hon HW (2001). *Spoken Language Processing: A Guide to Theory, Algorithm, and System Development*. Prentice Hall, Upper Saddle River, NJ.

Jefferson G (1989). Preliminary notes on a possible metric which provides for a "standard maximum" silence of approximately one second in conversation. In: Roger D, Bull P (eds.), *Conversation: An Interdisciplinary Perspective. Multilingual Matters*, Clevedon, UK.

Johnston M, Cohen PR, McGee D, Oviatt SL, Pittman JA, Smith I (1997). Unification-based multimodal integration. *Proceedings of the International Conference on Computational Linguistics and the 35th Meeting of the Association for Computational Linguistics (COLING-ACL'97)*, Madrid, pp. 281–288.

Johnston M, Bangalole S, Vasireddy G, Stent A, Eblen P, Walker MA, Whittaker S, Maloor P (2002). MATCH: An architecture for multimodal dialogue systems. *Proceedings of the 40th Annual Meeting of the Association for Computational Linguistics (ACL)*, Philadelphia, PA, July, pp. 376–383.

Jokinen K, Wilcock G (to appear). Confidence-based adaptivity and response generation in a spoken dialogue system. In: van Kuppevelt J, Smith R (eds.), *Current and New Directions in Discourse and Dialogue*. Kluwer Academic, Dordrecht.

Jokinen K, Kerminen A, Kaipainen M, Jauhiainen T, Wilcock G, Turunen M, Hakulinen J, Kuusisto J, Lagus K (2002). Adaptive dialogue systems – Interaction with interact. *Proceedings of the 3rd SIGdial Workshop on Discourse and Dialogue*, Philadelphia, PA, July 11–12.

Jurafsky D (2004). Pragmatics and computational linguistics. In: Horn L, Ward G (eds.), *Handbook of Pragmatics*. Blackwell, Oxford, UK.

Jurafsky D, Shriberg E, Biasca D (1997). Switchboard SWBD-DAMSL Shallow-Discourse-Function Annotation Coders Manual, Draft 13. University of Colorado, Boulder, CO. Institute of Cognitive Science Technical Report 97–02. Available at: http://www.colorado.edu/ling/jurafsky/ws97/manual.august1.html

Jurafsky D, Martin JH (2000). *Speech and Language Processing: An Introduction to Natural Language Processing, Computational Linguistics, and Speech Recognition*. Prentice Hall, Upper Saddle River, NJ.

Kamm C, Walker MA, Litman DJ (1999). Evaluating spoken language systems. *Proceedings of the American Voice Input/Output Society* (AVIOS).

Kamp H, Reyle U (1993). *From Discourse to Logic: Introduction to Model Theoretic Semantics of Natural Language, Formal Logic and Discourse Representation Theory*. Kluwer Academic, Dordrecht.

Kaplan J (1983). Co-operative responses from a portable natural language database query system. In: Brady M, Berwick RC (eds.), *Computational Models of Discourse*. MIT Press, Cambridge, MA.

Karsenty L (2002). Shifting the design philosophy of spoken dialogue systems: From invisible to transparent systems. *International Journal of Speech Technology* 5(2):147–157.

Kelsey Group (2002). Speech technology revenues to reach $2 billion by 2006 according to the Kelsey Group. Available at: http://www.kelseygroup.com/press/pr020430.htm

Kerminen A, Jokinen K (2003). Distributed dialogue management in a blackboard architecture. *Proceedings of the EACL Workshop Dialogue Systems:*

Interaction, Adaptation and Styles of Management, Budapest, Hungary, pp. 55–66.

Klabbers E, van Santen JPH (2003). Control and prediction of the impact of pitch modification on synthetic speech quality. *Proceedings of the 8th International Conference on Speech Communication and Technology (Eurospeech2003)*, Geneva, September, pp. 317–320.

Komatani K, Adachi F, Ueno S, Kawahara T, Okuno HG (2003). Flexible spoken dialogue system based on user models and dynamic generation of VoiceXML scripts. *Proceedings of the 4th SIGdial Workshop on Discourse and Dialogue*, Sapporo, Japan, July 5–6, pp. 87–96.

Kowtko J, Isard S, Doherty GM (1993). Conversational Games Within Dialogue. Research Paper HCRC/RP-31. Human Communication Research Centre, University of Edinburgh, Scotland, UK.

Krahmer E, Swerts M, Theune T, Weegels ME (2001). Error detection in spoken human–machine interaction. *International Journal of Speech Technology* 4(1):19–30.

Krahmer E, Swerts M, Theune T, Weegels ME (2002). The dual of denial: Two uses of disconfirmations in dialogue and their prosodic correlates. *Speech Communication.* 36(1):133–145.

Kurzweil R (2001). *The Age of Spiritual Machines: How We Will Live, Work and Think in the New Age of Intelligent Machines.* Texere Publishing, NY.

Lai J (2000) (ed.). Conversational interfaces. *Communications of the ACM* 43:9.

Lai J, Yankelovich N (2002). Conversational speech interfaces. In: Sears A, Jacko J (eds.), *The Handbook of Human–Computer Interaction.* Lawrence Erlbaum, Hillsdale, NJ.

Lambert T, Breen AP, Eggleton B, Cox SJ, Milner BP (2003). Unit selection in concatenative TTS synthesis systems based on Mel filter bank amplitudes and phonetic context. *Proceedings of the 8th International Conference on Speech Communication and Technology (Eurospeech2003)*, Geneva, September, pp. 273–276.

Lamel L, Bennacef S, Bonneau-Maynard H, Rosset S, Gauvain JL (1995). Recent developments in spoken language systems for information retrieval. *Proceedings of the ESCA Workshop on Spoken Dialogue Systems*, Vigsø, Denmark, pp, 17–20.

Larson JA (2000). Speech-enabled appliances. *Speech Technology Magazine*, November/December 2000. Available at:
http://www.speechtechmag.com/issues/5_6/cover/231-1.html

Larson JA (2002). *VoiceXML: Introduction to Developing Speech Applications.* Prentice Hall, Upper Saddle River, NJ.

Larsson S, Traum DR (2000). Information state and dialogue management in the TRINDI Dialogue Move Engine Toolkit. *Natural Language Engineering Special Issue on Best Practice in Spoken Language Dialogue Systems Engineering*, pp. 323–340.

Larsson S (2002). Issue-based Dialogue Management. PhD thesis, Goteborg University.

Leech G, Weisser M (2003). Pragmatics and dialogue. In: Mitkov R (ed.), *The Oxford Handbook of Computational Linguistics*. Oxford University Press, Oxford, UK.

Lehnert WG (1980). Question answering in natural language processing. In: Bolc L (ed.), *Natural Language Question Answering*. Hanser, Munich.

Levin E, Pieraccini R, Eckert W (2000). A stochastic model of human–machine interaction for learning dialog strategies. *IEEE Transactions on Speech and Audio Processing* **8**(1):11–22.

Levinson SC (1983). *Pragmatics*. Cambridge University Press, Cambridge, UK.

Litman DJ (2002). Adding spoken dialogue to a text-based tutorial dialogue system. *Proceedings of the ITS Workshop on Empirical Methods for Tutorial Dialogue Systems*, Biarritz, France, June.

Litman DJ, Pan S (1999). Empirically evaluating an adaptable spoken dialogue system. *Proceedings of the 7th International Conference on User Modeling (UM'99)*, pp. 55–64.

Litman DJ, Pan S (2002). Designing and evaluating an adaptive spoken dialogue system. *User Modeling and User-Adapted Interaction* **12**(2/3):111–137.

Litman DJ, Hirschberg J, Swerts M (2000). Predicting automatic speech recognition performance using prosodic cues. *Proceedings of the 1st Meeting of the North American Chapter of the Association for Computational Linguistics*, pp. 218–225.

Litman DJ, Walker MA, Kearns MS (1999). Automatic detection of poor speech recognition at the dialogue level. *Proceedings of the 37th Annual Meeting of the Association for Computational Linguistics (ACL'99)*, College Park, MD, June, pp. 309–316.

Mann W, Thompson S (1988). Rhetorical structure theory: Toward a functional theory of text organisation. *Text* **3**:243–281.

Markowitz JA (1996). *Using Speech Recognition*. Prentice Hall, Englewood Cliffs, NJ.

Matheson C, Poesio M, Traum DR (2001). PTT and EDIS. In: TRINDI Consortium, 2001. The TRINDI book (Draft). Available at: http://www.ling.gu.se/projekt/trindi/publications.html

Maudlin M (1994). Chatterbots, tinymuds and the Turing test: Entering the Loebner prize competition. *Proceedings of AAAI-94*, August, Seattle.

McKeown K (1985). *Text Generation*. Cambridge University Press, Cambridge, UK.

McKevitt P (1994–1996) (ed.). The integration of natural language and vision processing. Special issues of *Artificial Intelligence Review* **8**(2–3, 4–5), **9**(2–3, 5–6), **10**(1–2, 3–4). Also available as McKevitt P (1995/1996). *The Integration of Natural Language and Vision Processing*, Vols. 1–4. Kluwer Academic, Dordrecht.

McRoy SW (1998). Preface – Detecting, repairing and preventing human–machine miscommunication. *International Journal of Human–Computer Studies*, **48**:547–552.

McTear MF (1987). *The Articulate Computer*. Blackwell, Oxford, UK.

McTear MF (2002). Spoken dialogue technology: Enabling the conversational interface. *ACM Computing Surveys* **34**(1):90–169.

Milward D, Thomas J, Amores G, Bos J, Boye J, Cooper R, Ericsson S, Gorrell G, Hjelm D, Holt A, Knight S, Larsson S, Lewin I, Quesada JF (2001). A D'Homme Demonstrator in English, Swedish and Spanish. Dialogues in the Home Machine Environment: IST-2000-26280 Deliverable D2.2, October, 2001. Available at: http://www.ling.gu.se/projekt/dhomme

Minker W, Haiber U, Heisterkamp P (2002). Intelligent dialogue strategy for accessing infotainment applications in mobile environments. *Proceedings of IDS02*, Kloster Irsee, Germany, June.

Mitkov R (2003). (ed.). *The Oxford Handbook of Computational Linguistics*. Oxford University Press, Oxford, UK.

Moore RC (1994). Integration of speech with natural language understanding. In: Roe DG, Wilpon JG (eds.), *Voice Communication Between Humans and Machines*. National Academy Press, Washington, DC, pp. 254–271.

Murphy A (2001). Interactive Learning Using Speech: The use of speech as a tool for primary school children. MSc Dissertation Computing and Information Systems, University of Ulster.

Nakatani C, Traum DR (1999). Coding Discourse Structure in Dialogue (Version 1.0). Technical Report UMIACS-TR-99-03, University of Maryland. Available at: http://www.cs.umd.edu/users/traum/Papers/papers.html

Neal JG, Shapiro SC (1991). Intelligent multimedia interface technology. In: Sullivan J, Tyler S (eds.), *Intelligent User Interfaces*. ACM Press, New York, pp. 11–43.

Nickell J (2002). Are you being served? *Technology Review*, March 15. Available at: http://www.technologyreview.com/articles/print_version/nickell031502.asp

Nijholt A, Heylen D (2002). Multimodal communication in inhabited virtual environments. *International Journal of Speech Technology* **5**:343–354.

Nöth E, Batliner A, Warnke V, Haas J, Boros M, Buckow J, Huber R, Gallwitz F, Nutt M, Niemann H (2002). On the use of prosody in automatic dialogue understanding. *Speech Communication* **36**:45–62.

Novick DG (2002) (ed.). Special section on natural language interfaces. *International Journal of Speech Technology* **5**(2).

O'Neill IM, McTear MF (2002). A pragmatic confirmation mechanism for an object-based spoken dialogue manager. *Proceedings of the 7th International Conference on Spoken Language Processing (ICSLP'2002)*, Vol. 3, Denver, CO, September, pp. 2045–2048.

O'Neill IM, Hanna P, Liu X, McTear MF (2003). The Queen's Communicator: An object-oriented dialogue manager. *Proceedings of the 8th International Conference on Speech Communication and Technology (Eurospeech2003)*, Geneva, September, pp. 593–596.

Ousterhout JK (1994). *TCL and the TK Toolkit*. Addison-Wesley, Boston, MA.

Oviatt SL (1997). Multimodal interactive maps: Designing for human performance. *Human–Computer Interaction* (Special Issue on Multimodal Interfaces) **12**:93–129.

Oviatt SL (1999). Mutual disambiguation of recognition errors in a multimodal architecture. *Proceedings of the Conference on Human Factors in Computing Systems (CHI'99)*. ACM Press, New York, pp. 576–583.

Oviatt SL (2000). Taming recognition errors with a multimodal interface. *Communications of the ACM* 43(9):45–51.

Oviatt SL (2002). Multimodal interfaces. In: Jacko J, Sears A (eds.), *Handbook of Human–Computer Interaction*. Lawrence Erlbaum, Hillsdale, NJ.

Paek T, Horvitz E (1999). Uncertainty, utility, and misunderstanding. *AAAI Fall Symposium on Psychological Models of Communication*, North Falmouth, MA, November 5–7, pp. 85–92.

Paek T, Horvitz E (2000). Conversation as action under uncertainty. *Sixteenth Conference on Uncertainty in Artificial Intelligence*. Morgan Kaufmann, San Francisco, CA, pp. 455–464.

Page JH, Breen AP (1996). The Laureate text-to-speech system – Architecture and applications. *BT Technology Journal* 14(1):57–67.

Paris CL (1989). The use of explicit user models in a generation system for tailoring answers to the user's level of expertise. In: Kobsa A, Wahlster W (eds.), *User Models in Dialog Systems*. Springer-Verlag, London, pp. 200–232.

Peckham J (1993). A new generation of spoken dialogue systems: Results and lessons from the SUNDIAL project. *Proceedings of the 3rd European Conference on Speech Communication and Technology*, pp. 33–40.

Pellom B, Ward W, Pradhan S (2000). The CU Communicator: An architecture for dialogue systems. *Proceedings of the 6th International Conference on Spoken Language Processing (ICSLP'2000)*, Beijing, China, November.

Pellom B, Ward W, Hansen J, Hacioglu K, Zhang J, Yu X, Pradhan S (2001). University of Colorado dialog systems for travel and navigation. *Human Language Technology Conference (HLT-2001)*, San Diego, March.

Phillips M (2003). User interface design for spoken dialogue systems. Invited talk. *Proceedings of the ISCA Workshop on Error Handling in Spoken Dialogue Systems*, p. 145.

Pieraccini R, Dayanidhi K, Bloom J, Dahan JG, Phillips M (2003). A multimodal conversational interface for a concept vehicle. *Proceedings of the 8th International Conference on Speech Communication and Technology (Eurospeech2003)*, Geneva, September, pp. 2233–2236.

Poesio M, Traum DR (1997). Conversational actions and discourse situations. *Computational Intelligence* 13(3).

Poesio M, Traum DR (1998). Towards an axiomatization of dialogue acts. *Proceedings of Twendial'98, 13th Twente Workshop on Language Technology: Formal Semantics and Pragmatics of Dialogue*.

Portele T (2003). Interaction modeling in the SmartKom system. *Proceedings of the ISCA Workshop on Error Handling in Spoken Dialogue Systems*, pp. 89–94.

Portele T, Gorony S, Emele M, Kellner A, Torge S, te Vrugt J (2003). SmartKom-Home – An advanced multi-modal interface to home entertainment. *Proceedings of the 8th International Conference on Speech Communication and Technology (Eurospeech2003)*, Geneva, September, pp. 1897–1900.

Pulman S (2002). Relating dialogue games to information state. *Speech Communication* **36**:15–30.

Raman TV (1997). *Auditory User Interfaces – Toward The Speaking Computer.* Kluwer Academic, Boston, MA.

Raman TV, McCobb G, Hosn RA (2003). Versatile multimodal solutions: The anatomy of user interaction. *XML Journal* **4**(4).

Reilly R (1987) (ed.). *Communication Failure in Dialogue.* North-Holland, Amsterdam.

Reiter E, Dale R (2000). *Building Natural Language Generation Systems.* Cambridge University Press, Cambridge, UK.

Richards MA, Underwood K (1984). Talking to machines. How are people naturally inclined to speak? In: Megaw ED (ed.), *Contemporary Ergonomics.* Taylor & Francis, London.

Robertson S, Robertson J (1999). *Mastering the Requirements Process.* Addison-Wesley, London.

Roe DG, Wilpon JG (1994) (eds.). *Voice Communication Between Humans and Machines.* National Academy Press, Washington, DC.

Rooney E (2002). DKIT Voice Application. MSc Informatics Dissertation, University of Ulster.

Roth SF, Mattis J, Mesnard X (1991). Graphics and natural language as components of automatic explanation. In: Sullivan J, Tyler S (eds.), *Intelligent User Interfaces.* ACM Press, New York, pp. 207–239.

Rudnicky AI, Xu W (1999). An agenda-based dialog management architecture for spoken language systems. *IEEE Automatic Speech Recognition and Understanding Workshop (ASRU99)*, pp. 3–7.

Rudnicky AI, Thayer E, Constantinides P, Tchou C, Shern R, Lenzo K, Xu W, Oh A (1999). Creating natural dialogs in the Carnegie-Mellon Communicator system. *Proceedings of the 6th International Conference on Speech Communication and Technology (Eurospeech99)*, Budapest, Hungary, pp. 1531–1534.

Rudnicky AI, Bennett C, Black A, Chotomongcol A, Lenzo K, Oh A, Singh R (2000). Task and domain specific modelling in the Carnegie-Mellon Communicator system. *Proceedings of the 6th International Conference on Spoken Language Processing (ICSLP'2000)*, Beijing, China, October.

Russell SJ, Norvig P (1995). *Artificial Intelligence: A Modern Approach.* Prentice Hall, Upper Saddle River, NJ.

Rutten P, Fackrell J (2003). The application of interactive speech unit selection in TTS systems. *Proceedings of the 8th International Conference on Speech Communication and Technology (Eurospeech2003)*, Geneva, September, pp. 285–288.

Sacks H, Schegloff EA, Jefferson G (1974). A simplest systematics for the organization of turn-taking for conversation. *Language* **50**:696–735.

Sadek D, de Mori R (1997). Dialogue systems. In: de Mori R (ed.), *Spoken Dialogs with Computers.* Academic Press, New York.

San-Segundo R, Pellom B, Ward W, Pardo JM (2000). Confidence measures for dialogue management in the CU communicator system. *IEEE International Conference on Acoustics, Speech, and Signal Processing (ICASSP-2000)*, June.

Schank RC (1975). *Conceptual Information Processing.* North-Holland, Amsterdam.

Scheffler K, Young S (2002). *Automatic Learning of Dialogue Strategy Using Dialogue Simulation and Reinforcement Learning.* HLT, San Diego, CA.

Schegloff EA, Sacks H (1973). Opening up closings. *Semiotica* 8:289–327.

Schiffrin D (1994). *Approaches to Discourse: Language as Social Interaction.* Blackwell, Oxford, UK.

Schiffrin D, Tannen D, Hamilton H (eds.) (2001). *The Handbook of Discourse Analysis.* Blackwell, Oxford, UK.

Searle JR (1969). *Speech Acts.* Cambridge University Press, Cambridge, UK.

Searle JR (1975). Indirect speech acts. In: Cole P, Morgan JL (eds.), *Syntax and Semantics,* Vol. 3: *Speech Acts.* Academic Press, New York.

Seneff S, Hurley E, Lau R, Pao C, Schmid P, Zue V (1998). Galaxy-II: A reference architecture for conversational system development. *Proceedings of the 5th International Conference on Spoken Language Processing (ICSLP'98),* Sydney, Australia, November.

Sensory Inc. (2002). Sensory's new speech technologies for interactive kiosk avatars make shopping easy. *Speech Technology Magazine NewsBlast,* March 12. Available at: http://www.speechtechmag.com/pub/industry/159-1.html

Sidney S, Castellan NJ (1988). *Nonparametric Statistics for the Behavioural Sciences.* McGraw Hill, New York.

Sinclair JM, Coulthard M (1975). *Towards an Analysis of Discourse.* Oxford University Press, Oxford, UK.

Singh S, Litman DJ, Kearns MS, Walker MA (2002). Optimizing dialogue managment with reinforcement learning: Experiments with the NJFun system. *Journal of Artificial Intelligence Research* 16:105–133.

Sinha AK, Klemmer SR, Landay JA (2002). Embarking on spoken language NL interface design. *International Journal of Speech Technology* 5(2):159–169.

Skantze G (2003a). Error detection in spoken dialogue systems. Available at: http://www.speech.kth.se/~gabriel/courses/DialogueSystems5p/ErrorDetection.pdf

Skantze G (2003b). Exploring human error handling strategies: Implications for spoken dialogue systems. *Proceedings of the ISCA Workshop on Error Handling in Spoken Dialogue Systems,* pp. 71–76.

Smith RW (1998). An evaluation of strategies for selectively verifying utterance meanings in spoken natural language dialog. *International Journal of Human–Computer Studies* 48:627–647.

Smith RW, Hipp DR (1994). *Spoken Natural Language Dialog Systems.* Oxford University Press, New York.

Stent AJ (2000). The Monroe Corpus, TR728 and TN99-2. Computer Science Department, University of Rochester, March.

Stork DG (1998) (ed.). *Hal's Legacy:* 2001's *Computer as Dream and Reality.* MIT Press, Cambridge, MA.

Stubbs M (1983). *Discourse Analysis: The Sociolinguistic Analysis of Natural Language.* Blackwell, Oxford, UK.

Sturm J, den Os E, Boves L (1999). Dialogue management in the Dutch ARISE train timetable information system. *Proceedings of the 6th International Conference on Speech Communication and Technology (99)*, Budapest, Hungary, pp. 1419–1422.

Suhm B (2003). Towards best practices for speech user interface design. *Proceedings of the 8th International Conference on Speech Communication and Technology (Eurospeech2003)*. Geneva, September, pp. 2217–2220.

Sutton R, Barto AG (1998). *Reinforcement Learning: An Introduction.* MIT Press, Cambridge, MA.

Swerts M, Litman DJ, Hirschberg J (2000). Corrections in spoken dialogue systems. *Proceedings of the 6th International Conference of Spoken Language Processing*, Beijing, China.

Traum DR (1994). A Computational Model of Grounding in Natural Language Conversation. PhD thesis, University of Rochester.

Traum DR (1996). A reactive-deliberative model of dialogue agency. In: Muller JP, Wooldridge MJ, Jennings NR (eds.), *Intelligent Agents III: Proceedings of the Third International Workshop on Agent Theories, Architectures, and Languages (ATAL-96)*, Lecture Notes in Artificial Intelligence. Springer-Verlag, Heidelberg.

Traum DR (1999). Computational models of grounding in collaborative systems. *Proceedings of AAAI Fall Symposium on Psychological Models of Communication in Collaborative Systems*. North Falmouth, MA. AAAI Press, Menlo Park, CA, pp. 124–131.

Traum DR (2000). 20 questions for dialogue act taxonomies. *Journal of Semantics* **17**(1):7–30.

Traum DR, Allen JF (1994). Discourse obligations in dialogue processing. *Proceedings of the 32nd Annual Meeting of the Association for Computational Linguistics (ACL-94)*, pp. 1–8.

Traum DR, Larsson S (2001). The information state approach to dialogue modelling. In: *TRINDI Consortium, 2001, The TRINDI Book* (Draft). Available at: http://www.ling.gu.se/projekt/trindi/publications.html

Traum DR, Larsson S (to appear). The information state approach to dialogue management. In: Smith R, Kuppevelt J (eds.), *Current and New Directions in Discourse and Dialogue*. Kluwer Academic, Dordrecht.

TRINDI Consortium (2001). *The TRINDI Book* (Draft). Available at: http://www.ling.gu.se/projekt/trindi/publications.html

Turing AM (1950). Computing machinery and intelligence. *Mind* **59**:433–460.

Turunen M, Hakulinen J (2001a). Agent-based error handling in spoken dialogue systems. *Proceedings of the 7th International Conference on Speech Communication and Technology (Eurospeech2001)*, Aalborg, Denmark, pp. 2189–2192.

Turunen M, Hakulinen J (2001b). Agent-based adaptive interaction and dialogue management architecture for speech applications. Text, speech and dialogue. *Proceedings of the Fourth International Conference TSD*, pp. 357–364.

VoiceGenie (2003). Available at: http://www.voicegenie.com/pdf/Apps/VirtualAssistant.pdf

Wahlster W (1993). Verbmobil – Translation of face to face dialogs. *Proceedings of the Machine Translation SummitIV*, Kobe.

Wahlster W, André E, Finker W, Profitlich HJ, Rist T (1993). Plan-based integration of natural language and graphics generation. *Artificial Intelligence Journal* 63:387–427.

Wahlster W, Reithinger N, Blocher A (2001). SmartKom: Multimodal communication with a life-like character. *Proceedings of the 7th European Conference on Speech Communication and Technology*. Aalborg, Denmark, September, pp. 1547–1550.

Walker MA (2000). An application of reinforcement learning to dialogue strategy selection in a spoken dialogue system for email. *Journal of Artificial Intelligence Research* 12:387–416.

Walker MA, Litman DJ, Kamm C, Abella A (1997). PARADISE: A general framework for evaluating spoken dialogue agents. *Proceedings of the 35th Annual General Meeting of the Association for Computational Linguistics, ACL/EACL*, Madrid, Spain, pp. 271–280.

Walker MA, Litman DJ, Kamm C, Abella A (1998). Evaluating spoken dialogue agents with PARADISE: Two case studies. *Computer Speech and Language* 12(3):317–347.

Walker MA, Wright J, Langkilde I (2000a). Using natural language processing and discourse features to identify understanding errors in a spoken dialogue system. *Proceedings of the 17th International Conference on Machine Learning.*

Walker MA, Langkilde I, Wright J, Gorin A, Litman DJ (2000b). Learning to predict problematic situations in a spoken dialogue system: Experiments with How may I help you? North American Meeting of the Association of Computational Linguistics.

Walker MA, Rudnicky AI, Prasad R, Aberdeen J, Owen Bratt E, Garofolo J, Hastie H, Le A, Pellom B, Potamianos A, Passonneau R, Roukos S, Sanders G, Seneff S, Stallard D (2002). DARPA Communicator: Cross-system results for the 2001 evaluation. *Proceedings of the 7th International Conference on Spoken Language Processing (ICSLP2002)*, Denver, CO, pp. 269–272.

Ward W (1991). Understanding spontaneous speech: The Phoenix system. *Proceedings of the ICASSP'91*, pp. 365–367.

Webber BL (2001). Computational perspectives on discourse and dialogue. In: Schiffrin D, Tannen D, Hamilton H (eds.), *The Handbook of Discourse Analysis*. Blackwell, Oxford, UK.

Weinschenk S, Barker DT (2000). *Designing Effective Speech Interfaces*. Wiley, New York.

Weizenbaum J (1966). ELIZA – A computer program for the study of natural language communication between man and machine. *Communications of the Association for Computing Machinery* 9:36–45.

Whittaker SJ, Attwater DJ (1996). The design of complex telephony applications using large vocabulary speech technology. *Proceedings of the 4th Interna-*

tional Conference on Spoken Language Processing (ICSLP'96), Philadephia, PA, pp. 705–708.

Whittaker S, Walker MA, Maloor P (2003). Should I tell all?: An experiment on conciseness in spoken dialogue. *Proceedings of the 8th International Conference on Speech Communication and Technology (Eurospeech2003)*, Geneva, September, pp. 1685–1688.

Wilensky R (1981). PAM. In: Schank RC, Riesbeck CK (eds.), *Inside Computer Understanding*. Lawrence Erlbaum, Hillsdale, NJ.

Winograd T (1972). *Understanding Natural Language*. Academic Press, New York.

Winther M (2001). Leveraging Web Technologies to Achieve Customer-Centric Contact Centers. Voice Web Today. Available at: http://www.telera.com/news/newsletter/viewpoint.html

Woods WA, Nash-Webber BL, Kaplan RM (1972). The Lunar sciences natural language system final report. BBN Report 3438. Bolt, Beranek and Newman, Cambridge, MA.

Wooffitt RC (1991). The moral and inferential properties of silence: A warning note to designers of intelligent speech systems. ESPRIT Project P2218 (SUNDIAL) Working Paper.

Wright Hastie H, Poesio M, Isard S (2002). Automatically predicting dialogue structure using prosodic features. *Speech Communication* 36:63–79.

Yankelovich N, Levow G, Marx M (1995). Designing SpeechActs: Issues in speech user interfaces. *Proceedings of the SIGCHI Conference on Human Factors in Computing Systems*, Denver, CO, pp. 369–376.

Young SJ (2000). Probabilistic methods in spoken dialogue systems. *Philosophical Transactions of the Royal Society (Series A)* 358(1769):1389–1402.

Young SJ (2002). Talking to machines (Statistically speaking). *Proceedings of the 7th International Conference on Spoken Language Processing (ICSLP2002)*, Denver, CO.

Zue V (1997). Conversational interfaces: Advances and challenges. *Proceedings of the 5th International Conference on Speech Communication and Technology (Eurospeech97)*, Rhodes, Greece.

Zue V (1999). Talking with your computer. *Scientific American*, August 19, 1999.

Index